Lecture Notes in Computer

Edited by G. Goos, J. Hartmanis and J.

Springer

Berlin
Heidelberg
New York
Barcelona
Budapest
Hong Kong
London
Milan
Paris
Santa Clara
Singapore
Tokyo

Hanspeter Mössenböck   (Ed.)

Modular Programming Languages

Joint Modular Languages Conference, JMLC'97
Linz, Austria, March 19-21, 1997
Proceedings

 Springer

Series Editors

Gerhard Goos, Karlsruhe University, Germany

Juris Hartmanis, Cornell University, NY, USA

Jan van Leeuwen, Utrecht University, The Netherlands

Volume Editor

Hanspeter Mössenböck
Johannes Kepler Universität Linz, Institut für Informatik
Freistädterstraße 315, A-4040 Linz, Austria
E-mail: moessenboeck@ssw.uni-linz.ac.at

Cataloging-in-Publication data applied for

Die Deutsche Bibliothek - CIP-Einheitsaufnahme

Modular programming languages : proceedings / Joint Modular Languages
Conference, JMLC '97, Linz, Austria, March 19 - 21, 1997. Hanspeter Mössenböck
(ed.). - Berlin ; Heidelberg ; New York ; Barcelona ; Budapest ; Hong Kong ; London ;
Milan ; Paris ; Santa Clara ; Singapore ; Tokyo : Springer, 1997
  (Lecture notes in computer science ; 1204)
  ISBN 3-540-62599-2

NE: Joint Modular Languages Conference <1997, Linz>; Mössenböck, Hanspeter [Hrsg.]; GT

CR Subject Classification (1991): D.3, D.2, D.1, D.4

ISSN 0302-9743
ISBN 3-540-62599-2 Springer-Verlag Berlin Heidelberg New York

© Springer-Verlag Berlin Heidelberg 1997
Printed in Germany

Typesetting: Camera-ready by author
SPIN 10549488   06/3142 – 5 4 3 2 1 0   Printed on acid-free paper

Preface

The Joint Modular Languages Conference deals with languages, techniques, and tools for the development of modular, extensible, and type-safe software systems. It started out in 1989 as a Modula-2 conference but soon broadened its scope to include languages such as Modula-3, Oberon, Ada95, Eiffel, Sather, and Java, to name just a few. While other conferences such as OOPSLA and ECOOP focus on object-oriented software, JMLC encompasses all kinds of software relying on data abstraction, modular decomposition, and type-checked interfaces. The success of object-oriented technology and componentware is a clear indication that industry and academia are aware of the importance of modularity and extensibility. Although this is a good sign, much remeains to be done. The papers in this volume are a step in that direction.

For JMLC'97 we received 55 submissions from which the Program Committee selected 24 to be included in the proceedings. The submissions came from 21 countries spread over all continents. The selected papers deal not only with programming language issues such as language design, compilers, typing, and inheritance, but also with general aspects of software development such as distribution, concurrency, real-time programming, data structures, and teaching. The papers provide a well-balanced view on state-of-the-art software development techniques.

JMLC'97 featured not only technical papers but also two invited talks (included in the proceedings), four tutorials, and a series of short presentations (found in a separate proceedings volume). The short presentations were combined with posters and served as a forum for presenting ongoing research or results that were considered interesting to a more focused audience. Finally, the conference also included a report on the progress of the ISO Modula-2 standardization effort as well as a birds-of-a-feather session on Oberon.

As the Program Chair of JMLC'97 I would like to thank Springer-Verlag for publishing the proceedings as well as Addison Wesley Longman for sponsoring a Best Presentation Award encouraging high-quality presentations at the conference. Many people at the University of Linz and elsewhere helped us to make the conference as convenient as possible for the participants. Last but not least, the authors provided the spirit of the conference, and I would like to thank them particularly.

January 1997

Hanspeter Mössenböck
Program Chair JMLC'97
moessenboeck@ssw.uni-linz.ac.at

Program Committee

Chair: Hanspeter Mössenböck	University of Linz, A
Marwan Al-Akaidi	De Montfort University, UK
Frans Arickx	University of Antwerp, B
Ralph Back	Abo Akademi, FIN
Günther Blaschek	University of Linz, A
Andreas Borchert	University of Ulm, D
Laszlo Böszörmenyi	University of Klagenfurt, A
Jim Cooling	Loughborough University, UK
Antonio Corradi	University of Bologna, I
Jaques Farre	University of Nice, F
Michael Franz	University of California, USA
John Gough	Queensland University of Technology, AUS
Tibor Gyimothy	Academy of Sciences, H
Juerg Gutknecht	ETH Zurich, CH
Takayuki D. Kimura	Washington University, USA
Brian Kirk	Robinson Associates, UK
Herbert Klaeren	University of Tübingen, D
Kai Koskimies	University of Tampere, FIN
Jörg R. Mühlbacher	University of Linz, A
Libero Nigro	University of Calabria, I
Cuno Pfister	Oberon Microsystems, CH
Frantisek Plasil	Charles University Prague, CZ
Gustav Pomberger	University of Linz, A
Igor Pottosin	Academy of Sciences, RUS
Kees Pronk	Technical University Delft, NL
Peter Rechenberg	University of Linz, A
Beverly Sanders	University of Florida, USA
Peter Schulthess	University of Ulm, D
Marjan Spegel	Stefan Institute, SLO
Alfred Strohmeier	EPF Lausanne, CH
Clemens Szyperski	Queensland University of Technology, AUS
Pat Terry	Rhodes University, SA
Niklaus Wirth	ETH Zurich, CH
Alexandre Zamulin	Academy of Sciences, RUS
Heinz Züllighoven	University of Hamburg, D

Organizing Committee

Chair: Gustav Pomberger	University of Linz, A
Marwan Al-Akaidi	De Montfort University, UK
Jim Cooling	Loughborough University, UK
Alfred Lupper	University of Ulm, D
Hanspeter Mössenböck	University of Linz, A
Marjan Spegel	Stefan Institute, SLO
Niklaus Wirth	ETH Zurich, CH

Author Index

Sponsoring Organizations

OCG – Österreichische Computergesellschaft
GI – Gesellschaft für Informatik e.V., Fachausschuß 2.1
SI – Schweizer Informatikergesellschaft
BCS – British Computer Society, Modular Languages SIG
Addison Wesley Longman
Wirtschaftskammer Oberösterreich
Johannes Kepler Universität Linz

Contents

Active Objects, Real-Time Programming

Inheritance, Reflection

Languages

Miscellaneous

From Programming Languages to Program Construction

Gerhard Goos

Universität Karlsruhe
und
Forschungszentrum Informatik Karlsruhe

Abstract We argue that the notion of programming language semantics has perhaps played a larger role than needed. We illustrate the argument with examples taken from the object-oriented language *Sather-K*. Also, the role of program verification is critically reviewed. The discussion shows that the focus should gradually move from inventing ever better programming languages to topics such as configuration management which transcend the scope of a programming language.

1 Introduction

The history of programming languages is closely connected to the historic development of program design methodologies. Early languages supported the programmer by allowing high level expressions and statements instead of instruction sequences on the machine level. Then means for nested statements were added for representing even more complex program structures. These developments were all concerned with control flow and elementary data structures. Currently we explore the methodologies of modular and object oriented programming. The goal is to compose programs no longer from statements but from larger units.

Up to now the success of these attempts to programming-in-the-large has been doubtful at least when we relate them to questions of programming language design. This is not a surprise: Most of the arising problems cannot be solved within the framework of a programming language. Instead we must turn our attention to issues of library design, frameworks (in the object-oriented sense) and configuration management.

We analyze the requirements for program and software design and compare it to the means offered by modern programming languages. We concentrate on state oriented (or imperative) programming. We use *Sather-K*, [GOOS 1995], as an example. Finally we discuss means how to resolve some of the remaining problems by help of a configuration manager. This will especially lead to a constructive generalization of object oriented frameworks.

2 A view on programs

Programs may express algorithms for computing a mapping $f: A \rightarrow B$ from some input domain A to some output range B. A, B and all intermediate states of the computation represent data but the main interest rests with the computation proper expressed by the control flow in the program. Data structures such as integers, reals, records and arrays are used in this process.

Data abstraction may simplify the description of algorithms: they become more lucid when they are based on data structures such as stacks, queues, files, trees, or, generally speaking, on instances of abstract data types. Hierarchic program structures stress the same idea. We are now used to the idea of first identifying the objects and data structures on which a program should work for solving a given problem. Only afterwards we will formulate the central algorithm based on the operations defined for these objects. In many cases we may even reformulate the problem solution as a set of dialogs between participating objects, the basic idea of object-oriented design and programming.

This is particularly true for *reactive systems* such as operating systems, data base systems, process control systems etc. which map streams of input data to streams of output data under certain timing conditions.[1] A *stream* in this context is a potentially unbounded sequence of data or objects; its length is usually not known at the beginning of a computation. The data in an input stream may even depend on output data of the same computation.

Data abstraction and the object-oriented view enforce the principle of data encapsulation and information hiding by its very definition. The implementation of object interfaces should not be visible to the clients. By help of inheritance and polymorphism object-oriented programming is pushing this view to its extremes by allowing different object types to hide behind the same interface.

Whether or not information hiding is statically implemented by scope rules in a programming language or dynamically by help of name servers and the like is a different issue. Any static measure implements a rule *"for all* program runs it holds ... "* whereas a dynamic measure says *"for the particular* run at hand it holds ... "*. It may be that also the dynamic measure holds for all runs. But this may be very difficult to prove. To maintain understandability of long living programs static measures are therefore always preferable. This remark does not only hold for issues of information hiding.

These considerations lead to a very important insight: besides its bug-free execution we want to maintain understandability of programs over their whole lifetime. Otherwise the evolutionary development of a program and the derivation of slightly modified variants will eventually become impossible. To this end we impose at least the following requirements on the programming language:

1. As many program properties as possible should be statically expressible.
2. The "semantics" of a program should be easily derivable from the program text not only for the programmer but also for all his successors who would like to read and analyze the program later. The latter people are possibly not specially trained in the given programming language.
3. The interpretation of a program should be stable and independent of the particular implementation. If in doubt then as a measure of safety it is better

---

[1] This description grasps the essential content of the notion *reactive system* as defined in [MANNA and PNUELI 1992].

to declare certain features as implementation dependent so that nobody can rely on them.

4. The language should leave considerable freedom to variations of design and implementation styles since it (hopefully) will survive the state of the art at the time of its invention and also must accommodate the programming styles of programmers with a variety of backgrounds.

The semantics of the programming language must clearly describe the intended state transition for each language construct and for their combinations. A complicated semantic model of a language will most likely lead to wrong conclusions by the casual reader or writer of programs. Fancy semantic rules as derived from a consistent, theoretically clean model work, but only if the model is clearly understood by the programmer and the readers of the program.

3 Sather-K

For state oriented programming languages, from *Fortran* up to *Java*, we conclude that utmost simplicity, clarity and a safety margin against unexpected interpretations of pieces of a program are necessary ingredients of a successful language. We illustrate these points by examples from the programming language *Sather-K*:

Sather-K is an object-oriented, imperative language. A program consists of a collection of classes such as

```
class STACK(T); -- stack with elements of type T
   -- define some representation;
   procedure push(item: T): SAME is ... end;
   procedure pop: SAME is ... end;
   procedure top: T is ... end;
   procedure empty: BOOL is ... end;
end; -- class STACK
```

Classes as the only structuring element lead to a very simple program structure. We abstained from putting a module feature into the language. Such modules would have been non-recursive as in *Eiffel*, [MEYER 1992]. But system structures are recursively layered. Furthermore, on many occasions classes such as nodes in graphs or trees may belong to several modules at the same time and then create the additional problem of type equivalence between copies of the same class declaration.

Inheritance and substitution of generic parameters such as the element type T in the example above are explained by textual substitution.[2] This is a very pragmatic decision which is easily understood by practitioners but is considered theoretically unsatisfactory by others. E. g., multiple inheritance is provided on

---

[2] This corresponds to the method already used in *Sather-0*, [OMOHUNDRO 1991]. *Sather 1.1*, [STOUTAMIRE and OMOHUNDRO 1996], is taking a slightly different view.

a last-come-first-served basis: In case of several declarations of the same feature the last declaration overwrites the former ones.

Sather-K is leaving considerable freedom in deciding from which class to inherit which properties: There are presently two basic mechanisms, *include-inheritance* and *subtype-inheritance*. The first one includes the body of the superclass A by textually copying it into the subclass B (at least that is the way how it is explained). But this type of inheritance does not establish a semantic relation between classes A and B; it is only serving for code reuse. Subtype-inheritance on the other side is checking for conformity first before it includes the body of superclass A, i.e. it guarantees that, as far as typing is concerned, every object of the subclass B may be substituted when an object of the superclass is expected.

The distinction between code inclusion and subtyping removes the typing holes of *Smalltalk*, *Eiffel* and some other object-oriented languages; subtype-inheritance is the basis for type-safe polymorphism. Fig. 1 depicts the possible situations in terms of pre- and postconditions of a method m appearing in a class A and its subclass B. Horizontal arrows mean state transitions, vertical arrows logical implementation. The diagrams should commute. Conformant subtyping is type-safe. Specialization would be type-safe if only one subclass B would exist which is used throughout for implementing the interface defined by the (abstract) class A; for constructing object-oriented libraries it would be extremely useful to have specialization as a third distinguished kind of inheritance in a language; but presently we have no idea how type-safe use of specialization could be guaranteed. The covariant diagram is *Eiffel's* subtyping relationship, intuitively appealing but not type-safe. The contravariant case reverts the vertical arrows of the covariant diagram and is not shown. The general code inclusion is *Smalltalk's* standard case. It can only be used in a type-safe manner by runtime checking on a case by case basis and thus may lead to the infamous error message "method not implemented".

The main argument which in 1991 brought *Sather* into being was Steve Omohundro's dissatisfaction with the inefficiency of *Eiffel's* method calling mechanisms: *Eiffel* is always producing polymorphic calls. There is no sufficient language and compiler support for removing superfluous polymorphism. To remedy this situation *Sather* explicitly distinguishes between variables which may assume values of arbitrary conforming subclasses and variables which always carry the type given by their declaration. Methods of the later variables are always called monomorphically, i.e. without the overhead of dispatched calls. In a typical program they actually constitute the majority of all calls. In comparison, *Eiffel* is following a theoretically clean but costly principle whereas *Sather* is making a pragmatically motivated compromise.

In a similar vain *Sather* is using two different kinds of classes or types: value types serve for accommodating integers, reals, complex numbers and similar elementary objects whose values we would like to store in place; whereas reference classes are templates for objects which are stored elsewhere and represented by pointers. The alternative solutions would be to take such elementary types out of

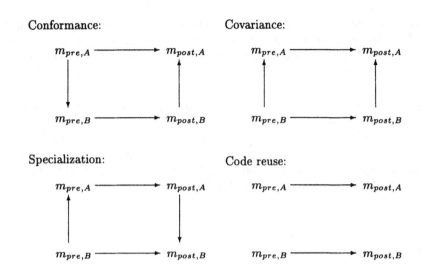

Figure1. Inheritance relations

the object-oriented class system or to handle them in the same way as reference types, a theoretically clean method but with a number of unwanted practical consequences.

An ongoing debate is the issue of implicit initialization of variables. Clearly non-initialized pointer variables must be avoided by all means because on some hardware the safety of the whole system may be endangered. For variables of a value type experience shows that programmers tend to omit explicit initializations if variables are automatically zeroed at creation time. This omission may reduce the readability of a program substantially. It seems therefore best to leave it implementation dependent whether and how variables are initialized so that programmers cannot rely on a specific rule.[3]

Clearly it must be specified when and for what operations a compiler is allowed to make use of the commutative or associative law. But even when the order of executing operations is fixed from, say, left to right, it does not follow that also the operands, or similarly the arguments of a procedure call, must be evaluated in the order from left to right. For optimization purposes it is best if this question is left unspecified, i.e. implementation-dependent. From the point of view of readability it is also best to leave it unspecified. Side effects which require a fixed evaluation order are rather pointing to a trick program then to a program which could be readable also 5 years from now. Imperative programming languages also have a sequencing operator, usually expressed by the semicolon; it is unclear why serialization of actions should also be enforceable by other means (except for data dependencies, of course).

---

[3] We are not concerned with the security holes which this decision may create in a distributed environment. Rightly, *Java* is deciding this problem in the opposite way.

Sather uses garbage collection for removing objects which are no longer needed from the heap. This frees programmers and program readers from the burden to understand how long an objects must remain allocated and is probably the single biggest advantage in slowing down performance degradation during maintenance.

These decisions illustrate the requirements discussed in the foregoing section. In particular, explaining inheritance and substitution of generics by textual replacement is an easily remembered rule compared to the often quite complicated semantics found in other object-oriented languages. It is, on the other hand, unavoidable that conformant subtyping requires a more complicated semantics than, say *Smalltalk's* onheritance rule; but this is the price to be paid for type safety.

3.1 Iterators and Streams

Information hiding requires that the client cannot navigate on his own through the elements of a data structure since this would require knowledge of the internal representation. To resolve this problem language constructs have been invented under various names such as *cursor, rider, iterator* or, in *Sather-K, stream.* Technically a stream is a set of three procedures **first**, **next** and **done** delivering the first and the next element respectively and testing whether all elements are dealt with. The application could look like

```
x := ds.first;
while not ds.done loop process x; x := ds.next end;
```

This approach has the drawback that only one stream in or out of a data structure can be used at a given time since the stream state indicating how far we have traversed the data structure *ds* is part of the data structure itself and cannot be duplicated. [GAMMA 1992] discusses at length how to remove the problem in $C++$ by moving the stream definition to a friend class. Given that we often want to traverse a data structure in a variety of ways, e.g. trees in prefix, infix or postfix order, this idea leads to a multitude of additional classes, one for each kind of traversal. In the presence of separate compilation this solution is also making optimizations very difficult. [LISKOV 1981] and *Sather-1* provide a more elegant but restricted solution: They consider a stream as a loop control and write

```
loop x := ds.elts!; process x end;
```

The *iterator* **elts!** takes one element after the other as its value. When no more elements are left then the loop is terminated. Iterators are declared in the class of the data structure to which they belong. Their state, however is stored on the run-time stack as part of the local context of their call. Thus multiple invocations of iterators at the same time are possible, see [MURER et al. 1993].

Iterators can especially be used for describing traditional for- and while loops as shown in fig. 2.[4]

```
loop while!(time_not_over); show_transparency(1.upto!(n)) end;
```

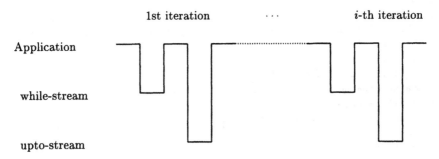

Figure2. Iterators are coroutines

Iterators as described can also produce output streams. The association with loop control is, however, often a severe restriction. E.g., in the standard merge procedure for merge-sort we compare elements until one of the input streams is terminated. Then we must collect the remaining elements of the other input stream. Thus, we need to know, how far this stream has been processed in the comparison loop. But with the above proposal the state information about this stream has also been deleted on termination of this loop! To avoid this problem *Sather-K* introduces explicit stream objects with state and distinguishes 3 items:

- Direct stream calls: These correspond to iterator calls in *Sather-1* and include loop control.
- Bound streams: they are closures in the same way as bound procedures; *Sather-1* also allows them.
- Explicit stream objects: these are local objects containing the state of an ongoing stream. They may be used like an iterator in a direct call; an unsuccessful call within a loop terminates the loop.[5]

The following program shows the use of explicit stream objects.

```
procedure merge(s1,s2: stream: T; s: stream(T)) is
-- type T must be ordered
-- merge two input streams into an output stream
-- establish explicit stream objects with state,
-- initialized with bound streams:
```

---

[4] It increases readability when iterator calls are marked with a special symbol, here the exclamation mark.

[5] Interestingly, implementing explicit stream objects caused less headache than the implementation of direct stream calls.

```
     sa: stream ! : T := bind s1;
     sb: stream ! : T := bind s2;
     ss: stream ! (T) := bind s;
     x1: T := sa!;
     x2: T := sb!;
     loop
        if x1 <= x2
        then ss! := x1; x1 := sa!;
        else ss! := x2; x2 := sb!;
     end; -- compare loop
     -- collect the remaining elements:
     if sa.terminated
     then ss! := x2; loop ss! := sb! end
     else ss! := x1; loop ss! := sa! end
     end; -- if
  end; -- merge
```

Stream objects are always local objects. There is no way of permanently storing the state of an ongoing stream as an attribute of an object. This reflects the dynamic nature of stream objects. It is related to the open question of how to define *robust* streams, i. e. input streams which behave as expected even when an output stream is changing the data structure underneath them. What is meant by *expected behaviour* is not universally clear, cf. [MESSERSCHMIDT 1996].

Streams or iterators are not some fancy additions to an object-oriented language but necessary ingredients for enforcing information hiding. They also lead to better readability of programs since they shorten the program by leaving out the mechanics of traversing data structures.

4 The Role of Program Verification

Hoare's axioms for program verification, [HOARE 1969], and the corresponding ideas about structured programming helped to simplify programming languages as far as programming-in-the-small is concerned. Conventional wisdom says that program verification based on these axioms or on Dijkstra's calculus of weakest preconditions is the right means for granting correctness of a program. But like any other methodology program verification has its weak and its strong points.

The examples given in class are all of this type. Nobody would doubt that Hoare logic is the adequate means, e. g. for proving the correctness of the program

```
{perm}
if a>b then h: INT; h := a; a := b; b := h end;
-- a <= b and perm
if c>d then h: INT; h := c; c := d; d := h end;
-- a <= b and c <= d and perm
if b>d then h: INT; h := b; b := d; d := h; h := c; a := c; c := h end;
-- a <= b <= d and c <= d and perm
if b>e
```

```
then if a>e then h: INT; h := e; e := d; d := b; b := a; a := h
   -- a <= b <= d <= e and c <= e and perm
  else h: INT; h := e; e := d; d := b; b := h end;
   -- a <= b <= d <= e and c <= e and perm
elsif d>e then h: INT; h := e; e := d; d := h end
   -- a <= b <= d <= e and c <= e and perm
end;
-- a <= b <= d <= e and c <= e and perm
if c>b
then
   -- a <= b <= d <= e and b < c <= e and perm
  if c>d then h: INT; h := c: c:= d; d := h end
   -- a <= b <= d <= e and b <= c <= d <= e and perm
elsif c>a then h: INT; h := b; b := c; c := h
-- a <= b <= d <= e and b <= c <= d <= e and perm
else h: INT; h := a; a:= c; c := b; b := h
-- a <= b <= d <= e and b <= c <= d <= e and perm
end
-- a <= b <= c <= d <= e and perm
```

---

for sorting 5 values a, b, c, d, e.[6] However, already in this small example verification could only help in establishing insights and in detecting programming mistakes. Should there be an error then we get hints where to make changes for arriving at a *functionally* correct solution. But for any additional goal such as solving the problem with the minimal number of 7 comparisons insights are needed which do not show up in the proof.

Indeed, we observe that algorithm designers rarely use program verification, stepwise refinement or similar means as their main way of thinking when creating new algorithms or data structures. The major reason is that this method does not naturally lead to considering the possible design alternatives. Program verification helps in producing *one* correct solution; but it does not help in producing the *best* solution when goals such as low time complexity, low storage consumption, portability, modifiability etc. are taken into account. The most impressive example is the well-known n-queens problem which is solved by stepwise refinement in all textbooks with a backtracking algorithm of exponential complexity. But on the path of design decisions why was the solution with linear complexity, known since 1874, [PAULS 1874], out of sight? We conclude that program verification certainly belongs to the tool box of algorithm designers. And verification as a final step will help to remove any remaining clerical errors. But the tool box contains many more means for analyzing the problem at hand and for deriving insights about the space of possible solutions.

This is becoming particularly clear when we consider the notions of partial and total correctness: Whenever the complexity $T(n)$ of an algorithm is analyzed then $T(n) < \infty$ will automatically imply termination of all loops and recursions.

---

[6] The predicate **perm** indicates that the current values are a permutation of the original ones.

Determining the time complexity is the better means than establishing total correctness.

Many people advocate writing pre- and postconditions of procedures and then proving the correctness of the procedure body from these assertions. However, this method is useful only in application domains such as combinatorics including graph theory for which it is easy to express theorems and their proof in predicate calculus. When we deal with application domains in mathematics, natural sciences, engineering or economics which are not fully formalized then there are application dependent assertions which must be used in the program proof. These assertions may take the form of a theorem from analysis or topology as in the subsequent example; but mostly they are assertions based on physical laws, economic insights or other sources of experience. The validity of the program is crucially dependent on the validity of these unproven assertions.

The following example, taken from [WELZL 1991], shows the difficulty in full glory: We want to compute the smallest enclosing disk $sd(p)$ of a point set $p \subseteq R$ in the Euclidean plane. We generalize the problem and write a procedure

```
sdb(p,r: $ SET($ POINT): DISK
```

solving the problem with the additional requirement that the point set r must be completely contained on the border of the disk. We get the solution to the original problem if r is empty. Of course, the original problem is always solvable whereas the generalized problem allows for inconsistent arguments, e.g. when r contains more then 3 points not all on the same circle. With some mathematical arguments WELZL arrived at the following solution:[7]

```
procedure sdb(p,r: $ SET($ POINT)): DISK is
    s: $ POINT; pminus: $ SET($ POINT);
    if p.empty or r.size >= 3 then res := DISK::create(r)
    else
        s := p.random_select;
        pminus := p.delete(s);
        res := sdb(pminus,r);
        if not res.contains(s) then res := sdb(pminus,r.add(s)) end;
    end; -- if
end; -- sdb
```

If p is empty or the border set r contains at least 3 elements then the solution, if it exists, is solely determined by r. Otherwise we remove a point s (at random) from p and solve the smaller problem. We are finished when s belongs to this solution; mathematics teaches us that otherwise s must be a point on the border and therefore we include s into r. Since in all recursive calls the size of p has been diminished the procedure will eventually terminate. But what is the precondition under which it is producing the correct result? The condition *problem is solvable* will do the job!

---

[7] The actual construction of a disk with a given set r of border points is not shown. Problems arising from the use of floating point instead of real arithmetic are neglected. WELZL proves that the algorithm has expected runtime $O(p.size)$.

This example is obviously not understandable if we do not know the precondition. But the existence proof for a solution depends on domain specific knowledge, the domain being geometry in this case. Also the proof that points not belonging to the previously constructed disk must lay on the border requires geometric knowledge.

Much has been made about including pre- and postconditions and class invariants into an object-oriented language. In the light of the foregoing example we have become rather reluctant about these assets:

- Pre- and postconditions expressed as executable Boolean expressions help in continuous supervision of correct runtime behavior. But successful checking only states that for the given arguments the conditions have been fulfilled. Especially beginners are inclined to believe that this is sufficient whereas they should really prove that *for all* admissible combinations of arguments the conditions are fulfilled.
- Many algorithms come with conditions which are not easily expressible with the limited means of Boolean expressions but need either the full power of predicate calculus or means for expressing domain specific knowledge such as the condition *problem is solvable* in the example. Such examples are then taken as an excuse for not writing pre- and postconditions at all. We thus prefer to insist that pre- and postconditions are written in all cases but as comments.
- In the presence of streams we observe cases where a class invariant must hold after each stream call, and others where it will only hold on termination of a stream. Both cases may occur within the same data structure and often indicate the difference between on-line and off-line algorithms.

In summary we conclude that program verification must be put in the proper perspective to value its merits:

- Standard verification techniques control the proper writing of a program and will uncover inconsistencies. Verification failures show the presence of a bug but not how to cure it.
- Loop invariants lead to a clearer understanding of the purpose of a loop and help in writing clean programs.
- Only partial correctness of an algorithm is of practical interest. Proof of termination is an implicit consequence of establishing bounds for the complexity (or better: the efficiency) of the algorithm. Such bounds should be be established anyway.
- Program understanding and verification proper depend on domain specific insights. The "real proof" crucially depends on the validity of this knowledge. Hoare logic or similar means are only formulating conclusions from this knowledge.
- The theories underlying the proof of propositions about the application domain are often extremely cumbersome to formally deal with as. For the majority of applications, e. g. business applications or the interaction of hard-

ware and software in real-time systems, formalized theories do not exist at all.

- The predicates occuring in pre- and postconditions and assertions must accomodate for formulating domain specific knowledge. Often the use of "pure" predicate calculus is rather obscuring this knowledge and thus does not help in bridging the gap between logic and application knowledge.
- For making a proof understandable all the application dependent assertions on which the proof relies must be carefully explained. Pre- and postconditions, class and loop invariants alone are not carrying the required knowledge when we leave the realm of toy problems used in teaching. This implies that assertions very often can be proven by hand only, not within an established logical theory.

These insights are raising severe doubts about the merits of program verification on the algorithmic level. Indeed, the algorithmics community is establishing the correctness of its results mostly in a different but nevertheless very rigid manner: they directly relate state transitions within the program to assertions in the application domain. The verification question "what is the meaning of a statement" is replaced by the question which of the assertions in the application domain should be exploited in a program.

The picture changes, however, as soon as we consider a purely combinatorial application domain such as VLSI-design or, in programming, as soon as we connect several modules on an abstract level. Information hiding dictates that the details of algorithms and the domain specific knowledge underlying these algorithms is hidden at the interface level. Checking the correct interfacing of modules is a task in which the power of program verification is the adequate means for establishing correctness.

We conclude again that programming semantics should be of the utmost simplicity as long as we consider design of algorithms since not the semantics of the programming language but the semantics of the application domain is of interest. We also conclude that the discussion of program verification on this level may lead to insights into the soundness, consistency and completeness of the tool set which a programming language is offering on this level. But important applications of program verification are not to be expected. This is in sharp contrast to what we teach about program verification where the examples remain mostly on this level. But when we consider programming-in-the-large then program verification is becoming an important tool for getting the interfaces right.

5 Programming Languages and Beyond

The main merits of object-oriented programming languages are not technical features such as inheritance, genericity and polymorphism but support for reusable libraries and evolutionary programming. Construction of libraries and frameworks for reuse is yet a difficult art, cf. [NÄHER and MEHLHORN 1990, GAMMA

1992, WEINAND 1992, GAMMA et al. 1994, FRICK et al. 1996, SPARKS et al. 1996] as a starting point. Proper support for such construction tasks very often exceeds the realm of language design since we must support the integration of modules from many different alnguages including binary code for which sources are not available.

A programming language is a set of mechanisms hopefully useful in writing interesting application programs. Likewise the environment of a language implementation should provide a set of mechanisms for dealing with the issues of program integration, library and framework design. In this section we explore some such mechanisms under the heading "configuration management" which we found useful in the context of implementing *Sather-K*. But the mechanisms are basically language independent.

From a compiler writer's point of view the use of large libraries, classes with many methods and the cooperation with program generators raises a number of issues:

1. How do we find the classes contributing to a specified main program without reading through all libraries?
2. How do we remove naming collisions between libraries and how do we structure the usually flat name space of class names?
3. How do we avoid translating methods which will never be called?
4. How could we avoid repeated checking of interclass relations such as conformity?
5. How could we automatically generate classes for which only specifications are given?

Many of these problems are well-known and arise also in the context of languages such as *C*. Disregarding these problems is significantly slowing down compilation and may create noticeable IO-overheads in networked environments. Problem (2) is considered by many as a problem of language design. We do not share this view since it also arises in multi-lingual contexts.

To solve such problems we propose to encapsulate compilation into an environment provided by a *configuration manager CM*:

1. *CM* is maintaining a data base controlling all the sources belonging to a specific project p. New or modified sources are entered at arbitrary times, e. g. by the *save* operation of the editor.
2. On entry *CM* is performing at least a syntactic analysis of each file for extracting the names of all class declarations and their features. This information is stored together with the source location in the data base.
3. All searches for class or feature declarations by the compiler are replaced by data base queries to be answered by the *CM*.

If all class names are unambiguous then this scheme implies that the compiler will only see those class and feature declarations which are needed. The idea may now be easily extended to cover also the other problems:

1. *CM* may use some of the well-known techniques for providing version- and variant-control and for dealing with other problems on the level of source code control.

2. We may augment the source code with *CM* instructions which describe dependencies between classes. In this way we can describe the grouping of classes to modules. Also overlapping modules and recursive groupings can be described. In general, arbitrary scope rules for class names can be represented by suitable relations and thus the problems of a flat class name space and of naming collisions can be resolved. E. g., in a framework f of classes $A, B, C, D, \ldots$ it may be specified that the occurrence of class specifier B always means class B of f whereas occurrence of a class specifier T may be bound to either class C of f or to a class defined by the user of the framework. Obviously by this relational approach arbitrary system architectures can be defined.

3. We may also allow for submitting specifications in any other suitable programming or specification language to the configuration manager. Such specifications must be accompanied by specifying a set of actions which the configuration manager should take for either generating source code from the specification or for generating linkable object code. Version control will warrant that such actions are executed whenever a specification is used the first time or is modified. Examples include the specification of an ftp address from which the required source may be obtained, the specification of an enumerated type

```
type weekday = (Sunday, Monday, ..., Saturday);
```

from which a class

```
class WEEKDAY is
  constant Sunday: INT := 0;
  constant Monday: INT := 1;
  ...
  constant Saturday: INT := 7;
  ...
end; -- WEEKDAY
```

together with suitable methods is generated, or the specification of a context-free grammar from which a framework for a parser is instantiated. The instantiation of generic classes in *Sather-K* or *Eiffel* and of class templates in $C++$ may be viewed as a special case of this more general procedure.

4. The *CM* may (partially) analyze the static semantics of any submitted source code. Of particular interest would be the analysis of inter class relations such as subtyping or other inheritance relations, and the extraction of a complete definition table of all submitted classes. This would further speed up compilation by avoiding repeated checking of unchanged source code. Extracting definition tables would be lead to very similar structures as the well-known data dictionaries used in data base applications.

The ideas may be easily extended to incorporate design methods for distributed systems based on CORBA's IDL specifications or Microsoft's ActiveX technology.

The last point of the list is of particular interest when all classes of a program are translated together and no separate compilation scheme is used. Our present *Sather-K*-compiler is using this method for exploring the potential of inter class optimizations.

We stress that this proposal is only providing mechanisms for resolving the above mentioned problems. We believe that policies of how to apply such mechanisms should not be part of a language implementation but fall into the responsibility of application and system designers.

A configuration manager for implementing parts of this proposal is currently in preparation as an extension of the *Sather-K*-system. The idea is, however, not generally new. [CLEMM and OSTERWEIL 1990] describes the ODIN-system for handling the dependency information in environment integration which we need. The compiler construction system ELI is based on ODIN and is demonstrating the viability of the approach. Our current configuration manager is also based on ODIN. The main differences are of a rather philosophical nature: Whereas earlier uses of the approach such as ELI consider their solution as a generalization of make we stress the vicinity to the use of data base management systems. Compared to even earlier approaches such as IPSEN, [NAGL 1996], GANDALF, [HABERMANN and NOTKIN 1986] or UNIBASE, [GOOS et al. 1988] the main emphasis here is on providing mechanisms applicable also in large-scale projects with libraries of many hundreds or thousands of classes. Experience shows that on this scale most of the detailed mechanisms so useful in smaller systems become inapplicable, cf. [DAUSMANN 1985].

References

[CLEMM and OSTERWEIL 1990] CLEMM, G. and OSTERWEIL, L. J. (1990): A Mechanism for Environment Integration. *ACM Trans. Prog. Lang. and Systems*, 12(1): 1–25.

[DAUSMANN 1985] DAUSMANN, M. (1985): *Informationen und Verfahren für die getrennte Übersetzung von Programmteilen*. PhD thesis, Universität Karlsruhe.

[FRICK et al. 1996] FRICK, A., ZIMMER, W. and ZIMMERMANN, W. (1996): Konstruktion robuster und flexibler Klassenbibliotheken. *Informatik, Forschung und Entwicklung*, 11: 168–178.

[GAMMA 1992] GAMMA, E. (1992): *Objektorientierte Software-Entwicklung am Beispiel von ET++: Klassenbibliothek, Werkzeuge, Design*. Heidelberg: Springer-Verlag.

[GAMMA et al. 1994] GAMMA, E., HELM, R., JOHNSON, R. and Vlissides, J. (1994): *Design Patterns: Elements of Reusable Software Components*. Addison-Wesley.

[GOOS 1995] GOOS, G. (1995): Sather-K — The Language. Interner Bericht 8/95, Fakultät für Informatik, Universität Karlsruhe.

[GOOS et al. 1988] GOOS et al. (1988): UniBase Abschlußbericht. Technical Report, Verbundprojekt UniBase.

[HABERMANN and NOTKIN 1986] HABERMANN, A. N. and Notkin, D. (1986): Gandalf: Software Development Environments. *IEEE Trans. Software Engineering*, 12(12): 1117–1127.

[HOARE 1969] HOARE, C. (1969): An axiomatic basis for computer programming. *Communications of the ACM*, 12: 576–583.

[LISKOV 1981] LISKOV, B. (1981): *CLU Reference Manual*, volume 114 of *LNCS*. Springer Verlag.

[MANNA and PNUELI 1992] MANNA, Z. and PNUELI, A. (1992): *The Temporal Logic of Reactive and Concurrent Systems Specification*. Springer Verlag.

[MESSERSCHMIDT 1996] MESSERSCHMIDT, H. J. (1996): List Iterators in C++. *Software — Practice and Experience*, 26(11): 1197–1203

[MEYER 1992] MEYER, B. (1992): *Eiffel: the Language*. Prentice Hall.

[MURER et al. 1993] MURER, S., OMOHUNDRO, S. M. and SZYPERSKI, C. (1993): Sather Iters: Object-Oriented Iteration Abstraction. Technical Report TR-93-045, ICSI.

[NAGL 1996] NAGL, M., editor (1996): *Building Tightly Integrated Software Development Environments: The IPSEN Approach*, volume 1170 of *LNCS*. Springer Verlag.

[NÄHER and MEHLHORN 1990] NÄHER, S. and MEHLHORN, K. (1990): LEDA — A Library of Efficient Data Types and Algorithms. In PATERSON, M., editor, *Proceedings of the 17th International Colloquium on Automata, Languages and Programming*, volume 443 of *LNCS*, pages 1–5. Springer Verlag.

[OMOHUNDRO 1991] OMOHUNDRO, S. M. (1991): The Sather Language. Report, 3. Juni 1991, International Computer Science Institute, Berkeley.

[PAULS 1874] PAULS (1874): Das Maximalproblem der Damen auf dem Schachbrett. *Deutsche Schachzeitung*, 29: 129–134;257–267.

[SPARKS et al. 1996] SPARKS, S., BRENNER, K. and Faris, C. (1996): Managing Object-Oriented Framework Reuse. *IEEE Computer*, 29(9): 52–61.

[STOUTAMIRE and OMOHUNDRO 1996] STOUTAMIRE, D. and OMOHUNDRO, S. (1996): The Sather 1.1 Specification. Technical Report TR-96-012, International Computer Science Institute, Berkeley.

[WEINAND 1992] WEINAND, A. (1992): *Objektorientierter Entwurf und Implementierung portabler Fensterumgebungen am Beispiel des Application-Framework ET++*. Heidelberg: Springer-Verlag.

[WELZL 1991] WELZL, E. (1991): Smallest Enclosing Disks (Balls and Ellipsoids). In MAURER, H., editor, *New Results and New Trends in Computer Science*, volume 555, pages 359–370. Springer Verlag.

Multi-language, Multi-target Compiler Development: Evolution of the Gardens Point Compiler Project

K.John Gough

Queensland University of Technology, Brisbane, Australia

Abstract. The Gardens Point project started in 1987 as an attempt to make *Modula-2* available on a variety of 32-bit Unix platforms. Since that time, it has evolved into a flexible platform for research into compiler construction and language implementation. Gardens point compilers are available on about a dozen platforms, and are mostly freeware.

Currently, the gardens point infrastructure is used for a variety of research projects in areas such as code selection, global optimization, register allocation, and exception handling. There are also a variety of language research issues which are being pursued by the group.

This paper sets out a brief history of the project, and describes the insights which have come from the implementation of a variety of languages on most of the major current computer architectures.

1 Introduction: Original Goals

The history of the gardens point project began in the mid 1980s, when QUT's School of Computing Studies decided to move a large part of their teaching onto *UNIX* servers. Until that point, teaching relied on PCs in the first year, and VAX and PDP-11 machines thereafter. We were already using *Modula-2* for introductory programming subjects, using Dave Moore's fast single-pass *FTL* compiler on the PCs, and the ETH five-pass M22 compiler for the PDP-11. By this time the author was maintaining the M22 compiler, ETH having moved their own compiler development onto Lilith machines.

As it turned out, the School decided to purchase the then very new HP Precision Architecture "RISC" machines. It soon became clear that the only way to get a *Modula-2* compiler for such a machine was to create one for oneself. The opportunity to create an entirely new compiler family targetted on the emerging 32-bit *UNIX* machines proved irresistible to the author, and to another old compiler hand, John Hynd. We decided to call the compiler **gardens point modula-2**, since QUT is sited at beautiful "Gardens Point" on the Brisbane river, in the heart of the City of Brisbane.

The main attraction, at first, was to create a complete compiler which could be entirely new. Thus the compiler would use no code or even architectural concepts from the various compilers on which we had previously worked. Instead, we would do a design which, from the start, would take advantage of the 32-bit flat virtual address spaces of the new generation of machines. Thus we planned to be free from what we saw as the tyranny of narrow address spaces. In retrospect it is clear that taking this approach allows for the design of a very clean software architecture, but that there are dangers in going too willingly down the inflationary path of memory gluttony. In our current generation of compilers, register allocation for certain pathological functions in the SPEC-92 benchmark suite causes the dynamic allocation of a single data structure which demands 3-Mb. Anyone who remembers writing a complete compiler which fitted in 56Kb is bound to slight nervousnous when faced with such a statistic.

Another prime goal was to create a compiler which would set new standards for user-friendliness in the area of compile-time and runtime diagnostics. We were simply dismayed at the prevailing standard of error messages which compilers produced. Most *Modula-2* compilers were better than most *C* compilers, for sound technical reasons, but were still rather primitive. Consider the following *Modula-2*-specific example —

> When a programmer imports two separate enumeration types, (say *Languages* and *Islands*) into a module, it is an unfriendly act for a compiler to respond —
>
> ```
>        FROM Atlas IMPORT Islands;
> ****                     ^-- doubly declared identifier
> ```
>
> What the user needs to know is that the identifier "java" appears as a value in both enumerations. The compiler *knows* the identity of the offending identifier, why not tell the user?

The dedication to better error reporting is not without cost, of course. In the case of static semantic errors, additional information needs to be propagated along the call chain. Thus the failure to insert a new identifier into a name scope cannot precipitate an immediate, generic diagnostic, but must be propagated back to a point where the declarative context is known.

In the case of runtime errors, **gpm** also makes valiant efforts. In the case of range errors, the **gpm** runtime produces a diagnostic which reports the out-of-range value, the limits of the permitted range, and the module and source line number at which the error occurred. With care, all of this can be done with no time penalty. All error jumps are vectored through intermediate locations where they pick up their individual information. This behaviour has a moderate space cost, and in very large programs may lead to somewhat worse paging behaviour.

1.1 The "via-C" compilers

The original compiler was designed to construct an abstract syntax tree (*AST*), for the whole of a compilation unit, in memory, at once. This choice was made to allow abitrary intra-module attributes to be evaluated. Code was to be emitted by a recursive tree-walker, with the original target language being Hewlett-Packard's proprietary version of "*Ucode*" [22]. For about one year it seemed that HP would make the interface available for third party developers, subject to the usual non-disclosure conditions. Eventually, negotiations broke down, due to what was said to be the rather unfamiliar legal territory into which such an agreement would have taken the company. Fortunately, we had been working on a contingency plan which involved traversal of the same *AST* to emit *ANSI-C*. As shown in Figure 1, by substituting a different tree-walker a different output

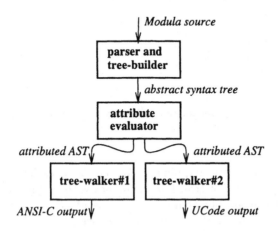

Fig. 1. Compiler frontend with multiple treewalkers

language could be produced. A small number of attributes were required for one tree-walker but not the other, but the majority of the effort was preserved.

The use of *ANSI-C* as an intermediate language is by now well established, but involves some rather tricky design considerations. One design issue which has seen a number of different attacks, is access to variables in non-local scopes (the so-called uplevel addressing problem). Some early designs, such as p2c allocate explicit activation records, so that explicit *static links* can be maintained. Currently, the most popular method to attack the problem seems to be to declare additional arguments in the *C* procedures, which explicitly pass references to each uplevel-accessed datum along the call chain. The "via-C" versions of **gpm** adopted an entirely different approach involving the maintainence of a version of Dijkstra's *display vector*[8]. In the usual organisation, the elements of the display vector point to the base of the stack-frames of the accessible scopes. Since *C* has no explicit concept of activation record, we make the display vector point to an arbitrary uplevel-addressed datum in the frame. In the unusual case where there are several such data, we dynamically compute address differences, and hold these in statically allocated locations. This rather baroque method is suprisingly efficient. In the case of the common idiom in Figure 2 the resulting object code is as efficient as any native code implementation. Note that with our method, no extra cycles are consumed in the calls of *Look*, and the single call of *Find* attracts the overhead of a save and restore of a single display element. In this example, the display vector element would point directly to the variable

```
PROCEDURE Find(key : INTEGER; VAR ok : BOOLEAN);
  PROCEDURE Look(k : INTEGER; t : Tree);
  BEGIN
    IF t = NIL THEN ok := FALSE; RETURN END;
    IF    k < t^.key THEN Look(k,t^.lOp)
    ELSIF k > t^.key THEN Look(k,t^.rOp)
    ELSE  ok := TRUE; RETURN
    END
  END Look;
BEGIN (* Find *)
  Look(key,root)
END Find;
```

Fig. 2. Binary tree lookup, with non-local variable access

parameter *ok*.

Another difficulty is the mapping of *Modula-2* types into *ANSI-C* types. More recent compilers which translate languages with polymorphic assignment into *ANSI-C* have invariably abandoned all use of *C*'s type system, and use casts everywhere. We would have been well advised to do the same. Different *C* compilers ascribe quite different semantics to recursive type declarations in complex cases involving function prototypes. Furthermore, in *ANSI-C* there is no way to declare a recursive type which does not involve a `struct` or a `union`. *ISO Modula-2*[18], on the other hand, allows recursion through procedure types, and also through arrays. None of these constructs has an analog in *C*.

At one time, while we were still developing our native code compilers, we offered the "via-C" compiler on no less than eleven platforms. Some of these did not have *ANSI-C* conformant compilers, and almost all had bugs or idiosyncrasies which turned support into a major challenge. We survived by using a preprocessor which selectively included code to step around the known bugs of each *C* compiler.

1.2 The Dcode compilers

Apart from a few remaining "via-C" compilers, all versions of **gpm** now generate native code based on the use of an intermediate program representation, which is the instruction set of an abstract stack machine. We call the intermediate form *Dcode*, as it was designed to be used to express Directed acyclic graphs. In principle, the use of such a form enables a clean separation between the language dependent (and target independent) **compiler frontend**, and the target dependent (and language independent) **code-generating backend**, as shown in Figure 3. Such an intermediate form is necessarily both language- and target-independent.

The use of abstract machine intermediate forms is the subject of much debate. One school of thought suggests that the separation of language and target

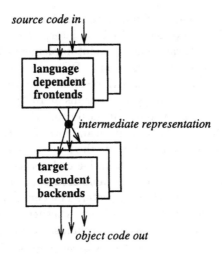

Fig. 3. Architecture of the compilers

concerns should be realised by the generation of orthogonal specifications, and the composition of such specifications within a tool framework, such as Eli [17]. It is true that for any given, single language-and-target combination, a monolithic compiler can be made smaller and faster than a two-part compiler based on a language- and target-independent intermediate form, but the abstract machine based design still has much to recommend it in practice. Some of the advantages and disadvantages are commented on here.

The first of the *Dcode* compilers was built for the *mips R-3000* architecture, with both big- and little-endian versions being created for *DecStation* and *Silicon Graphics* machines. Later versions were created for *Intel iapx86*, *SUN SPARC*, *Digital Alpha* and *IBM Power* architectures.

1.3 Mixed compilation and interpretation

One of the benefits of adopting an abstract stack machine as an intermediate representation is that it opens up the possibility of interpretation as an implementation strategy. Indeed, the exploitation of just this possibility was the key idea behind the *UCSD Pascal* compilers, which first brought high level language programming to the world of microcomputers in the 1970s.

By 1990, at QUT our first-year students were still predominantly using PC machines for their programming, and many at that time were still using 8088 or 80286 processors. The possibility of creating a native code version of **gpm** for these machines seemed remote. The design of **gpm** specified the whole-number types as 32-bits, and the profligate use of memory in the frontend made the goal of boostrapping a PC version unthinkable.

Instead, we translated the *Dcode* version of the frontend into *C* using the "via-C" compiler, and compiled it for the PC using *Turbo-C*. A vestigial backend performed some peephole compression of the *Dcode*, and cleverly combined this with some compiled code to achieve mixed compilation and interpretation. This version, which we dubbed **gpm-pc**, used an interpreter to emulate a 32-bit machine, and included a software floating point implementation. Students using **gpm-pc** could develop their programs on a PC, and then run them on the *UNIX* machines with absolutely identical results, other than execution speed. On computationally intensive code, **gpm-pc** runs at 10–20% of the speed of the same machine running compiled code (but also using the long datatypes).

The technology of this mixed compilation and interpretation has been covered in another paper[10]. Here is suffices to note the key concept. All procedure calls jump out of the interpreter to execute a native code procedure stub. This stub performs the usual entry prolog, copying value arrays, updating the display and so on, and then launches the *Dcode* interpreter. The consequences of this design are that the interpreter does not need to know whether the called procedure is interpreted or compiled, since the calling mechanism is identical. Furthermore, for programs which spend most of their time in the code of the compiled library modules, the speed penalty for interpretation is small.

Notice that with this design the interpreter indirectly is recursively activated. Interpreter and application may alternate their activation records on the runtime stack.

1.4 Parameterisation of the stack machine

During a short sabbatical visit to Tübingen by the author, a major cleanup of the **gpm** frontend was completed. After this rewrite, all implementations of **gpm** shared identical source code. That is still the situation today, despite the fact that the code runs on versions with different byte packing order, 32-bit or 64-bit word size, and with many different parameter passing conventions. It is worthwhile seeing how this is achieved.

Firstly, it should be noted that the situation illustrated in Figure 3 is somewhat of an ideal. Truly architecture-neutral forms, such as *OSF*'s *ANDF* and the bytecodes of the *Java* virtual machine[20] obtain their architecture neutrality by passing huge amounts of symbolic information along with their instructions. *Dcode* is intended to be a much lower-level form, and we wished for such things as offsets into data areas to be computed by the frontend.

In the final design, the **gpm** frontend is parameterised at runtime, by reading a small "configuration" file. The file specifies such things as the data alignment constraints, the byte packing order (*endian-ness*) of the target, and some technical details of the parameter passing mechanism. All of these specifications apply to the target machine, rather than to the host machine which is executing the frontend. Thus if **gpm** is running on an *INTEGER* = 64bits, little-endian *Alpha* machine, and is given the configuration file for the *INTEGER* = 32bits, big-endian *SPARC-Solaris* machine, then it will produce identical *Dcode* to a native *SPARC* version.

The frontend needs to know the target data alignment constraints, so that it can correctly compute offsets of fields on the target machine. On some machines the alignment rules are different for structures and for parameters, so that more than one alignment characteristic may need to be specified.

The problem of endian-ness is a difficult one, and became significantly more difficult with the introduction of value constructors in *ISO Modula-2*. Consider the following declarative code fragment —

```
CONST Foo = Table{ expression list };
      Bar = Foo[25] + 3.0;
```

Here is the problem: an image of the constant *Foo* needs to be constructed in the frontend, and output in correct byte-order in the output file. This argues for constructing the image using the representation conventions of the *target architecture*, so that a simple byte-by-byte dump of the image can be performed[1]. Unfortunately, the second line requires us to extract a component of the constant at compile time, in the representation conventions of the *host architecture*. The key issue here is not whether host and target are big- or little-endian, but whether they are *same-endian* or *cross-endian*. In the event, **gpm** constructs such values using target conventions. The endian-ness of the target is specified by the configuration file, and the compiler tests the endian-ness of its host during startup. Thus, for the above example the element extraction code of the frontend will be selected, "on the fly", according to the value of the initialisation *crossEndian* Boolean.

The parameter passing conventions are important to the frontend, since there are different constraints on parameter passing order for machines which push values on the stack, or pass values in machine registers. Stack discipline obviously demands a fixed order of "pushing", while machines which pass parameters in registers must serialise all calls. What this means, in the second case, is that *all* parameters which require function calls must be evaluated before *any* parameters are moved to the parameter assembly area (a set of designated registers plus the calling stack for additional parameters).

The passing of records and arrays by value is even more variable. Figure 4 shows three ways by which such parameters might be passed. In this diagram, the stack grows downward on the page, parameters are above *fp*, while local variables are between *fp* and *sp*. For value arrays, conformance with *C* is not an issue, so all versions of **gpm** currently use the method of diagram (a) for open arrays. Most architectures correspond to diagram (b) for value records, but *SPARC* conventions correspond to the method in diagram (c). Finally, for fixed arrays in *ISO Modula-2*, fixed-length arrays *must* be marshalled by the caller, since element-by-element value conversion and range checking may be required. Thus the method of diagram (c) is used for all such array parameters on all targets.

---

[1] Alternative approaches, such as dumping a symbolic representation of the structured constant, were rejected, since they would have required the backends to understand the semantics of value construction.

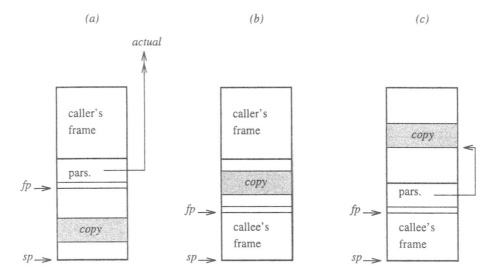

Fig. 4. Copying structured value parameters

(a) Passed by reference, copied by called procedure
(b) Copied by caller, passed by value
(c) Copied by caller, passed by reference

2 The Gardens Point Architecture

The overall architectural concept of the Gardens Point compilers was already shown in Figure 3. In principle, the instructions of the abstract machine might be passed from frontend to backend in a text file, a binary "byte-code" file, or via a procedural interface (but see Section 2.3 for a limitation). Figure 5 shows a *Dcode* interface with and without an intermediate file. The procedural interface into the *Dcode*-writer and out of the *Dcode*-parser are essentially the same.

The *Modula-2* frontends are well known, but we also use our backends on *Dcode* produced by frontends for other languages. A modified version of Fraser and Hansen's *lcc* [9] emits *Dcode* to create a rather nice *ANSI-C* compiler. Other languages which have been used are *Oberon-2*, *Sather 0.5* [21], and a number of experimental languages including various levels of *CLANG* [24], and a very minimal object-oriented *Oberon-2*-based language called *Luna* [6]. *Luna* is an interesting case, since despite the minimality, the frontend is written in its own language. *Java* [2] compilers for all supported platforms are currently under construction.

2.1 The abstract stack machine

The heart of the architecture is an abstract machine, the *D-machine*. The *Dcode* form is defined by the reference document [12], which is available publicly. The

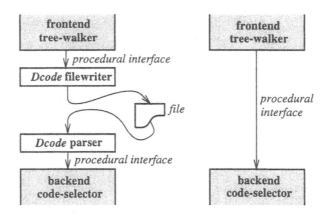

Fig. 5. Different implementation of the *Dcode* interface

form has undergone revisions on a regular basis, with major revisions occurring when 64-bit integer support was added, when more information was made available for global optimisers, and most recently when the exception handling model was upgraded to support *Java* exceptions. As it turns out, exception handling in *ISO Modula-2* fits comfortably into this new framework, although it does not utilise all of new capabilities.

Dcode is an instruction set for an abstract stack machine, much in the style of *Pcode*[25, 1] or *Ucode*[22]. All computation is performed onto an evaluation stack, and instructions implicitly take their operands from the stack. The semantic level of the instructions is a little lower in *Dcode* than in most such machines. The instruction set does not, for example, include any "load" instructions. Instead, there are "push address" and "dereference" instructions of various kinds which compose to create the operations of a typical load. The point of this choice is to expose more detail to the pattern matching capabilities of the backends. As well as the evaluation stack, the *D-machine* assumes an activation record, assumed to be placed on some runtime stack. The stack-frame abstraction assumed by *Dcode* is illustrated in Figure 6.

Abstract stack machines tend to be distinguished by the various mechanisms used to specify parameter passing, and the way in which non-top-of-stack values may be accessed. The *D-machine* is unusual in both respects, in an attempt to facilitate both interpretation and optimisation of its output.

The passing of parameters in the *D-machine* relies on a two step process. In the first, the actual parameter is evaluated onto the evaluation stack. In the second, a mkPar (*"make-parameter"*) instruction pops the top-of-stack value and moves it to an abstract parameter location. The called procedure finds these values in its own activation record, at known offsets relative to an abstract *argument pointer*. Each code-generating backend will know which locations in its activation record actually correspond to memory locations and which to register values. Interpreters implement the mkPar instruction by moving the top of the

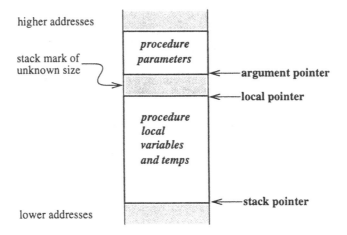

Fig. 6. Stack-frame abstraction used by *Dcode*

evaluation stack to the correct spot in the activation record. This particular design allows more freedom in the order of evaluation of actual parameters, since evaluated parameters may be stored on the stack.

Dcode does not allow access to values below the top of stack. Instead it provides a non-destructive "copy-to-temporary" instruction. These temporaries are assigned locations in the activation record. The *Dcode* definition guarantees that these locations will only be accessed via a corresponding "push-temporary" instruction, so that simple code-generators may, without further analysis, move such values to machine registers.

It is interesting that the *Java*-virtual-machine (*JVM*) makes rather different choices. The *JVM* passes arguments on the evaluation stack, thus pinning the computation order[2]. Similarly, the *JVM* has a number of instructions which access values at different depths below the top of stack. Of course, since *JVM* has no concept of offsets in the current activation record, the design choices were much more constrained.

The design of abstract machine instruction sets has two conflicting goals. The number of instruction may be made very small, but then many instructions will need additional "mode" information. This extreme is well suited to procedural interfaces in which each instruction is a separate procedure, and the mode values just become parameter values to the call. At the other extreme the instructions might have no modes at all, with separate instructions used for (say) *"add"*, *"add with signed overflow detection"*, and *"add with unsigned overflow detection"*. Provided that the number of instructions does not exceed 255, such a choice would lead to the simplest and fastest interpreted implementations, with the densest code.

---

[2] This fixing of the order is not an issue for *Java*, since the language definition demands fixed evaluation order in any case.

The *D-machine* lies intermediate between these two extremes, with a total instruction count of 134, but with many instructions still having mode information. At first sight, this number of instructions may seem rather high. Nevertheless, it must be remembered that the form provides facilities for achieving proper semantics for almost all kinds of languages. *Dcode* supports ten different storage data types, ranging from signed and unsigned bytes through to 64-bit integers. Whole-number arithmetic is supported at two precisions: *word-sized* and 64-bit, and two IEEE floating point types are supported.

In order to support various languages, arithmetic with and without overflow trapping is provided, together with multiple division and remainder operations. There are no less than 16 floating point conversion operations, 9 of which have both trapping and non-trapping versions.

If *Dcode* were being designed now, the benefit of hindsight would see the number of instructions sharply reduced, with more mode information attached to each instruction. This would trade speed for space in pattern matching code generators, and would not restrict interpreters, since it is a simple matter to expand the canonical form in a byte-code writer module.

2.2 The runtime support system

Almost all compiler systems depend on the presence of some kind of library support at runtime. For example, most *Modula-2* systems would implement intersection and union for large multi-word sets by means of a library function, rather than by generating inline code. Other languages require different language primitives to be supported by the runtime system.

It is a design goal that as far as possible frontends should be target independent, and backends should be language independent. With *Dcode* this goal is approached by parameterizing frontends for those target attributes which are unavoidable. Backends should be entirely language independent, at least for conventional procedural languages.

Both frontends and backends require knowledge of the facilities of the runtime support system. This poses a challenge, since most languages require language-specific runtime support, particularly if they attempt to provide error messages which are presented in terms of the source language semantics. Unless care is taken, knowledge of language specific runtime support diffuses into backends, defeating the objective of language independence.

In the Gardens Point compilers this challenge is met by separating the runtime support for any particular language into two parts. One part is language independent, and includes such things as range and index bounds checking, and the trap handler for hardware traps. This part is conventionally named gprts. The other part is language dependent, and contains such support procedures and traps as are specific to the particular source language. These modules are conventionally named gp*X*rts, where X denotes the particular frontend.

Backends are permitted to be dependent on the facilities of the generic runtime support system, but should never have knowledge of the language specific facilities. This implies that whenever a frontend wishes object code to reference a particular facility of the language dependent part of the runtime support, then the *name* of the facility must be passed as an explicit name in the *Dcode*.

Consider the occurrence of a runtime range test in a program. A range test instruction "test" is part of *Dcode*, and each backend knows how to best implement it on that target. Frontends specify the name of the trap which should be called if the test fails, so as to distinguish between index and range test traps for example. Typical *Dcode* for a test against the range [−5..7] would be —

```
<evaluate expression onto top of abstract stack>
test __gp_rTrpLHI, -5, +7
...
```

In the event that the test fails, the generic runtime will produce an appropriate error message.

Now consider the situation with a primitive specific to one language, but which requires runtime support. The string *LENGTH*() function of *ISO Modula-2* is just such an example. Because this is specific to one language the support is in gpmrts. The *Modula-2* frontend knows about the interface to this function, but backends cannot know about it. The function is invoked in *Dcode* by —

```
<evaluate address expression as first parameter>
<evaluate array or string HIGH as second parameter>
call __strLen,2
...
```

Of course, the implementation of this function may be quite different for different targets, but frontends need only to understand the calling convention.

The rules for enforcing the abstraction principles are as follows —

- facilities required by "all" languages are in the generic runtime and the names of the entry points are allowed to be known by frontends (see the use of __gpRTrpLHI above as an example)
- facilities required by "all" languages, but only on a particular target are in the generic runtime for that target. The names of the entry points must not be known to any frontend (machines which require a table of unit vectors to efficiently implement the *Dcode* setIn intstruction are an example)
- facilties required by a single language are implemented in a target-specific manner in the runtime module for that language. The frontend *must* explicitly generate calls to these facilities in the *Dcode*. Backends must not know of these facilities (support for large set intersections in *Modula-2* is an example)

This idea of separation of runtime support into generic and language specific modules has worked extremely well. In practice, the construction of mixed language programs which link the generic module and several of the language-specific support modules presents no problems, provided that an appropriate naming discipline has been enforced.

2.3 Interface bloat

One of the arguments against abstract machines as intermediate representations is that they create too narrow an interface. William Waite has compared such interfaces to a funnel through which all information must be forced to get from frontend to backend.

Against that view must be weighed the wide use of such forms in production compilers. Instructions for a stack machine are easy to generate, and provide an easy environment with which to experiment. For example, in the testing of our backends we have often used handwritten *Dcode* sequences. Typically we wanted to stress the backend with a pathological but legal *Dcode* sequence, but could not easily work out how to make any of our frontends generate such a sequence.

Nevertheless, in the last few years, we have started to suffer from what we call *interface bloat*. Each experimental optimisation which we wanted to apply required, or at least "wanted" just one more attribute from the frontend. In some cases it is possible to avoid the addition of attributes by the recomputation of information in the backend, but in other cases we have simply added more "noise" to the interface. Some of the optimisations in which we are currently interested require even more information from the frontends, to perform strong alias analysis, for example.

It would seem that much of the problem might be avoided if a procedural interface is provided between frontends and backends[3]. In this case, the procedure calls from the frontend to the backend implement the "instructions" of the bare *D-machine*, with optional attribute information obtained by the backend through callbacks to frontend enquiry functions. This is an option which we will probably implement, but it does not work for all languages for all targets.

Some machine code conventions require the visibility semantics of static locations to be known at the time of code selection in the backend. In effect, if a reference to a static variable occurs, then is must be known whether that object is exported or not. Of course this presents no problem for *Modula-2* or *Oberon-2*, but is hard to guarantee in language *C*. In *C*, variables or functions may be declared extern just as a trick to provide a forward reference. Until the last line of a *C* source file has been read, it cannot be known for sure whether such names are really imported, really exported, or just static and local. Language *C* frontends which do not buffer the whole of a compilation unit before starting to emit output, simply cannot resolve this problem. Of course a two-pass backend would also solve the problem. In our experimental, lcc-based *C* compiler we have adopted the sneaky policy of creating two output streams from the frontend. One has the declaration information, and is produced only after the last line of source has been read. The other is the *Dcode* instructions which are emitted incrementally as each function of the source is processed. At the start of this file we insert a file inclusion command —

· #include <*the declarations*>

It seems therefore that the *C* compiler is stuck with a file interface, unless a new

---

[3] Note that in this case the frontend and backend really become a single program.

frontend is produced which either buffers a whole compilation unit, or makes two passes over source files.

3 The Various Backends

Details of a typical frontend have been given in the introduction. In this section the design of the backends is described.

3.1 Architecture, commonalities and differences

All of the Gardens Point backends have the same overall structure, as shown in Figure 7. A parser, parses the *Dcode* emitted by the frontend, and an explicit

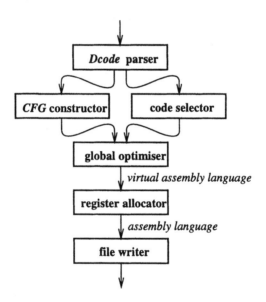

Fig. 7. Architecture of the backends

control flow graph (*CFG*) is created. The instructions of the *Dcode* are passed to a code selector. The code selector produces *virtual assembly language* (*VAL*), which is placed in a code buffer. Only one procedure is processed at a time, so that only one code buffer is used at any time.

The virtual assembly language form is the assembler for an idealised version of the target machine. Thus an indefinitely large number of registers are assumed to be available, with each temporary value being developed into a new register. We have also added instructions which are "missing" from the target instruction set, when the immediate expansion to multiple instructions would not uncover significant, additional optimisation opportunities. For example, for the

Intel iapx86 architecture, trapping arithmetic instructions are added. These instructions expand out later to the corresponding, available instruction, followed by a condition code test-and-branch instruction. Dealing with this pair as a single instruction significantly simplifies the backend, since if the *virtual* instruction is moved or deleted, then the test moves or disappears automatically.

On all 32-bit platforms 64-bit arithmetic instructions are added. These instructions are expanded, either inline (for addition and subtraction) or into a function call (for multiplication, division and remainder), *after* global optimisation, but *before* register allocation.

The *VAL* of each target is different, so that the code of all modules after the parser is unique to each target architecture. Of course, the code of the corresponding modules for each target is similar in structure, and differs according to the detailed semantics of each instruction in the target instruction set. This lack of commonality is an irritation, since the maintenance of so many different modules is difficult, particularly as some of the code depends on subtle features of each instruction semantic. One of our current research projects is to take a generalised description of the module, together with a declarative specification of each target instruction set, and automatically produce these modules. We consider this to be a more promising approach than, for example, the expansion of the internal form out to a register-transfer-list form.

The final, filewriter module emits assembly language for most targets, although we have produced object files directly also. The reason for this choice is simply one of convenience. For example, most of the *Intel iapx86* backends produce almost identical assembly language as output, with all details of the various object code formats hidden inside each assembler. Nevertheless, we are considering producing object code directly for some selected targets. There is particular benefit in going directly to object code for those targets for which the available assemblers do not process high-level language debugging information.

3.2 Shadow stack automata

Until 1995, all of our backends performed code selection using intepretative state machines, which emulate the abstract machine stack state at compile time. Such code generators are called *shadow stack automata*.

Despite their widespread use in production compilers, shadow stack automata have almost no written literature, with the design of the data types for the compile-time stack being a black art passed on from master to apprentice, and refined through a process of trial and error.

For the simplest possible *RISC* machines, the design of the automaton can be easily understood. During code selection, the shadow stack emulates the stack of the abstract machine. Thus values are pushed, operated on and popped from the shadow stack in response to the commands of the *Dcode*. Each entry in the shadow stack has a tag, which specifies in what *form* the value will be at runtime. Possible values are "literal", "value in register-N", "value in memory at address A". Whenever an operation is performed, the operands must be transformed into a state for which the required operation is defined, emitting one or more *VAL* instructions if necessary. Once a more complicated target machine is required, the design becomes much more murky. For example, suppose an add *Dcode* instruction is encountered, when the two top elements on the shadow stack are in registers. On a simple machine, the response would be to allocate a destination register, emit an add instruction to the *VAL* buffer, and replace the two top-of-stack values by the destination register value. Even on *SPARC* this would be the wrong response. On such machines, the emission of an add instruction should be deferred, since the add might be folded into a two-register address mode of a later instruction. Instead, a new type of symbolic entry must be placed on the shadow stack, encoding the fact that this value may be realised later (if necessary) by adding together registers N amd M.

It is an irony that the design of shadow stack automata can now finally be understood in terms of the non-terminal forms of the bottom-up tree rewriting code selectors that will surely replace them.

3.3 Bottom up rewriting

It is possible for shadow stack automata to generate extremely high quality code, but the quality comes at a price. Every "new" special pattern which is inserted into the code selector requires some localised code in the pattern recognition for those *Dcode* instructions which use the new pattern. Moreover, if a new pattern requires the invention of a new symbolic type for the shadow stack, then the changes are spread out over the patterns of *every* instruction.

Bottom up tree rewriting is currently the technology of choice for code selection[16]. Such code selectors use dynamic programming to select code which is locally optimal with respect to given instruction costs. Furthermore, such code selectors may be generated from declarative specifications of the tree rewriting grammar.

After some experimentation, we have begun changing over all of our code selection to this technology. We are using the tool *MBURG*[11, 14] which produces rewriters in *Modula-2* from specifications of tree grammars, which are annotated with associated semantic actions.

Early experience shows that *MBURG*-generated code-selectors take up approximately 50% more space than our shadow stack automata, and run more slowly by a few percent. The advantage of the change is that better output code is generated, and the code selectors are much more maintainable. In the case of the *SPARC* architecture, there appears to be an additional speed penalty, which we hypothesise results from the register-window spilling caused by the multiple deep recursions which these algorithms typically produce.

Although this technology is usually applied to tree-grammars which represent the instruction set and address modes of the target, much more is possible. Tree rewriters are able to recognise patterns which span several machine instructions. We have incorporated patterns into our grammars which arise from source language idioms, and make surprising savings.

It may seem ironic that current compilers walk over a well-formed tree in the frontend in order to produce a kind of flattened postfix representation which is then reconstructed into a tree in the backend. However, the two trees are not isomorphic, since trees in the frontends are language-specific, while the *code trees* in the backends are language-independent. Consider the *MOD* operation for integer operands in *Modula-2* and *Modula-3*. The same syntax in the two source languages would almost certainly be represented in the same way in the two frontends. However, as shown in Figure 8, the *Dcode* sequences are different, due to the different semantics of *MOD* in the two languages. Note here that

Modula-3
. . .
<push left operand>
<push right operand>
mod intOver
. . .
. . .
. . .

Modula-2
. . .
< push left operand>
<push right operand>
dup1
test __gp_ModTrp,0,*MaxInt*
mod intOver
. . .

Fig. 8. *Dcode* for *MOD* in *Modula-3* and *Modula-2*

the *Dcode* instruction "mod *TrapMode*" implements the general, four-quadrant modulus operation directly used by the *Modula-3* code. The *Modula-2* version duplicates the top-of-stack value holding the right operand, and then performs an explicit range check on the copy in order to exclude the half-plane over which *MOD* is not defined in *Modula-2*.

Thus the idea of creating a tree-rewriter which operates on an *AST* is doomed to failure, if the same tree grammar is to be used for rewriting trees arising from multiple languages. Instead, the tree-walker for each separate language frontend understands the transformation of it own *AST* form to the language independent *Dcode* form, or equivalently, the reconstructed *code tree* form.

3.4 Register allocation algorithms

The very first *Dcode* backends used a very fast bin-packing register allocation algorithm which worked very well, but placed constraints on the form of the control flow graph as it appeared in the *Dcode*. In particular, only forward control jumps were permitted, except for the back-edges of well-formed loops, which had to be explicitly marked in the code.

This constraint was trivial to satisfy for languages with well structured loops, but proved to be impossible to satisy with *C*. Since we were in any case interested in more powerful methods of global register allocation, we introduced graph coloring register allocators for all versions. These allocators find, for each computed value, the exact set of connected program locations at which the value is live. This set is the *live-range* of the value. The overlapping of live-ranges defines an "interference graph" the minimal coloring of which is isomorphic to the optimal register allocation problem.

For general graphs the exact solution of such graph coloring problems is known to be infeasible, but many excellent heuristic solutions are known[5, 4, 15]. Such register allocators sometimes use memory in a profligate fashion during compilation, but give excellent results.

As with much else in the backends, the designs of the register allocator modules in each version are essentially the same, but contain numbers of subtle differences which depend on the detailed semantics of the instruction set. A current research project seeks to automatically generate graph coloring register allocators from declarative machine specifications. The most challenging aspect of this work is to design the heuristics which must be used when the register supply is exhausted and values must be spilled to memory.

3.5 Global optimisations

Global register allocation algorithms such as the graph coloring methods perform register allocation for a whole procedure at a time. In order to do this, it is necessary to solve a dataflow problem on the *CFG* of the procedure.

Having gone to this effort for register allocation, it is a small step to provide a dataflow analysis framework for more general global optimisations. All of our backends perform global optimisations based on a program representation form called *static single assignment form*[7, 3].

All backends provide for global common subexpression elimination, constant propagation and value tracking. The effectiveness of these algorithms depends on the richness of the alias information which is passed from frontend to backend.

Placing the optimiser after code selection so that it operates on *VAL*, as shown in Figure ??, is an somewhat unusual choice. Indeed one of the original advantages claimed for the *Ucode* form, was that it allowed machine independent optimisations to be performed. Some production compilers, such as Hewlett-Packard's HPPA compilers, make the same choice as we do, but these examples are usually targetted on a single architecture. The argument in favour of placing the optimiser late, is that machine idioms are exposed to the optimiser in a way that would not occur if the optimisation was to be performed on the *Dcode*. Against that advantage must be weighed the fact that every backend must have its own, distinct version of the optimiser. In our case, the code which transforms the *VAL* into static single assignment form is *almost* identical from version to version, but is sprinkled with minor differences arising from semantic subtleties of the target instruction set. Part of our continuing research is to find ways of parameterising these semantic variations, so that the optimisers can be generated automatically from machine specifications.

Dcode still defines marker symbols which are used by frontends to signal the begining and end of structured loops. Since it is not possible to guarantee the accuracy of such information for languages with **gotos**, backends must now find all loops without reference to the hints from the frontend. This is an absolute necessity for all of those backends which perform loop optimisations. Within the next revision cycle all backends will include these loop optimisations.

Backends abandon all attempts to perform global optimisations on any procedure that is found to have the kind of irreducible flowgraph which arises from careless use of unstructured jumps in the source code. This avoids most problems, but the global register allocator must still be able to perform a correct register allocation in such cases. There are known algorithms for transforming irreducible flowgraphs so that they become tractable, but it is against our philosophy to go to extraordinary lengths to remove the result of programmer perversity.

4   Implementation Languages

For the most part, the frontends are all implemented in the language which they compile. An exception is Diane Corney's **gpo** and is is arguable that this compiler would have benefitted from the challenge of bootstrapping itself at an early stage.

All of the backends are implemented in the Gardens Point dialect of *Modula-2*. With a small number of differences, this is close to *ISO Modula-2*. In particular, our code makes frequent use of value constructors, both statically and dynamically assembled. We find the array constructor types very useful for mapping tables, with record constructors less so. However, we have stumbled into error on a number of occasions by using these constructors, and believe that their design is intrinsically flawed.

Consider a typical constructor which creates an array of values indexed on some enumeration type. Such a table might be useful, say, for mapping an enumeration of primitive datatypes to an opcode value —

```
TYPE  CodeTable = ARRAY DataType OF OpCode;
CONST loadCode  = CodeTable{lbu,lb,lhu,lh,lw, ... };
      ...
Emit(loadCode[type], ... );
```

where the opcodes mean "load byte unsigned", "load (signed) byte", and so on.

The problem with this, is that there is no inherent ordering for such enumerations. There is thus no logical reason that the order of values in the enumeration might not be changed. However, if the order ever is changed, then the constructor code will become incorrect in a way that no compiler can detect. We believe that this danger is so insidious that we have largely abandoned the use of constructors for tables indexed on enumeration types.

It seems that if constructors are to be both useful and safe, then a syntax extension allowing *named associations* of index values and component values is required, rather than the current *positional association*.

4.1   Minor extensions

gpm currently implements the following minor language extensions.

Executable assertions: From the start, **gpm** compilers have supported a low-cost executable assert function. This is a very simple facility, which produces an inline Boolean test in such a way that non-trapping code takes no branches. There are two versions, one which automatically produces a module-name and line-number message, and another which allows the program to specify an explicit message string. We use both forms prolifically within the compilers.

It is hard to think of any more useful single addition to any programming language. The use of these assertions has paid off time and again during the ten-year history of the compilers. Typically, some experimental modification of one of the components has violated an intrisic assumption of some other algorithm, and the failed assertion has given early diagnosis of this.

The *Assert* function must be explicitly imported from a system module, although we believe that it really should be pervasive, as is indeed the case for *Oberon-2*.

Additional conversion operations: **gpm** provides additional real to whole-number conversion modes, which allow for rounding to nearest (*ROUND*), and rounding to minus infinity (*ENTIER*), as well as the standard round to zero functions (*INT* and *TRUNC*). These non-standard functions are hidden in module *SYSTEM*, and are invisible unless implicitly imported.

Additional datatypes: **gpm** has always made the guarantee that the size of integers is at least 32-bits, and that the default real type should be *IEEE* double precision. We have provided for lower precision real types by means of a non-standard type *SHORTREAL*. For all current versions, *LONGREAL* is the same as the default real type, but in future some versions might provide extended double types, or the increasingly popular 128-bit reals.

Since our backends must be able to manipulate data of all the primitive types required by our various frontends, we decided that it was necessary to support the 64-bit integer type. We were reluctant to call this long type *LONGINT* since this name is already used by many thousands of our users programs which have been ported from 16-bit dialects to **gpm**.

We call our 64-bit type *HUGEINT*. It is a whole-number type, but is not classified as an ordinal type. Thus, variables of this type cannot be used as array indices or for-loop indices. The type has a full set of arithmetic operations, including both kinds of divisions and remainders. In keeping with the style of *Modula-2*, there are no implicit coercions to or from this type, but there are named conversions to and from the signed and unsigned type, and a full set of conversions to and from the real types with the usual choice of three different rounding modes.

All of the facilities of huge integers are invisible unless imported from the system module "*HugeInts*".

4.2 Extensible arrays

One of the very widely used data structures in the backends is the dynamically allocated, variably sized array. These are used for sets of virtual registers, interference graphs, code buffers and various list types.

In an experimental modification to **gpm**, we have added a new type constructor which provides for extensible arrays. These arrays automatically expand to accomodate append operations beyond their original capacity. A short technical

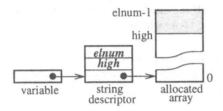

Fig. 9. *memory appearance of string variable*

report describes this extension in detail [13].

These *string types*, as we call them, can be declared for arbitrary element types. In particular, if the element type is another *string type* then a multidimensional, extensible array is created.

Accesses to elements of these string types uses the ordinary array index syntax, and are always index bounds-checked against the current length of the string, rather than the length of the container in which the string is embedded.

Figure 9 represents the runtime implementation of a string type. Each variable has a descriptor block, which records the current high limit of the string, as well as the number of elements of the container in which the string currently resides. If a string needs to expand beyond its current container size, a new container is allocated, and all of the current string copied across. With our current allocation strategy, strings implement lists and stacks using amortised doubling.

We are unsure whether the introduction of a new type constructor can be justified for general programming. It is true that the same effect could be obtained using an abstract data type, but each different element type would require a separate module to support it. In our case, given the ubiquity of extensible arrays in our code, we are finding the extension to be both efficient and convenient.

5 Current Projects

A number of research projects are based around the infrastructure of the Gardens Point compilers. The most ambitious of these is "Gardens"[23], a network of workstations project which involves both language and system design aspects. Associated projects are researching some aspects of garbage collection and of compiler-assisted heterogeneous task migration.

As as well as the ongoing work on code optimisation, a current project seeks to create tools for generating backend modules from specifications. Initially this project considers register allocators and some dataflow optimisations.

6 Conclusions

This paper has given an overview of a project which is now 10-years in the making. The original aims have been somewhat expanded, so that now the project supplies a framework within which a broad variety of research topics may be pursued, and a number of tools which are used every day by many people worldwide.

Many of the technical decisions which have been made turned out to be sound, others less so. There are a number of decisions which, given the benefit of hindsight would now have been taken differently. Some of these have been hinted at here.

To some degree compiler writing is at an interesting crossroad. For the computer vendors, there is an increasing emphasis on finding very specialised optimisations which apply to their own machines, or even to just specific configurations of their machine. Many of these optimisations require whole-of-program analysis, and involve such things as improving cache behaviour.

The other path is towards new compiler technologies which can be applied to "just in time" compiling techniques, and are applicable to extensible and dynamically configured applications.

While the Gardens Point project still has interests in optimisation algorithms, it seems that the second path is the more fruitful one, and the one which leads to the more interesting research opportunities.

6.1 Acknowledgements

The *Alpha* version of **gpm** was produced with the help of a Digital Equipment Corporation "Alpha Innovators Grant". The process of moving our code to our first 64-bit target is described in some detail in a report[19].

The current work on *Java* frontends is a project of the Distributed Sytems Technology Centre, a centre set up under the Australian Government's Cooperative Research Centre program.

Most of the papers and technical reports about the project referenced here are also available from the *URL* http://www.dstc.qut.edu.au/~gough/

References

1. U Ammann. *Pascal, the Language and its Implementation*, Chapter Code Generation for a Pascal Compiler. John Wiley and Sons, 1981.
2. Ken Arnold and James Gosling. *The Java Programming Language*. Addison-Wesley, 1996.

3. Marc M. Brandis and Hanspeter Mössenböck. Single-pass generation of static single assignment form for structured languages. *ACM Transactions on Programming Languages and Systems*, Volume 16, Number 6, pages 1684–1698, 1994.
4. P Briggs, K D Cooper, K Kennedy and L Torczon. Coloring heuristics for register allocation. In *Proc. ACM SIGPLAN'89 Confr. Programming Language Design and Implementation*, Volume 26 of *SIGPLAN Notices*. ACM, 1989.
5. G J Chaitin. Register allocation and spilling via graph coloring. In *Proc. ACM SIGPLAN'82 Symposium on Compiler Construction*, Volume 19 of *SIGPLAN Notices*, 1989.
6. Diane Corney. The Luna language report. http://www.fit.qut.edu.au/~corney/luna.ps. Language report for the Luna language.
7. Ron Cytron, Jeanne Ferrante, Barry K. Rosen, Mark N. Wegman and F.Kenneth Zadeck. Efficiently computing static single assignment form and the control dependence graph. *ACM Transactions on Programming Languages and Systems*, Volume 13, Number 4, pages 451–490, 1991.
8. E W Dijkstra. Algol 60 translation. *Supplement ALGOL Bulletin*, Volume 10, 1960.
9. C W Fraser and D R Hanson. *A Retargetable C Compiler: Design and Implementation*. Benjamin Cummings, 1995.
10. K J Gough, C Cifuentes, D Corney, J Hynd and P Kolb. An experiment in mixed compilation/interpretation. In *Proceedings of ACSC-14*, Hobart, Australia, 1992. Australian Computer Society.
11. K John Gough. Bottom up tree rewriting with MBURG: the mburg reference manual. ftp://ftp.fit.qut.edu.au/ in directory /pub/coco. Reference manual for version 0.8 of MBURG. Complete source code is available at the same URL.
12. K John Gough. The DCode intermediate program representation: Reference manual and report. ftp://ftp.fit.qut.edu.au/ in file /pub/papers/jmlc2.ps.Z. Online document specifying the intermediate form used by the gardens point compilers.
13. K John Gough. A new type-constructor for modular languages. ftp://ftp.fit.qut.edu.au/ in file /pub/papers/jmlc2.ps.Z. Technical report on extensible arrays.
14. K John Gough. Bottom-up tree rewriting tool MBURG. *SIGPLAN Notices*, Volume 31, Number 1, 1996.
15. K John Gough and Jeffrey Ledermann. Register allocation in the Gardens Point compilers. In *Proceedings ACSC18, Adelaide, Australia*. Australian Computer Science Society, 1995.
16. K John Gough and Jeffrey Ledermann. Optimal code-selection using MBURG. In *Proceedings ACSC20, Sydney, Australia*. Australian Computer Science Society, 1997.
17. R W Gray, W P Heuring, S P Levi, A M Sloane and W Waite. Eli: a complete, flexible compiler construction system. *Communications of the ACM*, Volume 35, pages 121–131, Feb 1992.
18. ISO SC22/WG13. *Modula-2—International Standard: IS 10154*. British Standards Institution, June 1996.
19. J Lederman, K J Gough, J Hynd and P Sinfield. The port of GPM to the ALPHA architecture. Technical report, Distributed Systems Technology Centre, Brisbane, Australia, 1994.
20. Tim Lindholm and Frank Yellin. *The Java Virtual Machine Specification*. Addison-Wesley, 1996.

21. Steven Omohundro. The Sather programming language. Technical report, ICSI, Berkley, California, 1994.
22. D R Perkins and R L Sites. Machine indepedent Pascal code optimization. In *Proc. ACM SIGPLAN'79 Confr. Programming Language Design and Implementation*, Volume 14 of *SIGPLAN Notices*, pages 201–207, 1979.
23. Clemens Szyperski. Gardens Project home page. http://www.fit.qut.edu.au/-~szypersk/Gardens. Includes an index to other Gardens related documents.
24. Pat Terry. *Programming Language Translation: A Practical Approach*. Addison-Wesley, 1985.
25. Niklaus Wirth. The design of the Pascal compiler. *Software: Practice and Experience*, Volume 4, pages 309–333, 1971.

Executable Assertions and Separate Compilation

K John Gough[1] and Herbert Klaeren[2]

[1] Queensland University of Technology, Box 2434 Brisbane 4001, Australia,
`j.gough@qut.edu.au`,
[2] University of Tübingen, Sand 13, 72076 Tübingen, Germany,
`klaeren@informatik.uni-tuebingen.de`

Abstract. The use of executable assertions is widely recognised as a useful programming technique for complex systems. In many cases static analysis of programs allows such assertions to be removed at compile time, thus removing the overhead of the test. The use of interprocedural analysis would often allow a larger number of such tests to be statically removed; intermodular analysis could even improve overall safety of the system. In general, however, such analysis is antithetical to separate compilation and extensible systems.

In this paper we offer a partial solution to this dilemma: We propose that preconditions become part of the interface definition of an encapsulated object. The implementation consequences of this technique are explored.

Keywords Executable assertions, separate compilation, value propagation, elimination of redundant checks.

1 Introduction

The use of preconditions and postconditions in the analysis of programs is by now firmly established. In a somewhat related development, many software engineers have found it useful to incorporate programmer-specified executable assertions into their software. This goes hand in hand with the claim for *secure languages* as described recently by Strom [11] who opposes insecure languages (where a bug in module A can damage data structures used by a (presumably) non-buggy module B in a way that B seems the culprit in a later system crash) to secure languages that would either make module A non-compilable or, to the least, raise an exception at the moment when A corrupts the data structure. Besides the usual measures taken by a type-safe language (such as overflow and array bounds checks and the like), programmer-defined pre- and postconditions can be a great help in making a language secure. Note that in the scenario described by Strom, we must be able to deal with such conditions across module boundaries.

For example, an assertion that a particular list is non-empty would prevent an algorithm depending on such a precondition from erroneously continuing in cases where the precondition isn't met. There are two consequences of this: Firstly, failure of the assertion at runtime can provide an explicit error message which highlights the exact nature of the programmer's misconception rather than allowing some arbitrary failure of later code, possibly even residing in a different module. Perhaps more importantly, the addition of such assertions keeps code evolution later in the software lifecycle from invalidating a necessary condition for correctness of some existing part of the code.

Some programming languages provide compiler support for such assertions; already Algol-W [12] had such provisions. Eiffel [8] introduced executable pre- and postcondition assertions as an intrinsic part of the *programming by contract* [9] paradigm. Oberon-2 now incorporates such assertions, and Gardens Point Modula (**gpm**) [10] has always had such a feature, although technically is not part of the Modula-2 language [6]. In the case of **gpm**, the *Assert* procedure takes either one or two arguments. The first is an arbitrary expression of type *Boolean*. If the optional second argument is present, it specifies an associated error message. If no message is specified, the compiler generates a default message which reports the compilation unit in which the assertion failed, and the respective line number in the source. The **gpm** compilers generate inline code for the Boolean evaluation, and indeed do not even cause any overhead in form of a taken branch in the case that the assertion evaluates to truth. All generation of error messages, and the trapping to the runtime system is done out of line of the main control flow; thus, the overhead of an assertion is never more than that of evaluating the Boolean expression plus a non-taken branch. It is possible to use a command line flag to turn off the generation of code for assertions, but we have never found a circumstance in which we have thought the modest saving in execution time was worthwhile. Our own code makes very substantial use of these assertions.

Examination of the code which arises from the use of the *Assert* facility shows that occasionally the dead-code removal algorithms of the compiler can eliminate the test entirely. This happens for example, when one assertion is logically implied by another, or when properties of the type system imply the truth of the assertion.

We have some experience with elimination techniques for redundant checks that are automatically introduced by type-safe language systems such as array bounds checks [3] or dynamic type tests [1]; obviously, all techniques used for this purpose are also suitable for elimination of redundant programmer-defined assertions.

Already Markstein et al. [7] observe that in addition to elimination of redundant checks it usually pays off to *move* the non-redundant ones to regions of lower execution frequency. Later it has been observed by Gupta [4, 5] that interprocedural analysis would enable an even larger number of tests to be eliminated. For this reason, he proposes to move tests from called procedure to the call site. The gain arises, because the *caller* of a procedure always has more static information about the arguments than the called procedure.[3] For example, the value of a literal constant argument is known to the calling procedure, but is just another variable to the *callee*. Thus the use of interprocedural analysis, or the use of procedure integration ("inlining") together with advanced *intraprocedural*

---

[3] Note the traditional abuse of terminology here: When we speak of what a procedure "knows" we use this as code to refer to the information that can be computed during compilation of the procedure.

analysis, might be expected to yield significant gains.

Unfortunately, the use of either procedure integration or whole program analysis is antithetical to separate compilation, and simply has no place in *extensible systems*. Indeed, we do not favour the use of such analysis either to propagate value information, or to patch up holes in the type system (as is required by some languages which allow covariant specialisation). Instead we are interested in exploring the strengthening of the static analysis which is available in the presence of separate compilation, and modular decomposition.

The rest of this paper is set out as follows. Section 2 introduces a motivating example. Section 3 sets out the essence of our proposal, while Section 4 discusses the semantic constraints on the method and section 5 discusses some implementation details. In the remaining sections, we discuss the extension to postconditions and procedure variables and draw some conclusions.

2   A Motivating Example

We consider the example of a generic matrix multiplication routine, using open arrays. The interface to such a routine might be

PROCEDURE *matmul*(**VAR** *res*:**ARRAY OF ARRAY OF** *REAL*;
$\qquad\qquad\qquad$ **VAR** *lOp*:**ARRAY OF ARRAY OF** *REAL*;
$\qquad\qquad\qquad$ **VAR** *rOp*:**ARRAY OF ARRAY OF** *REAL*);

Of course, the correctness of any call to this routine will depend on the proper conformance of the dimensions of the three arguments. In particular, if lOp is an $l \times m$ matrix, and rOp is $m \times n$, then the result matrix res must be $l \times n$. Using x_1, x_2 to denote the first and second upper bounds on parameter x, these conformance assertions are

$$lOp_2 = rOp_1 \qquad\qquad\qquad (1)$$
$$res_1 = lOp_1 \qquad\qquad\qquad (2)$$
$$res_2 = rOp_2 \qquad\qquad\qquad (3)$$

All of this is known to every student of algebra. What is not so well known is that the conformance assertions are sufficient to allow a compiler to statically eliminate all index bounds checks in the implementation of matrix multiplication. A typical body code might be

```
BEGIN
    FOR i := 0 TO lOp₁ DO
        FOR j := 0 TO rOp₂ DO
            sum := 0.0;
            FOR k := 0 TO lOp₂ DO
```

```
        sum := sum + lOp[i,k] * rOp[k,j]
    END;
    res[i,j] := sum
  END
END
END matmul;
```

The reasoning now is as follows. It is almost trivial for a compiler frontend to compute that if the FOR loop index k ranges over $[0 .. lOp_2]$ then the bounds check on k in $lOp[i, k]$ is never necessary. The bound on k, stated in terms of the dimensions of lOp, does not help by itself to eliminate the check on k in $rOp[k, j]$.

Equation (1), however, taken together with the FOR loop bounds on k, eliminates the second test on k in the summation line. Equations (2) and (3), taken together with the other FOR loop bounds eliminate both bounds checks on the final assignment. All of the other index bounds checks are directly eliminated by the FOR loop bounds, without the use of the conformance assertions.

It may be noted that the elimination of these bounds checks is quite influential, since the presence of the checks makes the loops harder to optimise. Once the tests are eliminated, the full power of induction variable analysis and invariant code motion are available to give very significant speedups in the code.

In our previous work [3] we have shown how a *symbolic computation* of range information for variables can be used for removal and relocation of overflow and array bounds checks. With a small extension of these techniques it is possible for our compilers to automatically eliminate all index checks in this example. If we begin the body of the procedure with three executable *Assert* statements equivalent to the conformance relations above, then the compiler links the values together. Whenever a new range interval is computed for (say) k in terms of lOp_2 then a check against rOp_1 is known to be equivalent, according to equation (1). The runtime cost of performing the Boolean evaluations is regained by the elimination of the index tests alone.

This leaves us with the question whether the called procedure should really be responsible for ensuring conformance with the dimension constraints. Meyer, in his "Design by Contract" paper [9] says that such contraints are part of the "contract" between client and server and continues by stating that there is a wide range of possible styles,

> "ranging from 'demanding' ones where the precondition is strong (putting the responsibility on clients) to 'tolerant' ones where it is weak (increasing the routine's burden). [...] The experience with Eiffel, in particular the design of the libraries, suggests that the systematic use of a demanding style can be quite successful. In this approach, every routine concentrates on doing a well-defined job so as to do it well rather than attempting to handle every imaginable case."

This is in perfect accordance with our own experience. In most cases, the code which calls the procedure knows the dimensions of the matrices, and is able with more or less (compiler) effort to establish the assertions without incurring any runtime cost. On the other hand, it is the matrix multiplication routine which can make the most valuable use of the information. Thus the *calling side* should be responsible for such checking, since more information is known about the actual arguments on the calling side. We also conclude that the called routine should be able to use the semantic content of any such assertions in the elimination of runtime checks, or in the computation of other static semantic properties, in other words: it should be allowed to assume that the client guarantees the precondition, and take advantage of this knowledge.

3   Assertions in the Definition

Consideration of the example in the previous section suggests the introduction of a formal mechanism for passing assertions between a library interface and its clients. We propose that assertions on the values of the arguments to a routine should form part of the declared interface.

The rules of the contract are as follows:

- the client of an interface is responsible for ensuring that the arguments passed to each procedure obey the Boolean conditions stated in the interface definition. The client may either eliminate these tests if statically computed information proves them redundant, or must otherwise perform tests at runtime,
- a procedure which is guarded by an advertised precondition on the values of its actual arguments may assume without tests that these preconditions hold. The procedure may use this information in the computation of static properties of the procedure body.

Note that at worst the runtime tests have been transferred from the body of the called procedure, back to the client. This can never use more machine cycles, but may cause an increase in code size proportional to the number of call sites due to code replication.

At best, the assertion may be statically satisfied in the caller, and may enable useful optimisations in the called procedure.

All of this occurs without compromising the type-checked separate compilation which is at the heart of modular languages. Indeed, it is possible to use these interface assertions as extensions to the type system.

Consider the case of languages such as the Oberon family, which do not have subrange and enumeration types. In such languages integer types are used to carry values which are semantically of restricted range. Thus a variable which holds a day-of-the-week value would be declared as an integer. At runtime the valid values would be only [0..6], and the interface to a procedure *WriteDay* might be declared with a precondition

PROCEDURE *WriteDay*(*day* : *INTEGER*);
    PRE $(0 \leq day) \wedge (day \leq 6)$;

In this case, the *WriteDay* procedure will certainly be able to use the assertion to eliminate the index test on the name-table access. The client of the procedure will often be able to eliminate the test, and when that is not possible will simply perform the prescribed range test.

This example shows that using an integer type, together with the range assertion leads to *exactly* the same tests and test-eliminations as would have occurred in Modula-2, for the call of a procedure

PROCEDURE *WriteDay*(*day* : *WeekDays*);

where *WeekDays* is either a subrange, or perhaps an enumeration type.

All of this is cognate with the point of view in which the notion of *datatype* is equivalent to a set of assertions on the permissible values of its object of that type.

4 What can be Asserted

In the case of Modula-2, assertions on exported procedures would occur in the definition part of a module. In this case, the scope in which the assertions are embedded is the scope of declarations of the formal parameters. Thus, the visible identifiers which can occur in the assertions include

- names of objects exported from this module
- formal parameters of the procedure in question
- identifiers explicitly imported into the definition.

Fortuitously, all of these names refer to values or types which are already available to all possible clients of the interface. Clearly, all of the objects exported from the definition are available to the client. Furthermore, any modules explicitly imported into a definition must also be indirectly imported by all clients of the definition, in order to check interface conformance. Thus the introduction of assertions according to these constraints does not require any broadening of the name scope in the client.

In languages such as Oberon, which do not have a separate definition part, the precondition assertions need to be treated with a little care. It would be simple for an assertion in an Oberon program to be perfectly well formed from the point of view of the compiler of the procedure, but to be ill-formed from the point of view of the client of the module. This would occur if the assertion referred to any identifier which was not publically available to the client.

The differences between the cases of Oberon and Modula thus relate to the name scopes in which semantic analysis of the definitions of the assertions must take place.

4.1   Handling opaque types

One of the benefits of encapsulation is that it is possible for the implementation of an abstract data type to ensure the integrity of all data values of that type.

Nevertheless, it may sometimes be the case that a procedure requires an assertion on value(s) of some opaque type, other than the implicit assertion that it *is* a valid value of the type. When such cases do arise, the assertions should not and need not break the encapsulation of the type. In such cases it seems that the module which encapsulates the type must also export the necessary procedure(s) to perform the value checking. Thus

DEFINITION MODULE *Foo*;
  TYPE *FooType*;   (* *opaque* *)

  PROCEDURE *Thing(x:FooType)*;
    PRE *IsOk(x)*;

  PROCEDURE *IsOk(x:FooType):BOOLEAN*;
END *Foo*.

Of course, in this case there is no real possibility of the client being able to eliminate this opaque test on the opaque type. After all, the use of an opaque type is intended to prevent the user of the code from making assumptions about the implementation. This is an important aspect of data abstraction, since it ensures that users are insulated from possible changes in the implementation of types. If the full benefit of separate compilation is to be maintained, then even the *compiler* of a module which uses an abstract type should not break the abstraction. Thus the compiler is prevented from performing optimisations based on implementation details.

Even in this case of assertions on the values of opaque types, when such an assertion is violated there is at least the advantage that the error message is sheeted home to the calling site, rather than requiring a stack trace to identify the culprit.

5   Implementation Issues

There are several important issues of implementation which require some consideration. Firstly, the format of the assertions themselves must be determined. We currently propose a syntax of the form given in Figure 1, which has the EBNF (leaning on [13])

$$ProcedureDeclaration \rightarrow \text{PROCEDURE } ident \, [FormalParameters]$$
$$[\text{``;''} PreCondition].$$
$$PreCondition \rightarrow \text{PRE } expression.$$

In effect, the identifier PRE is treated as a reserved word.

ProcedureHeading

PreConditions

Fig. 1. Syntax diagram for procedure headings with optional assertions

It suffices to provide for a single expression at this place because multiple assertions can be formed into a conjunct. The expression in the assert statement is parsed and statically checked within the scope of the current declarations, in exactly the same way that a constant declaration would be. The expression must be syntactically correct, and must be of the Boolean type. As pointed out earlier, because an Oberon compiler would have names in the scope of the assertions which would not be visible to the client of the module we believe that some additional analysis would be required in that case.

5.1 Symbol file representation

In most implementations of modular languages, information is passed between modules and their clients in a symbol file. These files are a compact representation of the static semantics of the interface. Typically, information such as the names of formal parameters are elided,[4] and constant expressions, no matter how complicated, are reduced to literals. This parsimony brings advantages, since it is a simple matter for a smart recompilation utility to detect when the source of a definition has changed but the symbol file has not. It is axiomatic that if a symbol file has not changed, then the interface is unchanged. Thus unnecessary recompilation of client modules can be avoided. Recent work [2] at ETH shows how a finer-grained view of change may reduce unnecessary recompilation even further.

In this context the representation of assertions in the symbol file becomes an issue. Clearly, some extension of the symbol file format is required to encode the additional information. In **gpm** the symbol file format completely folds constant expressions to literals, so there is no defined syntax for expressions or their operators. In our current experimental implementation we have dumped a simple preorder representation of the precondition expression as an addendum to the procedure type information. Globally visible names appear explicitly in the file, but the names of formal parameters, which are meaningless to the client, are replaced by positional indices.

---

[4] For Oberon-like languages the names of formal parameters may be retained, so that a browser can reconstruct a "virtual defininition module" from the symbol file.

A simple extension of the symbol file parser reconstructs the precondition expression trees, and attaches them as attributes of their corresponding type descriptors.

5.2 Client-side processing

Gardens Point compilers create abstract syntax trees for the whole of a compilation unit at once. For some languages the compilers bind names during tree creation, while for others, names are bound during a static semantic traversal of the tree.

In either case, during the static semantic traversal of the abstract syntax tree the referent of each procedure call is identified, and its type descriptor is retrieved. Each actual argument expression-tree is then type-evaluated, and tested for conformance against the corresponding formal parameter. The type-evaluator is also capable of quite aggressive constant folding, so that in many cases expressions are reduced to literals.

During static semantic checking, procedure call nodes with preconditions are modified by local tree rewriting. A new parent node is interposed above such nodes. This parent has an elaborated instance of the precondition attached to it. The precondition expression instance is type-checked in the normal way, and any constant expressions folded to literals. For our motivating example, the dimensions of statically declared arrays will probably be known, and the preconditions will be trivially satisfied at compile time.

When code is generated for the procedure call, intermediate language code to evaluate all arguments is emitted. If the precondition expression did not fold to the Boolean truth value, then code is emitted to evaluate the precondition at runtime, and trap if the assertion fails.

In **gpm** compilers all global dataflow analysis and global constant propagation is performed in the backend code generators.[5] Whether or not value range analysis is performed, there is further value propagation and dead code elimination in the backends, and further assertion tests will be optimised away.

6 Extension to Post-conditions

In this paper, we have concentrated on preconditions for purposes of exposition. It is, however, quite clear that postconditions can be treated symmetrically.

We have noted earlier that preconditions on the arguments to a function call are often able to be statically satisfied by the caller of a procedure, but are semantically relevant to the called function. Conversely, it is often the case that a function is able to statically ensure that some postcondition on its return value is satisfied. This assertion is perhaps of value to the caller who receives the returned value.

---

[5] Note however that backends, since they are language independent, do not understand the type system, but only untyped values. Thus we need to perform analysis in both front- and backends.

Thus we propose that post-conditions will place an obligation on the compiler of a procedure to either statically prove the test unnecessary, or generate code for a runtime test. The code which calls the procedure is then able to use the assertion of the postcondition to remove tests in the same way as for any other assertion. This establishes a symmetry in the client-server "contract": In the same way that the server relies on the client to check for the preconditions, the client can expect that the server has verified its postconditions before returning a result.

7 Treating Procedure Variables

Obviously, in a language like Modula-2 where we have *procedures as datatypes* and therefore assignable procedure variables, the scenario described so far cannot completely satisfy. Introducing pre- and postconditions to procedure types poses two interesting problems:

1. The *FormalTypeList* [13] used in the declaration of procedure types doesn't assign names to formal parameters but only types. However, the most natural way to express any assertions for procedure types is to use formal parameter names. Having both procedures with and without assertions means that we have to allow a mixture of the *FormalTypeList* and *FormalParameters* syntaxes; this will violate the LL(1) property. Of course, this poses no serious problem since an ad-hoc lookahead by a second symbol will resolve the ambiguity.

2. If we assign a procedure (constant) with given assertions to a procedure variable whose type has specified assertions, the question arises as to how to deal with the compatibility of these assertions. There are several tar pits lurking here, one of them being the theoretical incomputability of expression equivalence, one other the practical impossibility of incorporating a theorem prover into a compiler. In this case we resort to the *KISS* ("keep it simple, stupid") principle by allowing the said assignment only if

   (a) the procedure constant has no associated assertions at all (in which case it inherits those of the type it is being assigned to) or

   (b) the abstract syntax trees of the assertions belonging to the procedure constant and the left hand type are identical.

A small problem occurring in the implementation is that a precondition is expressed as a condition possibly referencing named formal parameter values, but is evaluated by referencing the corresponding actual values. These actual values may be mentioned multiple times, but must only be evaluated once because there may be side effects hidden in function calls. Furthermore, all such values are "used" at least twice, once by the parameter passing mechanism, and at least once by the evaluation. Our current solution to this is an implementation which defines local, internal names for the evaluated actual parameters, and converts all uses to references to those named "variables".

8 Conclusions

We claim that the technique described here has many advantages. Firstly, it creates enhanced safety, in that declaratively specified assertions form part of a module's contract, and are enforced by the compiler. It does so without losing any of the advantages of separate compilation, and is thus applicable to extensible systems which cannot use *whole-of-program* analysis even in principle.

Furthermore, we have shown that placing the assertions in the interface definition allows the preconditions to be checked by the caller, which has the greatest amount of information about the actual arguments. In addition, precondition assertions are processed by the compiler of the called procedure, and without any runtime cost can often eliminate code in the procedure.

Finally, we note that the addition of assertions to an interface may be seen as strengthening the type system of the language, by allowing constraints to be specified which the type system itself cannot express.

We have a working prototype compiler which tests the viability of the concept. Failure to honour the contract of the precondition of any procedure leads to a trap in this system. The increase in compiler size for the programmer-defined assertions is negligible; it amounts only to the small syntax additions and to the sketched enhancements of the symbol file reader and writer. All of the other ingredients have been present in the compiler anyway, which makes the proposed extension a very economic and sensible one.

Of course, the next step would be to obtain precise data about the impact on code size and execution speed; both of them being quantities that largely depend on properties of the specific program to be compiled, this could probably only done by a statistical analysis of a large number of programs from different application areas and programmer teams. The same can be said about the increase in program safety due to a thoughtful specification of pre- and postconditions; here, we still have some significant work in front of us.

Acknowledgement

The idea of moving preconditions into the interface definitions so as to achieve interprocedural code motion in the presence of separate compilation first arose while discussing [3] with Clemens Szyperski. His contribution is gratefully acknowledged.

References

1. Diane Corney and John Gough. Type test elimination using typeflow analysis. In Jürg Gutknecht, editor, *Proceedings Int. Confr. Programming Languages and System Architectures*, volume 782 of *Lecture Notes in Computer Science*, pages 137–150. Springer Verlag, 1994.
2. Régis Crelier. *Separate Compilation and Module Extension*. PhD thesis, Swiss Federal Institute of Technology, Zürich, Switzerland, 1994. Diss. ETH No. 10650.

3. K John Gough and Herbert Klaeren. Eliminating range checks using static single assignment form. In *Proceedings ACSC19, Melbourne, Australia*. Australian Computer Science Society, 1996.

4. Rajiv Gupta. A fresh look at optimizing array bound checking. In *Proc. ACM SIGPLAN'90 Confr. Programming Language Design and Implementation*, volume 25(6) of *SIGPLAN Notices*, pages 272–282, 1990.

5. Rajiv Gupta. Optimizing array bound checks using flow analysis. *ACM Letters on Programming Languages and Systems*, 2(1-4):135–150, 1993.

6. ISO. *Information Technology - Programming Languages - Modula-2. IS 10154-1*. International Standards Organisation, June 1996.

7. Victoria Markstein, John Cocke, and Peter Markstein. Optimization of range checking. In *Proc. of ACM '82 Symposium on Compiler Construction*, pages 114–119, 1982.

8. Bertrand Meyer. *Eiffel: The Language*. Englewood Cliffs, 1991.

9. Bertrand Meyer. Applying "Design by Contract". *IEEE Computer*, 25(10):40–51, 1992.

10. QUT. Gardens Point Modula Home Page. `http://www.fit.qut.edu.au/-CompSci/PLAS/GPM`. Information on gardens point compilers, their availability, and documentation.

11. Rob Strom. Do programmers need seat belts? *SIGPLAN Notices*, 31(3):6–7, 1996.

12. N. Wirth and C. A. R. Hoare. A contribution to the development of Algol. *Communications of the ACM*, 9:413–431, 1966.

13. Niklaus Wirth. *Programming in Modula-2*. Springer, 3rd edition, 1985.

Dynamic Runtime Optimization

Thomas Kistler

Department of Information and Computer Science
University of California at Irvine
Irvine, CA 92697-3425

Abstract. In the past few years, code optimization has become a major field of research. Many efforts have been undertaken to find new sophisticated algorithms that fully exploit the computing power of today's advanced microprocessors. Most of these algorithms do very well in statically linked, monolithic software systems, but perform perceptibly worse in extensible systems. The modular structure of these systems imposes a natural barrier for intermodular compile-time optimizations.

In this paper we discuss a different approach in which optimization is no longer performed at compile-time, but is delayed until runtime. Reoptimized module versions are generated on-the-fly while the system is running, replacing earlier less optimized versions.

In the first part of this paper we argue that dynamic runtime reoptimization will play an important role in future software systems and discuss the requirements for a modular, extensible operating system to support dynamic runtime optimization. In the second part we give an overview of promising intermodular and profile-guided reoptimizations. We also measure the characteristics of a modular, extensible operating system in order to estimate the potential of such optimizations.

1 Introduction

Generating high quality code is a challenge that has not just come into fashion recently. The first computer programs, written by hand in assembly code, had to be optimized to fit into the limited storage space and to complete their tasks within an acceptable period of time.

With the advent of high level programming languages and compilers that automatically translate user programs into machine code, this kind of "hand tweaking" of code more or less fell into oblivion. The primary goal of high level languages was to simplify program development and to free the programmer from writing machine dependent code. Generating optimized code was not of primary concern. Although the underlying hardware was seldom fully exploited, the generated instruction sequences were of fairly high quality. Besides, time-critical sections could still be written in assembler.

Only recently, with the introduction of more sophisticated processor architectures, the introduction of RISC computers, and the general availability of cheap hardware resources, have optimization techniques experienced a revival. Appropriate use of processor features, such as caches, pipelines, multiple instruction units, and register windows have lead to an increase in speed by an order of magnitude. Since the use of processor features cannot usually be influenced by the programmer, many efforts have been spent to increase the quality of the generated code by enriching the compiler with optimization techniques.

Except for optimizations that directly operate on instruction sequences (e.g. peephole optimization), most of today's algorithms are based on both semantic information that is collected statically at compile-time and precise knowledge about the underlying hardware architecture. Naturally, the more information that is available about a program, the better the results will be. Local optimizations, operating on basic blocks only, perform perceptibly worse than global optimization techniques that are based on modular dataflow analysis. Some strategies have even been implemented to optimize code patterns across compilation-unit boundaries — so called *intermodular optimizations*. Intermodular optimizations however are hardly feasible in modular systems. Key concepts like information hiding, data abstraction, or component reusability require hiding implementation details. Since the compiler cannot usually see what the programmer cannot see either, modularity can generally not be brought into line with the requirements of intermodular optimizations. These optimizations depend on global implementation knowledge. Only when a fixed number of modules is linked together to form a monolithic self-contained application (in which case global information is available to the compiler) can these systems profit from intermodular optimizations.

Today's optimization techniques have some other major drawbacks. First, they are all based on static program analysis and do not take into account the system's or even the program's dynamic behavior. Optimizations are applied uniformly to each section in the program, even though it is well known that only small portions of a program account for most of the execution-time [Knu70, Ing71].

Second, we are at the moment witnessing far-reaching changes in the field of software architecture. Applications of the next generation are very likely to come as a set of small software components instead of one large monolithic application. Such components, often called "applets", are loaded dynamically on demand and can be put together arbitrarily, forming new applications which are tailored to the specific needs of a user. Furthermore, new components can be downloaded and linked into the system at any time, immediately extending the functionality of an application. Although these systems have uncontested advantages, their highly dynamic nature imposes a natural barrier to interprocedural and intermodular optimizations. Since neither the end-user-configuration nor the components' interaction schemes are known to the optimizer at compile-time, code-optimization is limited to *intramodular* techniques.

Beside changes in the software architecture of future applications, we are also seeing major transitions in software distribution. Nowadays, applications are written to suit exactly one specific operating system and one specific processor type, forcing software vendors to maintain and distribute several different versions of their applications. However, in the near future, software components will be distributed in a portable format and will be able to run both on multiple operating systems and on multiple processor architectures. The components will either be interpreted at runtime, or machine code will be generated from the portable object file on-the-fly at load-time. Consequently, static optimization cannot be performed anymore during compilation of the source code since the compiler lacks information about both the target operating system and the target architecture.

Last but not least, computing power has soared dramatically during the past few years. Not only has the performance of new processor architectures increased from one processor to the next, but the time between generations has shortened as well, due to new innovative design and manufacturing techniques. This development diminishes the effects of optimizations that can be achieved. Applications optimized for one specific processor type cannot necessarily take full advantage of the new features of its successor models.

For all of the above reasons, we propose a new system architecture that delays program optimization until runtime. Optimization either takes place in the background while the system is running, or on explicit request of the programmer. Runtime optimization manages to combine the benefits of modular concepts and intermodular optimizations. It can utilize more information about user behavior or the target architecture than static optimizations and thus can achieve superior results for most optimizations.

2 A New System Architecture

We are currently implementing a system that performs optimization at runtime rather than at compile-time. By moving the optimization stage from compile-time to runtime we manage to eliminate all of the previously mentioned disadvantages of static optimizations and even improve on them with new techniques. Our system consists mainly of four parts that are shown in Fig. 1.

The *compiler* generates an object-file from the source code. In order to deal with all aspects of portability, each object file contains a portable intermediate representation of the program rather than native machine instructions. Except for constant folding, which is target-invariant and can be implemented in a straightforward manner, the compiler performs no code enhancements. Doing so might obstruct the potential for future dynamic runtime optimizations.

As soon as a module needs to be loaded, the *dynamic code-generating loader* transforms the intermediate representation into a native instruction sequence and executes the module body. Since many of the optimization algorithms have a great runtime complexity, optimizations are forgone at load-time in favor of fast module loading and short user response-time. This appears to be a good choice since the overall code-quality generated by our loader is quite good. In most cases, its code can compete with current non-optimizing compilers.

Once modules are loaded, the *adaptive profiler* starts collecting information about the system's runtime behavior. Its primary goal is to provide all the necessary background information upon which to base optimization decisions. It first monitors information on the level of procedures. In this context, the profiler takes a close look at call-frequencies, call-sequences, and call-durations. Furthermore, information about parameters and their dynamic types can be very valuable for certain optimizations. As soon as the measured results stabilize, monitoring is narrowed down to statement-blocks or even single statements in order to facilitate optimizations for long-running instruction sequences. It primarily keeps watch on variable-counts, execution-frequencies of loops and on how often conditional paths are executed.

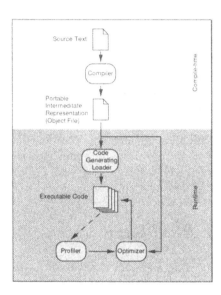

Fig. 1. System Architecture

The *dynamic optimizer* periodically recompiles modules that consume most of the execution-time in the *background*. The key idea is to profit from idle time (we have measured an average idle time of more than 90 percent in our interactive operating system) in order to perform optimizations that would take up a lot of user-time if performed on explicit demand. The optimizer operates on the intermediate program representation utilizing information accumulated by the profiler. Basing the optimizations on a profiler has one big advantage. If the profiler manages to pinpoint all the time-consuming parts (in general 5% of the code accounts for more than 50% of execution-time [Knu70, Ing71]), the optimizer is capable of spending more time on increasing the code quality of the sections that account for most of the execution-time. That way, most time is spent on highly optimizing a few important sequences rather than applying optimizations uniformly to each section of the program. Less frequently executed sections are optimized sparsely and no optimization is performed on barely executed sections. The challenging issue is to find the best balance between the number of blocks to optimize and the resulting speed-up. Still, in some cases, optimizations can take substantial time. To assume that the computing power is sufficient to recompile the whole system in one step, without impact on response-time, is rather optimistic, at least nowadays. Timings taken from existing compilers [Bra95] have shown that applying optimizations to a program takes at least 5 times as long as compiling the program. Therefore it may be preferable to perform optimizations gradually and to periodically reoptimize program parts.

Since the system knows exactly which modules are loaded at runtime and how they interact with each other, it is not restricted to local optimizations. Indeed, performing intermodular code improvements on loaded applications is made possible only now by the introduction of runtime code optimization.

As soon as a set of optimizations has been applied to a module, the system *replaces* the running instance with the optimized module version. This process requires updating intermodular dependencies.

3   The Importance of the Intermediate Representation

An important aspect that has not been discussed thus far is the choice of the intermediate representation. As we have seen earlier, it is used both for generating a first native version of a module and later on for supplying semantic information to the optimizer in order to achieve high code quality. Consequently the representation must hold enough information to perform the optimizations desired. It must also facilitate on-the-fly compilation that is fast enough to compete with loading of compiled code and that generates native code of high quality. Last but not least, the intermediate representation should not contain any machine dependent information in order to be highly portable.

For these reasons we base our system on slim binaries [Fra94, FK96]. Slim binaries are a form of intermediate representation that does not contain any object code at all, but a portable description of a module's contents. This makes these files completely independent of the eventual target machine. Slim binaries are based on an encoding of abstract syntax trees rather than on virtual instruction sequences as employed in the Java virtual machine representation [LYJ96]. Using a predictive compression algorithm to encode recurring sub-expressions, slim binaries facilitate storing and decoding programs efficiently, both in terms of space and time. Moreover, object code generation can be carried out on-the-fly and takes about as much time as loading traditional object files [FK96].

A tree-based encoding is different from a virtual machine representation in that it cannot be interpreted easily. Program interpretation was essential for efficient linking and loading of object files in operating systems with limited memory capacity and computing resources. However, with the recent increase of computing power and the advent of on-the-fly compilers, this argument loses force.

Tree-based encodings on the other hand have many valuable advantages over low-level representations. First of all, they are completely independent of any target machine, whereas chances of a virtual machine representation not suiting a specific processor type are reasonable. Second and even more important, the abstract syntax-tree preserves all the semantic program information which is essential for effective optimization algorithms. It keeps all the control-flow and maintains the notion of basic blocks. Tree-based encodings also contain all the information necessary for debugging tools that operate on the language level rather than on the instruction level.

In order for low-level representations such as byte-codes to achieve comparable optimization results, a tree or control-flow graph must be reconstructed before performing optimizations. In the past, object files have therefore been instrumented with hints about block boundaries [Han74]. Even worse, the absence of type information in such low-level representations prevents a complete set of optimizations like polymorphic inline caches [HCU91] or runtime type feedback [HU94].

4 Promising Intermodular Optimizations

In this section, we will present optimizations that can profit specifically from the execution profiles and semantic information available at runtime. Generally this applies to all optimizations that are based on heuristics. They tend to achieve much better results in our experimental system than on any statically compiled system since they now are based on exact, measured execution profiles rather than on imprecise assumptions and since they now can be applied to the whole system rather than to single procedures. Optimizations that only rely on local information will not be discussed here because they are fundamental in every system (e.g. copy propagation, common subexpression elimination, peephole optimizations, strength reduction, instruction scheduling).

4.1 Intermodular Inlining

Perhaps one of the most auspicious optimizations is *intermodular inlining*. The basic idea of inlining is to replace a call to a procedure by the body of that procedure. This not only avoids the costs of calling and returning from a procedure (i.e. copying parameters to registers or on the stack, and allocating and disposing of the parameter-passing area) but also increases the potential for successive optimizations (e.g. common subexpression elimination) since it allows the inlined body to be improved within the context of the caller. In general, separately compiled systems are restricted to inlining procedures within module boundaries. Only by neglecting extensibility and portability can inlining be performed across compilation units. This case is called *intermodular inlining*.

In our architecture, in which optimization is performed while the system is running, there are no restrictions. In addition, the idea can be taken even one step further by inlining calls to *procedure variables* if a procedure is bound to only one variable at runtime. The same idea holds for method calls, given that the method is never overridden at runtime. For object oriented systems, even hardcoding method calls without actually inlining the calls results in noticeable speed-ups as no method lookups are required as a result.

In most compilers, inline decisions are based on size heuristics since it is extremely difficult to estimate how inlining affects runtime performance. No simple rule can be given as to which procedures to inline. For example, while the number of instructions that can be saved is easy to precalculate, the effect of modified code locality on cache performance is very hard to predict. Only with the availability of an integrated profiler can the system further refine these decisions. Issues to take into account are call frequencies, call-durations, or even the results of previous inline steps.

Instead of actually copying the call bodies into the call site, *procedure cloning* [IBM94] and *partial evaluation* [Sur93, Jon93] are related techniques that generate multiple versions of the procedure body, each customized for a specific set of callers. These optimizations are usually preferred to inlining for larger procedures that are called frequently with multiple, but partially fixed parameter lists. These parameter lists are then hardcoded into the corresponding procedure clones in order to benefit from further optimizations. Since dynamic type information is also present at runtime in our system, even dynamic types can be hardcoded into call-chains and thus speed up message sends dramatically in object oriented systems. As for inlining, we expect procedure cloning and partial evaluation to do perceptibly better when applied to the whole system.

4.2 Intermodular Register Allocation

A second optimization from which we expect improved speed-ups is *intermodular register allocation*. Recent RISC machines have been built with small and simple instruction sets and fast instructions that operate on registers only. The few provided load and store instructions are, however, an order of magnitude slower because they access main memory. Hence chip manufacturers rely on smart compilers that keep as much data as possible in the large provided register sets. Unfortunately non-optimizing compilers use only a small subset of these registers, wasting a lot of computing power. Even popular register allocation schemes, like the ones developed by Chaitin and Chow [Cha82, CH84], fail to yield satisfactory results for systems applying separate compilation. The main problem is that register allocation has to be applied separately to every single module instead of to the whole system. This results in different registers being assigned to the same global variable or the same register being assigned to different local variables. Only late code optimization can avoid these problems.

In our experimental system, registers are assigned at link-time over the entire system, hence the same set of registers can be assigned to procedures that are not alive at the same time. In addition when one procedure calls another, the optimizer can make sure that they use different registers. The same principle holds for parameters. No particular parameter passing mechanism is enforced. Rather parameters are assigned to disjunctive register sets for fast argument passing, and in order to avoid saving and restoring data around procedure calls. In some cases it might even be worth storing constants in particular registers.

In our runtime optimizer, all allocation strategies are based on an intermodular call graph as proposed by Wall [Wal86] and on execution profiles. The latter are particularly useful in estimating which registers to spill in case of shortcomings.

4.3 Intermodular Code Elimination and Code Motion

A completely different group of optimizations deals with intermodular code elimination and code motion. The idea is to either remove code in case it cannot be reached or to relocate it to program parts that are less frequently executed. Well known optimizations are *loop invariant code motion* — which tries to move loop-invariant code outside of loops — and *partial dead code elimination* or *partial redundancy elimination* — that tries to move statements into conditional paths.

Just as with register allocation and inlining, good algorithms have been around for single procedures and single modules, but only poor solutions have been presented so far for intermodular analysis. We hope to improve this situation by the introduction of dynamic runtime optimization.

4.4 Cache Optimizations

Today's new processor designs use fast on-chip caches and somewhat slower off-chip second level caches in order to improve system performance. In the near future, these caches will become dramatically faster than main memory. Even today, it typically takes ten times longer to retrieve data from main memory than from a cache. It is therefore very important to avoid cache misses whenever possible. With the availability of on-the-fly compilers and runtime optimizers *cache optimizations* can now try to meet these requirements.

Basically there are three groups of possible cache optimizations: data cache optimizations, instruction cache optimizations, and optimizations that take into account cache parameters but don't have the explicit goal of improving cache performance. *Data cache optimizations* on the one hand are easy to implement and achieve good results. The idea is to improve the temporal data locality by grouping variables that are repeatedly used in the same period of time. Spatial locality can also be improved and the size of the working set decreased by re-ordering and compacting records. Cache blocking is a further, but much more complicated technique to improve data cache behavior, especially for numerical programs [WL91]. All of the above data cache optimizations have in common that they are based either on statically weighted access computations or on execution profiles.

Instruction cache optimizations, on the other hand, are very hard to implement and not at all feasible at compile-time. Only if a time-critical section consists of a small number of procedures that call each other can we ensure that the bodies are located in separate cache lines. If, on the other hand, a time-critical section spans over many procedures, as is normally the case for object oriented systems, it is hardly possible to avoid line conflicts. Therefore, we adapt existing optimizations to take into account cache parameters (e.g. size, line size, degree of associativity) instead of writing new ones with the sole goal of improving instruction cache performance. Consider loop unrolling as an example, where the primary goal is to remove unnecessary control structures and to overlap the execution of several loop iterations. Unfortunately, if the unrolled loop results in more cache misses, the runtime performance may even be decreased by this optimization. Hence cache characteristics should be considered in this kind of code improvement.

5 Optimization Potential for an Extensible Modular Operating System

In order to quantify the potential achievements of the presented optimizations, we have collected statistics about the Oberon System [WG89] for Power Macintosh computers. The Oberon System is an interactive, extensible operating system. It not only includes representative applications like a graphical user interface, a native and portable compiler, a text- and a graphics-editor but also smoothly integrates Internet services that will be essential parts of future operating systems (e.g. e-mail, WWW-browser, ftp, news, telnet, gopher). The included native compiler translates programs written in the programming language Oberon [Wir88] to PowerPC 601 machine instructions. Its code quality can be roughly compared to the quality of non-optimizing C compilers.

Table 1 gives a general overview of the system. There are two interesting points to be observed. First, there are more calls to external procedures than to local ones. This might be surprising at first sight but actually reflects the achievement of two key goals of modular systems: abstraction and reuse. Hence, our claim that intermodular optimizations are very important to achieve good speed-ups can be reemphasized at this point.

Number of modules	229
Number of procedures	6660
Number of external procedure calls	20299
Number of local procedure calls	17217
Number of indirect procedure calls	3411
Number of references to external variables	7756
Number of references to local variables	43540

Table 1. General Static System Information

Second, unlike in dynamically typed object oriented systems, there are very few indirect calls in our system. As a result, many code improvements that could be implemented to accelerate message-calls like polymorphic inline caches [HCU91] or runtime type feedback [HU94] would have very little effect on our system.

Table 2 and Table 3 show average counts of various properties per procedure. The numbers given in Table 2 have been collected during compilation of all modules. Thus they do not take into account the fact that some procedures are executed more frequently than others.

Procedure size (bytes)	422.14
Number of statements per procedure	17.10
Number of external calls per procedure	3.05
Number of local calls per procedure	2.59
Number of indirect calls per procedure	0.51
Number of references to external variables per procedure	1.16
Number of references to local variables per procedure	6.54
Number of unused registers per procedure (on PowerPC)	15.82

Table 2. Static Procedure Information

Weighting the values with the effective execution-time spent in a procedure during an average working session yields slightly different values (Table 3). The most interesting result here is that almost 50% of the available registers are unused during execution-time (the PowerPC architecture defines 32 user-level, general-purpose registers). Consequently there is an enormous potential for register related optimizations. Not only would it be worthwhile to keep local variables in registers since they are accessed ten times more often than external variables, but we could also keep local variables and parameters of two successively called procedures in disjunctive register sets to avoid expensive parameter-passing and register-saving. In comparison to statically optimized code, speed-ups in the range of 10-25% have been reported for similar register allocation schemes [Wal86].

Number of external calls per procedure	4.79
Number of local calls per procedure	3.25
Number of indirect calls per procedure	1.64
Number of references to external variables per procedure	1.02
Number of references to local variables per procedure	10.55
Number of unused registers per procedure (on PowerPC)	11.82

Table 3. Dynamic Procedure Information

We have also examined the distribution of procedure sizes which is given in

Fig. 2. In general, procedures in our system are small. Half of all procedures are smaller than 240 bytes which corresponds roughly to 60 instructions or 10 Oberon source-code statements. The great potential for inlining is evident. Even when considering only to inline leaf-procedures (i.e. procedures that do not call any other procedure) still every tenth procedure would be a potential candidate.

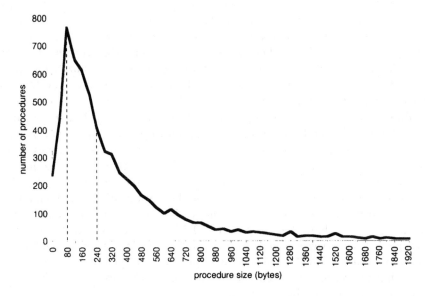

Fig. 2. Procedure Size Distribution

The results that we have measured during test runs were very promising.In some cases, when inlining frequently-executed procedures, a speed-up factor of 9 could be achieved. In addition, small procedures have a second positive impact on inlining. If the optimizer inlined every second call, the overall code size would only grow by about 25%.

6 Related Work

Pioneering research in program reoptimization was done by Knuth [Knu70], Ingalls [Ing71], and Jasik [Jas71]. Their work can be classified as *iterative optimization* and involves a feedback loop between the system and the programmer. A profiler monitors the execution of a program and creates data upon which the programmer bases further optimizations. The program is then run again to obtain updated profiles. The disadvantages of this approach are obvious. Not only does the inclusion of the programmer in the compile-load-run cycle make the results dependent on his knowledge, but also input values may vary from run to run, diminishing previous optimizations.

A group at the University of Washington examined value-specific data-dependent optimizations [KEH93], where code is optimized at runtime around particular input values. This strategy can best be compared to partial evaluation that is applied at runtime. Unfortunately the programmer is still involved in that he/she has to explicitly identify the bottlenecks in the application. This is done by marking sections using templates or fragments in the source code.

Removing the programmer from the feedback loop was one of the main ideas in Hansen's [Han74] automated optimization system. For speed considerations, his system was based on a non-portable intermediate representation that could be interpreted directly. Only when exceeding a certain runtime threshold was the representation translated *just-in-time* to native code and optimized for speed. He reported that the new reoptimizing FORTRAN-IV system did better than any single compiled system he examined.

Rather than optimizing programs at runtime, the Titan/Mahler project at Digital Western Research Laboratory attempted to perform optimizations only at the time of linking. In order to avoid expensive loading, program analysis was performed completely by the compiler. The results were then integrated into the object files which were represented in a portable register transfer language. The results confirmed the importance of intermodular optimizations. Although inlining or procedure cloning was not integrated, the built-in intermodular register allocation scheme achieved a speed-up of 10-25% [Wal86]. Another speed-up in the range of 5-10% was reported by the implementation of intermodular code motion. In addition [SW93] stressed the importance of dynamic profiles and described that previously collected variable-use profiles almost invariably achieve better results than compiler estimates.

In order to make object oriented languages competitive with traditional languages, eliminating the overhead of dynamic dispatching at runtime is probably the most important and the most promising optimization. Several techniques have been presented in the last few years to achieve this goal, such as class prediction [Höl94] and iterative class analysis [CU90] (both of them have been integrated into the SELF-system [US87]). Interprocedural class analysis, a related technique, was proposed by Grove [Gro95]. However it is still an open question whether traditional statically-typed languages can profit from these techniques.

7 Conclusion

Traditional static optimization algorithms suffer from two important deficiencies. First, they cannot be applied to portable code, and second, intermodular optimizations can only be performed on statically linked monolithic applications, thus thwarting extensibility and reducing the applicability for modular systems.

Since extensibility and portability will play an important role in future software systems, we are currently implementing a system architecture in which program optimization is performed in the background while the system is running. Unlike earlier proposals, optimizations are not applied uniformly to each section of the program but rather take into account the program's dynamic behavior and are only applied to the parts that account for most of the execution-time. The system utilizes object files that are based on a tree-based intermediate representation, and is guided by an adaptive profiler. A tree based encoding has many advantages over most commonly used low-level intermediate representations.

Finally, we have presented some examples of intermodular optimization techniques and illustrated their enormous potential for modern extensible operating systems.

8 Acknowledgments

Michael Franz and Martin Burtscher provided many helpful comments on an earlier version of this paper. Martin Burtscher also developed a prototype algorithm for intermodular inlining upon which some of the presented statistics are based. More information about the Oberon project and research related topics at the University of California at Irvine can be found on the World Wide Web at http://www.ics.uci.edu/~oberon.

References

[Bra95]   M. M. Brandis; *Optimizing Compilers for Structured Programming Languages*; (Doctoral Dissertation) Eidgenössische Technische Hochschule Zürich; 1995

[Cha82]   G. J. Chaitin; Register Allocation & Spilling via Graph Coloring; In *Proceedings of the ACM SIGPLAN '82 Symposium on Compiler Construction*, pp 98–105. Published as *SIGPLAN Notices 17(6)*; June 1982

[CH84]   F. C. Chow, J. L. Hennessy; Register Allocation by Priority-Based Coloring; In *Proceedings of the ACM SIGPLAN '84 Symposium on Compiler Construction*, pp 222–232. Published as *SIGPLAN Notices 19(6)*; June 1984

[CU90]   C. Chambers, D. Ungar; Iterative Type Analysis and Extended Message Splitting: Optimizing Dynamically-Typed Object-Oriented Programs; In *Proceedings of the ACM SIGPLAN '90 Conference on Programming Language Design and Implementation*, pp 150–164. Published as *SIGPLAN Notices 25(6)*; June 1990

[Fra94]   M. Franz; *Code-Generation On-the-Fly: A Key to Portable Software*; (Doctoral Dissertation) Verlag der Fachvereine, Zürich; 1994

[FK96]   M. Franz, Th. Kistler; *Slim Binaries*; Technical Report 96-24, Department of Information and Computer Science, UC Irvine; 1996

[Gro95]   D. Grove; The Impact of Interprocedural Class Analysis on Optimizations; *CASCOM '95 Proceedings*; November 1995

[Han74]   G. J. Hansen; *Adaptive Systems for the Dynamic Run-Time Optimization of Programs*; (Ph.D. Dissertation) Department of Computer Science, Carnegie-Mellon University; 1974

[HCU91]   U. Hölzle, C. Chambers, D. Ungar; Optimizing Dynamically-Typed Object-Oriented Languages With Polymorphic Inline Caches; In *ECOOP '91 Conference Proceedings*. Published as *Springer Verlag Lecture Notes in Computer Science 512*; 1991

[Höl94]   U. Hölzle; *Adaptive Optimization for SELF: Reconciling High Performance with Exploratory Programming*; (Ph.D. Dissertation) Department of Computer Science, Stanford University; 1994

[HU94]   U. Hölzle, D. Ungar; *Optimizing Dynamically-Dispatched Calls with Run-Time Type Feedback*; In *SIGPLAN '94 Conference on Programming Language Design and Implementation*, pp 326–336. Published as *SIGPLAN Notices 29(6)*; June 1994

[IBM94]   IBM; *PowerPC and POWER2: Technical Aspects of the New IBM RISC System/6000*; IBM Order Number SA23-2737-00

[Ing71]   D. Ingalls; The Execution Time Profile as a Programming Tool; In *Design and Optimization of Compilers*, pp 107–128, Prentice-Hall; 1971

[Jas71]   S. Jasik; Monitoring Execution on the CDC 6000's; In *Design and Optimization of Compilers*, pp 129–136, Prentice-Hall; 1971

[Jon93]   N. Jones; Special Issue on Partial Evaluation; *Journal of Functional Programming 3(4)*; 1993

[KEH93]   D. Keppel, S. J. Eggers, R. R. Henry; *Evaluating Runtime-Compiled Value-Specific Optimizations*; Technical Report 93-11-02, Department of Computer Science and Engineering, University of Washington; 1993

[Knu70]   D. E. Knuth; *An Empirical Study of FORTRAN Programs*; IBM Report RC 3276; 1970

[LYJ96]   T. Lindholm, F. Yellin, B. Joy, K. Walrath; *The Java Virtual Machine Specification*; Addison-Wesley; 1996

[Sur93]   R. Surati; *A Parallelizing Compiler Based on Partial Evaluation*; Technical Report AITR-1377, Artificial Intelligence Laboratory, Massachusetts Institute of Technology; 1993

[SW93]   A. Srivastava, D. W. Wall; A Practical System for Intermodule Code Optimization at Link-Time; *Journal of Programming Languages*; 1993

[US87]   David Ungar, R. B. Smith; SELF: The Power of Simplicity; In *OOPSLA '87 Conference Proceedings*, pp 227–241. Published as *SIGPLAN Notices 22(12)*; December 1987

[Wal86]   D. W. Wall; Global Register Allocation at Link Time; In *Proceedings of SIGPLAN '86 Symposium on Compiler Construction*, pp 264–275; July 1986

[WG89]   N. Wirth, J. Gutknecht; The Oberon System; In *Software-Practice and Experience 19(9)*, pp 857–893; September 1989

[Wir88]   N. Wirth; The Programming Language Oberon; In *Software-Practice and Experience 18(7)*, pp 671–690; July 1988

[WL91]   M. Wolf, M. Lam; A Data Locality Optimization Algorithm; In *Proceedings of the SIGPLAN '91 Conference on Programming Language Design and Implementation*, pp 30–44, Published as *SIGPLAN Notices 26(6)*; June 1991

Type Inference for Late Binding: The SmallEiffel Compiler

Suzanne COLLIN, Dominique COLNET and Olivier ZENDRA
Campus Scientifique, Bâtiment LORIA,
Boîte Postale 239,
54506 Vandoeuvre-lès-Nancy Cedex
France
Tel. +33 03 83.59.20.93
Email: colnet@loria.fr

Centre de Recherche en Informatique de Nancy

Abstract. The SmallEiffel compiler uses a simple type inference mechanism to translate Eiffel source code to C code. The most important aspect in our technique is that many occurrences of late binding are replaced by static binding. Moreover, when dynamic dispatch cannot be removed, inlining is still possible. The advantage of this approach is that it speeds up execution time and decreases considerably the amount of generated code. SmallEiffel compiler source code itself is a large scale benchmark used to show the quality of our results. Obviously, this efficient technique can also be used for class-based languages without dynamic class creation : for example, it is possible for C++[10] or Java and not possible for Smalltalk.

1 Introduction and Related Works

Object-oriented languages, by their very nature, pose new problems for the *delivery of applications* and the construction of time-efficient, type-safe, and compact binaries. The most important aspect is the compilation of inheritance and late binding. The distinctive feature of late binding is that it allows some freedom about the exact type of a variable. This flexibility of late binding is due to the fact that a variable's type may dynamically change at run time. We introduce an approach to compilation which is able to automatically and selectively replace many occurrences (more than 80%) of late binding by static binding, after considering the context in which a call is made. The principle we will detail in this article consists in computing each routine's code in its calling context, according to the concrete type of the target. The computation of a specific version of an Eiffel [7] routine is not done for all the target's possible types, but only for those which *really exist* at run time. As a consequence, it is first necessary to know which points of an Eiffel program may be reached at run time, and then to remove those that are unreachable.

Our compilation technique, which requires the attribution of a type to each object, deals with the domain of type inference. Ole Agesen's recent PhD thesis

[2] contains a complete survey of related work. Reviewed systems range from purely theoretical ones [13] to systems in regular use by a large community [8], via partially implemented systems [11] [12] and systems implemented on small languages [5] [9].

Using Agesen classification [2], SmallEiffel compiler's algorithm can be qualified as *polyvariant* (which means each feature may be analyzed multiple times) and *flow insensitive* (no data flow analysis). Our algorithm deals both with *concrete types* and abstract types. The Cartesian Product Algorithm (CPA) [1] is a more powerful one. However, the source language of CPA is very different from Eiffel : it is not statically typed, handles prototypes (no classes) and allows dynamic inheritance ! The late binding compilation technique we describe for Eiffel may apply to any class-based language [6], with or without genericity, but without dynamic creation of classes. The generated target code is precisely described as well as the representation of objects at run time.

Section 2 introduces our technique's terminology and basic principle. Section 3 explains in detail and with examples the technique we used to suppress late binding points. Section 4 considers the problem of genericity. Section 5 show the impact of late binding removal. Our examples are written in Eiffel, and we use the vocabulary which is generally dedicated to Eiffel [7].

2 Overall Principles and Terminology

2.1 Dead Code and Living Code

In Eiffel, the starting execution point of a program is specified by a pair composed of an initial class and one of its creation procedures. This pair is called the application's *root*. The first existing object is thus an instance of the root class, and the very first operation consists in launching the root procedure with that object. First of all, our compilation process computes which parts of the Eiffel source code may or may not be reached from the system's root, without doing any data flow analysis. The result of this first computation is thus completely independent of the order of instructions in the compiled program. With regard to conditional instructions, we assume that all alternatives may a priori be executed. Starting from the system's root, our algorithm recursively computes the *living code*, that is code which may be executed. Code that can never be executed is called *dead code*. Living code computation is closely linked to the inventory of classes that may have instances a run time. For example, let's consider the following root :

```
class ROOT creation root feature
   a: A;
   root is
      do io.put_string("Enter a number :"); io.read_integer;
         !!a;                               -- (1)
         a.add(io.last_integer);           -- (2)
         a.sub(1);                         -- (3)
      end;
end -- ROOT
```

Of course, the root procedure of class ROOT belongs to the living code. Since this procedure contains an instantiation instruction for class A (at line (1)), instances of class A may be created. The code of routines **add** and **sub** of class A may be called (lines (2) and (3)). Consequently, the source code of these two routines is living code, from which our algorithm will recursively continue. In the end, if we neither consider input-output instructions nor the source code of routines **add** et **sub**, only two classes may have instances at run time: class A and class ROOT. By analogy with the terms dead and living code, a *living class* is a class for which there is at least one instantiation instruction in living code: A is a living class. Conversely, a *dead class* is a class for which no instance may be created in living code.

2.2 Goals and Basic Principles

Object-oriented programming (OOP) is largely based on the fact that an operation always applies to a given object corresponding to a precise dynamic type. In Eiffel, as in Smalltalk, no operation may be triggered without first supplying this object, called *target* or *receiver*. Named **current** in Eiffel, the target ob-

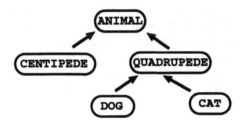

Fig. 1. Simple inheritance graph used in all the article.

ject determines which operation is called. Let's consider the simple inheritance example of figure 1, which will be used all along this article. Let's also assume that each sub-class of ANIMAL has its own routine **cry**, which displays its own specific cry. If the target is of type CAT, the routine **cry** of class CAT is used. If the target is of type DOG, it is the routine of class DOG. And so on... The main goal of our compilation technique consists in *statically* computing either — at best — the only routine which corresponds to a target object, or the reduced set of routines that are potentially concerned.

2.3 Representation of Objects at Run Time

Only living types are represented at run time. Basic objects corresponding to Eiffel's types INTEGER, CHARACTER, REAL, DOUBLE and BOOLEAN are directly represented with simple types of the target language. For example, an Eiffel object of type INTEGER is directly implemented with a C **int**. All other objects are represented by a structure (C **struct**) whose first field is the number that identifies the corresponding living type. Each of the object's living attributes is implemented inside this structure as a field bearing the attribute's name. If the attribute is directly an object (**expanded**), the field's type corresponds to the living type considered. If the attribute is a reference to another object, the field's type is "pointer to anything"((**void** *) in C). For example, for the previously described class ROOT, the C structure is:

structure ROOT {int id; void *a;};

If attribute a of class ROOT is declared as **expanded** A, that is without intermediate pointer, the C structure would be:

structure ROOT {int id; A a;};
structure A {int id; ...; ...;};

3 Adapting Primitives

Considering that we know the set of living types, our compilation technique consists, for each of these types, in computing a specific version of primitives that can be applied to the type. The adaptation of a primitive is mainly based on the fact that the target's type is known: it is the living type in which the adaptation is realized. For all the following examples, we refer to the source text of classes ANIMAL, QUADRUPEDE, DOG, CAT and CENTIPEDE given in appendix.

To avoid needlessly complicating our explanations, the target language used is a pseudo-code close to Pascal or C. The actual C code produced by Small-Eiffel can be obtained by compiling those examples, which are available with the compiler itself by **ftp** at address **ftp.loria.fr** in directory **/pub/loria-/genielog/SmallEiffel**.

3.1 General Example

```
class ROOT1 creation root feature
dog: DOG;
root is
   do   !!dog;                         - (1)
        dog.set_name("Snowy");         - (2)
        dog.introduction;              - (3)
   end;
end - ROOT1
```

Fig. 2. The only living types are ROOT1 and DOG. Other types are dead.

The first root given in figure 2 is deliberately very simple. If we omit input-output instructions and class STRING, only types DOG and ROOT1 are alive. Type

```
structure ROOT1 {int id; void *dog;};
structure DOG {int id; void *name;};
procedure DOGset_name(DOG *target,void *my_name) {
  target->name = my_name;};
procedure DOGintroduction(DOG *target) {
  write("My name is :");
  write(target->name);};
procedure ROOT1root(ROOT1 *target) {
  target->dog = new(DOGid);                          - (1)
  DOGset_name(non_void(target->dog),"Snowy");        - (2)
  DOGintroduction(non_void(target->dog));}           - (3)
procedure main {
  ROOT1root(new(ROOT1id));}
```

Fig. 3. Generated code for the root of figure 2.

ROOT1 is alive, as well as the **root** operation which serves as main program. Only class DOG may be instantiated (at line (1) figure 2). Procedures **set_name** and **introduction** of type DOG are alive, since they are used in operation **root** at lines (2) and (3). Operation **set_name** uses attribute **name** (cf. definition of class ANIMAL), which is thus also alive. Let's note that classes ANIMAL and QUADRUPEDE are abstract ones (**deferred**) and may never correspond to a living type. Eventually, the generated pseudo-code is composed of two structure definitions and four procedures, including the launching procedure **main** (figure 3). Structures ROOT1 and DOG both begin with an **id** field that contains their type identifier. Field **dog** of structure ROOT1 corresponds to attribute **dog**, which is an object pointer. Similarly, attribute **name** of structure DOG is also an object pointer. The adaptation of procedure **set_name** in type DOG is procedure DOG-**set_name**. The latter always applies to a pointer to a structure DOG (the living type corresponding to the target). The body of this routine consists in setting field **name** in the target object's structure. In this procedure as in all others, we consider that argument **target** may never be a "pointer to nothing" (C NULL or Eiffel **void**). This choice is perfectly coherent with an elementary principle of OOP: without target, no operation may be executed. The target's existence test is done by the caller, as can be seen in the code produced for instructions (2) and (3) of procedure ROOT1root. Function **non_void** has to verify that the target exists. If it does not, this function raises a run time error. Otherwise, this function returns its argument unchanged. Considering that we do not perform any data flow analysis, the call to **non_void** is always done, even when the previous instruction (the one in line (1)) gives the target a value.

3.2 Routines that Do not Use the Target

Let's now consider the root given in figure 4. In this example, only classes

```
class ROOT2 creation root feature
 centipede: CENTIPEDE; quadrupede: QUADRUPEDE;
 root is
  do
   !!centipede;                    - (1)
   centipede.cry;                  - (2)
   !DOG!quadrupede;                - (3)
   quadrupede.cry;                 - (4)
  end;
end - ROOT2
```

Fig. 4. Living types : ROOT2, CENTIPEDE and DOG. Other types are dead.

```
structure ROOT2 {int id; void *centipede; void *quadrupede};
structure CENTIPEDE {int id;};
structure DOG {int id;};
procedure DOGcry() { write("BARK");};
procedure CENTIPEDEcry() { write("SCOLO");};
procedure ROOT2root(ROOT2 *target) {
  target->centipede = new(CENTIPEDEid);           - (1)
  non_void(target->centipede); CENTIPEDEcry;      - (2)
  target->quadrupede = new(DOGid);                - (3)
  non_void(target->quadrupede); DOGcry; }         - (4)
```

Fig. 5. Target code generated for the root of figure 4.

CENTIPEDE and DOG are instantiated in the living code (instructions (1) and (3)). The two corresponding types are thus living ones. No instance of class CAT may exist at run time, since the living code does not contain any instantiation instruction for that class: type CAT is dead, as well as types ANIMAL and QUADRUPEDE. Indeed, these two types correspond to abstract (**deferred**) classes whose instantiation is forbidden. Code is thus produced only for the 3 living types ROOT2, DOG and CENTIPEDE. The full resulting code, given in figure 5, contains 3 structures and 4 procedures. Each living type structure comprises only living attributes. Consequently, type DOG does not contain field **name** any more, since attribute **name** is not used. Procedures DOGcry and CENTIPEDEcry do not use the target object (**current**) which corresponds to their living type. They always print the same message, whatever their living target. Such routines that do not use their target are thus coded without any **target** argument. However, it is necessary to keep the target's existence test in the caller routine, by calling function **non_void** just before the actual call (cf. lines (2) and (4) of figure 5). For the instruction of line (4), DOGcry must be called, even if the static type of variable **quadrupede** is QUADRUPEDE and not DOG. Indeed, the only living type which conforms to (dead) type QUADRUPEDE is DOG.

3.3   Late Binding

```
quadrupede: QUADRUPEDE;
root is
  local x: STRING;
  do
    x := get_user_answer("Dog or Cat? ");
    if equal("Cat",x) then !CAT!quadrupede else !DOG!quadrupede end;
    quadrupede.cry;  - (1)
  end;
```

Fig. 6. Instruction of line (1) need late binding.

```
procedure root(ROOT *target) {
  ...
  switchQUADRUPEDEcry(target->quadrupede); }      - (1)
procedure switchQUADRUPEDEcry(void *target) {
  switch (non_void(target)->id){              - (a)
    DOGid:   DOGcry; break;                    - (b)
    CATid:   CATcry; break;                    - (c)
    else error("non-conforming type");} } - (d)
```

Fig. 7. Generated code for instruction (1) of figure 6.

In the example of figure 6, CAT and DOG are living types. The static type of
the target of instruction (1) is QUADRUPEDE. Since the 2 living types conform to
the target's type, a late binding operation is required to select either procedure
cry of type CAT, or procedure **cry** of type DOG. When a late binding point exists
in living code, an appropriate switching routine is defined (figure 7). For a given
type, dead or alive, this routine performs the selection corresponding to a given
operation name. Given the role of switching routines, their names remind the pair
which corresponds to the selection (*type × operation_ name*). In our example, the
switching procedure must realize this selection among living types that conform
to QUADRUPEDE, in order to call the suitable procedure **cry**. Hence the name
switchQUADRUPEDEcry. In order to factorize it, the target's existence test is
realized into the switching routine's body (line (**a**)). The operation called is the
one which corresponds to the number that identifies the living type (lines (**b**) and

(c)). Finally, to guard against all contingencies, an error is raised (line (d)) if the target does not correspond to any living type that conforms to QUADRUPEDE. Error "non-conforming type" of line (d) allows the detection of a potential problem of *system-level validity* .

Of course, this error may never occur for example of figure 6, because the target is always either of type CAT or of type DOG. Furthermore, the target is always an existing object, thanks to the call to **non_void**. More generally, the root of example 6 is said to be *system-valid* according to corresponding rules that are defined in the Eiffel reference manual [7] (*system-level validity*, page 357). A compiler which would be able to detect that a program is correct with regard to these rules could omit the run time error of line (d).

To simplify our presentation, we use a sequential switch in figure 7. Actually, one of our compiler's strong points is its ability to generate a dichotomic selection code, after sorting out the type identifiers. This speeds up the selection, which may have more than 2 alternatives, by decreasing the average number of tests performed. We may note that other compilers generally use a function pointer table whose goal is to realize the selection in a constant time. For reasons we will explain later (§3.5), we did not choose that solution.

3.4 Calls on Target current

```
animal: ANIMAL;    quadrupede: QUADRUPEDE;
root is
  do
    x := get_user_answer("Dog or Cat? ");
    if equal("Cat",x) then !CAT!quadrupede else !DOG!quadrupede end;
    x := get_user_answer("Dog, Cat or Centipede ? ");
    if equal("Cat",x) then !CAT!animal
    elseif equal("Dog",x) then !DOG!animal
    else !CENTIPEDE!animal end;
    quadrupede.chameleon(animal);                - (1)
  end;
```

Fig. 8. Procedure chameleon is alive for types CAT and DOG (line (1)).

As a living operation is always adapted in the corresponding living type, calls on the receiver (target current) are coded as immediate calls : there is no target's existence test, since current may never be a pointer to a non-existent object, and there is also no need for any selection by switching routine. Let's consider the root given in figure 8. The set of living types is composed of 4 types : ROOT4, CAT, DOG and CENTIPEDE. Instruction (1) is a call to procedure **chameleon** with a target whose static type is QUADRUPEDE. This procedure is

```
procedure root(ROOT *target) {
  ...
  switchQUADRUPEDEchameleon(target->quadrupede,target->animal);}    - (1)
procedure switchQUADRUPEDEchameleon(void *target, void *other) {
  switch (non_void(target)->id)
     DOGid:DOGchameleon(target,other); break;                      - (a)
     CATid:CATchameleon(target,other); break;                      - (b)
     else error("non-conforming type");} }
procedure DOGchameleon(DOG *target, void *other) {
  DOGcry;                                                          - (c)
  write(" imitates ");
  switchANIMALcry(other);                                          - (d)
  write(" = ");
  switchANIMALcry(DOGimitation(target,other)); }                   - (e)
```

Fig. 9. Switch (QUADRUPEDE × chameleon) and the code of procedure chameleon for type DOG. Coding for the root of figure 8.

thus alive in types CAT and DOG, and dead in type CENTIPEDE because CEN-TIPEDE is not a type that conforms to QUADRUPEDE. The code for instruction (1) given in figure 9 includes the corresponding switch and the version of procedure **chameleon** adapted to type DOG. This procedure, whether it is adapted to type CAT or type DOG, uses its target. Consequently, internal calls to the switch (lines (a) and (b) in figure 9) pass down 2 arguments: the target, and argument **other**. Operation **chameleon** adapted to type DOG begins with a call to procedure **cry** on target **current** (see class ANIMAL). As each living operation is duplicated in the corresponding living type, target **current** is always a non-void pointer to an object of the corresponding living type. A call whose target is **current** is thus coded with a direct — static — call, without even checking that the pointer exists (line (c)). The call to **cry** with target **other** of static type ANIMAL relies on the corresponding switch (line (d)). To follow Eiffel's order of evaluation (left to right for qualified calls), the leftmost elements in Eiffel become the rightmost and most nested arguments in the generated C code. So, instruction "**current.imitation(other).cry;**" is coded (line (e)) by a direct call to **imitation** (adapted to type DOG), which serves as an argument of the switch (ANIMAL×**cry**). Using this switch is mandatory, because in DOG's context, one has to consider the definition of **imitation** given in class QUADRUPEDE.

3.5 Further Optimizations

When a program is considered to be valid, either because it was intensively tested or because it has been proven system-valid, the produced code may be simplified in several ways:
- The test of target existence **"non_void"** may be suppressed.

– In a switch, the default test "non-conforming type" may be omitted.

– Simple operations, such as procedures that set or functions that read an attribute, may be inlined.

The various alternatives in a switch may thus result in different forms of coding: function calls, inlined function calls or mere variable accesses. This explains why we decided not to use function pointers arrays to realize our switching routines. Another advantage of our choice is that it is possible to factorize alternatives which correspond to the same C code.

4 Dealing with Genericity

```
root is
  local
    pussy:CAT; cat_ar:ARRAY[CAT]; doggy:DOG; quad_ar:ARRAY[QUADRUPEDE];
  do
    !!pussy; !!doggy;
    cat_ar := «pussy»;
    cat_ar.item(1).cry;                    - (1)
    quad_ar := «pussy,doggy»;
    quad_ar.item(1).cry;                   - (2)
    cat_ar.item(1).set_name("Felix"); - (3)
  end;
```

Fig. 10. Using genericity . Types ARRAY[CAT] and ARRAY[QUADRUPEDE] are alive.

```
procedure root {
  ...
  non_void(ARRAYofCATitem(cat_ar,1)); CATcry;                        - (1)
  ...
  non_void(quad_ar);
  switchQUADRUPEDEcry(ARRAYofQUADRUPEDEitem(quad_ar,1));             - (2)
  ...
  non_void(cat_ar);
  CATset_name(ARRAYofCATitem(cat_ar,1),"Felix");}                    - (3)
```

Fig. 11. Code generated for the root of figure 10.

To handle genericity, we also apply a similar technique, considering that several types derived from a same generic class are all *distinct* living types. A given generic class is alive if there is at least one living generic derived type for that class. For example, in figure 10, **‹pussy›** represents an instantiation of type ARRAY[CAT] by creation of an array initialized with one single element. Type ARRAY[CAT] is thus alive. Notation **‹pussy,doggy›** corresponds to a 2-element array whose type is ARRAY[QUADRUPEDE]. Indeed, QUADRUPEDE is the smallest type to which **pussy** and **doggy** conform. So type ARRAY[QUADRUPEDE] is also a living type.

The living operations of types ARRAY[CAT] and ARRAY[QUADRUPEDE] are copied and adapted separately in each of these 2 types. For example, function **item**, which returns an element, has two possible adaptations: one in AR-RAY[CAT] and the other in ARRAY[QUADRUPEDE]. This function's static type is CAT in ARRAY[CAT] and QUADRUPEDE in ARRAY[QUADRUPEDE]. In this way, the code for instruction (1) given in figure 11 is a direct call to procedure **cry** of type CAT, since the static type of the target (which is the result of function **item**) is CAT. For instruction (2), the static type of function **item**'s result is QUADRUPEDE. Using a switch is thus mandatory, because CAT and DOG are both living types that conform to QUADRUPEDE.

5 Results and Conclusion

5.1 Results Using Eiffel Source Code of SmallEiffel

boost	check	require	Number of ...
17666	19736	23039	direct calls without any test of target existence
0	7190	8289	direct calls with the target's existence test
3379	5138	5899	switched calls
194	203	211	defined switches
83	319	258	functions which do not use the target
27	82	36	procedures which do not use the target
1434	1436	1698	functions which do use the target
1010	1589	1758	procedures which do use the target
1010	0	0	inlined functions
266	0	0	inlined procedures

Fig. 12. Compiling SmallEiffel with itself (45000 lines / 250 classes).

The results we present here are obtained when compiling SmallEiffel compiler's root itself. Obviously, such a root is a significant benchmark, with about 250 classes and 45000 lines of Eiffel source code. Figure 12 gives a general survey of our results. We used 3 different compilation modes:

boost: Compilation mode which includes all optimizations. There is no target's existence test, and no system-level validity checking. Some routines are inlined, and switches are simplified. There is no assertion check.

check : Compilation mode in which no Eiffel assertion is checked. The target's existence test is performed. Some code is generated for the system-level validity checking, and to produce an execution trace. There is no inlining and no assertion check.

require : Compilation mode in which Eiffel preconditions are checked. The generated code is similar to the previous one, but also includes code to test preconditions (**require** clause).

Results are extremely positive concerning the number of calls without switch compared to the total number of calls. For example, in boost mode, the total number of calls is 21045, including only 3379 switched calls. This means that 84% of the calls are direct, fast calls.

In the 2 other modes (check and require), this ratio is similar (respectively 83% and 84%) if one admits that a call with only a target's existence test may be considered as a direct call. The ratio of routines (procedures and functions) that do not use the target is 5% in boost mode, 13% in check mode and 8% in require mode. This relatively low proportion in all modes comes from the fact that, generally, a routine which is put into a class is designed to operate on instances (targets) of this class. This is a basic principle of object-oriented programming. Figure 13 gives a survey of results obtained about the size of the generated code

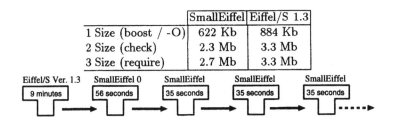

	SmallEiffel	Eiffel/S 1.3
1 Size (boost / -O)	622 Kb	884 Kb
2 Size (check)	2.3 Mb	3.3 Mb
3 Size (require)	2.7 Mb	3.3 Mb

Eiffel/S Ver. 1.3	SmallEiffel 0	SmallEiffel	SmallEiffel	SmallEiffel
9 minutes	56 seconds	35 seconds	35 seconds	35 seconds

Fig. 13. Executable size and compilation times: SmallEiffel vs Eiffel/S 1.3.

as well as the compilation time to obtain C code from Eiffel. As before, the code of SmallEiffel is used as a benchmark. All the results shown in figure 13 were obtained from tests realized on the same machine (HP 9000/887), with the same C compiler and the same options (cc -O). Since we used the Eiffel/S compiler (Release 1.3, from SiG Computer GmbH) to initiate SmallEiffel's bootstrap, we compare our results with this compiler. The size of the optimized code given in line 1 corresponds to SmallEiffel's boost mode and option -O of Eiffel/S compiler. The size comparisons of lines 2 and 3 are given for information only, since we should compare without including the code used to trace execution errors. This code is different from one compiler to an other, and varies with the level of detail of the trace. We can nonetheless note that the code size of Eiffel/S is constant, whereas the size of SmallEiffel's code increases. The latter point is due to the fact that SmallEiffel produces *only* the code which is strictly necessary for a specific compilation mode.

In order to evaluate the benefit that directly comes from our processing of late binding, we may examine more closely SmallEiffel's bootstrap process. Bottom of figure 13 shows how SmallEiffel is obtained, through a succession of compilations on the same source code (SmallEiffel's Eiffel code). After each compilation, the compiler produced is used for the next compilation, and so on... The first compilation (9 minutes) corresponds to an execution of the Eiffel/S compiler. The second one (56 seconds) uses SmallEiffel's compilation algorithm, but late binding still relies on Eiffel/S indirection algorithm. The third compilation (35 seconds) is the first that uses our implementation of late binding by switches. The fourth compilation and the following show that the process has stabilized [3]. The actual benefit when compiling the SmallEiffel compiler code is given by the ratio 56/35. SmallEiffel runs 1.6 times as fast as Eiffel/S for this big benchmark.

5.2 Comparison with C++ and Other Eiffel Compilers

Results presented in this section are available in `comp.lang.eiffel` on the Internet. This comparison was done by Dietmar Wolz. See archives files available at `http://www.cm.cf.ac.uk` for details. The Eiffel program consists of 13 classes where one (dynamic arrays, inheriting from ARRAY[G]) was adapted to the different compilers for performance optimization. The C++ program uses the same algorithm, a similar structure and is based on the Standard Template Library. The test was realized on the same machine with the same C compiler. The following compilers have been tested : (a)-gnu g++ 2.7.2 with STL from gnu libg++2.7.1 (b)-gnu g++ 2.7.2 with commercial STL from Object Space (c)-ISE ebench 3.3.7 finalize, no garbage collection (d)-ISE ebench 3.3.7 finalize, with garbage collection (e)-SmallEiffel, no garbage collection (f)-SmallEiffel, with Boehm-Demers-Weiser garbage collector (g)-Sig Eiffel 1.3S no garbage collection (h)-Sig Eiffel 1.3S with garbage collection (i)-Tower Eiffel 1.5.1 no garbage collection.

Results of figure 14 include run time, compilation time, memory used in MByte and code size of the executable file in kByte. According to Dietmar Wolz's test, SmallEiffel is really the most efficient Eiffel compiler. The C++ program does memory management by hand, but there are some leaks. Thus one cannot compare the memory usage between Eiffel and C++, but only between the different Eiffel compilers.

5.3 Conclusion and Work in Progress

Each time it is possible, the dynamic dispatch is used into the SmallEiffel source code for various kinds of expressions as well as for various kinds of instructions, various kinds of names and so on. We were ourselves very surprised by the excellent score of 84%. Obviously, the 100% limit cannot be reached for all programs whatever the quality of the inference algorithm used : a simple ARRAY[ANIMAL]

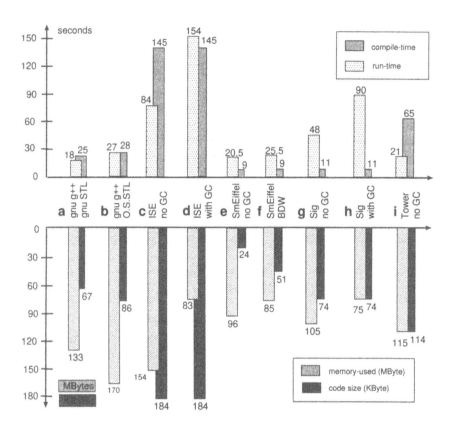

Fig. 14. Results between different compilers.

with mixed DOG and CAT entered at the keyboard is enough to break down any type inference system. Adding flow sensitivity to our compiler will increase the actual score [4]. This is a work in progress. SmallEiffel — as all other Eiffel compilers — is currently unable to check the system-level validity rules of Eiffel. This issue is also our present research theme.

Appendix: Eiffel Source Code

```
deferred class ANIMAL feature
  cry is deferred end;
  imitation(other: ANIMAL): ANIMAL is do Result := other; end;
  choose(other: QUADRUPEDE): ANIMAL is do Result := other; end;
  chameleon(other: ANIMAL) is
    do Current.cry; io.put_string(" imitates "); other.cry;
       io.put_string(" = "); Current.imitation(other).cry; end;
  name: STRING;
  set_name(my_name: STRING) is do name := my_name; end;
  introduction is
    do io.put_string("My name is:"); io.put_string(name); end;
```

```
end -- ANIMAL
deferred class QUADRUPEDE inherit ANIMAL redefine imitation feature
    imitation(a: ANIMAL): ANIMAL is do Result := a.choose(Current); end;
end -- QUADRUPEDE
class DOG inherit QUADRUPEDE feature
    cry is do io.put_string("BARK"); end;
end -- DOG
class CAT inherit QUADRUPEDE redefine choose feature
    choose(quadrupede: CAT): CAT is do Result := Current; end;
    cry is do io.put_string("MEOW"); end;
end -- CAT
class CENTIPEDE inherit ANIMAL feature
    cry is do io.put_string("SCOLO"); end;
end -- CENTIPEDE
```

References

1. Ole Agesen. The Cartesian Product Algorithm: Simple and Precise Type Inference of Parametric Polymorphism. In *Proceedings of the 9th European Conference on Object-Oriented Programming (ECOOP'95)*, pages 2–26, 1995.

2. Ole Agesen. *Concrete Type Inference : Delivering Object-Oriented Applications.* PhD thesis, Department of Computer Science of Standford University, Published by Sun Microsystem Laboratories (SMLI TR-96-52), 1996.

3. A.V. Aho and J.D. Ullman. *Principles of Compiler Design.* Addison-Wesley, Reading, Massachusetts, 1977.

4. Diane Corney and John Gough. Type Test Elimination using Typeflow Analysis. In *PLSA 1994 International Conference, Zurich. Volume 782 of Lecture Notes in Computer Sciences, Springer-Verlag*, pages 137–150, 1994.

5. J. Graver and R. Johnson. A Type System for Smalltalk. In *Proceedings of POPL*, pages 139–150, 1990.

6. G. Masini, A. Napoli, D. Colnet, D. Léonard, and K. Tombre. *Object Oriented Languages.* Academic Press Limited, London, 1991.

7. B. Meyer. *Eiffel, The Language.* Prentice Hall, 1994.

8. R. Milner. A Theory of Type Polymorphism in Programming. In *Journal of Computer and System Sciences*, pages 348–375, 1978.

9. Jens Palsberg and Michael I. Schwartzbach. Object-Oriented Type Inference. In *Proceedings of 6th Annual ACM Conference on Object-Oriented Programming Systems, Languages and Applications(OOPSLA'91)*, pages 146–161, 1991.

10. B. Stroustrup. *The C++ Programming Language.* Addison-Wesley Series in Computer Science, 1986.

11. N. Suzuki. Inferring Types in Smalltalk. In *Eighth Symposium on Principles of Programming Languages*, pages 187–199, 1981.

12. N. Suzuki and M. Terada. Creating Efficient System for Object-Oriented Languages. In *Eleventh Annual ACM Symposium on the Principles of Programming Languages*, pages 290–296, 1984.

13. J. VitekN, N. Horspool, and J.S. Uhl. Compile-Time Analysis of Object-Oriented Programs. In *International Conference on Compiler Construction. Volume 641 of Lecture Notes in Computer Sciences, Springer-Verlag*, pages 237–250, 1992.

An Object-Oriented Database Programming Environment for Oberon

Jacques Supcik[1], Moira C. Norrie[2]

[1] Institute for Computer Systems, Department of Computer Science, ETH Zürich
[2] Institute for Information Systems, Department of Computer Science, ETH Zürich

Abstract. We describe a system designed to provide database programming support for Oberon programmers. The system is based on a generic object-oriented data model which supports rich classification structures and an algebra over collections of objects. We describe how support for the constructs and operations of this model is provided to the programmer without changes to the Oberon language and with minimal changes to the run-time system. In particular, we consider issues of support for object evolution, constraint maintenance and query optimisation.

1 Introduction

Database functionality is necessary for a large category of modern computer applications. This is the case for not only traditional commercial applications such as payroll systems or personnel record management systems, but also the complex management of documents or computer aided engineering. In most of these applications, the relational data model is not appropriate because of the complex structure and processing of the information that has to be managed.

The more recently developed object-oriented data models are much more appropriate for these sorts of applications and the goal of our project is to provide Oberon programmers with the constructs and functions needed to support such a model. In order to realize this goal, we adapted the *OM* generic object data model [7] and made it available to the programmer through a set of Oberon modules. Since our primary goal is to provide Oberon programmers with database programming support, it was a basic requirement that no change be made to the Oberon-2 language [12] and minimum changes to the run-time system. This we achieved and our experiences show that the extensibility of the Oberon System [11] provides an elegant solution to the problem of integrating the underlying database engine in the operating system.

Two important aspects of database systems are the classification of objects and the ability of objects to evolve over time. Classification is important because it helps organize the database as collections of similar objects. In our model, we support multiple simultaneous classifications; that is, that the same object can be, at the same time, in many collections. Further, in our model classification has another fundamental role, namely the attribution of properties to objects. The second important aspect is object evolution. This is important because, usually, the objects will persist for a long time and, as we cannot predict the future, we cannot know in advance all the roles that the object may play during its life time. Even if we could predict the future, we still would like to have the evolution mechanism because we may not want to always store the whole history of all objects. This paper discusses the problems of supplying constructs and operations to support classification and evolution in the Oberon environment, and how these were solved.

Persistence in Oberon has already been dealt with in other research works. In [5], Templ shows an implementation of persistence in Oberon using meta-programming. In Oberon System-3, the concept of objects and persistence is a central part of the system. Knasmüller, in his *Oberon-D* project also added persistence to the Oberon System [8]. What makes our system different is that persistence itself was not the main goal, but rather a secondary goal required to support our data model. Consequently, contrary to Oberon-D, our persistent store does not need to be orthogonal to the Oberon types since, in our model, we make an explicit distinction between *database objects* that persist and *transient objects* that do not.

The next section of this paper motivates our approach and describes our object data model and the solutions found for the evolution problem. It also explains the idea of *"Typing by Classification"* which is a central concept in our model. The third section describes the operations on the model in terms of an algebra. Section four gives an overview of the query mechanism. Section five describes briefly the implementation and some key aspects of the persistent store. Concluding remarks and a discussion of further work are given in the last section. Throughout the paper, an example of a document management system shows how the constructs and operations needed to implement a database application are made accessible to the Oberon programmer.

2 The Data Model

The role of a database is to store and manipulate information about the application domain. To specify how this information is mapped in a database, we need to specify the constructs and the operations of the database system. These constructs and operations are specified in terms of a *data model* and this section describes the data model underlying our system.

The model is a generic, object-oriented model, offering a rich classification scheme. The advantage of such a generic model is that we can use it for both conceptual modeling of the application domain and for the implementation of the database system. In the following subsections, we describe in what ways the model is "object-oriented" and what the concept of *classification* means. We also describe our support for constraints. Many existing object-oriented database management systems, for example O_2 [13], lack any support for constraints.

2.1 An Object-Oriented Model

The term "object-oriented" is still used in several ways, so we start by stating what it means in the context of the model presented here. Let us begin with the definition of "Object". An object, in our model, is an abstract representation of a thing (concrete or abstract) or of a being. This representation is abstract because outside any context, an object has no visible attribute. It has no name, no colour, no size. In fact, the only global attribute of an object is an internal unique identifier used by the system to find the object and to differentiate it from the others. Such an object with no attributes does not seem very useful in a database but, in the next subsection, we show how to place the object in a context and how this context will be used to associate attributes with the object.

Contrary to a relational database management system, an object-oriented database management system should first be able to manage objects that are more complex than simple records. Such complex objects are found, for example, in computer aided engineering databases. Second, the system must be able to deal with *inheritance* between classes. With inheritance, we mean a mechanism to allow a class to be defined as an extension of a previously defined one. The system described in this paper meets these two requirements.

2.2   The Classification

Classification is used to organize and to structure a database by placing objects in different collections. A collection represents a *semantic* grouping of objects, i.e. a set of objects with a common role in the application system. For example, a collection "Professors" could contain a set of persons giving a course in a university. In our model, a collection is itself an object. Thus, it is possible to make collections of collections and to build a nested structure in the database system. The set of all collections in a database, together with the rules that control these collections, is called the *schema* of the database. An interesting consequence of this notion of collection as a semantic grouping is that the collection now gives a *context* or a *role* to the objects it contains and, in such a role, the objects share some common attributes related to it. For example, all members of the "Professors" collection could have an attribute such as the name of their university or the number of courses they are giving. This implementation of roles using semantic grouping is an interesting alternative to the other solutions proposed for example in [1] where they have implemented the concept in a new language, namely Fibonacci, or in [2] where they implemented, in Smalltalk, a role hierarchy for evolving objects.

With this view, collections are somehow similar to Oberon *types*. The main difference is that, in Oberon, an object has only one type, and in our model, an object can be in many collections and in every collection it will exhibit attributes relative to the role represented by that collection. Our classification model is not only more powerful than the one of the Oberon language, but also than most commercial object-oriented database systems, such as O_2 [13]. Another difference is that the classification is not a rigid structure: that is, an existing object can be inserted in or removed from existing collections. An object can also be moved from one collection to another. This mechanism, called *object evolution*, allows the objects to *evolve* during their life in the database. For example, in a university database, an object representing a person could first be considered as a student, then later as an assistant and then as a professor. In each of these three phases, the object would have attributes related to the corresponding role.

Some basic attributes such as integers or strings are already implemented in the basic system, but the user is not restricted to use only these types. Actually, he can define any new attributes he wants, provided that he also implements the methods for loading and storing the attributes in the persistent store. This makes the model much more flexible than the relational model in which the first normal form [14] disallows multivalued attributes, composite attributes and their combinations.

The general idea can be summarized as "Typing by Classification", which is contrary to the usual idea of "Classification by Typing". It is the most novel concept in our system, and represents an interesting solution to the object-evolution problem. Besides this, the mechanism also offers a solution to the *Schema evolution* problem because it is always possible to add or to remove collections. We also are able to add, remove or change the attributes associated with a collection, without changing all the objects in the collection. The details concerning this feature are beyond the scope of this paper. Another interesting theme concerning collections is how to control object evolution in the database. For example, how to forbid an object to evolve from the "Professors" to the "Students" collection. This theme is covered in [9].

We can illustrate this concept of classification using the example of a document management system. Figure 1 is a graphical representation of the schema of the database. In this figure, the collections are represented by rectangles and the subcollection relation by arrows between rectangles.

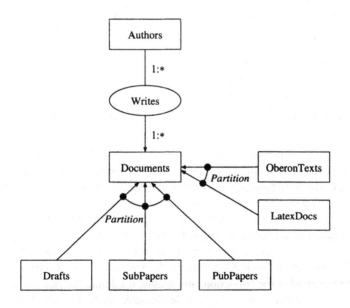

Fig. 1. Schema of the Document Management Database

In this schema, we see that "Documents" is a central collection. Actually, this collection contains all documents managed by the system. Then we have a first classification on the status of the document. In this classification, a document can be a draft, a submitted paper or a published one. We represent this classification using the three subcollections "Drafts", "SubPapers" and "PubPapers". This classification is a partition in that a document must belong to exactly one of these collections. The second classification over the documents is based on their form, or their file format. In our system, the documents we manage can be written in LaTeX or in Oberon Text Format. We represent this classification using the two collections "LatexDocs" and "OberonTexts". This classification is also a partition. Besides these two classifications on documents, we also have a collection to represent the "Authors" of these documents. The oval-shaped box labelled "Writes" represents an association between "Authors" and "Documents" and will be discussed in detail later.

Now that we declared the collections, we can define the attributes that the objects will have in these collections. For example, all members of "Documents" have a title. This attribute is represented as a string of characters. They also have methods to print the document and to edit it. These methods are generic and may be overridden by those defined in "LatexDocs" and in "OberonTexts". The attributes of the "Documents" collection are summarized in Table 1 and those of the "Drafts" collection in Table 2. As you can see, the only attribute defined for the "Drafts" collection is date giving the deadline for the submission of the document.

Documents	
Attribute	Type
title	String
print	Method
edit	Method

Table 1. Documents Attributes

Drafts	
Attribute	Type
deadline	Date

Table 2. Drafts Attributes

In an Oberon application, collections are created by calling procedures of the database management system. For example, to create the "Documents" collection, the application first calls the Collections.NewCollection procedure with a first parameter saying that this collection is not a subcollection, and a second parameter saying that this collection has three attributes. The application then defines the name of each attribute. Program 1 shows the creation of the "Documents" and "Drafts" collections.

The creation of an object is done in a similar way. For example, to create an author, we first call the function Objects.NewObject, then we add the object to the collections using the Add method of the collection, and finally, we define the value of the attributes of the object in each collection using the SetObjectAttribute method of the collection. Program 2 shows this process for an author and a draft document written in LaTeX.

As we have described, classification supports the structuring of a database but, until now, we have not discussed how to prevent the structure being misused. For example, it would be possible for a person to be at the same time in the collection "Men" and in the collection "Women". Of course, one could say that this problem is under the responsibility of the application managing the database, but it is better to integrate a mechanism into the system to detect these integrity inconsistencies in the model itself. This is the only way to globally guarantee the logical consistency of the database.

Program 1 Creating the collections

```
VAR docs, drafts, subPapers,... , authors: Collections.Collection;

PROCEDURE CreateCollections*;
BEGIN
    docs := Collections.NewCollection(NIL, 3);
    docs.SetCollectionAttribute(0, "name");
    docs.SetCollectionAttribute(1, "print");
    docs.SetCollectionAttribute(2, "edit");
    drafts := Collections.NewCollection(docs, 1);
    drafts.SetCollectionAttribute(0, "deadline");

    ...
END CreateCollections;
```

In our system, the logical consistency is defined by a set of rules called *constraints*. A constraint is an invariant that must be valid at the beginning and at the end of each *transaction*. A transaction is an atomic sequence of operations: that is, a sequence of operations that are considered as a whole. We know that the constraints are valid before the beginning of a transaction, so the only place where we check constraints is at the end of each transaction. The transactions here are used to ensure *logical* consistency of the information, but we will see later that our system also supports transactions to ensure the *physical* consistency of the data.

In our model, the consistency constraints are specified by algebraic expressions. The formal definition of a constraint is given by the following syntax:

constraint = expr "=" expr.
expr = term { "∪" term}.
term = factor { "∩" factor}.
factor = "("expr")" | collection | ∅.

For example, to impose that the collection Men and Women must be disjoint, we write following constraint: Men ∩ Women = ∅. In our example of the document management system, we have a partition constraint over the three collection Drafts, SubPapers and PubPapers. To specify this, we declare a *partition constraint* over these three collections. Program 3 shows how this may be coded in Oberon.

Drafts ∩ SubPapers = ∅
Drafts ∩ PubPapers = ∅
SubPapers ∩ PubPapers = ∅
Drafts ∪ SubPapers ∪ PubPapers = Documents

With this type of constraint, it is now possible to check logical consistency at the collection level, but it would also be useful to check logical consistency at the object level when an object is added to a collection. For example, one could wish to restrain the age of the members of the "Employees" collection to be a number between sixteen and

---

Program 2 Creating the objects

```
VAR albert, josef, physicPaper, OberonPaper, CPaper: Objects.Object;

PROCEDURE CreateObjects*;
    VAR strAttr: Objects.StringAttr; dateAttr: Objects.DateAttr;
      prtAttr: PrintMthAttr; editAttr: EditMthAttr
BEGIN
    albert := Objects.NewObject();
    authors.Add(albert);
    strAttr.value := "Albert";
    authors.SetObjectAttribute(albert, "name", strAttr);
    ... (* similar for josef *)
    physicPaper := Objects.NewObject();
    documents.Add(physicPaper);
    strAttr.value := "Physic Paper";
    documents.SetObjectAttribute(physicPaper, "docName", strAttr);
    prtAttr.method := NIL (* no generic method *);
    documents.SetObjectAttribute(physicPaper, "print", prtAttr);
    ... (* similar for the edit method *)
    drafts.Add(physicPaper);
    dateAttr.value := Today();
    drafts.SetObjectAttribute(physicPaper, "deadline", dateAttr);
    latexDocs.Add(physicPaper);
    prtAttr.method := LatexPrint;
    latexDocs.SetObjectAttribute(physicPaper, "print", prtAttr);
    ... (* similar for the other documents *)
END CreateObjects;
```

---

seventy-five. It is also possible to define such constraints in our model. These are specified by a Boolean function that takes an object as argument and returns a value indicating whether or not the object conforms to the constraint. In Oberon, this function is defined by:

PROCEDURE (o: Objects.Object): BOOLEAN

In the preceding section, we specified how to define a constraint, but we did not explain what happens when a constraint is violated at the end of a transaction. Two solutions are possible: either the transaction is simply rejected and the database is reset to the state before the transaction, or the system first tries to restore the constraint by updating the database and, only in the case where the system is not able to restore it in an unequivocal way, is the transaction rejected. In our system, we chose to investigate the second approach dealing with constraint *propagation*.

When a constraint over collections is violated, the system tries to restore the database to a consistent state by propagating the changes made during the transaction. Suppose, for example, that the constraint "Men ∪ Women = Persons" is defined in a database and that, at the end of a transaction, the system detects that an object has been added to the "Women" subcollection, but not to the collection "Persons". The constraint

---

Program 3 Definition of Constraint

```
PROCEDURE DefineConstraint;
   VAR c1, c2, c3, c4: Constraints.Constraint;
BEGIN
   c1 := Constraints.NewConstraint(Constraints.NewIntersection(
      Drafts, SubPapers), Collections.emptyCollection);
   c2 := Constraints.NewConstraint(Constraints.NewIntersection(
      Drafts, PubPapers), Collections.emptyCollection)
   c3 := Constraints.NewConstraint(Constraints.NewIntersection(
      SubPapers, PubPapers), Collections.emptyCollection)
   c4 := Constraints.NewConstraint(Constraints.NewUnion(
      Drafts, Constraints.NewUnion(SubPapers, PubPapers) , Documents)
END DefineConstraint;
```

---

is thus violated, but the system can restore it by propagating the insertion of the object to the collection "Persons".

In the case of constraints on objects, the solution of how to deal with violation is left to the procedure checking the constraint. The function can either signal an error by simply returning FALSE or modify the object and return TRUE to signal that the object is valid.

Finally, we describe how relationships between objects are represented in our model. For example, we would want to represent the relation between the husband and his wife, or between an author and the documents he wrote. In our model, relationships are represented by *"associations"*. An association is a collection in which members are special objects, called *pairs*, representing the two related objects. The associations also have a direction. A link always goes from the *source* of the association to its *destination*. For example, the collection "Authors" is the source of the association "Writes" and "Documents" its destination. Our model supports only *binary* associations, but since it is always possible to represent associations with more than two members using many binary associations, this restriction does not limit the expressiveness of the model.

There is another type of constraint for associations, namely the *cardinality* constraint. This constraint verifies that neither too many nor too few objects are related through a given association. Such a constraint is given by two pairs of numbers: (m:n $\rightarrow$ o:p). The first pair (m:n) specifies that every member of the collection at the source of the association must participate in at least m and at most n instances of the relationship represented by the association. If n is replaced by a star ($*$), this means that there is no maximum limit. The second pair is similar but for the collection at the destination side of the association.

In our document management example, the cardinality constraint of the "Writes" association is ($1:* \rightarrow 1:*$). This means that an author has to write at least one document, and that a document needs to have at least one author.

Now consider the following scenario in our document management system: Albert is writing a paper on Physics using LaTeX and Josef is writing two papers, one on Oberon and the other on C++, using the Oberon Text Editor. Then Albert submits his paper, which has to "evolve" from the Drafts collection to the SubPapers one. Later on, the paper of Albert is accepted and thus will evolve again from the SubPapers collection to the PubPapers one. Josef does the same, but his paper on C++ is rejected. He decides then to rewrite part of it, convert it to LaTeX and send it to another conference. So his document moves from the OberonTexts to the LatexDocs one, moves back from the SubPapers collection to the Drafts one and then from the Drafts one to the SubPapers one again. Now the paper is submitted for the other conference, and this time the paper is accepted and it can then move from the SubPapers collection to the PubPapers one.

The object evolution mechanism in our system can easily support such a scenario. For example, if a paper has to evolve from the "Drafts" to the "SubPapers" collection, we first remove it from "Drafts", then add it into "SubPapers". We can then define the new attributes that the object has in its new collection. Program 4 shows this evolution process.

Program 4 Submit a Paper

```
PROCEDURE SubmitPaper*(paper: Objects.Object);
   VAR dateAttr: Objects.DateAttr;
BEGIN
   drafts.Remove(paper); subPapers.Add(paper);
   dateAttr.value := Today();
   subPapers.SetObjectAttribute(paper, "submissionDate", dateAttr);
END SubmitPaper;
```

---

3   The Algebra

In the past, one of the main criticisms made against object-oriented database systems was their lack of an associated algebra and query language. In this section, we present an algebra, based on [6], [7], in which the operations on collections of our model are defined. Algebra operations always generate collections of objects. For other operations such as aggregation, the user has to write specific Oberon code. For example, if we are interested in the number of papers written by a given author, we can use the algebra to retrieve the corresponding papers, then use an Oberon procedure to compute the cardinality, that is the number of the members, of the result.

The three basic operations on collections are those from set theory. They are the *intersection*, the *union* and the *difference*. These operations are valid on all collections. Two other operations are defined for all collections: the *select* operation used to extract objects that satisfy a given predicate from a collection and *flatten* that takes a collection of collections and flattens them to a single collection.

The *select* operation comes in different flavours depending on how the predicate is defined. For simple queries, the selection can be done by searching for a given value, or a range of values, in an index, but the system allows also for more complex selections, or for selections for which no index exists. In this case, the predicate is specified by an Oberon function, similar to the one we used for constraints, that takes an object as parameter and returns a boolean indicating if the object satisfies the select condition or not. This form of selection is very powerful because the only limiting factor for the predicate expressiveness is the expressiveness of the Oberon language itself.

Some operations of the algebra are defined only for associations and using them with unary collections is forbidden by the system. The *Domain* function, which extracts the source of an association and *Range*, which extracts its destination, are typical examples. Here is the formal definition for these operations:

- Domain: dom $S = \{x \mid \exists\, y : (x,y) \in S\}$
- Range: rng $S = \{y \mid \exists\, x : (x,y) \in S\}$

Range restriction is also such an operation. It takes an association A and a collection C and forms an association comprising all those pairs of A with second value in C. Formally, we can write:

- Range Restriction: $A \text{ rr } C = \{(x,y) \mid (x,y) \in A \wedge y \in C\}$

In addition to these, the algebra also has operations to compute the *inverse* of an association, to *compose* associations and to *nest* or *unnest* associations.

Each operation is made available to the application programmer as an Oberon procedure. Program 5 shows how, in our document management system, we can find all published documents written in LaTeX. In this program, the result of the **Algebra.Intersection** function is a temporary collection C. The **Collections.Enumerate** procedure is an evaluator that applies the function DisplayDoc to every member of the temporary collection C.

Program 5 find Published Documents Written in LaTeX

```
PROCEDURE FindPubDocInLatex*;
    VAR C: Collections.TempCollection;
BEGIN
    C := Algebra.Intersection(pubDocuments, latexDocs);
    Collections.Enumerate(C, DisplayDoc);
END FindPubDocInLatex;
```

---

4 Query Processing

Having outlined the algebra, we can now describe how queries are evaluated. This process can be divided into three phases: A *front-end* reads and analyses the query given by the user and generates an intermediate structure representing the query in question. An *optimizer* transforms this structure to make its evaluation more efficient. Finally, a *back-end* evaluates the query represented by the intermediate structure and returns to the user a collection of objects matching the query. The functioning of the front-end is straightforward and will not be described further here. However, in this section, we describe briefly the intermediate structure, the functioning of the optimizer and of the evaluator.

To handle a query easily and efficiently, the system needs to represent it in an appropriate form. We use a *"syntax-tree"* to represent the queries. In such a tree, each operation previously defined in the algebra, and each reference to a collection, is represented by a node.

For example, consider the following query: "Find all authors who have published a document written in LaTeX". An algebraic representation of this query would be:

$$\text{dom}(Writes \text{ rr } (PubPapers \land LatexDocs))$$

Then we have to build the syntax tree representing the query. Figure 2 shows a graphical representation of that tree. There are two ways of introducing queries into an application. We can either write a string representing the query in a query language and give the string to the front-end, or we can bypass the front-end and build the tree directly using procedures from the system. Program 6 shows a procedure that directly builds the syntax-tree. The advantage of this second method is that the validity of the query is checked at compile-time and not only at run-time.

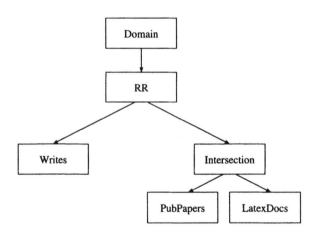

Fig. 2. Example of the internal representation of a query

The optimization phase transforms the tree to make its evaluation by the back-end more efficient. The tree being modified will possibly contain special "optimized" nodes that could not have been produced by the front-end. For example, a closure operation followed by a selection will be replaced by a special "ClosureSelect" node. This special node will prevent the back-end from producing huge intermediate collections.

The last phase of the query processing is the evaluation of the syntax-tree representing it. This last phase is similar to the evaluation of an arithmetic expression, but with collections instead of numbers.

Program 6 Procedure to Build a Syntax-Tree

```
PROCEDURE BuildQuery*;
    VAR n: Queries.Node;
BEGIN
    n := Query.Intersection(PubPapers, LatexDocs);
    n := Query.RR(writes, n);
    n := Query.Domain(n);
END BuildQuery;
```

---

5   Overview of the Implementation

The persistent store is implemented using the *"log principle"* [3]. Each time an object is written to the store, a new space is allocated and the object is written in this new space. In other words, an object is never changed "in place" but always completely rewritten. With this mechanism, the system is very robust because every operation can be undone allowing the system to always recover by restoring a previous status. This is used to implement transactions and to recover in the case of physical failures such as power failure or a disk crash.

The disadvantage of this mechanism is that a lot of "dead objects" stay in the store, using a lot of space. Therefore, the mechanism also requires a good garbage collection process to eliminate the garbage from the memory. However, if the garbage collector process tries to re-organize the whole store, the length of time of database unavailability would be too great. We solved this problem by implementing an *incremental* garbage collector. Using this method, only a small part of the storage is reorganized and the system remains available for other transactions. Details of the transaction mechanism is beyond the scope of this paper.

In the persistent store, the address of an object may change over time. In fact, it will change each time the object is written and each time the garbage collector relocates the object. So, to find the object without having to scan the whole database, we implemented an *id table*. This table is indexed by the identifier of the object and gives its physical location. When an object is moved, the corresponding entry in the table is modified. The table itself must persist, so we divide the persistent store into two domains: the id-table, which starts at the beginning of the store and grows toward the end, and the space for the objects which starts at the end of the store and grows towards the beginning. Figure 3 shows this structure. When a program needs to load an object from the store, it can either access it through its identifier or using a root-table, similar to the one used in PS-algol[10]. This table is nothing more than a collection of pairs <name, id> which allows an object to be found using a name instead of its id.

Having described the structure of the persistent store, we now show how the objects themselves are represented. Figure 4 shows the implementation of an object representing a draft document. The belongsTo structure is a dynamic array that indicates which collections contain the object, and for each collection, it defines the attributes that the object has in the collection. In this figure, we see that the object (ID=35) belongs to

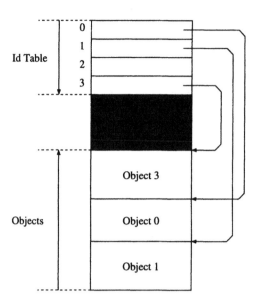

Fig. 3. Structure of the Persistent Store

Documents (ID=7), Drafts (ID=12) and OberonDocs (ID=47). In Documents, it has the attributes Relativity (Name), PrintMth (Print) and EditMth (Edit). In Drafts, it has 1.9.97 (Deadline). In OberonDocs, it has OPrintMth (Print) and OEditMth (Edit).

Figure 5 shows the implementation of a collection. As we can see, a collection has not only the ID as a predefined attribute, but also the ID of the parent collection in the case of a subcollection. In addition, it has a list of attribute names defined for this collection and an extension containing the references of the members of the collection. In this example, the collections Drafts (ID=12) is a subcollection of Documents (ID=7), it has only one attribute ("deadline") and contains the objects 35, ...

We implemented this system using the original Oberon-2 Compiler with no changes to the Oberon run-time system. The system now runs under HP-Oberon [4] V4.4, but since we developed it with portability in mind, it should be easy to port it to other Oberon systems, such as Oberon System 3 or Oberon/F.

6   Conclusion

We have presented an environment to provide database programming support for Oberon programmers. This support is realised through a combination of a module library for the management of collections of database objects and an extended run-time system for the implementation of a persistent store.

The underlying data model is an adaptation of an existing generic object-oriented data model. The key features of this model are its support for conceptual modelling in terms of classification and association constructs and for query processing in terms of its algebra over collections of objects. As a result, unlike most other object-oriented

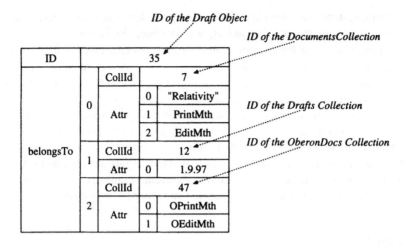

Fig. 4. Structure of a Draft Object

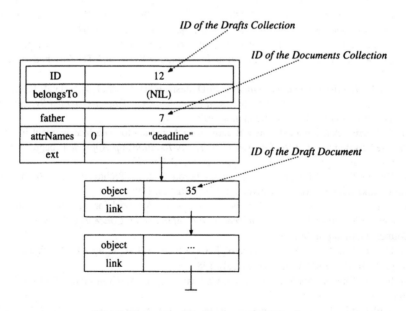

Fig. 5. Structure of the Documents Collection

programming systems, we provide not only data persistence, but also constraint maintenance, programming by querying and support for object evolution.

The current status of the system is that we have implemented a first version of the persistent store together with the basic modules for the management of database collections and their associated constraints. Investigations on the performance of the persistent store and refinements for performance are to be undertaken.

While all aspects of both algebraic and physical query optimisation are outside the scope of the current project, a general framework that enables query optimisation has been established and some simple optimisation strategies investigated. It is hoped that the topic of query optimisation will be investigated thoroughly in future work. Other issues for future research include distribution, concurrency control, advanced transaction management and additional support for schema and database evolution.

References

1. A. Albano, R. Bergamini, G. Ghelli and R. Orsini. An object data model with roles. In *Proceeding of the 19th VLDB Conference*, pages 39–51, Dublin, Ireland, 1993. Morgan Kaufmann.
2. G. Gottlob, M. Schrefl and B. Röcki. Extending object-oriented systems with roles. *ACM Transactions on Information Systems*, 14(3), July 1996.
3. J. Ousterhout and F. Douglis. Beating the I/O bottleneck: A case for log-structured file systems. *ACM Operating Systems Review*, 23(1):11–28, January 1989. Also appears as University of California, Berkeley, Technical Report UCB/CSD 88/467.
4. J. Supcik. HP-Oberon™: The Oberon implementation for Hewlett-Packard Apollo 9000 Series 700. Technical Report 212, Institute for Computer Systems, ETH Zürich, Switzerland, 1994.
5. J. Templ. *Metaprogramming in Oberon*. PhD thesis, ETH Zürich, Switzerland, 1994.
6. M. C. Norrie. *A Collection Model for Data Management in Object-Oriented Systems*. PhD thesis, University of Glasgow, Scotland, 1992.
7. M. C. Norrie. An Extended Entity-Relationship Approach to Data Management in Object-Oriented Systems. In *12th Intl. Conf. on Entity-Relationship Approach*, pages 390–401, Dallas, Texas, December 1993. Springer-Verlag, LNCS 823.
8. M. Knasmüller. Adding persistence to the Oberon-System. Technical Report 6, Institut für Informatik, Johannes Kepler Universität Linz, Austria, 1996.
9. M. Norrie, A. Steiner, A. Würgler and M. Wunderli. A model for classification structures with evolution control. In *15th International Conference on Conceptual Modelling. ER 96*, Cottbus, Germany, 1996.
10. M. P. Atkinson, K. J. Chisholm and W. P. Cockshott. PS-algol: an Algol with a persistent heap. *ACM SIGPLAN Notice*, 17(7), July 1981.
11. M. Reiser. *The Oberon System. User Guide and Programmer's Manual*. Addison-Wesley, 1991.
12. N. Wirth and M. Reiser. *Programming in Oberon. Steps beyond Pascal and Modula*. Addison Wesley, 1992.
13. O. Deux. The O_2 system. *Communication of the ACM*, 34(10):34–48, October 1991.
14. R. Elmasri and S. B. Navathe. *Fundamentals of Database Systems*. Benjamin/Cummings, second edition, 1994.

Adding Persistence to the Oberon-System

Markus Knasmüller
Institute for Computer Science (Systemsoftware)
Johannes Kepler University, Altenbergerstrasse 69, A-4040 Linz
knasmueller@ssw.uni-linz.ac.at

Abstract

Oberon and Oberon-2 [MöW91] are general purpose programming languages in the tradition of Pascal and Modula-2. Oberon [WiGu89] is also a modular, single-threaded operating system for single-user operation of workstations. It is used in daily work as well as in programming courses. One missing point of Oberon is the existence of database functionality such as persistence or recovery.

This report describes the project Oberon-D, which adds database functionality to the Oberon system. The first step of this project is to include persistence, i.e., the object's property to outlive the program that created it.

Persistence in the Oberon system is obtained by a persistent heap on the disk. Persistent objects are on this heap, while transient objects are in the transient memory. Transient and persistent objects can access each other mutually. Accessing a persistent object leads to loading the object into the transient heap. If persistent objects are not accessed from transient objects any more, they are written back to the persistent heap. Persistent objects, which are not referenced by other persistent objects, are reclaimed by a garbage collector. We show the use of persistence as well as its implementation.

1 Introduction

In today's software engineering projects the advantages of object-orientation such as reusability and extensibility are well-known. While object-orientation is a very common feature of modern software development environments, persistence is not. This is rather surprising since in most applications the objects do not only exist temporally but persist beyond the execution of some program. Examples are user interface objects of a graphical editor, design objects of a CAD system, and document objects of a workflow system, to mention just a few. If persistence is not supported by the chosen development environment, the software engineer has two possibilities: On the one hand, he can change the environment. But this is often impossible, because high efforts and costs are combined with the used environment. On the other hand, he can try to add persistence to the chosen environment by implementing read and write mechanisms for various object types. It would be advantageous, however, to add persistence as a general feature to the object-oriented development environment, instead of reimplementing it repeatedly for ever program that needs it. The main contribution of this paper is to demonstrate the ease of integrating persistence into an object-oriented development environment, in our case into the Oberon system [WiGu89].

The work described in this paper is part of the ongoing research project Oberon-D in which database functionality, like persistence, schema evolution or query languages, is added to the object-oriented development environment. The paper concentrates on the first step, namely the introduction of persistent objects.

Persistence is a characteristic describing an object's lifetime. In a language with persistence, objects may survive between program runs. In contrast to persistent objects, transient objects only exist during one run of a program. The design goals behind integrating persistence into the Oberon system have been driven by the following principles by Atkinson and Buneman [AtBu87] for designing a database programming system:

- Persistence should be orthogonal to the type system, i.e., it should be a property of arbitrary values and not limited to certain types.
- All values should have the same rights concerning persistence, i.e., persistence should be regarded as a property of data orthogonal to its type.
- If a value persists, its description (type) should persist, too.
- Furthermore, the programmer should be able to manipulate the persistent objects with normal expression syntax, i.e., physical I/O should be transparent to the programmer.

These principles were taken into account when developing our project. Based on these principles, our main design goals underlying the "persistent" extension have been the following:

- It should be as simple as possible.
- There should be no changes to the used language.
- There should be no (unnecessary) changes to the used run-time system.
- It should impose minimal memory overhead.
- There should be no interference with other tasks and no noticeable delays.
- Both persistent and transient data should be allocated, accessed, and deallocated in exactly the same way.

In the rest of the paper, we demonstrate how these design goals have been met by Oberon-D.

2 Oberon as Baseline Object-Oriented Development Environment

This section lays the foundations for understanding the rest of the paper. It describes parts of the object-oriented development system Oberon, which was chosen because it offers powerful mechanisms for extending software, such as dynamic module loading, commands, and extensibility.

Oberon-2 [MöW91] is a general purpose programming language in the tradition of Pascal and Modula-2. It combines the well-proven type system and module concept of its ancestors with the new concept of record type extensions. Additional improvements like basic string operations and type-bound procedures make the language more convenient to use. In the following the concepts of record type extension and type-bound procedures will be used regularily. Therefore, these features will be shortly outlined below.

```
TYPE
    Object = POINTER TO ObjectDesc;
    ObjectDesc = RECORD objectfields END;
    SpecializedObject = POINTER TO SpecializedObjectDesc;
    SpecializedObjectDesc = RECORD (Object) additional fields END;
```

Figure 1. Type definition

A record type may extend another record type and introduce additional fields. In the example in Figure 1, the type *SpecializedObject* is a direct extension of type *Object*. An extended type inherits all fields of its base type and is therefore upward compatible with it. Roughly speaking, anything that can be done with the base type can also be done with the extended type, but not vice versa.

Oberon-2 type-bound procedures can be used to express dynamic binding in a convenient and efficient way. Procedures associated with a record type are said to be bound to the record type.

```
    PROCEDURE (o: Object) Draw (x, y: INTEGER); ...
    PROCEDURE (o: SpealizedObject) Draw (x, y: INTEGER); ...
```

Figure 2. Type-bound procedures

Procedures bound to a base type are inherited by a derived type but may be overridden by binding a procedure with the same name to the more specific type. This is illustrated in Figure 2.

Oberon [WiGu89] is also a run-time environment providing Mark & Sweep garbage collection, dynamic module loading, run-time types, and commands. Commands are procedures that can be called interactively from the user interface by clicking on their names. They provide multiple entry points into a module, and their invocation may cause the dynamic loading of modules.

3 How to use Persistence in Oberon-D

Persistence is obtained by a persistent heap on the disk. Persistent objects are on this heap, while transient objects are in the transient memory. Transient and persistent objects can access each other mutually. Accessing a persistent object leads to loading the object into the transient heap. If persistent objects are not accessed from transient objects any more, they will be written back to the persistent heap. Persistent objects which are not referenced by a persistent root are reclaimed by a garbage collector. This section discusses the use of persistence while its implementation is introduced in the next section.

All objects are allocated with Oberon's standard procedure NEW. They become persistent as soon as they are referenced (directly or indirectly) from a persistent root. A persistent root is any object that has been registered using the procedure *Persistent.SetRoot (obj, key)*, where *obj* is (a pointer to) an object that should become a persistent root and *key* is a user-defined string that serves a unique name for the root.

Applications may access a root object with the name *key* by using the procedure *Persistent.GetRoot (obj, key)*. Having the root, persistent objects which are directly or indirectly referenced from the respective root object can simply be accessed by pointer dereferencing.

The following code fragment shows how to make a list of objects persistent by registering its root with the key *"myroot"*:

```
TYPE
   Node = POINTER TO NodeDesc;
   NodeDesc = RECORD data: INTEGER; next: Node END;
VAR
   p, q: Node;
...
NEW (p); p.data := ...;
NEW (q); q.data := ...;
p.next := q; q.next := NIL;
Persistent.SetRoot (p, "myroot")
```

This persistent list can be accessed as follows:

```
Persistent.GetRoot (p, "myroot");
WHILE p # NIL DO
   Out.Int (p.data, 10);
   p := p.next
END
```

Many other systems (e.g., ODE [AgGe89]) require that persistent objects are allocated with a special operator such as *pnew*. We feel that our solution is simpler and more flexible, because it does not require a language extension, and because transient objects may become persistent (and vice versa) at any time.

In order to make an object persistent, it has to be mapped onto an external representation. In most cases the object's fields can be written to a file in some standard way. Normally the system knows the structure of all objects and can therefore decide how to write them to a file. However, there are cases in which automatic mapping is unsatisfactory ([Tem94, p. 115ff]):

- Closure Control: Following all references is sometimes not reasonable. For example, if an object contains a reference to a font, it is sufficient to store the font name instead of the whole font data.
- Implicit Dependencies: Externalized objects, i.e., persistent objects on the disk, may have implicit dependencies on other data structures. An implicit dependency is the interpretation of a long integer value as address information. This dependency has to be handled properly, e.g., by adjusting the address during externalizing or internalizing the object.
- Partially used Arrays: Sometimes, array structures are only used partially. There may be a counter outside an array which determines how many elements are used or there may be a sentinel in one of the array elements. It is unneccessary to externalize the unused elements.

Because of these problems we allow the user to specify a mapper for each type. A mapper is a procedure variable with the following structure

```
Mapper = PROCEDURE (m: Map; o: SYSTEM.PTR);
```

A mapper reads or writes an object *o* from or to a persistent medium *m* using operations from a module *PersMaps*, which offers methods for reading or writing basic types. The type SYSTEM.PTR is compatible with any pointer type. User-defined mappers for reading and writing an object have to be registered with the procedure *Persistent.RegisterType (t, readMapper, writeMapper)*. After that, *readMapper* and *writeMapper* are used instead of the default mappers for mapping objects of type *t*. Note that if type *t* has extension level *n*, i.e., it has been derived from a type *t1* with extension level (*n* - 1), the registered mappers are only responsible for handling the fields introduced at level *n*.

The following example shows how to use user-defined mappers. A module *Lists* (see Figure 3) implements a list of nodes with the fields *name* and *number*. A module *Client* (see Figure 5) offers the commands *Init* (to allocate the list), *Insert* (to insert elements in the list) and *Print* (to print the list). Each list has a header containing the field *font*, which determines the printing font (see Figure 4).

```
MODULE Lists;

    IMPORT SYSTEM, Fonts, Persistent, PersMaps;

    TYPE
        List* = POINTER TO ListDesc;
        Elem* = POINTER TO ElemDesc;

        ListDesc* = RECORD
            first*: Elem;
            font*: Fonts.Font
        END;

        ElemDesc* = RECORD
            number*: LONGINT;
            name*: ARRAY 32 OF CHAR;
            next*: Elem
        END;

    PROCEDURE WriteMapper (m: PersMaps.Map; o: SYSTEM.PTR);
        VAR l: List; str: ARRAY 32 OF CHAR;
    BEGIN
        l := SYSTEM.VAL (List, o); (* o interpreted as of type List *)
        m.WriteObj (l.first);
        IF l.font # NIL THEN COPY (l.font.name, str) ELSE str := "" END;
        m.WriteString (str)
    END WriteMapper;

    PROCEDURE ReapMapper (m: PersMaps.Map; o: SYSTEM.PTR);
        VAR l: List; str: ARRAY 32 OF CHAR;
    BEGIN
        l := SYSTEM.VAL (List, o); m.ReadObj (l.first); m.ReadString (str);
        IF str # "" THEN l.font := Fonts.This (str) ELSE l.font := Fonts.Default END
    END ReadMapper;

BEGIN Persistent.RegisterType ("Lists.ListDesc", ReadMapper, WriteMapper)
END Lists.
```

Figure 3. Example module Lists

The objects of type *Elem* are mapped automatically, the objects of type *List* are mapped by the registered mappers *WriteMapper* and *ReadMapper*. Note that the procedures *Insert* and *Print* of the module *Client* access persistent data by ordinary pointer operations.

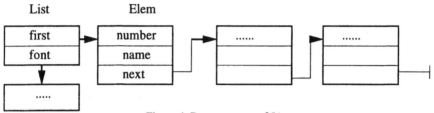

Figure 4. Data structure of *List*

The separation in two modules *Lists* and *Client* shows that the mappers need not be defined in each client, but only in the module which defines the type. It can be seen that clients have just little work with persistence.

Another central point is the deallocation of unused persistent data. Transient data is reclaimed automatically by a garbage collector that frees programmers from the non-trivial task of deallocating data structures correctly and thus helps to avoid errors. We also use a garbage collector for persistent data. All disk objects that are not accessible from a persistent root are garbage and will therefore be removed in the next run of the garbage collector. The garbage collector is started explicitly by calling a command. A persistent root with memory name n can be removed by the function *Persistent.RemoveRoot (n)*.

4 Implementation

Each object is identified by a unique key, the object identifier *OID*. In order to make an object persistent it is necessary to map it into an external representation. There are three decisions involved: When should the object be externalized, where should it survive, and how should this mapping work?

• When?
This point was easy to decide. An object should be externalized when it is no longer referenced by a transient object. There is only one possible time to map such objects: between the Mark and the Sweep phase of the garbage collector. All persistent objects that are unmarked after the Mark phase are externalized. Externalizing an object earlier would allow that it could still be changed afterwards via references to it. Externalizing an unreferenced object after the Sweep phase is impossible, since the object does not exist any more.

```
MODULE Client;

    IMPORT Fonts, Oberon, Persistent, Texts, In, Out, Lists;

    VAR w: Texts.Writer;

    PROCEDURE Init*;  (* root font *)
    (* allocates a list, named root. The list header contains the property font *)
        VAR l: Lists.List; root, font: ARRAY 32 OF CHAR;
    BEGIN
        In.Open; In.Name (root); (* persistent list can be identified by a key: root*)
        In.Name (font); (* printing font *)
        IF In.Done THEN
            NEW (l); l.first := NIL; l.font := Fonts.This (font);
            Persistent.SetRoot (l, root);
            IF Persistent.res = Persistent.alreadyExists THEN
                Out.String ("This root already exists"); Out.Ln
            END
        END
    END Init;

    PROCEDURE Insert*;  (* root {name nr} *)
    (* inserts the tuples (name nr) into the list named root *)
        VAR l: Lists.List; e: Lists.Elem; nr: LONGINT;
            name, root: ARRAY 32 OF CHAR;
    BEGIN
        In.Open; In.Name (root);  (* persistent list can be identified by a key: root *)
        IF In.Done THEN Persistent.GetRoot (l, root) END;
        IF In.Done & (l # NIL) THEN
            In.Name (name); In.LongInt (nr);
            WHILE In.Done DO
                NEW (e); COPY (name, e.name); e.number := nr; e.next := l.first; l.first := e;
                In.Name (name); In.LongInt (nr)
            END
        END
    END Insert;

    PROCEDURE Print*; (* prints the list with the name root *)
        VAR l: Lists.List; e: Lists.Elem; root: ARRAY 32 OF CHAR;
    BEGIN
        In.Open; In.Name (root); (* persistent list can be identified by a key: root *)
        IF In.Done THEN Persistent.GetRoot (l, root) END;
        IF In.Done & (l # NIL) THEN
            e := l.first; Texts.SetFont (w, l.font);
            WHILE e # NIL DO
                Texts.WriteString (w, e.name); Texts.WriteInt (w, e.number, 10);
                Texts.WriteLn (w); e := e.next
            END;
            Texts.Append (Oberon.Log, w.buf)
        END
    END Print;

BEGIN Texts.OpenWriter (w)
END Client.
```

Figure 5. Example module *Client*

• Where?

All persistent objects are stored in a single persistent heap. Their positions are reflected in their OID. In future versions we plan to investigate the use of multiple heaps (see also Section 6).

• How?

When mapping an object between the Mark and Sweep phase, one is not allowed to allocate memory and to use type-bound procedures (methods), because allocating memory could possibly start another garbage collector run, which could loop forever.

Therefore a simple externalization technique was used [Tem94, p.83ff]. All objects which should be externalized (mapped) before being reclaimed by the garbage collector are automatically registered in a list. Between Mark and Sweep all registered objects are marked in a special way. After the Sweep phase an externalization procedure is called for all specially marked objects, which maps them to their external presentation.

Another interesting question is how persistent objects are loaded. This has to be done when a pointer to such an object is dereferenced. Before that, loading is not necessary and references to such objects are just represented as OIDs. Dereferencing an OID, however, causes a trap, since an OID is an illegal pointer value. A customized trap handler then loads the object.

4.1 Writing Objects to the Disk

When the transient garbage collector finds out that a persistent memory object is not referenced any more, it writes it to the persistent heap using the procedure *Persistent.Fin*. This procedure has the following responsibilities:

- Determine the object's OID. This is done with the OID table that stores the memory addresses and the OIDs for all persistent memory objects. This table is implemented as a hash list.
- Set the writing position within the persistent heap file at the position defined by the object's OID.
- Write an indication whether the object is an array or a record.
- Write the object's type. In most cases only a number identifying the type is written compactly encoded (for details see below). This type information is necessary to restore the object, when reloaded.
- Write the object's data. This means to call the mappers for each extension level of the object's type. If the object is an array, additional information (number of dimensions, number of elements for each dimension) is written to the heap.

The object's data is written with methods of the class *PersMaps.Map*. In most cases, these procedures call the corresponding procedures of the underlying run-time system, but there are two special cases:

- *map.WriteObj (o)* writes only the OID of the object *o* to the persistent heap. If *o* is not a persistent object it becomes one by executing the following tasks:
  - The persistent type *pt* of the object is determined (and registered if necessary).
  - A block of *pt.size* is allocated at the end of the persistent heap.
  - The object's OID and its memory address are stored in the OID table.

• *map.WriteProc (proc)* writes only the name of the procedure and the defining module to the persistent heap.

4.2 Reading Objects from the Disk

The trap handler is responsible for reading persistent objects. Every time an OID is dereferenced, an illegal pointer trap is caused. The trap handler determines the register whose contents caused the trap. If the register contains NIL the standard trap handler is called, otherwise the absolute value of the register's contents is equivalent to a persistent object's OID. In this case the trap handler loads the object into the transient heap by executing the following steps:

• Determine if the object is already loaded: For this purpose a relation (OIDs to memory addresses) must be available. This relation is stored in a hash list in module *PersRel*. If the object is already loaded, the contents of the register is set to the memory address of the object.
• If the object is not already loaded, set the loading position within the persistent heap file at the position defined by the object's OID.
• Read the start sign (array or record) and the type information (analogous to writing, see above).
• Allocate enough memory to store the object.
• Read the object's data by calling the appropiate mapper(s) (analogous to writing, see above).
• The loaded object is marked as a persistent object. This means it must be registered in the two relations (memory addresses to OIDs and OIDs to memory addresses, respectively).
• Set the contents of the register to the memory address of the object.

Only the register contents is set to the memory address. This means that further accesses to this persistent object will again trap. To prevent this, three optimizations are implemented:

• The machine instructions are scanned backwards, to get the load instruction where the patched register is loaded from memory. Thus it is possible to get the memory address of the pointer and set the memory pointer to the correct value preventing further traps. Unfortunately, there are some algorithms (e.g iterating a list) where the loading instruction is not easily found. Furthermore this optimization is highly system dependent, for example, because of byte ordering.
• A persistent object may have references to other objects. If an object is loaded into memory it is checked whether it contains OIDs of an already loaded object. In that case the OIDs are replaced with the actual pointer values. This prevents further traps when the pointer is dereferenced again.
• The last optimiziation keeps a list (cache) of the most recently loaded objects. When a trap occurs, the requested persistent object is loaded and an iteration over the list shows whether these objects have references to the newly loaded object. If this is the case, the references are set to the correct memory address.

These optimizations prevent a considerable number of traps, which has also been demonstrated by our performance tests. The two last optimiziations are especially suited for iterations over lists and similar algorithms.

4.3 Persistent Memory Management

The persistent memory management consists of the root management, the list of persistent types and the persistent garbage collector.

A list of all persistent roots is maintained in module *PersKernel*. When initializing the database this list is loaded from a file which is updated whenever the list is changed.

For externalizing and internalizing persistent objects, information about their types is needed. This information is stored in module *PersTypes*. For every type the type name, the defining module, a unique number (for a shorter type identification), the registered read and write mappers (if there are any), the size, and the pointer offsets on the disk are stored. If mappers are registered, the size and pointer offsets can differ between the transient and persistent representation. The pointer offsets are needed for persistent garbage collection (see below).

Types can be registered explicitly by a procedure call, or implicitly if an object of an unregistered type is made persistent. In the latter case, the type of the object is automatically registered with default values (e.g. default mappers) as its properties.

We use Stop & Copy garbage collection [Wil92] to delete obsolete persistent data. This algorithm uses two heaps (files) and copies all accessible objects from the old heap to the new heap. Garbage collection must not be started, as long as there exist transient references to persistent data, because garbage collection may change the OIDs.

Garbage collection on a persistent heap must not fragment the heap. This condition is not so important for a garbage collector on a transient heap, because there the heap is rebuilt every time the system is started again. Stop & Copy compacts the heap and has some additional advantages: memory allocation becomes straightforward, the locality of memory accesses is increased, and no mark bits are needed in objects. The disadvantages of Stop & Copy are that only half of the heap can be used for memory allocation and that copying needs time. But these drawbacks are not so important for a garbage collector on the persistent heap, because the whole disk can be used for the two heaps and the garbage collector does not run very frequently.

The algorithm can be optimized by caching the old and the new heap in the transient memory. Nearly all of the memory can be taken for this purpose.

5 Related Work

In the last few years many papers about object-oriented database systems (OODBS) have been published. Most of them describe specific database programming languages, which are extensions of existing languages. This has the disadvantage of needing a new compiler. Others describe totally new systems which are not platform independent. We have implemented another approach using an existing language and an existing system, which is platform independent with minor exceptions (for details see [Kna96, p. 26]). This section compares our approach to related work.

5.1 ODE

ODE [AgGe89] is a database system using the programming language O++, which is an extension of the programming language C++. It provides facilities for creating persistent and versioned objects, organizing persistent objects into clusters, defining and manipulating sets, iterating over sets and clusters, and specifying constraints and triggers.

Persistent objects are allocated in persistent store and they continue to exist after the program that created them has terminated. There is no difference between accessing and manipulating persistent and volatile objects. It is also possible to move objects from persistent store to volatile store in much the same way as it is possible to move objects from the stack to the heap and vice versa. The objects are written to the disk in the same format as they are in memory.

In O++ persistent objects are declared with the keyword *persistent*, allocated with the operator *pnew*, and deallocated with the operator *pdelete*. An O++ compiler translates an O++ program into a C++ program that contains calls to the ODE object manager library.

In contrast to our approach there is no possibility to register user defined mappers. Furthermore, no garbage collector is supported.

5.2 GemStone

GemStone [Bre89] is an OODBS which combines the concepts of the Smalltalk object-oriented programming language [GoRo83] with the functionality of a database management system.

GemStone falls into the category of systems in which persistence is an orthogonal property of the objects. Not all the objects created are automatically persistent. The simplest way of making an object persistent is to associate an external name with it, similar to a root key in our system. Each object which can be 'reached' by a persistent object is, in turn, persistent. To delete an object all references to the object have simply to be removed. At that point, the system automatically deletes the object. As in our system GemStone does not provide an explicit delete operation but uses garbage collection. GemStone has two possibilities for shrinking the database files: An on-line method and an off-line method. The latter method, which needs an off-line state of the database, results in greater shrinkage. The former method removes only the garbage after the last used object.

5.3 O_2

O_2 [Deu90] is an OODBS, which did not originate from an object-oriented programming language. In particular, the language for implementing methods, referred to as CO_2, is an extension of the C programming language. The extensions are used for manipulating objects and for sending messages to objects. The approach of persistence is similar to GemStone's approach, however, no garbage collector is supported.

5.4 Persistent Sets in Modula-3

Böszörmenyi and Eder added parallel and persistent sets to the Oberon related language Modula-3 [BöEd94]. Sets are unordered collections of objects. These sets can be made persistent by defining them in a domain interface. The general form of a domain interface is:

DOMAIN DomainName INTERFACE InterfaceName;
   Declarations
END InterfaceName.

Operations like union, difference, insert, delete and set iteration, are defined. Also the all quantifier and the existential quantifier are implemented. The sets are stored in a memory-resident parallel object store, called PPOST.

Whereas this approach introduces new keywords, our approach does not change or extend the used language.

5.5 ObjectStore

ObjectStore was designed to simplify the conversion from existing non-database applications to database applications and for application areas such as interactive modelling and computer-aided analysis and design. Oberon-D is highly influenced by this approach. One of the system's specific objectives has been to provide high performance. In order to achieve this, an architecture based on virtual memory with page faults was adopted. Essentially, when an application refers to data which is not in main memory, a page fault occurs. ObjectStore intercepts the page fault and loads the segment of the database containing the required data into main memory. This technique is different from the one we used. By using virtual memory, the objects have the same identifier on the transient and on the persistent heap. The result is that the optimization, which has been essential in our work, is not necessary in ObjectStore. However, ObjectStore has been a bit more difficult to implement. Furthermore, not all run-time systems offer a virtual memory management with this functionality. Another disadvantage is that in case that only one object of a memory page has been changed, the whole memory page must be written back. In our system only the modified object must be written back. Therefore we decided not to use the virtual memory but to use a relation (memory addresses to OIDs).

ObjectStore is accessible by programs written in C and C++ with an interface library. Persistent data can be accessed directly and transparently within C++ programs. One way to specify persistent data involves an overloading of the C++ *new* operator to allow creation of persistent objects. Alternatively, objects can also be declared persistent using the specifier *persistent*:

   persistent <control-variable> classtype object-name;

where *control-variable* specifies the database in which the variable's storage is to reside. The keyword persistent is used in the ObjectStore data manipulation language to specify objects that behave as root objects. Each object has to be deleted explicitly, which means that there is no garbage collector.

5.6 Summary

Table 1 shows the principal characteristics of the discussed object-oriented database systems regarding persistence and compares them with Oberon-D (shadowed entry = advantage).

	ODE	Gem-Stone	O_2	Persistent Modula-3	Object-Store	Oberon-D
special NEW necessary	yes	no	no	no	yes	no
special Compiler necessary	yes	yes	yes	yes	yes	no
Garbage Collector	no	yes	no	no	no	yes
Different declaration of persistent and transient objects	yes	no	no	no	no	no
User defined mappers	no	no	no	no	no	yes

Legend: ▓ advantage ☐ disadvantage

Table 1. Comparison of different approaches to persistence

6 Outlook

Recalling the design goals we can say that these goals have been reached:

- Working with Oberon-D is simple; just one procedure has to be called in order to make objects persistent.
- The Oberon language could be used unchanged.
- Only minor changes were necessary in the Oberon system (for details see [Kna96, p. 26]).
- Only a simple entry in two relations is necessary for a persistent object.
- Other tasks are not affected by persistent objects.
- Persistent and transient data can be allocated, accessed, and deallocated in exactly the same way.

Oberon-D is an ongoing project. Adding persistence was just the first step. The next steps will be to add the following items (see also http://www.ssw.uni-linz.ac.at/Projects /OberonD.html):

- Schema Evolution: Many object-oriented database systems allow the user to modify type definitions. However, they vary considerably in the amount of assistance they offer in handling such modifications. For example, when a new attribute is added to an object type, is it necessary to explicitly "fix" all the existing objects of the changed type to include the new attribute? Is it possible to add a new supertype when instances of a type exist? [Cat94, p.116ff].
- Recovery: Another interesting point is the occurrence of a system crash. In that case the system must guarantee that the database is in a consistent state at the next system start.
- Query Languages: Query languages are an important functionality of database systems. The user can retrieve data simply by specifying the conditions the data must meet. In relational database systems, query languages are the only way to access data, whereas object-oriented database systems, in general, have two ways. The first way, which we have already implemented, is navigational and exploits object identifiers and aggregation hierarchies. Given an OID, the system directly accesses the corresponding object and navigates through the other objects referred to by its attributes. The second way refers to associative access through a query language with a textual or a graphical [Kna95] representation.
- Concurrency: Concurrency control limits simultaneous reads and updates by different users to give all users a consistent view of the data [Cat94, p.69ff].

Additionally, the implementation of persistence will be improved in the future. The most important points are:

- Optimization of the persistent garbage collection: Garbage collection can be optimized by caching the old and the new heap of the copy collector in transient memory. Nearly all of the memory can be taken for this purpose. Depending on the number of cache blocks and the size of each block the time profit is over eighty percent. The best values for these two parameters have yet to be found.
- Usage of more than one heap: In the current version all objects are stored on one persistent heap. In future versions the user should have the choice between different heaps, e.g., each application can have its own persistent heap.

Acknowledgements

I wish to thank Prof. Hanspeter Mössenböck and Prof. Gerti Kappel for their support of this project. My thank goes also to Markus Hof, Christoph Steindl, and Josef Templ for many stimulating discussions on Oberon-D.

References

[AgGe89] R.Agrawal and N.H.Gehani,
"Ode: The Language and the Data Model"
Proc. ACM-SIGMOD 1989 Int'l Conf. Management of Data, Portland, Oregon, May - June 1989, pp. 36-45

[AtBu87] M.P.Atkinson, O.P.Buneman,
"Types and Persistence in Database Programming Languages"
ACM Computing Surveys, 19, 2, 1987, pp. 105-190

[BöEd94] L.Böszörmenyi, K.H.Eder
"Adding Parallel and Persistent Sets to Modula-3"
Proc. of the Joint Modular Languages Conference 1994
Universitätsverlag Ulm, 1994

[Bre89] R.Breitl, "The GemStone data management System"
In "Object-Oriented Concepts, Databases, and Applications"
W.Kim and F.Lochovsky, eds., pp. 283-308,
Reading MA: Addison-Wesley, 1989

[Cat94] R.G.G.Cattel, "Object Data Management"
Addision-Wesley, 1994

[Deu90] O.Deux, "The story of O2"
IEEE Trans. on Knowledge and Data Engineering, 2, 1, 1990, pp. 91-108

[GoRo83] A.Goldberg and D.Robson,
"Smalltalk-80, the language and its implementation"
Reading MA: Addison-Wesley, 1983

[Kna95] M. Knasmüller, "Oberon Dialogs: A User Interface for End Users"
Proc. of the GI/SI Annual Conference, Zurich,
Springer, 1995

[MöW91] H.Mössenböck, N.Wirth: "The Programming Language Oberon-2"
Structured Programming, 12, 4, 1991, pp. 179 - 195

[Tem94] J.Templ, "Metaprogramming in Oberon"
PhD Dissertation. ETH Zürich 1995

[WiGu89] N.Wirth, J.Gutknecht, "The Oberon System"
Software - Practice and Experiences, 19, 9, 1989

[Wil92] P.Wilson, "Uniprocessor Garbage Collection Techniques"
Lecture Notes in Computer Science 637, Springer 1992, pp. 1-42

An Abstract Data Type for Freezable Lists and DAGs

Wolfgang Weck

Åbo Akademi University, Lemminkäisenkatu 14A, FIN-20520 Turku, Wolfgang.Weck@abo.fi

Abstract. We propose an abstract data type for freezable data structures. A frozen data structure is immutable. In contrast to general immutable data structures, freezable data structures can be mutated efficiently until they are frozen. Our abstract data type relies on the Carrier-Rider Pattern and information hiding in a module.

1   Introduction

One of the old realms of modular programing languages is the implementation of abstract data types. Modules are used to encapsulate information for the purpose of asserting system wide invariants.

In this paper, we present an abstract data type that asserts immutability of lists and graphs. One example of an application of immutable DAGs is symbolic computation. For instance, in Maple [3] the interpreter of the Maple user level language asserts DAGs to be immutable.

Immutable data structures are also a basis for recursive data structures as defined in [6] and used e.g. in LISP. Immutability is required because structures can share substructures. For instance, a single list can be used as the tail of two different lists.

As a consequence, data structures must not be modified. Instead of changing existing data, it has to be copied. Whenever, in other circumstances, a sequence of mutations of some data would be done, this will now lead to additional copying. These intermediate copies introduce undesired overhead.

This situation can be improved by introducing the notion of *freezing* a data structure. As long as a data structure is not frozen, it can be changed, allowing for efficient operations. Only after it is frozen it may be shared. Obviously, a structure once frozen must remain frozen forever.

It is the purpose of the abstract data type presented in this paper to assert correct usage of such freezable data structures. In particular, it has to be asserted that only frozen data structures can be refered to more than once.

Our design is related to modular languages in two ways. On the one hand, modules as units of encapsulation are an important tool for the solution. On the other hand, part of the motivation for the abstract data type comes from open and extensible systems, which are a modern application of modular languages.

The rest of this paper is organized as follows. Section 2 gives three motivations for immutable data structures. Section 3 states the design goals that we want to achieve. Section 4 describes our solution for immutable lists in detail. It contains a definition of the abstract data type, an implementation, and an outline of how to use it. Section 5 extends this solution to graphs and shows how to modify it such that graphs can even be guaranteed to be DAGs. Section 6 presents an example of a client module. Section 7 discusses some related work and Section 8 concludes.

2 Motivation: Why Immutable Data Structures?

In this section we will discuss three cases in which it is needed to asserted that some data will not be changed, i.e. that it is immutable. It is common to all three cases that references to individual objects are shared and that this sharing cannot be statically analyzed. If the shared data is more than a single object, namely a graph consisting of several objects and references between them, immutable data structures are required.

2.1 Concurrent Processing

The most commonly known example of statically not controllable data sharing is concurrent processing. Several processes (or threads) operating on the same data must be asserted not to interfere. It must be prohibited that two processes change the same data at the same time. Furthermore, a process reading data may come to inconsistent results if another process changes the data in the meantime.

The traditional solution to these problems is to assert mutually exclusive access to the data, e.g. by using *Monitors* introduced in [5]. Locking data leads to run-time overhead. Extra instructions need to be executed. Furthermore, processes are suspended while waiting for a requested lock to become available. This synchronizes the entire system which, therefore, may significantly lose efficiency. Finally, data locking is error-prone, as deadlocks may be created accidentally.

In some applications locking and the associated efficiency loss can be avoided by disallowing any changes of the data. This means that the data has to be immutable. Immutable data can only be read, which can be done in parallel without interference problems.

An example of this are the immutable texts used in the Cedar system. Each text is represented by an immutable object, called a *Rope* [2]. Every change of a text creates a new Rope. Existing Ropes are never changed and thus can be shared between different processes.

2.2 Sharing Nodes in Directed Acyclic Graphs

In some applications, large directed acyclic graphs (DAGs) have to be maintained in memory. A typical example of such graphs are mathematical expressions in symbolic computation software. Such expressions can either be represented as trees or as DAGs. DAGs are usually preferred as they lead to much better efficiency in both memory and computation time. ([10] provides an analysis of this.)

Any number of references may exist to a node within a DAG. It is this property which makes DAGs superior to trees, but requires sharing of subgraphs.

If a symbol x occurs several times within an expression, it is usually represented by a single node with multiple references to it. Consider further, that one of the occurrences of x is to be changed to a y. Altering the node that represents the x would change all occurrences of x simultaneously. This is not desired. Therefore, the node must not be changed.

Generally, it cannot be statically decided when a particular node may be changed without affecting other paths through the DAG. Therefore, such nodes and also the DAGs themselves must be immutable.

Two examples of mathematical software based on immutable DAGs are Maple [3] and a framework for mathematical component software in Oberon described in [13].

2.3 Open Systems

One purpose of a modular programming system is to create units of analysis, namely modules. Modules are to be analyzed and described independently of their context.

This idea is carried on by open systems, or extensible systems, where the context can still change at run time. [15] discusses the importance of extensibility. The Oberon System [14] is an example of extensible systems.

It has been stated in [12] that open systems cannot be analyzed as a whole. Therefore, if references to data objects are shared between modules, this sharing cannot be detected statically.

If several modules can refer to some data at the same time, these modules must either be aware that the data may be changed by another module, or the data must be immutable.

It depends on the application which of the two scenarios is appropriate. For instance, the Model-View-Controller Pattern for extensibles editors [7] requires that the model is shared between modules. Changes of the model cause changes of the corresponding views, involving a notification mechanism. On the other hand, mathematical component software, as described in [13], requires immutable DAGs to represent mathematical expressions. Subgraphs of these DAGs represent subexpressions.

3 Design Goals

Before presenting a method, or a design pattern, how to implement immutable lists and DAGs, we will list the goals to be achieved.

The four goals stated below have driven the design. All these goals are more or less required from an abstraction of immutable DAGs. Safety and efficiency are necessary to make it useful at all. Generic nodes and inhomogeneous structures allow for better reuse of the abstraction. Finally, the abstract data type must not be too cumbersome to use in order to be accepted.

3.1 Immutability Shall be Asserted

We propose an abstract data type for immutable lists, which can also be used to create immutable DAGs. This abstract data type shall not only discourage mutations, it shall make them impossible. No client shall be able to destroy this system-wide invariant. The module, in which the abstract data type is implemented, shall hide all the information that could be used to alter the data.

3.2 The Implementation Shall be Efficient

Neither access to the data nor creation of new lists shall be slowed down considerably. Furthermore, copying shall be avoided as far as possible. This contrasts for instance the *Ropes* approach for immutable texts [2]: with this approach a new Rope object is created for *every* operation. In practical systems, changes occur often in bursts. In particular, when creating a new list by sequentially inserting all the entries, it would not be wise to create a copy of the list for every insertion operation. However, this is what Ropes would do.

3.3 Lists and DAGs Shall be Generic and Inhomogeneous

The abstract data type for immutable lists shall be a generic service. It shall be possible to use it with arbitrary nodes. This means that the node type itself must be extensible.

3.4 Usage Shall be Convenient

The client programmer shall not be confronted with a set of difficult interfaces and rules. Instead, an abstraction shall be offered that lends itself to the appropriate usage. It shall be possible to operate on the data as if it were mutable. The necessary copy-on-demand operations shall be hidden behind the scene. This contrasts e.g. Hoare's recursive data structures and the way lists are manipulated in LISP.

4 Freezable Lists

In this section the we will describe how the above design goals can be achieved. We will start with lists. These are simpler than DAGs and, therefore, easier to understand. Also, freezable lists are the fundamental building block for freezable DAGs, as we will see later.

The requirement to assert certain system-wide correctness as stated in 3.1 seems to be in contradiction with the requirements stated in 3.2 and 3.4, namely efficiency and convenience of usage. The latter would be met best if data could be changed freely, whereas the former forbids exactly this.

The center of our proposal is to present an interface to the user that virtually allows the data to be changed, but behind the scene asserts all the needed properties.

Why is this not self-contradictory? To answer this question, we must consider encapsulation of data. Encapsulation allows to distinguish between what really exists (inside the encapsulation) and what can be observed (from outside the encapsulation). A data structure can be changed and still be considered immutable as long the changes cannot be observed.

To observe an inplace change, more than one reference to the same data must exist. Otherwise, it cannot be distinguished whether data is being changed or whether data is being replaced by a new version just generated. To distinguish these cases, the old data structure needs to be observable after an operation, what requires a second reference to it. (This fact is used for instance by functional language compilers to optimize memory usage.)

As an example, consider p to be a reference to a data structure that is not refered to elsewhere. After executing the assignment $p := f(p)$ the data structure, to which p had refered so far, becomes unreachable, since no further reference to it exists. Hence, it cannot be observed if the original data has been altered.

As a consequence: data may be changed inplace as long as only a single reference to it exists. This is more efficient than always copying the data structure. Hence, the key to our solution is to control whether a data structure can be accessed only by the mutator itself. The way to do this is to hide the references to the data structures within a module.

4.1 Carrier-Rider Separation to Hide References

The remaining question is: how can a client be enabled to manipulate a list without having a direct reference to the list? A solution is provided by the *Carrier-Rider Pattern*.

The Carrier-Rider Pattern originates from the Oberon system [14] where it has been invented as an access mechanism to sequential structures, like files and texts. Its purpose has been to separate access information (e.g. the current reading position) from the data structure. The Carrier contains the bare data, whereas all access information is stored in the Riders. As a result, several clients can access the same Carrier simultaneously at different positions. For this, each client uses its own Rider which is connected to the common Carrier. Later in [11] the Carrier-Rider Pattern was generalized to allow for independent extension of Carriers and Riders.

We will use Riders to hide references to non frozen Carriers. A client holding a Rider can manipulate the corresponding Carrier, but it is asserted that no direct reference to the Carrier exists outside the module in which both Rider and Carrier are implemented. A direct reference can only be obtained through a special procedure. This procedure marks the Carrier as frozen. In other words: for a client of our module Carriers are asserted to be immutable, but Riders can virtually change a list after implicitly copying it.

To enforce this, the module does not export the means to access lists directly. Only Riders, which therefore are implemented within the same module, have access to these operations. Riders have to take care that the data in the lists is copied if required, i.e. if the list is frozen.

4.2 The Interface

To illustrate the above we show the interface of a module implemented in Oberon:

```
DEFINITION Immutables;

TYPE
   Node = POINTER TO NodeDesc;
   NodeDesc = RECORD END;              (* extensible, abstract entry type *)

   List = POINTER TO ListDesc;         (* immutable lists of nodes *)

   Rider = RECORD                      (* Rider to access Lists *)
     pos-: LONGINT;                    (* current position *)
     node-: Node;                      (* Node at this position *)
     eol-: BOOLEAN                     (* End Of List *)
   END;

VAR
   emptyList-: List;

(* operations on Lists *)
PROCEDURE LengthOf(l: List): LONGINT;      (* length of list l *)
PROCEDURE Excerpt(from: List; beg, end: LONGINT): List;
                                           (* copy of from[beg ... end[ *)

(* operations with Riders *)
PROCEDURE OpenRider(VAR r: Rider; l: List);    (* open r on l at position 0 *)
PROCEDURE Set(VAR r: Rider; pos: LONGINT);     (* re-position an open Rider *)
PROCEDURE Forward(VAR r: Rider);               (* forward r by 1 *)

PROCEDURE Replace(VAR r: Rider; n: Node);      (* replace node at r.pos *)
PROCEDURE Insert(VAR r: Rider; n: Node);       (* insert n at r.pos; forward r by 1 *)
PROCEDURE Delete(VAR r: Rider; len: LONGINT);(* remove [r.pos...r.pos + len[ *)

PROCEDURE ThisList(VAR r: Rider): List;        (* freeze list, do not change r *)

END Immutables.
```

Three types are involved so far: *Node, List,* and *Rider. Node* is meant to be extended to store application dependent data. *List* and *Rider* in turn are not intended to be extended. According to the design pattern, lists can be manipulated through Riders only. Therefore, the implementation details of Type *List* are not exported. It is only allowed to determine the length of a list (Procedure *LengthOf*) and to copy a sublist (Procedure *Excerpt*).

Riders can be opened and positioned on lists. They allow the user to replace, insert, or delete entries in a single copy of the list they were connected to. A reference to the new list can be obtained through Procedure *ThisList*. This procedure marks the list as frozen before returning the reference.

A global, read-only exported variable makes an empty list available. It is used as the starting point to create new lists. New data can be inserted into (an implicit copy of) the empty list through a *Rider*. Behind the scene the changes of the empty list lead to the allocation of a new list. We use this mechanism instead of an explicit creation since it follows the model of virtual changing an existing list discussed so far.

4.3 Generating a New List (Example of a Client Module)

As an example of how to use the above interface, we will show part of a simple application module that generates immutable lists of some objects. We will leave out the details of the objects' type and creation, as they are of no importance for this paper.

It is the application module's task to assert immutability of the application-related data stored within each object. Therefore, the extra data fields defined for objects will typically be exported for read access only.

The following sample module exports a new type *Object* and a procedure *NewList*. The latter returns an immutable list of objects, which are immutable themselves if all fields are exported for reading only.

A client of Module *Application* may (virtually) mutate lists generated by Procedure *Application.NewList*. For this a Rider has to be connected to the list, which implicitly causes a copy to be generated before the change is done.

```
MODULE Application;

IMPORT Immutables;

TYPE
  Object* = POINTER TO RECORD(Immutables.NodeDesc)
    (* application specific data, exported for reading only *)
  END;

PROCEDURE GenerateNextObject(VAR obj: Object);
  (* some algorithm working here *)
END GenerateNextObject;

PROCEDURE NewList*(): Immutables.List;
  VAR obj: Object; r: Immutables.Rider;
BEGIN
  Immutables.OpenRider(r, Immutables.emptyList);
  GenerateNewObject(obj);
  WHILE obj # NIL DO
    Immutables.Insert(r, obj); GenerateNewObject(obj)
  END;
  RETURN Immutables.ThisList(r)
END NewList;

END Application.
```

4.4 The Module's Implementation

To complete the presentation of immutable lists, we will give excerpts from an implementation of Module *Immutables* in Oberon. Below, the complete type definitions can be found, as well as the complete implementation of some typical examples of the exported procedures:

```
MODULE Immutables;

TYPE
  Node* = POINTER TO NodeDesc;
  NodeDesc* = RECORD END;            (* extensible, abstract entry type *)

  Entry = POINTER TO RECORD
    next: Entry;
    node: Node
  END;

  List* = POINTER TO ListDesc;       (* immutable lists of nodes *)
  ListDesc = RECORD
    entries: Entry;                  (* first entry *)
    len: LONGINT;                    (* number of entries *)
    frozen: BOOLEAN                  (* = list must not be changed *)
  END;

  Rider* = RECORD                    (* Rider to access Lists *)
    pos-: LONGINT;                   (* current position *)
    node-: Node;                     (* Node at this position *)
    eol-: BOOLEAN;                   (* End Of List *)
    buf: Entry;                      (* current link in list, holding node *)
    list: List                       (* head of current list *)
  END;

VAR
  emptyList-: List;

PROCEDURE OpenRider*(VAR r: Rider; l: List);    (* open r on l at position 0 *)
BEGIN
  r.list := l; r.pos := 0; r.buf := l.entries;
  IF l.len # 0 THEN r.node := r.buf.node; r.eol := FALSE
  ELSE r.node := NIL; r.eol := TRUE
  END
END OpenRider;

PROCEDURE CopyList(r: Rider);
  (* copy the list attached to r, attach the copy to r and mark it as not frozen *)
END CopyList;
```

```
PROCEDURE Replace*(VAR r: Rider; n: Node);        (* replace node at r.pos *)
BEGIN
   ASSERT(n # NIL);
   IF r.list.frozen THEN CopyList(r) END;           (* copy on demand *)
   r.buf.node := n; r.node := n                      (* change entry's value *)
END Replace;

PROCEDURE ThisList*(VAR r: Rider): List;           (* freeze list, do not change r *)
BEGIN
   r.list.frozen := TRUE; RETURN r.list
END ThisList;


BEGIN
   NEW(emptyist); emptyList.len := 0; emptyList.frozen := TRUE
END Immutables.
```

5   From Immutable Lists to Immutable DAGs

Once immutable lists are available, it is easy to implement immutable graphs. To do so, with each node a list of the direct successors is associated. This list represents the outgoing edges. It must be assigned to each node upon creation and this assignment must not be changed afterwards. This kind of assignment is sometimes called *snappy*. The procedure performing it is called an *initialization procedure*. It asserts that it is not called more than once on every object.

Since the lists are immutable and the assignments of lists to nodes are immutable too, the entire graph structure is immutable.

The interface of Module *Immutables* needs two extensions. A list of successors must be added to Type *Node* and an initialization procedure for nodes must be introduced. The successor list is exported for reading only and can only be set by a call to Procedure *Init*. Procedure *Init* in turn aborts if the node has already been initialized before.

```
TYPE
   Node* = POINTER TO NodeDesc;
   NodeDesc* = RECORD                               (* extensible, abstract entry type *)
      successors-: List                             (* list of successors *)
   END;

PROCEDURE InitNode*(n: Node; successors: List);
   (* initialization, to be called only once per node *)
```

An implementation of Procedure *Init*:

```
PROCEDURE Init*(n: Node; successors: List);
BEGIN
   ASSERT(n.successors = NIL);                      (* Init not called on n before *)
   ASSERT(successors # NIL);                        (* parameters are valid *)
   n.successors := successors                       (* set values *)
END Init;
```

Remark: Immutable graphs implemented with immutable lists of successors can easily be guaranteed to be DAGs. Cycles can be excluded by a single, easy to assert requirement: each node to be inserted into a list needs to be initialized, i.e. a list of successors must already have been assigned to it. Consequently, an initialized node can only refer to other already initialized nodes. This applies transitively. Hence, it is not possible to build a cycle. Such a guarantee may be advantageous in certain applications.

6   A Sample of how to Use Immutable DAGs

With immutable DAGs the following pattern is typical for many operations. First, a node is identified which shall be changed. During this identification process, the path leading to the node is recorded. Next, a new graph is built. Doing so, every node on the path recorded before is reproduced. Only for the edges on this path, new references are included; all other subgraphs can be shared by copying the references to them.

Some operations change several nodes within a graph. Consider for instance an operation that replaces all occurrences of nodes with a certain property. Such a command will traverse the entire graph and apply changes in several places.

Below, we will show such a procedure to illustrate how to use our abstraction of immutable DAGs. It has three parameters: the graph to operate on, a pattern node to search for, and a pattern node to substitute for all occurrences of the search pattern.

The operation itself is programmed to recurse on the DAG's structure. The recursion terminates if a node has no successors. The algorithm works for DAGs only, as a cycle in the graph would lead to infinite recursion.

The root of the graph to operate on is passed as a variable parameter. It is changed if and only if the graph rooted by it mutates. During the recursion, a successor list is changed only if an entry mutated. A new node is generated only if it matches the search pattern, or if the successor list mutated. It can be easily verified that no unnecessary copying takes place, i.e. that all objects generated during the entire process are part of the final structure.

```
PROCEDURE ReplaceAll(VAR in: Immutables.Node; search, replace: Immutables.Node);
   (* replace all nodes equal to search by replace *)
   VAR r: Immutables.Rider; n: Immutables.Node; l: Immutables.List;
BEGIN
   Immutables.OpenRider(r, in.successors);
   WHILE r.eol DO
      n := r.node; ReplaceAll(n, search, replace);
      IF n # r.node THEN Immutables.Replace(r, n) END;    (* update list if necessary *)
      Immutables.Forward(r)
   END;
   l := Immutables.ThisList(r);                           (* build new node if necessary *)
   IF Equal(in, search) THEN
      in := Clone(replace); Immutables.Init(in, l)
   ELSIF l # in.successors THEN
      in := Clone(in); Immutables.Init(in, l)
   END
END ReplaceAll;
```

7 Related Work

The work presented in this paper can be related to various other projects.

7.1 Recursive Data Structures

Recursive data structures as introduced in [6] rely on sharing substructures, like in our DAGs. This requires substructures to be immutable. Every manipulation on such data requires that a new object is generated. Assuming that operations will often occur in bursts, this is not optimal.

A solution to this problem may be to bundle operations explicitly by having the client to call special procedures to announce begin and end of operation groups (as done e.g. in the Oberon/F framework [9]). We consider such explicit calls an extra burden on the client programmer and as error-prone (the call to the end-procedure may be forgotten, for instance).

An example with the same disadvantage are Ropes to represent immutable text [2]. With this approach, a new object is allocated for every operation carried out on a text.

7.2 Piece Lists

The piece-list-based text system of the Oberon system [14] is based on immutable files, in which the text data is stored. Here, immutability is employed to share data, as discussed in Section 2.2. However, the data in files can be mutated, if the file system is used directly, i.e. not through the text system. Further, the data structure presented to the user, namely texts, is shared and mutable in the usual way. The problems caused by reference sharing as discussed in Section 2.3 cannot be solved this way.

7.3 Linear Types, Use-Once Variables

Linear types (e.g. [8]) or Use-Once Variables [1] can be used to assert that only a single reference to an object exists at any point in time. This allows to implement lists which are asserted to be refered to only once. To implement DAGs, however, linear types are too strong, since multiple references to nodes within a DAG must be allowed. Also, even for lists, more data replication may be necessary than with our solution. Linear types only help to assert that the necessary copies are created.

7.4 Immutable Data Structures in the Programming Language

Computer algebra systems like Maple [3] have immutable recursive data structures (for expressions) built into their user level programming language. Within this language only operations can be expressed that do not invalidate this invariant. This requires to use a higher abstraction level than the system itself is built in, namely the Maple language. By programming at the same level at which the language interpreter is implemented, the invariant can be violated. Programming an abstract data type in an add-on module is much more light-weight than introducing a new programming language.

7.5 Copy-On-Write or Smart Pointers

It has been suggested, for instance in [4], to use Proxy objects to assert that data is replicated when changes are attempted. This application of Proxy objects is refered to as *Copy-On-Write* or as *Smart References*.

This design pattern, however, is less powerful than ours. Smart Pointers can be compared to our Rider objects, but our List objects have no counter part in the Smart Pointer Pattern. Having two types is important to guarantee correctness and efficiency at the same time. Riders allow efficient data manipulation and Lists allow immutability to be asserted. Depending on the current needs of a client either type is being used.

With only one type, like a Proxy, one either looses efficiency or safety. One way would be to treat the data as generally immutable and to replicate it before every change. This would cause a loss of efficiency, as unnecessary copies may be generated. The way to avoid this, would be to require the client to explicitly freeze the data by calling a special operation. Before that, the data can be changed freely. This compromises safety, since it is hard to detect it if the call to the freezing operation is forgotten.

8 Conclusions

We have shown how to implement an abstract data type for immutable lists of objects. The design pattern has been extended for immutable graphs. It can be modified to assert that graphs are DAGs.

The design pattern has been derived from the general Carrier-Rider Pattern described in [11]. Assertion of the system-wide invariant relies on encapsulation and information hiding within a module.

Efficiency has been emphasized, in particular unnecessary copying of objects was to be avoided. This makes *freezable* data structures superior to *immutable* data structures. Arbitrary changes to the data are allowed as long they cannot be observed by anyone except by the mutator. This requires the module implementing the abstract data type to control when a data structure may possibly be referred to by more than one client.

The design pattern can either be implemented separately for each application, or it can define a generic node type (as shown in this paper). In the latter case, the module can be used as a generic service module, but the immutability of the individual objects within the data structure must be asserted by the modules defining these objects.

The design has been used in a specialized form within a framework for mathematical software described in [13].

Acknowledgements

The author wishes to thank Ralph Back for commenting on an earlier version of this paper and in particular for pointing out the relationship to Hoare's recursive data structures.

The work described in this paper has been carried out at the Institute of Scientific Computing at ETH Zürich while the author was employed as a research assistant.

References

1. H.G. Baker: Use-Once' Variables and Linear Objects - Storage Management, Reflection and Multi-Threading. ACM Sigplan Notices 30, 1, 1995
2. H.J. Boehm, R. Atkinson, M. Plass: Ropes Are Better Than Strings. Technical Report CSL-94-10, Xerox Corporation, Palo Alto Research Center, 1994
3. B. Char, K. Geddes, G. Gonnet, B. Leong, M. Monagan, and S. Watt: Maple V Language Reference Manual. Springer-Verlag, New York, 1991
4. E. Gamma, R. Helm, R. Johnson, J. Vlissides: Design Patterns. Addison Wesley, Reading, MA, ISBN 0-201-63361-2, 1995
5. C.A.R. Hoare: Monitors: An operating system structuring concept. Comm. ACM 17, 10, Oct. 1974
6. C.A.R. Hoare: Recursive Data Structures. International Journal of Computer and Information Sciences, June 4, 2, 1975
7. G. E. Krasner, S. T. Pope: A cookbook for using the Model-View-Controller user interface paradigm in Smalltalk-80. Journal of Object-Oriented Programming, Vol. 1, No. 3, August 1988, pp. 26..49, 1988
8. Naftaly Minsky: Towards Alias-Free Pointers. Proceedings of the Tenth European Conference on Object-Oriented Programming (ECOOP'96), Linz, Austria, July, 1996, LNCS 1098, Springer-Verlag, 1996
9. The Oberon/F User's Guide. Oberon microsystems, Inc., Basel, Switzerland, (http://www.oberon.ch/customers/omi) 1994
10. N. Soiffer: The Design of a User Interface for Computer Algebra Systems. Doctoral Dissertation Report No. UCB/CSD 91/626, Computer Science Division, University of California at Berkeley, April 1991
11. C.A. Szyperski: Insight ETHOS - On Object-Orientation in Operating Systems. PhD Thesis. Diss. No. 9456, ETH Zürich, 1991
12. C.Szyperski: Independently Extensible Systems - Software Engineering Potential and Challenges. Proceedings of the 19th Australasian Computer Science Conference, Melbourne, Australia, January 31 - February 2, 1996
13. W.Weck: On Document-Centered Mathematical Component Software. PhD Thesis. Diss. No. 1181, ETH Zürich, 1996
14. N. Wirth, J. Gutknecht: Project Oberon. The Design of an Operating System and Compiler. Addison-Wesley, Reading, MA, 1992
15. N.Wirth: A Plea For Lean Software. IEEE Computer, pp. 64-68, Febr. 1995

Types That Reflect Changes of Object Usability

Franz Puntigam

Technische Universität Wien, Institut für Computersprachen
Argentinierstr. 8, A-1040 Vienna, Austria. E-mail: franz@complang.tuwien.ac.at

Abstract. Strong, static typing is useful because it can improve the readability, reliability and optimizability of programs. The usability of an object may change over time. However, conventional type systems for object-oriented languages presume that objects are always used in the same way. In this paper an extension of Ada's type concept is presented: Possible changes of object usabilities can be specified as part of type declarations for passive and active objects. This extension is compatible with inheritance and supports static type checking.

1 Introduction

Statically typed programming languages associate each expression in a program with a type statically derivable from the program. Strongly typed languages ensure that type errors cannot occur at run time [2]. Most programming languages used in practice are (at least in part) statically and strongly typed because static, strong typing can increase the readability and reliability of programs and supports optimizations. In object-oriented languages, types of objects specify contracts between objects (servers) and their users (clients) [11]. These contracts play an important role in the maintenance and reuse of software.

An object's type is usually regarded as the object's signature, often associated with a name as an abstract description of the object's behavior. Clients can call the object's methods as specified in the signature in arbitrary ordering. The promised results are returned if appropriate concrete input parameters are provided. This type concept works fine for a large class of applications.

Sometimes methods shall be called only in certain circumstances depending on the object's state or history. For example, a method "iconify" that replaces a window with an icon shall be called only when the window is open. A buffer is another example: Elements can be put only into nonfull buffers and got only from nonempty buffers. Preconditions as in Eiffel [9] specify conditions under which methods are applicable. Unfortunately, preconditions are not "history sensitive" and cannot always be checked statically, loosing the advantages of strongly typed languages. Furthermore, the semantics of preconditions has to be changed in concurrent environments, causing many further troubles [8, 10].

Concurrent active objects like tasks in Ada show a reason for these problems: For example, if each of two concurrent clients sends a message "iconify" at about the same time to a window open at that time, one of these messages is still in the queue when the window is already replaced with an icon; this message may not be handled at all or, worse, may be handled in a completely different context. In such cases, preconditions can ensure only that "iconify" is handled while the window is open; they cannot prevent that two conflicting messages are sent. In current programming languages and type models, a type specifies a contract only between an individual client and a server, but not between the unity of all clients and the object. In the example, the contract cannot specify that all clients of the window must coordinate themselves before one of them sends "iconify". (The notion of sending messages is used in a broad sense, including method calls.)

In the present paper a solution of this problem is proposed as an extension of a practically usable language. Ada [6] was chosen as the basis of this work because it is widely known and supports static, strong types for both, passive objects (records, etc.) and active objects (tasks). Furthermore, it turned out that Ada's concept of discriminants provides a reasonable syntactical basis for the extensions. A programmer shall be able to specify a contract between each object and the object's set of clients as part of the object's type. This type specifies all possible orderings of messages the object can deal with as well as type constraints on the input parameters and results. A type checker shall be able to ensure statically that

- each object actually behaves as specified by the object's type;
- each client is coordinated with the other clients so that only messages specified by the object's type are sent to the object in an expected ordering.[1]

As a consequence, all objects shall be able to deal properly with all received messages, i.e., there are no "message-not-understood-errors", unintended behaviors or deadlocks caused by wrong messages or wrong message orderings.[2]

Types with these properties became possible only recently by theoretical work on behavioral types for concurrent object-oriented languages [14, 15, 16]. The proposed language extensions are based on the process type model [19, 20, 21] described informally in Sect. 2. The formalism introduced for the theoretical analysis of this model is not practically usable in imperative languages. A more suitable formalism is introduced in Sect. 3 as Ada extensions. Some implementation issues, especially concerning static type checking, are addressed in Sect. 4. A discussion of this work and related work follows in Sect. 5.

2 Foundation: The Process Type Model

With the process type model [19, 20, 21] a programmer is able to specify not only what messages are accepted by an object, but also constraints on the expected orderings of them. Types are represented as communicating processes in a process calculus (like CCS [13], the π-calculus [12], CSP [4] and ACP [1]). The calculus is constrained so that a compiler can check the required properties.

---

[1] The programmer has to specify how clients are coordinated. The compiler rejects programs where the type checker cannot prove that all clients cooperate.

[2] Static typing cannot prevent all kinds of deadlocks. But it ensures that objects don't block with non-empty message queues, while expected messages are not received.

Syntax and semantics. Each atomic action in a process type represents the receipt of a message. Syntactically, an action consists of a message name and a parameter list profile, similar to procedure headers in Ada (e.g., "put (**in** Elem)"). Each action is a process type. If σ and τ are process types, $\sigma \cdot \tau$, $\sigma + \tau$ and $\sigma \parallel \tau$ also are process types. The dot ($\cdot$) stands for sequential composition: Messages specified by σ are expected to be received before those specified by τ. Alternative composition ($+$) means that clients can send messages according to either σ or τ. A parallel composition ($\parallel$) states that the actions of σ can be arbitrarily interleaved by those of τ.

The representation of types is enhanced by recursive equation systems. For example, the solution of the equation $x = a \cdot x$ (where a is an atomic action and x a process type variable) is $x = a \cdot a \cdots$, and the solution of $y = a \parallel y$ is $y = a \parallel a \parallel \cdots$. Equations on type expressions are treated, for example, in [1, 13].

Some examples demonstrate the use of process types. The first example specifies the type of a buffer with a capacity of only one element:

$$\text{Buffer1} = \text{put}(\textbf{in } \text{Elem}) \cdot \text{get}(\textbf{out } \text{Elem}) \cdot \text{Buffer1}.$$

Each instance of "Buffer1" first accepts the message "put", then "get" (each with a parameter of type "Elem") and then repeats this cycle. It is not possible to put an element in a full buffer or get an element from an empty buffer.

A buffer able to hold three elements uses parallel composition:

$$\text{Buffer3} = \text{Buffer1} \parallel \text{Buffer1} \parallel \text{Buffer1}.$$

The next example uses parallel composition in the specification of an infinitely large buffer which always accepts the message "put", but only as many "get" messages as there are elements in the buffer:

$$\text{BufferI} = \text{put}(\textbf{in } \text{Elem}) \cdot (\text{get}(\textbf{out } \text{Elem}) \parallel \text{BufferI}).$$

The final example accepts "put" and "get" messages in arbitrary ordering:

$$\text{BufferU} = (\text{put}(\textbf{in } \text{Elem}) + \text{get}(\textbf{out } \text{Elem})) \cdot \text{BufferU}.$$

The semantics of process types are essentially trace semantics [1, 21]: A type corresponds to a set of traces, each describing a sequence of messages accepted by an object of this type. Two process types are equivalent if their trace sets are equal. (The parallel composition operator is in fact syntactic sugar: Each type expression containing "$\parallel$" is equivalent to one without "$\parallel$".)

Subtyping. It is straight forward to define the subtyping relation $\leq$ on process types. ($\sigma \leq \tau$ if σ is a subtype of τ.) The principle of substitutability says that an instance of a subtype can be used wherever an instance of a supertype is expected [23]. A type is a partial specification of an object's behavior [7]; a subtype is a more complete specification of the same behavior. Following this argumentation, a type σ is a subtype of a type τ essentially if the trace set of τ is a subset of that of σ. Input parameter types are contravariant, output parameter types covariant, and through-parameter types invariant. A subtype extends a supertype by adding alternatives (at any part of the supertype) and arbitrary type expressions at the end of the supertype. A formal definition and axiomatization of $\leq$ as well as type equivalence can be found in [21]. With process types it is, for example, possible to derive

$$\text{BufferU} \leq \text{BufferI} \leq \text{Buffer3} \leq \text{Buffer1}.$$

These relationships are intuitively clear: An instance of BufferU can be used as if it were an instance of BufferI, Buffer3 or Buffer1, etc. The additional properties (i.e., the ability to deal with additional message orderings) are not needed by the client. Such relationships cannot be proved in any other approach to subtyping for concurrently active objects proposed in the literature.

Type updating. Each occurrence of a variable is annotated with a process type. Whenever a message is sent to an object referred to by a variable, this variable's type annotation is updated implicitly. The update reflects the expected state change on receipt of the message. For example, when the message "put" is sent to an empty buffer of type "Buffer1", the sender can expect that the variable's type constraint becomes "get(**out** Elem) · Buffer1", the type of a full buffer. The next occurrence of the variable has to be annotated with this type expression. Type updating occurs at compile time: The compiler updates its type information while walking through the code. Other approaches to behavioral types for concurrent languages also use type updating [15].

Controlling aliases. Using process types, it is necessary to control aliases. Aliases can be spread out all over a program during execution; it is in practice impossible for a compiler to know all aliases statically. As a solution of this problem, the allowed interactions with an object are restricted further whenever a new alias for the object is introduced: Each variable gets a limited type constraint so that the combination of the type constraints of all variables referring to an object does not exceed (i.e. is a supertype of) the object's type. The communication with the object through a variable is limited by the variable's type constraint. Whenever a new alias for a variable is (or may be) introduced, the original type constraint of the already existing variable is split into two parts; the existing variable is associated with one part, the new alias with the other. Hence, the right to send messages to an object is divided among all aliases. Type constraints must be split along parallel compositions so that the object is able to accept all messages sent in arbitrary interleaving. For example, if a variable annotated with the type expression "get(**out** Elem) ‖ BufferI" occurs as a message parameter and also later in the program, the type constraint can be split so that the occurrence as parameter is associated with "get(**out** Elem)" and the later occurrence with "BufferI". The object receiving the message can send a single "get", and the object sending the message can send further messages according to "BufferI". Since "BufferI" is directly recursive via parallel composition, we can show "BufferI = BufferI ‖ BufferI". Hence, it also is possible to split the type constraint into "get(**out** Elem) ‖ BufferI" and "BufferI".

Process types are frequently of the form $(\sigma \parallel \tau) \cdot \varphi$. Expressions of this form cannot be split easily into σ and τ without loosing φ. For this reason the concept of "type renewal" was introduced: Two variables have the type constraints σ and τ; then, after sending all messages according to $\sigma \parallel \tau$, the type constraint of one of these variables is renewed to φ. We do not describe this concept in detail because the formalism of the proposed Ada extension provides a much simpler solution of the problem.

Relationships with conventional types. The process type model comprises the essential parts of conventional object-oriented type models based on the λ-calculus [3]. For example, for two records of functions σ and τ with

$$\sigma = \{f_1{:}\tau_1{\to}\sigma'_1, \ldots, f_m{:}\tau_m{\to}\sigma'_m, \ldots, f_n{:}\tau_n{\to}\sigma'_n\}$$
$$\tau = \{f_1{:}\sigma_1{\to}\tau'_1, \ldots, f_m{:}\sigma_m{\to}\tau'_m\}$$

we have $\sigma \leq \tau$ if $\sigma_i \leq \tau_i$ and $\sigma'_i \leq \tau'_i$ $(1 \leq i \leq m \leq n)$. The corresponding process expressions are

$$\sigma = (f_1(\textbf{in } \tau_1; \textbf{out } \sigma'_1) + \cdots + f_m(\textbf{in } \tau_m; \textbf{out } \sigma'_m) + \cdots + f_n(\textbf{in } \tau_n; \textbf{out } \sigma'_n)) \cdot \sigma$$
$$\tau = (f_1(\textbf{in } \sigma_1; \textbf{out } \tau'_1) + \cdots + f_m(\textbf{in } \sigma_m; \textbf{out } \tau'_m)) \cdot \tau$$

with $\sigma \leq \tau$ under analogous conditions. But in the conventional models it is not possible to constrain the expected orderings of received messages.

The process type model can be applied together with synchronous and asynchronous message passing as well as procedure call and rendezvous semantics. If asynchronous message passing is used, the messages must be received in the same ordering they were sent.

3 Language Extensions

Since the (usually highly recursive) formalism of the process type model does not fit very well into type declarations in Ada, we introduce a new formalism, step by step using examples. The type of a buffer for a single element can be declared in Ada as follows:[3]

```
type State is (empty, full);
type Buffer1a is record s: State; e: Elem; end record;
function put (b: in out Buffer1a; x: in Elem) return Boolean;
function get (b: in out Buffer1a; x: out Elem) return Boolean;
```

Each function returns "true" if the function was executed successfully and "false" if the operation did not change the state of the first parameter, b, because the buffer was in the wrong state. This approach corresponds to dynamic type checking: "False" returned by a function indicates a violation of a type constraint. It is our goal to replace dynamic type checking by static type checking. Ada already offers a solution for simple cases: The component s of "Buffer1a" is used as a known discriminant, stated explicitly in type constraints:

---

[3] The simple buffers used as examples in this text are perhaps not very useful. But they show the problems to be tackled, and their solutions.

type Buffer1b (*s*: State) **is record**
    case *s* **is when** full => *e*: Elem; **when** empty => **null**; **end case**;
end record;
type EmptyBuffer1b **is** Buffer1b (*s* => empty);
type FullBuffer1b **is** Buffer1b (*s* => full);
function put (*b*: **in** EmptyBuffer1b; *x*: **in** Elem) **return** FullBuffer1b;
function get (*b*: **in** FullBuffer1b; *x*: **out** Elem) **return** EmptyBuffer1b;

A small advantage of this version is that the record component *e* is needed only if the buffer is full. But there are some important disadvantages: The buffer cannot be used as an **in out** parameter because of different discriminant values; and this method cannot be used if type checking depends on more than a single binary variable. The reason is that discriminants are immutable.

Modificative discriminants. Having this knowledge it is rather easy to find a solution by extending Ada: Modificative discriminants, distinguished by the word **mod**, are added. They are mutable in a restricted way so that the compiler knows their values in each expression in a program. Changes of the discriminants' values are equivalent to type updates in the process type model. These changes are expressed explicitly as in the following version of the buffer example:[4]

type Buffer1c (**mod** *s*: State := empty) **is** ...   -- like Buffer1b
procedure put (*b*: **in out** Buffer1c (*s* => empty **then** full); *x*: **in** Elem);
procedure get (*b*: **in out** Buffer1c (*s* => full **then** empty); *x*: **out** Elem);

The discriminants' values state under which conditions a function, procedure or entry can be called and how discriminant values are changed. Syntactically, a discriminant constraint list contains combined discriminant value checking and modification expressions of the form

$$discriminant => old\_value \ [\textbf{then} \ new\_value]$$

where *old_value* is the expected value of the discriminant at the time when the corresponding function, procedure or entry is called, and *new_value* the discriminant's new value after execution. The part containing *new_value* can be omitted if the state is not changed; it must be omitted for **in** and **out**-parameters.

Discriminants are immutable in Ada because they can determine the structure of records, as in the above examples. For modificative discriminants the compiler has to reserve space for all possible discriminant values that may occur. The discriminants' values determine which parts of the data structures are visible. The compiler can ensure that only visible data are accessed because it must statically know the discriminant's values in each expression. Changes of discriminant values are specified explicitly by assignments. Within the body of a procedure, function or accept statement, there must be an appropriate assignment of a new static value for each discriminant. Here is an example of an implementation of "put":

---

[4] We assume that parameter types can contain discriminant constraints.

procedure put (*b*: **in out** Buffer1c (*s* => empty **then** full); *x*: **in** Elem) **is**
begin
    b.s := full;   -- *b.e* becomes visible; earlier values of *b.e* are lost
    b.e := *x*;
end put;

Partitioning of discriminant sets. There is a need for an equivalent of type splitting: The set of discriminants given in a variable's type constraint is an appropriate means to express what can be done with the variable. A type constraint can specify any number of discriminants declared for the type. Functions, procedures and entries can be called only if the discriminant lists associated with these functions, procedures or entries do not exist or contain only values of specified discriminants. For example, "*v*: Buffer1c (*s* => ...)" specifies *s*; either "put(*v*, *x*)" or "get(*v*, *x*)" can be called, depending on the value of *s*. For "*w*: Buffer1c" neither "put(*w*, *x*)" nor "get(*w*, *x*)" can be called because the discriminant *s* is not specified and the appropriateness of the call cannot be checked. The type constraints of all variables referring to (i.e., being aliases of) an object specify disjoint subsets of the discriminant set declared for the object's type. Thus, type splitting corresponds to partitioning a set of discriminants.

Without further language extensions, there is still a notational problem as shown by type declarations for buffers able to hold three elements:

    type Buffer3a (**mod** *s, t, u*: State := empty) **is** ...

This type shall be splittable into three parts, each describing a behavior like that of a buffer for a single element. A type "Buffer3a (*s* => v_1, *t* => v_2, *u* => v_3)" can be split into "Buffer3a (*s*=>v_1)", "Buffer3a (*t*=>v_2)" and "Buffer3a (*u*=>v_3)", where each v_i is either "full" or "empty". Unfortunately, it would be necessary to implement three versions of "put" and "get" because the three types have different discriminants. This problem is solved with multiple discriminants as shown by a further example:

    type Buffer3b (**mod** *s*(3): State := (empty, empty, empty)) **is** ...;
    procedure put (*b*: **in out** Buffer3b (*s* => empty **then** full); *x*: **in** Elem);
    procedure get (*b*: **in out** Buffer3b (*s* => full **then** empty); *x*: **out** Elem);
    procedure d (*b*: **in out** Buffer3b (*s*(2) => (full, empty) **then** (full, full)));

The number *n* with *n* ≥ 1 added to a discriminant's name specifies multiple discriminants, i.e., there are *n* instances of the discriminant's type, all with the same name but (possibly) different values. A simple modificative discriminant *s* is a shorthand for *s*(1). From a theoretical point of view, multiple discriminants are multisets. For initializations, assignments and value checks, multiple discriminants are handled like arrays with indices in the range from 1 to *n*. "Buffer3b (*s*(3) => (v_1, v_2, v_3))" can be split into "Buffer3b (*s* => v_1)", "Buffer3b (*s* => v_2)" and "Buffer3b (*s* => v_3)". Thus, "put" and "get" require only a single implementation each. The procedure "d" (which duplicates an arbitrary element in the buffer) demonstrates the use of multiple discriminants in conditions; there must be a filled and an empty slot in the buffer when the procedure is called, and both slots are filled on return.

In many cases (e.g., for the declaration of a Buffer without fixed size) multiple discriminants with infinite multiplicity are useful:

type BufferIa (**mod** $s(*)$: State := (**others** => empty)) **is** ...

An important property of infinitely multiple discriminants is that they can be split into any number of infinitely multiple discriminants. For example, the type "BufferIa $(s(*)$ => (**others** => empty))" can be split as often as needed, and this expression remains unchanged.

With these extensions, all possible message orderings can be expressed. (Each regular process expression has a representation using modificative discriminants.)

Using type updating and type splitting. As in the process type model, these two principles are applied while walking through the program code. For a human reader of a program it is easy to understand how discriminants are modified:

```
procedure foo1 (in b: Buffer3b (s(2) => (full, empty)));
procedure foo2 (out b: Buffer3b (s(2) => (full, empty)));
b: Buffer3b;   x, y, z: Elem := ...;
...            -- b's discriminants: s(3) = (empty, empty, empty)
put (b, x);    -- s(3) = (full, empty, empty)
put (b, y);    -- s(3) = (full, full, empty)
foo1 (b);      -- s = full ("foo1" absorbs two discriminants)
get (b, z);    -- s = empty (z need not be equal to x or y)
foo2 (b);      -- s(2) = (full, empty) (b is replaced)
...
```

The variable b initially has the three discriminants declared for "Buffer3b" with the corresponding default values. Each call of "put" changes the value of one discriminant from "empty" to full"—type updating because "put" takes b as an **in out** parameter. After putting two elements into the buffer, two buffer slots are "full" and one is "empty". The ordering of these discriminant values does not matter. The procedure "foo1" takes b as input parameter. When calling "foo1", this procedure becomes responsible for dealing with two buffer slots— type splitting because of the mode **in**—, an empty and a full one. Only one full slot remains. An element z got back from b need not be equal to one of those put in previously because "foo1" may have put a further element into b. For type updating it is not necessary to know anything about the behavior of "foo1". The call of the procedure "foo2" replaces the old buffer with a new one having a new set of discriminants. It is possible that "foo2" returns the very same buffer given as parameter to "foo1", equal to the old value of b. The corresponding discriminants are replaced in each case because it is not known whether or not the buffers are equal.

As shown above, type updating is applied for **in out** parameters, type splitting for **in** parameters, and replacement for **out** parameters. If a procedure, function or entry has several parameters, they are dealt with as follows: First, **in** parameters are handled. Since type splitting is associative and commutative, the ordering does not matter. Then, **in out** and **out** parameters are considered in arbitrary ordering. The concrete parameters must be different variables. For type checking it does not matter if some of them refer to the same object; type splitting ensures that aliases are always handled correctly.

In conditional expressions, each alternative path is dealt with separately. When alternative pathes are joined again, the types of all variables in use after joining must have got compatible types within the alternatives. Types are compatible trivially if they are equal. They also are compatible if the set of modificative discriminants of one type is a subset of those of the other type, the values of these discriminants are equal, and the subset is used in further computations. Loops are handled similarly: The discriminant set at the begin of the loop has to be a subset of the discriminant set at the end of each iteration. An example demonstrates these relationships:

```
b: BufferIa;  x: Elem := ... ;
...                    -- b's discriminants: s(*) = (others => empty)
loop                   -- for each iteration: s(*) = (others => empty)
    put (b, x);        -- s(*) = (full, others => empty)
    if ... then
        put (b, x);    -- s(*) = (full, full, others => empty)
    end if;            -- s(*) = (full, others => empty)
end loop;
```

For loops with statically known numbers of iterations, more complex rules can be used. These rules are not elaborated here because the same effects can always be achieved with loop unrolling.

In a conditional expression executed only if two variables are equal, these variables' types are regarded as unified, i.e., the union of the corresponding modificative discriminant sets is used. This simple mechanism is a full substitute for the complicated "type renewal mechanism" in the process type model.

Tasks. In principle, tasks can be handled in the same way as passive objects. However, while a called procedure or function is executed immediately, an entry call is appended to a list; the execution of a corresponding **accept** statement can be delayed, possibly forever. The ordering in which (different) messages are sent does not necessarily reflect the ordering in which these messages are processed. One might conclude that, therefore, it is not useful to describe an ordering on messages. But, on the other hand, a successful computation of a task can depend on a given ordering of messages. For example, a buffer can expect to receive the messages "put" and "get" in alternation. Such task type declarations (and single task declarations) shall be possible:

```
task type Buffer1d (mod s: State := empty) is
    entry put (x: in Elem) when (s => empty then full);
    entry get (x: out Elem) when (s => full then empty);
end;
```

Since an entry declaration does not contain the task as a parameter, a list of constraints on discriminant values is given in a **when** clause. Modificative discriminants in tasks must have a default initialization. The **when** clauses in the example ensure that the messages "put" and "get" are sent in alternation, beginning with "put". However, they cannot ensure that the task actually accepts the messages in this sequence. It is easy to get a deadlock if client and server assume different message orderings. A further language extension is needed to deal with this unsufficient safety: The key word **limited** is put in front of a task body in order to indicate that the task must be able to accept the messages in each sequence they can arrive. The compiler has to check this property. This is a possible task body for "Buffer1d":

```
limited task body Buffer1d is
    y: Elem;
begin
    loop
        accept put (x: in Elem) do y := x; s := full; end;
        accept get (x: out Elem) do x := y; s := empty; end;
    end loop;
end Buffer1d;
```

It reflects the requested ordering directly. The implementation may accept additional message orderings:[5]

```
        select accept put (x: in Elem) do y := x; x := full; end;
        or     accept get (x: out Elem) do x := y; s := empty end;
        end select;
```

Messages are handled in the same sequence as they have been sent. Because of the restricted sequence of received messages, the above two implementations are equivalent.

Inheritance. All language extensions introduced above are compatible with inheritance. It is easy to see how modificative discriminants can be used in extending tagged types:

```
    type Buffer3c (mod s(3): State) is tagged record ... end record;
    procedure put (b: in out Buffer3c (s => empty then full); x: in Elem);
    ...
    type BufferIb (mod s(*): State) is new Buffer3c (s(3)) with null record;
```

If the implementation of "Buffer3c" can deal with an arbitrary number of elements, extending the set of modificative discriminants is sufficient for increasing the size of the buffer; the procedures of "Buffer3c" are inherited by "BufferIb" and can be called using all discriminants of "BufferIb". Of course, it is also

---

[5] Only the part within the loop differing from the previous example is given.

possible to provide new implementations of the operations (with the same constraints on discriminants) and add further operations and record components if necessary.

These extensions are compatible with subtyping in the process type model: By extending discriminant sets and adding operations, instances of subtypes can deal with additional messages and message orderings. Of course, all extensions can be combined equally well with abstract types, class-wide types and access types. In each case the set of available modificative discriminants specifies which massages a client can send to a server.

4 Implementation Issues

Christof Peter implemented a small subset of Ada extended with behavioral types for active objects as part of his master's thesis [17]. First experience with this implementation shows that the concept is feasible, although only small examples could be tested. The extension to passive objects seems to be natural and does not introduce further difficulties from an implementer's point of view.

Modificative discriminants require additional type checking. Beside the usual type checking the compiler has to

- assign information about the modificative discriminants' values to each expression where this information is accessed;
- ensure that procedures, functions and entries are called only if the discriminants' values are appropriate;
- ensure that in the body of each procedure, function and accept-statement the discriminants' values are changed (or not changed) as stated in the corresponding procedure, function and entry declarations;
- ensure that only those record components are accessed which are visible according to the discriminants' values;
- ensure for each limited task body that the task can deal with all message orderings specified by the **when** clauses in the task type declaration (or single task declaration);
- optionally perform optimizations that are possible because of the additional static program information (e.g., dead code elimination, and removing code for unnecessary select statements in tasks).

A compiler can perform these computations and checks on the control flow graph. It associates a set of modificative discriminants with each procedure, function and task body as well as each variable (including parameters), initialized as specified by the procedure or function headers, task types and variable declarations. The discriminant sets associated with variables are used by the activities described in the first two items in the above list, those associated with procedures, functions and tasks by those of the remaining four items. The values of these discriminants are updated while walking through the code.

The most important aspects of updating the discriminants associated with variables have already been explained in Sect. 3. Special care must be taken to ensure that type splitting is applied in all cases where aliases can be introduced. For example, aliases are not only introduced by calls taking input parameters, but also by assigning the address of an object to an access variable.

Subsequently, a (simplified) algorithm computing the variables' discriminant sets and their discriminant values for each instruction is briefly outlined: At the root of the control flow graph, the discriminants of all declared variables have their initial values. Each path in this graph is followed, starting at the root. For each instruction passed on this graph walk and each variable, the set of discriminants is updated appropriately. A copy of all variables' discriminants is stored in each node (i.e., for each instruction) with more than one incoming edge when this node is passed the first time. Whenever this node is passed again, the current set of all variables' discriminants is compared with the stored copy. Three cases can occur:

- If for some variable the stored discriminant set is incompatible with the current one (i.e., neither set is a subset of the other, e.g. because discriminant values are different), a type error has been detected.
- If for each variable the stored discriminant set is equal to or a subset of the current set, the computation for this path can be stopped because the node was already examined appropriately.
- Otherwise (for each variable) both, the stored discriminant set and the current discriminant set, are replaced with the intersection of these two sets and the computation continues with this node.

This algorithm terminates because the discriminant set stored in a node becomes smaller whenever a loop is entered.[6] The appropriateness of calls is checked on the fly. This algorithm can be improved in several ways. For example, repeated computations for loops can be avoided by computing the differences on discriminant sets caused by one run through the loop and interpolating the results to a sufficiently large number of runs in a single step.

As for checking discriminants associated with variables, the discriminant values associated with procedures, functions and tasks are updated when a new value is assigned. It is checked if the values assigned in alternatives fit together at a join, and the values at the begin of a loop are the same as those at the end. When returning from a procedure, function or accept statement, the values assigned to discriminants must be those specified in the declarations. It is easy to check on the fly if occurring accesses of record components are allowed.

While walking through the control flow graph of a limited task body, the compiler has to ensure that this task is able to accept messages in all specified orderings. For each enabled message, i.e., for each message that can be sent according to the current set of discriminant values, there must be a corresponding accept statement in each alternative path in the control flow graph. This accept statement must be reachable without reaching an accept statement for another message first.

---

[6] Infinitely multiple discriminants do not affect this termination property. Because of space limitations, the reasons cannot be explained in this paper.

An important detail is the representation of modificative discriminant sets associated with variables: Each discriminant can be—and often is—of large or infinite multiplicity; and it shall be easy to check type conformance and perform type splitting and type updating. Usually, the set of values a discriminant can have is rather small. The following representation turned out to be useful: For each variable of a type with modificative discriminants there is a container. The container holds information about the number of discriminants having a given discriminant name and value. (A simple list or tree works fine because usually there will be only few entries if entries holding the number zero are removed.) Comparing such data structures during type checking is as easy as verifying that there is a sufficient number of appropriate discriminants. Type splitting is simply done by subtracting the needed number of discriminants, and type updating by subtracting from one set of entries and adding to another set of entries.

5   Discussion and Related Work

A large amount of work on object-oriented type systems was done in theory as well as for practical programming languages. Much of this work deals with increasing the expressiveness of types by adding information about the behavior of the types' instances. For example, Meyer's work on types as contracts [9, 10, 11] and Liskov and Wing's work on behavioral subtyping [7, 8] had a large influence. There also is a large amount of theoretical work on object-oriented type systems based on the λ-calculus [2, 3] and (more recently) types for concurrent object-oriented languages [14, 15, 16, 18, 22]. In types for concurrent languages it is important to consider the ordering of messages, as in the process type model [19, 20, 21].

The results of this theoretical work on types for concurrent languages have not yet been made available in procedural languages. Making some of these results available in an understandable way compatible with existing languages is probably the most important contribution of the work presented in this paper. Major notational changes as well as some important changes in the substance were necessary to achieve this goal.

An important property of the process type model differentiates this approach from all other approaches: A type is understood as a contract between an object and the whole unity of its users. This property implies that aliases are controlled by a language mechanism. The need for protecting objects against aliasing was detected earlier, and mechanisms for alias protection like "islands" were proposed [5]. Unlike the islands approach, the process type model does not restrict aliasing to small islands.

Aliasing also plays an important role in the work of Liskov and Wing [7, 8]: They restrict subtyping so that an alias of an object can assume an arbitrary supertype of the object's type even if the type expresses the object's behavior at a very high level. Since Ada's types with the extensions presented in this paper cannot express object behavior at such a high level, the result of their work cannot be used for type checking in Ada. The integration of information about high level behavior into the proposed approach is regarded as an important future work.

Strong, static typing is a useful software development tool. It is natural that software developers ask for more expressive types which support readability, reliability and optimizability at even higher degrees. However, the more expressive a type language is, the more restrictive it usually is and the more typing discipline it requires from a programmer. Especially in early phases of a project a programmer may want to have more freedom than given by a restrictive type system. The type concept proposed in this paper is very expressive and restrictive. It is not yet clear if, under which conditions and for which applications its advantages compensate for the reduced freedom. The author thinks that such a restrictive type system is especially useful for safety-critical applications because many properties of an object's dynamic behavior are statically determinable. Furthermore, the proposed type system may be quite helpful in detecting errors in message driven and concurrent systems early.

6 Conclusion

In practice many objects assume that clients send messages in fixed orderings. An extension of Ada was presented that allows programmers to specify orderings of messages as parts of type declarations: The values of an object's modificative discriminants represent an abstraction of the object's state and determine which messages the object expects to receive. Changes of these values reflect changes of the state. But changes are restricted so that a compiler statically knows the values of these discriminants during the execution of each statement. The compiler can ensure statically that each object can deal with all messages sent to it. The mechanism of partitioning discriminant sets ensures that aliases cannot destroy system consistency. The proposed approach can be used in sequential as well as concurrent and distributed applications and supports subtyping (inheritance). Compared with the difficulty of the solved problem, one of the most appealing properties of this approach is its simplicity.

References

1. J. C. M. Baeten and W. P. Weijland. *Process Algebra*. Number 18 in Cambridge Tracts in Theoretical Computer Science. Cambridge University Press, 1990.
2. Luca Cardelli and Peter Wegner. On understanding types, data abstraction, and polymorphism. *ACM Computing Surveys*, 17(4):471–522, 1985.
3. Carl A. Gunter and John C. Mitchell, editors. *Theoretical Aspects of Object-Oriented Programming; Types, Semantics, and Language Design*. The MIT Press, 1994.
4. C. A. R. Hoare. *Communicating Sequential Processes*. Prentice-Hall, 1985.
5. John Hogg. Islands: Aliasing protection in object-oriented languages. *ACM SIG-PLAN Notices*, 26(10):271–285, October 1991. Proceedings OOPSLA'90.
6. ISO/IEC 8652:1995. Annotated ada reference manual. Intermetrics, Inc., 1995.

7. Barbara Liskov and Jeannette M. Wing. Specifications and their use in defining subtypes. *ACM SIGPLAN Notices*, 28(10):16–28, October 1993. Proceedings OOPSLA'93.
8. Barbara H. Liskov and Jeannette M. Wing. A behavioral notion of subtyping. *ACM Transactions on Programming Languages and Systems*, 16(6):1811–1841, November 1994.
9. Bertrand Meyer. *Eiffel: The Language*. Prentice Hall, 1992.
10. Bertrand Meyer. Systematic concurrent object-oriented programming. *Communications of the ACM*, 36(9):56–80, September 1993.
11. Bertrand Meyer. *Reusable Software: The Base Object-Oriented Component Libraries*. Prentice-Hall, Englewood Cliffs, NJ, 1994.
12. R. Milner, J. Parrow, and D. Walker. A calculus of mobile processes (parts I and II). *Information and Computation*, 100:1–77, 1992.
13. Robin Milner. *Communication and Concurrency*. Prentice-Hall, New York, 1989.
14. Flemming Nielson. The typed lambda-calculus with first-class processes. In *Proceedings PARLE'89*, number 366 in Lecture Notes in Computer Science, pages 357–373. Springer-Verlag, 1989.
15. Flemming Nielson and Hanne Riis Nielson. From CML to process algebras. In *Proceedings CONCUR'93*, number 715 in Lecture Notes in Computer Science, pages 493–508. Springer-Verlag, 1993.
16. Oscar Nierstrasz. Regular types for active objects. *ACM SIGPLAN Notices*, 28(10):1–15, October 1993. Proceedings OOPSLA'93.
17. Christof Peter. Typüberprüfung von aktiven Objekten mit Prozeßtypen. Master's thesis, Technische Universität Wien, Austria, 1996. In German.
18. Benjamin Pierce and Davide Sangiorgi. Typing and subtyping for mobile processes. In *Proceedings LICS'93*, 1993.
19. Franz Puntigam. Flexible types for a concurrent model. In *Proceedings of the Workshop on Object-Oriented Programming and Models of Concurrency*, Torino, June 1995.
20. Franz Puntigam. Type specifications with processes. In *Proceedings FORTE'95*. IFIP WG 6.1, October 1995.
21. Franz Puntigam. Types for active objects based on trace semantics. In *Proceedings of the 1st IFIP Workshop on Formal Methods for Open Object-based Distributed Systems*, Paris, France, March 1996. IFIP WG 6.1.
22. Vasco T. Vasconcelos. Typed concurrent objects. In *Proceedings ECOOP'94*, number 821 in Lecture Notes in Computer Science, pages 100–117. Springer-Verlag, 1994.
23. Peter Wegner and Stanley B. Zdonik. Inheritance as an incremental modification mechanism or what like is and isn't like. In S. Gjessing and K. Nygaard, editors, *Proceedings ECOOP'88*, number 322 in Lecture Notes in Computer Science, pages 55–77. Springer-Verlag, 1988.

Lightweight Parametric Polymorphism for Oberon

Paul Roe and Clemens Szyperski

Queensland University of Technology, Brisbane, Australia
{p.roe,c.szyperski}@qut.edu.au

Abstract. Strongly typed polymorphism is necessary for expressing safe reusable code. Two orthogonal forms of polymorphism exist: inclusion and parametric, the Oberon language only supports the former. We describe a simple extension to Oberon to support parametric polymorphism. The extension is in keeping with the Oberon language: it is simple and has an explicit cost. In the paper we motivate the need for parametric polymorphism and describe an implementation in terms of translating extended Oberon to standard Oberon.

1 Introduction

A key goal of Software Engineering is to support the production and use of reusable code. Reusable code, by definition, is "generic" i.e. applicable in a number of different contexts. To guarantee that code is reused correctly strong typing is desirable. Genericity in code can best be expressed by polymorphic types. Two different forms of polymorphism have been identified: inclusion and parametric [2]. In theory inclusion and parametric polymorphism are orthogonal concepts and neither can be used to satisfactorily replace the other.

The Oberon language supports inclusion polymorphism via subtyping. This permits a certain degree of safe code reuse to be achieved. However parametric polymorphism cannot be safely expressed. This paper describes how parametric polymorphism can be incorporated into Oberon. The following results are achieved:

- strict extension to Oberon
- relatively simple extension in the style of Oberon
- orthogonal to subtyping
- polymorphic routines can be statically type checked
- requires no change to a compiler back-end or run-time system
- polymorphic code is compiled to real object code shared by all instantiations
- polymorphic libraries can be separately compiled e.g. for DLLs
- incurs no run-time overhead, and can eliminate some type tests

The rest of this paper is organised as follows. Section 2 briefly describes Oberon and its subtyping, for further information see e.g. [10, 12]. Section 3 describes the extension to Oberon. The implementation of parametric polymorphism is described in Section 4. The final sections describe further work, related work and conclusions.

2 Motivation: Inclusion Polymorphism and Oberon

In Oberon we may define a list of heterogeneous objects (records) thus:

```
TYPE Base     = POINTER TO BaseDesc;
     BaseDesc = RECORD END;


     List     = POINTER TO ListDesc;
     ListDesc = RECORD elem: Base; next: List END;
```

The **Base** type is the type of list objects. For the list to support different sized objects, objects must be represented via a reference. By extending the **Base** type we can support lists of different objects, for example:

```
     Point     = POINTER TO PointDesc;
     PointDesc = RECORD (BaseDesc) x,y: REAL END;


     Emp       = POINTER TO EmpDesc;
     EmpDesc   = RECORD (BaseDesc)
                     name, address: String;
                     eno, level: INTEGER
                 END;
```

The Oberon syntax RECORD (BaseDesc) ...END indicates that the record type extends an existing record type (namely **BaseDesc**). It is also possible to further extend the **EmpDesc** and **PointDesc** objects.

To process a heterogeneous list of objects we need to distinguish between different objects in order to determine how to process them. This is achieved by dynamic type inspection or dynamic dispatch. Different procedures (methods), but all with the same interface, may be bound to different types; thus depending on the type, different procedures may be invoked. For example we may bind a print method to each of the objects in the previous example, thus:

```
PROCEDURE (r: Base) Print;
END Print;

PROCEDURE (r: Emp) Print;
BEGIN Out.String(r^.name)
END Print;

PROCEDURE (r: Point) Print;
BEGIN Out.Real(r^.x,0); Out.Real(r^.y,0)
END Print;
```

In the examples above r is the receiver object, *self*. (Note, strictly the dereferencing operation (^) used above is redundant, but we leave it for those readers more familiar with Pascal or Modula-2.) An object of type **Base**, **Emp** or **Point** can be printed thus: **x.Print**. A general list printing procedure can be written as follows:

```
PROCEDURE ListPrint(l: List);
   VAR t: List;
BEGIN
   t := l;
   WHILE t # NIL DO
      IF t^.elem # NIL THEN t^.elem.Print END;
      t := t^.next
   END
END ListPrint;
```

This procedure is polymorphic, it will work on lists of any objects having type at least **Base**. Furthermore it may be reused with new types of objects unknown at the time **ListPrint** was written. If a new type is created which is a subtype of **Base**, lists can be formed containing such objects, and they can be printed using the above procedure: without any re-compilation or modification of **ListPrint**. This kind of reuse arises from inclusion polymorphism (subtyping).

We may also define other useful routines such as a list length function:

```
PROCEDURE ListLen(l: List): INTEGER;
   VAR len: INTEGER; t: List;
BEGIN
   t := l; len := 0;
   WHILE t#NIL DO INC(len); t := t^.next END;
   RETURN len
END ListLen;
```

and a list prepend procedure:

```
PROCEDURE ListPrepend(VAR x: List; y: Base);
   VAR z: List;
BEGIN
   NEW(z); z^.elem := y; z^.next := x;
   x := z
END ListPrepend;
```

This list prepend procedure will prepend any object of type **Base** to any **List**. Thus it always allows a heterogeneous list to be constructed. However sometimes a more constrained version of prepend is required. For example an application may utilise a list of employee descriptions (**Emp**), and it may be that the list should only contain **Emp** or its subtypes. Thus we would like to prevent **Base** type, **Point** type or any other type of element not a subtype of **Emp** from being prepended to the list. This constraint should be statically enforceable by the type system. However this is not possible in Oberon, all we can do is define a new list type to contain **Emp** elements, and new functions on the type: thereby eliminating code reuse – our goal.

Another example of a routine which cannot be adequately expressed in Oberon is the list map operation. This operation invokes a procedure on all elements of a list:

```
TYPE BaseProc = PROCEDURE (x: Base);

PROCEDURE ListMap(p: BaseProc; l: List);
   VAR t: List;
BEGIN
   t := l;
   WHILE t#NIL DO
      p(t^.elem); t := t^.next
   END
END ListMap;
```

Unfortunately the procedure argument must have an argument of type **Base**; this is necessary since the list may be heterogeneous. However if we have a list of at least **Point** type elements, and we wish to rotate them, we *cannot* use the following procedure:

```
PROCEDURE Rotate(r: Point);
   VAR t: REAL;
BEGIN
   t := r^.x; r^.x := -(r^.y); r^.y := t
END Rotate;
```

Instead we must use a type test to dynamically check that the type really is at least **Point**:

```
PROCEDURE BRotate(r: Base);
BEGIN Rotate(r(Point))
END BRotate;
```

(The type guard r(Point) asserts that r has at least type **Point**, if not the program aborts.) This is a poor solution for implementing homogeneous lists. We have no static guarantee that a homogeneous list will be constructed, and even if it is we must pay the cost of unnecessary type tests and extra procedure calls. Effectively what the above example has done is to simulate parametric polymorphism in Oberon. However in doing so we are programming in an untyped way, with no static checking, rather like programming in Smalltalk. For example there is nothing to stop a program being compiled with an invocation like **ListMap(BRotate,l)** where l is a list of **Emp**. The following section describes an extension to Oberon which supports type checked parametric polymorphism.

3 Parametric Polymorphism for Oberon

We introduce parametric polymorphism via our previous example. A type may be parametrised on types in much the same way as a procedure may be parametrised on values and variables. For example our previous list example may be parametrised on an element type thus:

```
TYPE Ptr(A)     = POINTER TO A;
    List(A)     = Ptr(ListDesc(A));
    ListDesc(A) = RECORD elem: Ptr(A); next: List(A) END;
```

We term `List` and `ListDesc` polymorphic (or poly) types and similarly we term a type with no type parameters a monomorphic (or mono) type. Actual type parameters of poly types may be "forward-declared". We shall use the poly type `Ptr` in place of `POINTER TO` in the remainder of this paper. In general a type may have multiple type parameters. Some example lists are declared below:

```
VAR emplist       : List(EmpDesc);
    pointlist     : List(PointDesc);
    listpointlist : List(ListDesc(PointDesc));
```

A list having type `List(EmpDesc)` is statically guaranteed by the type system to only contain elements of type at least `EmpDesc`. In addition to parametrising types we can also parametrise procedures on types, for example:

```
PROCEDURE <A> ListPrepend (VAR x: List(A); y: Ptr(A));
    VAR z: List(A);
BEGIN
    NEW(z); z^.elem := y; z^.next := x;
    x := z
END ListPrepend;
```

Procedure type parameters are listed before the procedure name, enclosed in angle brackets. The reason for this is that, unlike poly types, procedures do not have actual type parameters supplied to them when they are used (invoked). Procedure type parameters are scoped over the whole of the procedure body. The type parameter in `ListPrepend` enables the procedure to operate on different types of lists; furthermore the prepended element is guaranteed (by the type system) to have the same, or a more specific, type as the list. For example the polymorphic list prepend procedure can be invoked thus: `ListPrepend(emplist,e)`. Although no actual type parameters are supplied each invocation is statically checked to ensure the element being prepended matches the type of list elements.

The previous map function may be rewritten:

```
TYPE Proc(A) = PROCEDURE (x: Ptr(A));

PROCEDURE <A> ListMap (p: Proc(A); l: List(A));
    VAR t: List(A);
BEGIN
    t := l;
    WHILE t#NIL DO
        p(t^.elem); t := t^.next
    END
END ListMap;
```

For example, this may be invoked thus: `ListMap(Rotate,pointlist)` or `ListMap(IncLevel,emplist)`, where `IncLevel` is defined thus:

```
PROCEDURE IncLevel(e: Emp);
BEGIN INC(e.level)
END IncLevel;
```

By combining Oberon's inclusion polymorphism (subtyping) with parametric polymorphism, the map procedure can be abstracted to work for entire families of collections, not only lists:

```
TYPE Collection(A) = Ptr(CollectionDesc(A));
     CollectionDesc(A) = RECORD
        elem: Ptr(A)
     END;

     List(A) = Ptr(ListDesc(A));
     ListDesc(A) = RECORD (CollectionDesc(A))
        next: List(A)
     END;

     Tree(A) = Ptr(TreeDesc(A));
     TreeDesc(A) = RECORD (CollectionDesc(A))
        left, right: Tree(A)
     END;

PROCEDURE <A> (c: Collection(A)) Map (p: Proc(A));
BEGIN p(c.elem)
END Map;

PROCEDURE <A> (l: List(A)) Map (p: Proc(A));
BEGIN
   l.Map^(p);  (* "super call" to overridden procedure *)
   IF l.next # NIL THEN l.next.Map(p) END
END Map;

PROCEDURE <A> (t: Tree(A)) Map (p: Proc(A));
BEGIN
   IF t.left # NIL THEN t.left.Map(p) END;
   l.Map^(p);
   IF t.right # NIL THEN t.right.Map(p) END
END Map;
```

For example, it is now possible to abstractly map `Rotate` over a collection of points `Collection(PointDesc)`, regardless of whether the collection is actually a list, a tree, or any other structure derived from the base type `Collection(A)`.

3.1 Language Extension

This section describes details of the parametric polymorphism extension to Oberon. The syntax of Oberon [10] is extended, by modifying TypeDec, ProcDec and Type thus:

TypeDec   = IdentDef [TypePars] ”=” Type
TypePars = ”(” [Ident {”,” Ident}] ”)”
ProcDec   = PROCEDURE [PTypePars] [Receiver] IdentDef [FormalPars] *etc.*
PTypePars = ”<” [Ident {”,” Ident}] ”>”
Type   = Qualident [TypeActs] | *etc.*
TypeActs = ”(” [Type {”,” Type}] ”)”

Our language extension is a minimal one; a particular goal was to make explicit any costs associated with parametric polymorphism, in keeping with Oberon. A polymorphic value, by its very name, may have any shape and size. Some languages support arbitrary use of polymorphism. However, supporting this either entails an implicit run-time cost or prevents compilation of polymorphic routines. This is discussed further in Section 5.

Our solution to the problem is a simple one. We only support references to poly values, analogous to subtyping restrictions in Oberon. That is all poly values must be: explicitly referenced via pointers to poly values, implicitly referenced via **VAR** parameters or procedure types. Thus all costs of polymorphism are explicit.

Our approach could be broadened to also support polymorphism over any pointer sized objects. This trick is used by C programmers and for supporting Modula-2 opaque types. However this is rather implementation dependent, and may necessitate the introduction of procedure wrappers and closures, hence we prefer not to do this.

The following describes our language extension. Two new forms of type abstraction (type parametrisation) are introduced:

1. Parametrised type declarations, e.g. **TYPE List(A)** = T_{exp}; . The type parameter **A** is scoped over the single type declaration T_{exp}.
2. Parametrised procedure declarations, e.g. **PROCEDURE <A> Foo (1: List(A))**, but not parametrised procedure type declarations[1]. For example a procedure type may be declared thus: **P(A) = PROCEDURE (1: List(A))**, but the following is *illegal:* **P = PROCEDURE <A> (1: List(A))**.

The following restrictions on the use of poly types and type parameters guarantee the explicit cost model previously described. A poly type or type parameter can only be used in the following type contexts:

1. a pointer to a type parameter, e.g. **POINTER TO A**
2. a var parameter, e.g. **PROCEDURE <A> Foo (VAR x:A)**
3. a poly type application, where the actual type parameter is:

---

[1] This restricts our system to rank one polymorphism.

(a) a record type, e.g. List(EmpDesc)

(b) a type parameter, e.g. List(B)

4. an uninstantiated polymorphic receiver object, for example: PROCEDURE <A> (List(A)) Foo, is legal, but an instantiated one is *illegal*, e.g. PROCEDURE <A> (List(EmpDesc)) Foo.

Instantiated poly record types do not have subtype relationships induced by their actual type parameters; this follows naturally from standard Oberon, and is strictly necessary to be type safe. For example although PointDesc is a subtype of BaseDesc, List(PointDesc) is *not* a subtype of List(BaseDesc). This is the reason why methods cannot be bound to instantiated poly types.

A variable of poly type has no accessible methods or fields, unless its type is constrained via a type guard or WITH statement. The type guard, type test and WITH constructs can all operate on polymorphic values, e.g.:

```
PROCEDURE <A> Foo (p:Ptr(A));
BEGIN
    IF (p#NIL) & (p IS Emp) THEN p(Emp)^.eno := 123 END
END Foo;
```

A procedure may introduce new type parameters. Type parameters are scoped over the whole procedure definition. Angle brackets are used to distinguish type parameters from procedure receiver objects, and also to indicate that they do not need to be, and indeed cannot be, supplied on procedure invocation. This latter point is important, we do not want to overburden the program or programmer with specifying types; actual types of actual parameters are supplied implicitly to procedures, so are poly types. We wish to encourage the reuse of parametric poly procedures; thus syntactically they should be no more expensive to use than ordinary monomorphic procedures.

3.2   Type Checking Rules

The instantiation of a poly type does not create a new type; therefore poly types are type equivalent by structure. Type aliasing of poly types follows that of ordinary Oberon types.

Within a procedure declaration, a type parameter is only type compatible with itself; thus the following is type correct:

```
PROCEDURE <A> Foo (x: Ptr(A)): Ptr(A);
BEGIN RETURN x
END Foo;
```

but the procedure below is type *incorrect*:

```
PROCEDURE <A,B> Foo (x: Ptr(A)): Ptr(B);
BEGIN RETURN x
END Foo;
```

since x has type Ptr(A) which is not type compatible with Ptr(B). The procedure header states that A and B may be different types; therefore they are not type compatible. Effectively in the procedure, A and B are abstract types which cannot be manipulated other than by: inspecting their type with type tests and type guards, and passing them to other polymorphic procedures.

To understand how a procedure invocation is typed it is necessary to explain what type a poly procedure has. Polymorphic procedures may be used with different types, therefore we can represent a poly procedure's type as a universally quantified type. For example consider the three procedure headers below:

```
PROCEDURE <A> Id(x: Ptr(A)): Ptr(A);
PROCEDURE <A,B> K(x: Ptr(A); y: Ptr(B)): Ptr(A);
PROCEDURE <A> Pick(x,y: Ptr(A)): Ptr(A);
```

We may give them the following formal types:

$$\forall A. \ (\text{Ptr}(A)): \ \text{Ptr}(A)$$
$$\forall A, B. \ (\text{Ptr}(A), \ \text{Ptr}(B)): \ \text{Ptr}(A)$$
$$\forall A. \ (\text{Ptr}(A), \ \text{Ptr}(A)): \ \text{Ptr}(A)$$

To type the use of a procedure (call or assignment to a procedure variable) its type must unify with the types of its context and any actual parameters. Consider the program fragment below:

```
TYPE S = Ptr(Srec); Srec = RECORD END;
     T = Ptr(Trec); Trec = RECORD (Srec) END;
     U = Ptr(Urec); Urec = RECORD (Srec) END;
VAR s:S; t:T; u:U;
```

An expression such as Id(t) will type with the unifier $A \mapsto$ T, and hence t:=Id(t) or s:=Id(t) will type correctly. Similarly K(t,u) will type with unifier $A \mapsto$ T, $B \mapsto$ U. However in general subtyping requires a more sophisticated form of unification to be used. For example the expression s:=Pick(t,s) should type, but the expression t:=Pick(t,s) should not (a valid implementation of Pick is to simply return its second argument). To handle these cases unifiers need to be refined using a least upper bound rule for subtypes. For example consider the expression Pick(t,s), matching the type of t to A, in the type of Pick above, should produce a unifier $A \mapsto$ T. Subsequently matching s to A with the previous unifier $A \mapsto$ T should produce a refined unifier (least upper bound of T and S) of $A \mapsto$ S. Thus the result of Pick(t,s) has type S, not T. Similarly the result of Pick(t,u) has type S; since the least upper bound of T and U is S.

4 Implementation

In this section we describe an implementation of the parametric polymorphism extension to Oberon. The implementation of the extended type system is briefly described and code generation is described in terms of rewrite rules, which map extended Oberon to standard Oberon. The rewrite rules show how our extension can be implemented, that the extension has no associated run-time cost, and that no modifications to the run-time system or compiler back-end are necessary.

4.1 Type Checking

Type checking can be performed by a modified Oberon type checker which performs unification and refinement of unified subtypes. It is desirable to reduce all poly types to normal form. This aids type checking by eliminating any unnecessary intermediate poly types. The body of a poly procedure can be simply checked by treating all poly types as new types. Poly procedures can be used with different types. Therefore when a poly routine is typed, its type parameters must be distinguished from those of different uses of the same routine. Furthermore when a context constrains an instance of a type parameter all other related instances must also be constrained. To implement this when a poly procedure is used its formal type is copied and fresh type variables are substituted for bound type parameters. This is a standard technique, see e.g. [1]. Type variables are instantiated, like Prolog variables, during type checking, and are also subject to refinement, as described in Section 3.2.

4.2 Rewrite Rules

Our rewrite rules map extended Oberon to standard Oberon. Poly values (instantiated or not) are restricted to be references; these fall into three categories: explicit record pointers, implicit record pointers via var parameters or function pointers in the case of poly procedure values. Poly values in each category have the same representation for different record types; this is already required in order for standard Oberon's subtyping to work. Thus, there is no difference between the run-time representation of ordinary values in each category from poly ones; since all values in each category have the same representation. (Note that not all mono values can be used in poly contexts.) Therefore all that is required is to map an extended Oberon program to correct standard Oberon. We assume that the program has already been type checked by the extended Oberon type checker which checks poly and mono types.

We can identify two places where the rewrite rules must map extended Oberon to standard Oberon: type declarations and type expressions, and program statements and expressions. In the first case all poly type declarations of the form: TYPE $T(A_1 \ldots A_n)$ = TE are rewritten to TYPE T = TE', where TE' is the result of recursively rewriting the type expression TE. Any instance of a type parameter in a type expression is rewritten to ANYRECORD the standard base record type[2]. Similarly any procedure declaration introducing poly types is

---

[2] We assume a standard type ANYRECORD that is the base type of all records that have no declared base type. If unavailable, such a type can be introduced as part of the rewriting process.

rewritten without them, recursively mapping any instances of type parameters to ANYRECORD.

The second case concerns program statements and expressions. As previously mentioned all poly types, instantiated or uninstantiated, have the same representation as their mono type instances. Thus to coerce values between poly types and mono types (and vice versa) requires no change of representation; all that is required is a cast between the appropriate types. This can be achieved using SYSTEM.VAL; a caveat is that the exact behaviour of this operation is undefined[3]. The following rewrites are necessary:

1. Any dereference or NEW operations on instantiated poly pointer types require the pointer to be cast to the appropriate pointer type.
2. A procedure object may be used in a more specific or more general context than its type would allow; in which case it must be cast to the type required by its context.

An example rewrite is shown below; the extended Oberon program:

```
TYPE Ptr(A)     = POINTER TO A;
    List(A)     = Ptr(ListDesc(A));
    ListDesc(A) = RECORD elem: Ptr(A); next: List(A) END;
    Proc(A)     = PROCEDURE (x: Ptr(A));

VAR el: List(EmpDesc); pl: List(PointDesc);

PROCEDURE <A> ListMap (p: Proc(A); l: List(A));
   VAR t: List(A);
BEGIN
   t := l;
   WHILE t#NIL DO
      p(t^.elem); t := t^.next
   END
END ListMap;
...
NEW(el); NEW(el^.elem);
```

is rewritten to:

```
TYPE Ptr      = POINTER TO ANYRECORD;
    List     = Ptr;
    ListDesc = RECORD elem: Ptr; next: List END;
    Proc     = PROCEDURE (x: Ptr);

VAR el: List; pl: List;
```

---

[3] We utilise SYSTEM.VAL in a completely general way. For some compilers we would need to translate some casts a little differently.

```
PROCEDURE ListMap (p: Proc; l: List);
   VAR t: List;
BEGIN
   t := l;
   WHILE t#NIL DO
      p(SYSTEM.VAL(ListDesc,t^).elem);
      t := SYSTEM.VAL(ListDesc,t^).next
   END
END ListMap;
...
NEW(SYSTEM.VAL(POINTER TO ListDesc,el));
NEW(SYSTEM.VAL(Emp,(SYSTEM.VAL(POINTER TO ListDesc,el))^.elem));
```

5 Related Work

Many languages have facilities for supporting some sort of parametric polymorphism. Table 1 categorises some prominent examples by the properties of their respective facilities.

language group	generics are type checked	coexistence with inclusion polymorphism	real object code generated from generics	all run-time costs are explicit
CLU, Ada 83	yes	none	no	yes
ML, Napier-88	yes	none	yes	no
C++, Modula-3	no	orthogonal	no	yes
Ada 95	yes	orthogonal	no	no
Eiffel, Sather, Theta	yes	bounded poly	yes	no
Extended Oberon	yes	orthogonal	yes	yes

Table 1. Categories of Parametric Polymorphism

Approaches that neither support type checking of polymorphic code, nor generation of shared object code really are just glorified macros (Modula-3 generic modules, C++ templates).

Constrained parametric polymorphism was first introduced for CLU [6, 7]. Parametric polymorphism for a Pascal like language was proposed by Tennent in [16]. All functional programming languages in the tradition of ML, and some related languages, such as Napier-88 [9] support parametric polymorphism. Many modern object-oriented languages also support parametric polymorphism, including Eiffel [8], Sather [14, 15], or Theta [3, 5]. In all these languages the run time cost of using parametric polymorphism is hidden.

Hidden costs are caused by the use of uniform representations for all values in shared polymorphic code. Such representations have to cater for all types, irrespective of size. Usually the uniform representation is an indirection to the natural representation: often called a *boxed representation*. When a value is moved between a poly and mono context, coercion is used to convert values between representations: often called boxing/unboxing. However boxing and unboxing is an implicit cost involving hidden operations such as heap allocation. Furthermore boxing can necessitate the use of closures to support partial applications of procedures to types. In extended Oberon we avoid these hidden costs by restricting poly types to references.

In untyped languages such as Lisp or Smalltalk, where every context is polymorphic, a uniform representation must be used everywhere, e.g. Lisp *S-expressions*. However this is rather inefficient. Optimisation, such as dynamic compilation, is possible, but still incurs hidden costs.

A way to avoid hidden costs without restricting instantiations is to give up on sharing code and instead generate code for each instantiation, e.g. Ada style generics. This leads to code explosion and prevents construction of generic dynamically linkable libraries. In addition to leading to code explosion, Ada-style generics are relatively heavyweight, as they require explicit instantiation before use and therefore make extensions to existing generics subtle and complicated[4].

Various unsafe practices that do not cause any run-time cost and allow for the sharing of object code are in common use to simulate parametric polymorphism in languages that do not support it, demonstrating the *need* for safe and efficient language-level support. Examples are unsafe type casts in C or unsafe constructs closed off by multiple safe interfaces such as Gough's Device (Chapter 7 in [4]).

Recently some work similar to ours has investigated parametric polymorphism for an abstract imperative language called Polymorphic C [13]. This also restricts parametric polymorphism to pointers. However, the emphasis of this work is more theoretical than ours: a formal type system is presented and type soundness proven, but no implementation exists. Our work concentrates on the smooth practical integration of parametric polymorphism with an existing language, Oberon. The relationship between our work and Polymorphic C requires further investigation.

6   Further Work

There are several areas which we wish to pursue further. It is desirable to support parametric polymorphism over arrays. The present implementation strategy could support this providing references to arrays (explicit and implicit) have the same representation as references to records; since a poly procedure must be capable of accepting either references to records or arrays. An alternative would be to perform a run-time test, but this is not in keeping with our zero cost implementation strategy.

More general combinations of inclusion and parametric polymorphism are possible, for example bounded polymorphism [2]. With the polymorphism introduced effectively all poly types must be at least ANYRECORD, for example:

---

[4] Extensions have to define a local instantiation that is parametrised with the type parameters of the extending generic.

```
PROCEDURE <A> ListMap (p: Proc(A); l: List(A));
```

the `ListMap` procedure will operate on all values of type **A**, from **ANYRECORD** downwards in the subtype hierarchy. The procedure can assume nothing about the type of **A**, and hence its fields and methods. Thus it is rather like saying **A** must be at least of type **ANYRECORD**. A more powerful form of polymorphism than that proposed here allows the type of **A** to be bounded. However, there are also known pitfalls of general bounded polymorphism [11].

It is desirable to develop a library of poly routines and poly types for Oberon, as has been successfully done for Smalltalk and C++ (STL).

We are currently incorporating extended Oberon into our standard Oberon compiler; for further information on the progress of the project refer to: `http://www.fit.qut.edu.au/~szypersk/Gardens.html`.

7 Conclusions

Parametric polymorphism supports type parametrisation, just as procedures support code parametrisation. As such, this is a proven and well-established concept and part of many languages. Parametric polymorphism does not interfere with or substitute inclusion polymorphism (subtyping), but the two mutually benefit from each other. When properly designed and implemented, parametric polymorphism improves type safety, maintainability and reusability of code.

In current languages, parametric polymorphism comes at one of two costs. Either polymorphic code cannot be separately compiled into shared generic object code, or the use of such shared code incurs significant hidden costs. Languages in the former category simply generate code for each instantiation of a generic, leading to code explosion and, possibly worse, preventing the construction of generic dynamic link libraries. Languages in the latter category, which hide run-time costs, can significantly affect the programmer's control over execution cost in time and space.

In this paper we presented a simple extension to the language Oberon that is lightweight in all dimensions. The extension is carefully restricted to simultaneously support type checking and full separate compilation of polymorphic code *and* to not introduce any run-time cost in time or space. The extension is not only simple but also strictly upwards compatible with Oberon. The extension only affects the front-end of a compiler: after type checking, extended Oberon can be rewritten into standard Oberon.

Acknowledgements

We would like to thank Jürgen Wendel for contributing to the implementation of our ideas, and for his comments on a draft of this paper. This work was partially funded by ARC grant ARCSG 55, 7056.

References

1. A V Aho, R Sethi, and J D Ullman. *Compilers, principles, techniques, and tools.* Addison-Wesley, 1986.
2. L Cardelli and P Wegner. On understanding types, data abstraction, and polymorphism. *Computing Surveys*, 17(4):471–522, December 1985.
3. M Day, R Gruber, B Liskov, and A Myers. Subtypes vs. Where Clauses: Constraining parametric polymorphism. In *Proc, 10th Conf on Object-Oriented Programming Systems, Languages, and Applications (OOPSLA '95)*, pages 156–168, October 1995.
4. K J Gough and G M Mohay. *Modula-2: A Second Course in Programming.* Prentice Hall, 1988.
5. B Liskov, D Curtis, M Day, S Ghemawat, R Gruber, P Johnson, and A C Myers. Theta Reference Manual, preliminary version. Programming Methodology Group Memo 88, MIT Laboratory for Computer Science, Cambridge, MA, February 1995.
6. B Liskov and J Guttag. *Abstraction and Specification in Program Development.* MIT Press, 1986.
7. B Liskov, A Snyder, R Atkinson, and C Schaffert. Abstraction mechanisms in clu. *Comm ACM*, 20(8):564–576, August 1977.
8. B Meyer. *Eiffel – The Language.* Prentice Hall, 2 edition, 1992.
9. R Morrison, A Dearle, R C H Connor, and A L Brown. An ad-hoc approach to the implementation of polymorphism. *ACM TOPLAS*, 13(3):342–371, 1991.
10. H Mössenböck. *Object-Oriented Programming in Oberon-2.* Springer Verlag, 1993.
11. B C Pierce. Bounded quantification is undecidable. *Information and Computation*, 112(1):131–165, July 1994.
12. M Reiser and N Wirth. *Programming in Oberon – Steps beyond Pascal and Modula.* Addison-Wesley, 1992.
13. G Smith and D Volpano. Towards an ML-style Polymorphic Type System for C. In *1996 Eurpoean Symposium on Programming*, Linköping, Sweden, April 1996.
14. D Stoutamire and S Omohundro. Sather 1.1. Technical report, International Computer Science Institute, Berkeley, CA, 1996.
15. C Szyperski, S Omohundro, and S Murer. Engineering a Programming Languager— the Type and Class System of Sather. In *Proc, 1st Intl Conf on Programming Languages and System Architectures*, number 782 in Springer LNCS, Zurich, Switzerland, March 1994.
16. R D Tennent. *Principles of Programming Languages.* Prentice Hall Int., 1981.

Static Type Checking and Method Lookup in Plop!

P.G.Kluit, C.Pronk, R.Verver
e-mail: {P.G.Kluit/C.Pronk}@twi.tudelft.nl

Delft University of Technology
Faculty of Technical Mathematics and Informatics
Department of Technical Informatics
Postbus 356, 2600 AJ Delft, Netherlands.

Abstract. The language Plop![1] is an experimental object oriented language, with a functional flavor. It combines in one language the following features: prototyping, multiple delegation, multi-methods and static type checking.

1   Introduction

The design of a language starts with balancing between freedom and flexibility on one hand, and safety on the other hand. As we consider safety not an item for bargaining, we insisted on static type checking. That decision taken, we tried to obtain as much dynamical freedom, and freedom of extension as possible. Evidently this freedom could never go beyond what can be checked statically.

We will not give a full description of the language Plop!. We introduce a minimal subset, sufficient to convince (we hope) that our concepts are sane.

2   Overview of Plop!

Plop! is an object-oriented language. It was designed with the following goals in mind:

Modularity. Software is built from independently developed components.

Generality and Incrementality. Software components should be build as general as possible, so as to be applied and reused in as many situations as possible. Extension of a system should be done exclusively by adding code, so editing of code should be reserved for correcting errors [11], [13]. In other words, we adhere to the principle of 'Separate Authority', stating that the only person allowed to modify code is the author of the code. Any other person who wants to adapt the behavior of a component to his personal needs should do so solely by adding code. This implies indeed that the behavior of a component *can* be changed by adding code. To obtain a very general level of re-usability we prefer delegation over inheritance.

---

[1] The name Plop! has no meaning whatsoever. It is even not a brand of coffee.

Safety. Plop! is statically typed. The unit of type checking is the module. Once a module is (statically) declared type safe, no typing errors may occur during run time. Moreover, the type system is designed to obey the *open world assumption*[12], which implies that adding code may change the behavior of a component, but not its type safety.

2.1 The elements of Plop!

The language Plop! provides prototyping, multi-methods, delegation and static type-checking. We believe this combination to be new.

Four components play a role in a Plop! program: types, objects, methods and expressions. We discuss three of them in short.

Types. Plop! programs are statically type-checked. The *subtype*-relation imposes a partial order on the types, which is conveniently represented by the *type graph*. This type graph is statically fixed.

Objects. All data is represented by objects, which can be manipulated exclusively by calling methods. Plop! has a prototype-based object model, so there is no class concept, but every object has a type. The programmer can define new *prototypical* objects from 'scratch'. An object, other than a prototype, is created by *cloning* an other object (possibly a prototype). The newly created object has the same type as the original one.

Objects may have other objects as their delegates. Using delegation, objects may directly share the state and behavior of other objects. This delegate relation gives rise to the *object graph*, in which each directed edge goes from an object to one of its delegates. This object graph may grow dynamically, but it is always acyclic. A relation (to be described later) between the type graph and the object graph restricts the shape of the object graph.

Methods. Methods in Plop! are multi-methods. A method has (among others) a name, and a vector of formal parameter types. A method may be applied to a vector of actual parameter objects only if each of the objects has the correct type. However, when an object is an actual parameter in a method call, it may be replaced by one of its delegates or one of the delegates of its delegates, etc.. This way in addition to the original vector of actual parameter objects, we obtain a collection of alternative vectors of actual parameter objects consisting of delegates of the original vector's objects. For some of these vectors an applicable method may exist. This imposes some problems with respect to method lookup (evidently we have multiple-dispatching method lookup). No method might be applicable, or many methods might be applicable. The typing system should ensure that in type-safe programs there is at least one applicable method for any call. The method lookup mechanism should contain rules to select a 'best' method, in case more than one is applicable.

The *open world assumption* enlarges this problem. In a language like Modula-2, type checking a module statically is not too hard, as binding is static. In Plop!

binding is dynamic, but we want to declare a component statically type safe although we do not know in advance what definitions will be in scope during run time. New method definitions might have been added making a previously unambiguous call ambiguous. Addition of new methods can (and should!) not be prevented, but we can prevent ambiguity. To guarantee type safety we supply each method call expression with 'blinders', to make disturbing definitions invisible.

More specific (well, just a bit), each method call is statically supplied with a totally ordered search set (or search route). With each element of this search route a statically applicable method may be associated. We statically check that at least one statically applicable method is present, otherwise the type checker rejects the program. When the call is actually executed the search route is expanded to a totally ordered run time search route. With each element of this run time search route an applicable method may be associated. Moreover, every statically applicable method is present. During method lookup we pass along the run time search route. The first applicable method we encounter is then selected for application. This search never fails, as at least one applicable method is present (the one that was found during type checking). This search is never ambiguous, as the search route is totally ordered. Newly added methods that might cause ambiguity are simply ignored, as they are not found along the search route.

The static search route is constructed by the type checker in creating a *type path* for every parameter in the call.

To construct the run time search route we start with the set of possible actual parameter vectors, obtained by 'delegating' the original actual parameter vector. A subset of this set (based on the statically created type paths) is selected and supplied with a total order. To this purpose, for each actual parameter a search path in the object graph is constructed (in run time). For each parameter this search path linearizes the search for delegates. We then impose an ordering from left to right upon the parameter positions . Replacing actual parameters with delegates starts with the rightmost parameter; only if this one has reached the end of its search path its left neighbor is replaced (and the rightmost parameter starts over again). This way we obtain (lexicographically) a total order on the possible vectors of delegates to be used in a method call.

3 Details of Plop!

A program statically consists of type definitions, methods and expressions. Each program contains a designated method named *main* that takes no parameters and returns no result. That is where the program starts.

3.1 Types in Plop!

A program defines a finite set of *types*. Each type may have zero or more *parent types*. The *type graph* conveniently represents the set of types and the parent relationship between types. Every node in the type graph corresponds to a type. Every (directed) edge in the type graph points from a type to one of its parents. The type graph should contain no cycles and no multiple edges between types. The *subtype relation* between types is the transitive closure of the parent relation. So the type t is a subtype of the type u (notation $t \leq u$) if in the type graph a path exists from t to u. Then u is a *super-type* of t. The graph contains one designated type called Object, which is a super-type of all other types.

As Plop! is a prototyping language, new types are derived from prototype definitions. The following definition introduces (among others) the new type Person and a prototypical object of type Person.

```
object Person
object Student
object Sporter
object SportyStudent
object Rower
```

Parent type relations are derived from *delegate definitions*.

```
delegate Student : Person
delegate Sporter: Person
delegate SportyStudent : Student
delegate SportyStudent : Sporter
delegate Rower : Sporter
```

This adds (among others) Person as a parent type to Sporter. Or, the other way round, it defines Sporter as a subtype of Person. The type graph now looks as follows:

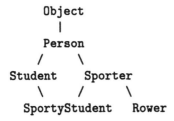

3.2 Methods

A program contains a finite set of methods. A method consists of

- a name,
- a vector of formal parameter names and types,
- a result type, and,
- a body expression.

Methods having the same name should be different in their formal parameter types. Some examples of method definitions (bodies are omitted):

```
method name(p1: Person) -> String is ...
method set-name (p: Person, s: String) is ...

method train(s: Student) is ...
method train(s: Sporter) is ...
method train(r: Rower) is ...

method compete(r: Rower, s: Sporter) -> Sporter is ...
method compete(s: Sporter, r: Rower) -> Person is ...
```

(The last definition lacks some realism, for the sake of the example). Where result types are absent, the default type Object is assumed.

3.3 Expressions

The body of a method is an expression. In a complete language many kinds of expressions will occur. We will not go into the details of all possible expressions, but restrict ourselves to the following:

- a formal parameter name is an expression,
- a local name is an expression,
- a prototype name is an expression,
- a cloning expression (see 3.4) is an expression,
- a method call is an expression. It has the form: $msg(exp_1, ..., exp_n)$.

3.4 Objects

A running program consists of a set of objects. This set dynamically grows as new objects are created (it never shrinks). Every object is an instance of a particular type. An object, other than a prototype is created by *cloning* an other object (eventually a prototype). The newly created object has the same type as the original one. The following expression describes a new object of type Student.

```
Student[]
```

Observe the difference with the expression

```
Student
```

which designates the prototype itself.

Objects may have other objects as delegates. Within a cloning expression new delegates may be assigned. A new student with a new clone as Person-delegate is constructed as follows:

```
Student[Person = Person[]]
```

The first occurrence of the type name **Person** indicates that it is the Person-delegate that is to be replaced. The expression **Person[]** generates a new clone.

When an object occurs as actual parameter of a method call, the type of the object itself might be a subtype of the required type. In that case we (recursively) have to consult the delegates. Type safety guarantees that an object of the required type can be found between the delegates. An object may have several delegates, however, these possibly having several delegates themselves, so we might end up with multiple candidates. As the delegation graph not necessarily represents a total order, we must realize some mechanism to make a choice.

The way this problem is solved, is inspired by the Point of View notion for multiple inheritance [5]. Assume we have an object o_0, having type t_0. We hand this object over to a method, on a parameter position where type t_1 is required. This is allowed, as t_0 is a subtype of t_1, so at least one of the (direct or indirect) delegates of o_0 has type t_1. To narrow the choice of this delegate we provide a path in the object graph, instead of just o_0 . This path starts in o_0 and ends in o_2, having type t_2, say. Type t_2 should be a subtype of t_1. When the method actually is applied, the path is extended to end in an object o_1 of type t_1. We call such a path a *view*.

Definition 1. A *view* is a sequence of objects.

Every object is supplied with a fixed (possibly empty) vector of *delegate views*, or *parent views*. These vectors should obey certain restrictions, to be described soon If object o has view $< o_1, o_2, , \ldots >$ as a delegate view, we call o_1 a *parent object* of o. This induces a relation between objects, the parent relation, giving rise to the object graph, in the same way as the type graph. As every type is a prototype, and every prototype is an object, the type graph in subsection 3.1 is an instance of an object graph.

Definition 2. The *type* of a view $< o_1, o_2, , \ldots, o_n >$ is the type of its *last* object o_n.

Using the object graph, we conveniently can formulate the restrictions for delegates.

The delegate views (and the object graph derived from these) should obey the following conditions:

- The object graph is acyclic.
- An object has as many parent views as its type has parent types. that is, it has one parent view for each parent of its type.
- Every view describes a path in the object graph.
- Let r_1 be a parent view of object o. Let t_1 be the corresponding parent of the type t of o. Then r_1 has type t_1.

In fact, an object not only represents itself, but also all its delegates, and their delegates, etc.. The purpose of a view as a sequence instead of a single object is to restrict the part of the object graph that is represented. The object graph (like the object set) grows dynamically during program execution. Objects never disappear. Moreover, parent views are created, but never changed during program execution. Evidently the type graph restricts the way in which the object graph may grow. The object graph will never grow to violate its restrictions. Below we give an example of an object graph. For the sake of simplicity instances of type Object are not represented in the object graph. Person indicates the prototype Person considered as an object. An object named student1 is a new object of type Student.

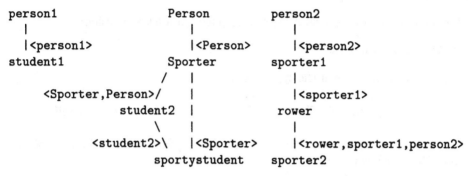

```
person1                Person           person2
  |                      |                |
  |<person1>             |<Person>        |<person2>
student1                Sporter          sporter1
            /   |                          |
<Sporter,Person>/   |                     |<sporter1>
         student2 |                       rower
              \    |                        |
  <student2>\   |<Sporter>     |<rower,sporter1,person2>
           sportystudent   sporter2
```

The leftmost graph is constructed from the type graph in subsection 3.1 by the expression mentioned above:

    Student[Person = Person[]]

This is how the second graph may be constructed:

    SportyStudent[Student = Student[Person = Sporter]]

Finally sporter2 in the third graph is made as follows:

    Sporter[Person = Rower[Sporter = Sporter[Person = Person[]]]]

This construction is unambiguous, as a Rower is a Person in a unique way.

An arbitrary object does not know which other objects refer to it, nor does it know in which views it occurs. Changing dynamically one of its parent views would imply changing the object graph and all (unknown) views in which the object and its parent occur. In short, keeping the object graph consistent forbids changing it.

3.5 Type checking

All computation in Plop! is achieved by method calling. The only error that may occur during the execution of a program is method lookup failure. Method lookup may fail in two ways: no method is applicable, or several methods are applicable, and no choice can be made. In general it is impossible to predict statically which method will be applied for a particular method call, for two reasons. First, the method selected for application depends upon the actual parameters of the call, which are not statically known. Second, the method actually applied may not be known during type checking.

Definition 3. A module is *type-safe* if no method lookup failures may occur during its execution.

The purpose of the type checker is to statically analyze the program and either reject it, or declare it type-safe.

Typing formal parameters. Formal parameters occur in the body of a method. The signature of the method defines the type of the formal parameter.

Typing local names. A local name is introduced in a let expression:

Let *name* = *exp* in

The type of *name* is then the type of *exp*.

Typing prototype names. The type of a prototype is the prototype itself.

Typing cloning expressions. The type of a cloning expression is the type of the object being cloned.

Typing method call expressions. Typing a method call expression is a strictly bottom-up process. First we derive types for all argument expressions. Based upon these types we supply every argument expression with a path in the type graph. These paths have two purposes. Statically they are needed to find a type for the method call expression. At run time they support message lookup.

Assume we have a method call expression $msg(exp_1, ..., exp_n)$. Let $t_1, .., t_n$ be the types derived for the argument expressions $exp_1, ..., exp_n$. For every parameter position i we proceed as follows:

- First we select all methods having name msg and arity n.
- From these methods we select the methods whose i-th formal parameter type is a super-type of t_i.
  If no method is selected we reject the program as being not type-safe. (We cannot statically guarantee that an applicable method exists).
- Consider all i-th formal parameter types for all selected methods. All these formal parameter types are super-types of t_i. Consider all possible paths in the type graph starting in t_i, and passing through one of these formal parameter types. Thus we obtain a bundle of paths starting in t_i.
- We reduce this bundle into a single path in two steps. First we remove prefixes, using the following 'algorithm':

```
Whenever a path in the bundle is a prefix
of an other path in the bundle:
    remove the shortest one.
```

Next we take the longest common prefix of all the remaining paths. This prefix is the longest unambiguous search path.

After this process, every parameter position of the call is supplied with a path in the type graph (or the program is rejected). Denote these paths $< t_{1,1}, t_{1,2}, \ldots >$ $\ldots < t_{n,1}, t_{n,2}, \ldots >$. Choosing a type in each path we obtain type vectors: $t_{1,k1}, t_{2,k2}, \ldots, t_{n,kn}$. The set of all these type vectors is totally ordered in the following way: Let j be the index of the first position where two type vectors are different. Assume the types at this position are $t_{j,kj}$ and $t_{j,lj}$, respectively. Then the order of the vectors is then determined by the order of the types $t_{j,kj}$ and $t_{j,lj}$ in the type path. (This is the lexicographical order, derived from the ordering in the type paths). This ordered collection of type vectors is the static search route. Along this search route we check for every type vector whether a method exists having this vector as its formal parameter type vector. If no method is found along this route, we reject the program (or module). The first method we find along this route we declare the *most specific statically applicable method* and call it m_{static}. The result type of m_{static} is then the type of the call expression.

Example 1. Type check the expression:

```
train(Student[Person = Person[]])
```

The argument expression has type **Student** (it is a cloning expression). There is only one parameter. Going through the type checking algorithm:

- We have three methods with name **train**.
- Only one of them has as formal parameter type (a super-type of) **Student**.
- So we obtain just one path, of zero length.

It turns out that a best static candidate is present. The type for the full expression is the default type **Object**.

Example 2. Type check:

```
name(SportyStudent[])
```

The argument type is **SportyStudent**. Again we have one formal parameter.

- Only one method with name **name** is known.
- The type it requires is **Person**, which indeed is a super-type of **Sporter**.
- We obtain in the type graph two paths:<SportyStudent, Sporter, Person> and <SportyStudent, Student, Person>
- The algorithm gives as longest unambiguous type path: **SportyStudent**.

Searching along this path we find no applicable method, so the expression is rejected as not being type safe. The reason is that it is not clear whether a sportystudent obtains his name from his sporter delegate or from his student delegate. The type checker is not allowed to assume that they both delegate to the same **Person**. The expression:

```
name(SportyStudent[]: Student)
```

forces the argument to be considered as a **Student**, so the ambiguity is resolved. This raises the question as to how an expression **a: t** should be type checked. The answer is that the expression **a: t** is syntactic sugar for: **as-t(a)**. For every type **t** the method **as-t** is (implicitly) defined as follows:

```
method as-t(x: t) -> t is x
```

We will see in 3.6 that this method realizes the required type-conversion, provided that a unique type conversion exists.

Example 3. We conclude with a two parameter example:

```
compete (Rower, Rower)
```

The first argument has type **Rower**.

- two methods are available.
- One needs a **Rower** in its first argument, the other one a **Sporter**, so both will accept a **Sporter**.
- The type paths we obtain are: **Sporter** and **<Rower, Sporter>**.
- The algorithm gives us as the longest unambiguous type path for the first argument: **<Rower, Sporter>**.

The second argument gives along the same lines as the longest unambiguous type path for the second argument: **<Rower, Sporter>**. We obtain the following type-vectors, (in this order!):

1. **<Rower, Rower>**
2. **<Rower, Sporter>**
3. **<Sporter, Rower>**
4. **<Sporter, Sporter>**

It turns out that both methods are applicable, but the first one we encounter is the one fitting with the second vector. This method has result type **Sporter**, so this will be the type of the expression as well.

3.6 Program Execution

Executing a Plop! program consists of evaluating the body expression of its **main()** method.

Method Calling. The evaluation of a method call expression $msg(exp_1, \ldots, exp_n)$ gives rise to a message call. Method calling is divided in three steps:

1. The actual parameter expressions $exp_1, \ldots, exp_n$ are evaluated, producing views $ref_1, \ldots, ref_n$, the actual parameters of the call.
2. The next step (*method lookup*) consists of selecting *applicable* methods and choosing the most specific one (say m).
3. Finally the selected method m is *invoked* on the actual parameters.

It is important to realize that the result of a method call will be not just an object, but a view.

Method Lookup. Method lookup starts with

- a message name
- a vector of views (the actual parameters).
- for each formal parameter position a path in the type graph (created by the type checker) starting in the type of the actual parameter.

For every parameter we extend the view to a search path, using the path in the type graph that was statically constructed. For the i-th parameter, let t be the type of the actual parameter. Recall that this means the actual parameter is a view $< o_1, o_2, \ldots, o_n >$, where t is the type of o_n. Let $t, t_1, .., t_k$ be the type path associated with the i-th parameter position. (Now the index no longer indicates the parameter position). As t_1 is a parent of t, and o_n has type t, the object o_n has a delegate view of type t_1, that is, a path $o_{n+1}, \ldots o_r$ such that o_r has type t_1. Simultaneously we shorten the type path to $t_1, .., t_k$ and extend the object path to $o_1, \ldots o_r$, where t_1 is the type of o_r. We repeat this process of extending the object path and shortening the type path, until the type path is reduced to one single type, being the type of the object path. In fact we 'lift' the type path to an object path.

Applying this process to every parameter position, we find for every parameter position an object path. We denote $o_{i,1}, o_{i,2}, \ldots$ the object path (extended view) for the i-th parameter position.

Choosing an object from each path we obtain an object vector: $o_{1,k1}, o_{2,k2}, \ldots$. The objects in each path are totally ordered (by the path). We extend this ordering lexicographically to an ordering on the object vectors as follows:

Let $o_{1,k1}, o_{2,k2}, \ldots$ and $o_{1,l1}, o_{2,l2}, \ldots$ be two (different) object vectors. Let i be the first position for which $ki \neq li$. Then $o_{1,k1}, o_{2,k2}, \ldots$ precedes $o_{1,l1}, o_{2,l2}, \ldots$, iff. $ki < li$.

This gives a total ordering on the possible object vectors. Obeying this ordering we pass along all possible object vectors, until we find one that matches a method. That method is selected. Recall that a method consists of:

1. a name,
2. a vector of formal parameter types,
3. a result type,
4. a body expression.

For method lookup, (1), (2) and (3) are relevant. To be applicable, a method first of all must have the right name. Next, its result type must be a *subtype* of the type assigned to the method call expression at hand, and it must be so in a unique way. That is: there exists a unique path in the type graph from the result type of the method to the required type of the expression.

We say that an object vector $o_{1,k1}, o_{2,k2}, \ldots$ matches a method, if for every parameter position i the type of $o_{i,ki}$ equals the type required by the method on this position. From the construction of the type path we know that at least one matching method exists. The (total) ordering of the object vectors imposes a total order on the applicable methods, from which we choose the first one.

The result of the method lookup process is a method and a vector of objects $o_{1,k1}, o_{2,k2}, \ldots$, one in each search path, having the type required by the method chosen.

Method Application. Method application (or rather *invocation*) consists of two phases. During the first phase the formal parameters are bound to the actual parameters. We bind the formal parameter on the i-th position to the view: $o_{i,1}, o_{i,2}, \ldots, o_{i,ki}$, being the appropriate prefix of the search path.

During the second phase the body of the method is evaluated, using this binding. The result of this evaluation will be a view. This view is a subtype of the required type, and a unique path in the type graph exists from this view to the required view. Again we can lift this path to a path in the object graph. Extending the (preliminary) result view with this path we obtain a view having the required type.

Example. We go through the execution of the call: name(SportyStudent[] : Student), which is read as:

name(as-Student(SportyStudent[]))

First we have to go through the evaluation of the argument expression, that is the call as-Student(SportyStudent[]). The cloning expression SportyStudent[] returns a clone of the SportyStudent prototype, having type SportyStudent. Method lookup is simple: only one method as-Student exists. This method is applicable, and the type checker supplied the type path <SportyStudent, Student>. This is lifted to an object path <sportystudent, Student>, and this is the view given to the method as-Student as its argument. The method as-Student returns nothing but its argument view, so the argument view for the name method is <sportystudent, Student>.

The type checker calculated a type Student for the argument of the name-call and supplied a type path <Student, Person>. Using this type path the argument view is extended to: <sportystudent, Student, Person>, This view is handed over to the method name, which will return the name of the prototype Person.

3.7 Type safety

We call an arbitrary expression *well typed* if evaluation of that expression at run time always returns a view having the same type as the type checker assigned to that expression. Local names, prototype names and cloning expressions are well typed by definition.

Definition 4. A formal parameter is well typed if evaluation at run time always returns a view having the type of the parameter.

The last paragraph of 3.6 explained how actual parameter views are extended at run time to match the statically required type. This shows that all formal parameter expressions are well typed.

Definition 5. A method call expression $msg(exp_1, \ldots, exp_n)$ is well typed iff

1. the method call succeeds for every vector of actual parameter views having the required type,
2. the result of the call has the type assigned to the expression by the type checker.

During the search for an applicable method, we certainly will encounter the method m_{static}, (end of 3.5). As we have linearized the search, ambiguity may not arise so method call will not fail. The mechanism discussed at the end of 3.6 to create the result view assures that this view has the required type.

3.8 Modules in Plop!

Multi methods exist outside objects. Objects should make all their contents available for these methods, and for other methods, to be added later in possible extensions of the system. Hence the object can no longer be the unit of encapsulation, so we need other means for encapsulation. Apart from that, modules are the units of reuse. According to the principle of Separate Authority, a programmer delivers and maintains a complete module. Consequently, the module is also the unit of type checking.

4 The benefits of Plop!

In the language Plop! several features are combined, each one having its own reason for existence.

Multi-methods. As multi-methods exist outside objects, adding functionality to existing types is allowed. Covariance problems do not occur. Method lookup is flexible.

Dynamic delegation. This allows us to dynamically extend the interface (and hence the functionality) of an existing object. Moreover it allows us to provide different interfaces for one and the same object For example, one and the same person could be considered either as a student, or as a sporter. So objects may be reused dynamically, and supplied with additional behavior. For example, an existing object might be supplied with a Graphical User Interface.

Multiple Delegation. Without duplication of code we can reuse the code of several objects. On the other hand, this mechanism gives rise to possible ambiguities. For example the call name(SportyStudent) is ambiguous. If the compiler cannot resolve the ambiguities, the programmer should supply sufficient extra information (type annotation). The call name(SportyStudent: Student) is unambiguous, as the argument is to be considered as a Student).

Static Type Checking. The advantages of static type checking are well known. We realize type safety, even under the open world assumption. Modules may be type checked separately, and once checked remain type safe, even when reused in an extended context. On the other hand we must mention some restrictions:

- Ambiguities in method lookup are resolved by the system solely. The programmer has no way to interfere. This is unavoidable, as these ambiguities can not statically be foreseen.
- Dynamic inheritance may change the behavior of objects. The interface of an object is statically fixed.

5 Related work

Although we believe that the combination of features we offer in Plop! is unique, no doubt each of these features can be found in some other language[2]. We will pay some attention here to languages based on related principles.

Omega. The language *Omega*, introduced by Günther Blaschek in [2] has a prototype-based object model and static typing, single dispatching and single inheritance. New prototypes can be derived from existing prototypes in a way that resembles class inheritance. Prototypes can be changed, these changes are propagated to (shared by) all clones. There is no delegation in Omega.

Cecil. The language Cecil, designed by Craig Chambers [6], [7], is based upon multiple dispatching and multiple inheritance. Cecil has inheritance rather than delegation. The object-model is classless (prototype based). Sub-typing and inheritance are different (though related) concepts in Cecil. Cecil has dynamic type checking. If the programmer supplies sufficient annotations some static type checking is possible, in which case ambiguities are reported at compile time.

Mixins. In [4], Gilad Bracha and William Cook discuss the concept of *mixin-based inheritance*. In most OO-languages, inheritance involves the creation of new classes by extending existing classes. These extensions are a part of the new class. With mixin-based inheritance, the extensions are abstractions of their own, that can be applied on a variety of parent classes. Thus, inheritance can be seen as a composition of mixins. The construction of the type graph using mixins strongly resembles the construction of the object graph in Plop! using delegation, except that the type graph in Plop! is constructed statically rather than dynamically, and that mixins support only single inheritance. In their paper, Bracha and Cook extend the strongly typed language Modula-3 with mixins, and also provide typing rules.

Agora. In the language Agora[14], Patrick Steyaert et. al. introduce the concept of *dynamic Mixins*. These Mixins are not applied to classes, but to existing objects in order to extend those objects. Agora is statically typed, features single inheritance and single dispatching method lookup.

---

[2] we do not have a reference for multiple delegation.

6 Conclusion

In Plop! we succeeded in obtaining a high level of extendibility and reuse, without sacrificing the benefits of static type checking. Evidently, something had to be sacrificed. A delegate can be replaced during creation of an object, but it can not be changed afterwards. We had to restrict (in the search path as well as in the result type) the way in which a method call may obtain another meaning.

Some slight improvements could be made. Type checking is strictly a bottom up process. When a message call is the body of a method, some result type is required. This information is not propagated downwards in the expression tree. Further there are no generic types, although in principle genericity should be possible.

References

1. Agrawal, R. et al. Static Type Checking of Multi-Methods, OOPSLA '91, pp. 113-128.
2. Blaschek, G. Object-Oriented Programming with Prototypes, SPRINGER-VERLAG BERLIN HEIDELBERG, 1994.
3. Borning, A.H. Classes Versus Prototypes in Object-Oriented Languages, PROCEEDINGS OF THE IEEE/ACM FALL JOINT CONFERENCE, 1986, pp.36-40.
4. Bracha, G. and Cook, W. Mixin-Based Inheritance, ECOOP/OOPSLA '90 PROCEEDINGS, October 1990, pp.303-311.
5. Carre, B and Geib, J-M. The Point of View Notion for Multiple Inheritance. ECOOP/OOPSLA '90 PROCEEDINGS, October 1990, pp.312-321.
6. Chambers, C. Object-Oriented Multi-Methods in Cecil. ECOOP '92 CONFERENCE PROCEEDINGS, Utrecht, the Netherlands, July 1992.
7. Chambers, G. and Leavens, G.T. Typechecking and Modules for Multi-Methods, ACM TRANSACTIONS ON PROGRAMMING LANGUAGES AND SYSTEMS, Vol.7, No.6, pp.805-843, November 95.
8. Dony, C. et al. Prototype-Based Languages: From a New Taxonomy to Constructive Proposals and Their Validation, OOPSLA '92, pp.201-217.
9. Hölzle, U. Integrating Independently-Developed Components in Object-Oriented Languages, ECOOP '93 PROCEEDINGS, Springer Verlag Lecture Notes on Computer Science.
10. Lieberman, H. Using Prototypical Objects to Implement Shared Behavior on Object-Oriented Systems, OOPSLA '86 PROCEEDINGS, September 1986, pp.214-223.
11. Ossher, H and Harrison, W. Combination of Inheritance Hierarchies, OOPSLA '92, pp.25-40.
12. Palsberg, J. and Schwartzbach, M.I. OBJECT-ORIENTED TYPE SYSTEMS, Wiley Professional Computing, 1994.
13. Stein, L.A., Lieberman, H. and Ungar, D. A Shared View of Sharing: The Treaty of Orlando, OBJECT-ORIENTED CONCEPTS, APPLICATIONS AND DATABASES, 1989
14. Patrick Steyaert et. al., Nested Mixin-Methods in Agora, FTP, VRIJE UNIVERSITEIT BRUSSEL

CDCS: A New Development Approach for Distributed Applications in Java*

Igor Vel'bitsky, Sergey Yershov, Igor Netesin

International Scientific Centre of Software Engineering TECHNOSOFT
of The National Agency on Informatization by the President of Ukraine,
Ukrainian National Academy of Sciences,
44, Acad. Glushkova Avenue, Kiev, 252187, Ukraine

Abstract. The Communication Design and Control System (CDCS) provides computer assistance for the communication aspects of a distributed program in a network environment. The CDCS supports the static definition of kind of structure of shared objects, exchanged messages, remotely called procedures and remotely invoked methods. It identifies client and server processing units together with the involved services and puts produced Java and C++ code into essential program units. Automatically generated headers and program skeletons containing Java interfaces and C++ definitions for the communication ease object-oriented programming and improve the program reliability. Similar tools set is delivered for UNIX and Windows NT.

1 Introduction

The Java architecture provides a portable, robust, high performance environment as an underlying basis for the development of distributed applications [1]. The Java language is familiar, being fashioned after C++. The Java developers have provided native multithreading facilities as well as the *net Sockets* Class Library for incorporating communication across network nodes. Unfortunately, using this library, programmers must themselves develop all low-level details of RMI (remote method invocations), message exchange and synchronization between different network hosts. Although JDK supports remote loading of bytecode across the Internet, this doesn't resolve the problem of designing of communicating applications that run concurrently on different Java stand-alone interpreters that do not "know about" network protocols supported by Java Library classes. CDCS provides a set of tools and APIs for the development of the communications aspects of Java (and C++ [2]) applications, ensuring that both the client and the server sides of a distributed application are generated based upon the extended RMI Specification Language.

* This research has been funded by the EC under the EUREKA framework, project HPPC/SEA-DOMAIN. Special thanks goes to Dr.Ivan Futo (ML Consulting, Hungary) and Gyorgy Strausz (Budapest Polytechnic University) for help on the development of the CDCS project.

Many articles have been written to describe how to add concurrency and distributed application facilities to the C++ language [3, 4, 5, 6, 7, 8]. Unfortunately, the described approaches suffer from the unreasonable limitations of the underlying object model, as well as from a lack of computer-aided support for migration from nondistributed systems to distributed ones (applications reengineering).

In contrast with many previous attempts (for instance, [7]), in the approach used in CDCS, the facilities of OOP are used to encapsulate the lower-level details of network communications, concurrency and synchronization.

2   CDCS Overview

The main goals within the CDCS project are fourfold:

1. To provide computer assistance for the development of the communication aspects of distributed object-oriented programs written in both the Java and the C++ languages.
2. To deliver a structure for shared object, exchanged messages, and remotely invoked methods (RMIs).
3. To reduce the amount of user effort during reengineering of previously created applications when making them distributed. To provide this both for object-oriented applications written in Java as well as for the usual C++ applications.
4. To provide network transparency to the user of CDCS. Configuration facilities of distributed application should be separated from source code and the user should be able to make an assignment of services without recompilation of application.

Remote method invocations (RMIs) between objects are based on the standard method invocation of the Java (C++) language. Invocations among objects in different address spaces use the proxy class model. A type of proxy, called a proxy class, is used to trap the normal function invocation and replace it by a remote invocation which marshals the parameters, issues a message to the remote object, receives a message in response, and unmarshals the results, if necessary. At the remote object, a dispatch method, which is associated with the remote object, is used to call the appropriate method.

The CDCS agent is a Java class that is run by an interpreter on a remote host. A CDCS agent could create a new class instance (server) in a separate address space in response to a request from the other process (client). After this, the client and server could communicate directly.

The combination of the notion of a thread and a class (an object in C++) results in the conception of a shared class. Such a Java class (or C++ object) is shared among a number of client threads (or class instances), e.g. a shared class is a server that could serve requests from any number of clients. All pending requests are serialized, e.g. a shared class can process only one request each time. The user of a shared class can provide client-side synchronization of RMI.

It is possible to define either a synchronous or an asynchronous RMI using the Shared Class API.

The server-side synchronization is delivered by the notion of a precondition[9]. A precondition should be satisfied just before a service is delivered in response to the RMI. If the precondition is not satisfied, then the server suspends this service until the other RMI will change the object state and the precondition will be satisfied. Additionally, the precondition can support the integrity of a distributed application as a collection of abstract data types.

The RMI Specification Language delivers an extension of the disciplined exception mechanism [1, 10] to distributed processing. An exception transmission between remote shared classes and the client is invisible to the client. Therefore, the client may handle exceptions in shared classes in way that is similar to usual Java classes (or C++ objects).

Since class instances exchange messages, the Message Exchange API library delivers the underlying level of distributed programming. The user of the Message Exchange library can create his own message by describing all the compound parts of a large variety of data types. There is the capability of creating one's own specific data types and anyone can use the newly created types in messages. Thanks to the semantics of combining the usual in-line copying with deep copying the user can control copying of data segments between processes. Therefore, this gives the user the possibility of restricting the transmission of data to the necessary entity only, and the result could be a great improvement of the general application performance.

The free combination of communication methods (blocking or nonblocking, buffering or nonbuffering) provides a large choice for the user of the Message Exchange library. Using this set of methods, the application implementer may obtain significant performance improvements through tailoring the communication schema to his own needs.

The RMI Server Generator can be designed to automatically generate methods in Java and C++ to pack and send, or receive and unpack the messages used to communicate between threads that are running on different hosts. The generated servers deliver some services, as prescribed in the RMI Specification Language, including RMIs for specified classes. It is similar to the interfaces description in the Java language, with the exception of full-fledged data transmission and synchronization facilities that are out of the scope of Java. The generated code has two advantages: separation of interface and implementation, and network transparency. In the network environment, the server, generated by the Server Generator, both encodes messages to be transmitted, and decodes them upon arrival at the destination node, taking into account the dissimilarities in machine architectures.

Additionally, the RMI Server Generator makes it possible to automatically create specification files from Java packages or C++ projects. The Server Generator creates the specifications of a synchronous RMI without default temporal restrictions about service delivery.

The Distributed Application Configurator is an important tool that can provide distributed application configuration before the application is run on a target set of network nodes, or even during application execution. Any shared class should be attached to some network node before this class instance (or server) starts to "live" through a standard *Thread* class. Configuration information is outside of the application and, therefore, the application does not need to be recompiled to make the desired reconfiguration.

The Graphical user interface (GUI) of the CDCS makes communication design easy to grasp. It supports convenient manipulation of communication units during application design.

The CDCS consists of four main parts: the Distributed Application Configurator, the RMI Server Generator, the CDCS Shared Class API library, and the CDCS Message Exchange API library. The *Thread Class* and *net Class Library* are used for implementation of the Java APIs of the CDCS. The *KW C++ UNIX-TCP/IP Distributed Programming Primitives Library, KW C++ DDE, KW C++ DDML* and *KW C++ NetDDE Distributed Programming Primitives Library* are used for implementation of C++ APIs. KW libraries are compound parts of the HPPC/SEA-DOMAIN project.

3 CDCS Shared Classes Library

The CDCS uses the Java environment and an existing object-oriented language C++[10], and provides concurrency abstractions through an external Java class library. The main concurrency abstractions provided by this library are classes as threads – shared classes – and an asynchronous remote method invocation (RMI) with data-driven synchronization. We call the class instance invoking the method a client, and the invoked class instance a server in accordance with [9].

The proposed view of distributed programming is based on the notion of a thread and its integration with the notion of a Java class. This unification of the notion of a thread and a class results in the concept of a shared class. Class instances can become shared only if they extend the *SharedObject* class. Distributed calculation then can be viewed as the parallel execution resulting from the creation of these shared class instances (objects) and their interactions with one another in a networked environment.

The parallel model requires that all the objects referenced (using method calls) by at least two threads (shared classes) are also threads. This rule leads to the identification of new shared threads.

For several reasons this provides an important methodological guideline. First, this rule points out the need for synchronization between method invocations for the same class instance. Second, a default FIFO synchronization is provided automatically when using the RMI Server Generator tool. Third, a control thread for a shared Java class should be provided in future system versions.

For a class that extends the *SharedObject* class, the constructor semantics of Java classes is preserved. First, a sequential intermediate proxy class instance is created, using the Java constructor. The actual creation of a shared class with its own process is achieved by invoking the *MakeSeparate()* method of the proxy class. The *MakeSeparate()* method starts a new process with an independent control thread, and returns back to the client after the active class instance is created and communication channels are established and initialized. Then the shared server object begins executing a special start-up method called *Synchronizer()*. Each class that extends *SharedObject* must implement a method called *Synchronizer()*. The implementation of the abstract method *Synchronizer()* demonstrates how to serve the requests generated by client class instances. All requests are delivered as actual messages to the server using a transparent Java (C++) CDCS Message Exchange API mechanism. Since multiple clients can simultaneously request services, the communication is buffered.

After a *MakeSeparate()*, the server object in the client's address space acts as an agent for the actual shared server class instance. This proxy class instance asynchronously relays the requests to the shared server object's *request_queue*, and returns the results of requests which are asynchronously delivered to its *result_queue* by the server.

Since a server class instance has been made shared, via a *MakeSeparate()* method, new clients that want to invoke the server's methods must create their own proxy class instances and use the *MakeAttachable()* method to set up the association between the proxy object and the shared server object. *MakeAttachable()* is significantly cheaper than *MakeSeparate()*, since it does not involve the creation of a class instance on a remote host. *MakeAttachable()* is the only mechanism to share shared classes.

In the Java object-oriented paradigm, method invocation is a synchronous procedure call, and objects are passive entities, doing work only when their methods are invoked. The *Message* class extends to the *SharedObject* class a nonblocking, asynchronous method invocation mechanism called *BufferedSend()*. The client does not wait for the completion of the invoked method, but concurrently continues executing its own code until the point in its own execution where it actually uses the result of the remote execution of the method. This is a data-driven synchronization scheme, based on asynchronous message passing.

The *SharedObject* class provides two methods to access the results of a remote method invocation. Both of the methods take a single argument, a *receipt*, which is returned by the corresponding remote invocation as a handle to obtain the actual result in the future. The first method, *GetResult()*, returns the result delivered by the server. If the result is not available, then *GetResult()* blocks until it becomes available. The other method, *ResultAvailable()*, is a nonblocking test for the availability of the result of the remote invocation associated with the *receipt*. All the underlying IPCs are encapsulated and hidden from the application.

Since shared class instances reside in separate address spaces, classes that appear as parameters of remote methods cannot be passed as in Java but must either be (deep) copied, or the proxy class instance in the server address space that is attached to classes-parameters in the client space must be provided automatically.

```
Receipt receipt; T return_value;
receipt = shared_object.method(arg1, arg2, ...);
    .
    .   // concurrent execution with shared_object
    .
return_value = receipt.GetResult();
        // implicit GetResult from shared_object
```

Above we show a way to indirectly call a buffered send function using the same syntax of a sequential call in Java. Using the *Receipt* class provides a simpler and more transparent way of accessing the result of the remote invocation.

Two types of synchronization are supported by this mechanism: reply synchronization and request synchronization. Reply synchronization is the control the client has over the delivery of the reply, and request synchronization is the control the shared class server has over the acceptance of the request. Reply synchronization is addressed by the *BufferedSend()*, *GetResult()* and *ResultAvailable()* methods, as presented in this section.

One of the requirements of this approach for designing shared classes is to define a start-up method, called *Synchronizer()*. A *MakeSeparate()* method call to a proxy class instance eventually starts a new thread execution using the *Synchronizer()* method of the active class. The *Synchronizer()* has exclusive access to the concurrency-related internal state of the shared class, and specifies its behavior.

Message acceptance is asynchronous and explicit. Also, accepting a message is separated from actually serving the request. A queue of request messages, called *request_queue*, contains all the accepted requests of the client class intances. Messages delivered to the communication buffer, but not yet accepted into the *request_queue*, are called pending requests. Each entry in the queue contains all of the parameters of the client's remote invocation request, including *request_identifier* and reply address. The server class explicitly needs to show intent to accept messages: *Receive()* is a potentially blocking method that places all pending requests into the *request_queue*, and blocks if no pending request exists until the first one arrives. A nonblocking version of *Receive()* is *ImmediatelyProbe()* method.

The *Synchronizer()* has unrestricted access to the *request_queue*, and it can inspect the parameters and names of the requests in the queue in order to select and serve one of them. It can also choose to wait for a certain type of request to arrive, or for a certain condition before it selects a request to service. Sending a result back to a client after the servicing of a request is also done asynchronously and explicitly, using the *SendResult()* method.

Since there is a single thread inside the *Synchronizer()*, the *Synchronizer()* serializes the execution of its methods. This eliminates the need for synchronization inside the methods of the Java class but does not restrict this possibility.

4 A Dinner Philosophers Example

The following example illustrates how the RMI Specification Language is used for producing a simple Java distributed application from an existing nondistributed (nonconcurrent) one. In addition, it shows the use of the CDCS Java Shared Classes library.

Let the Java classes *Fork* and *Philosopher* be developed and tested by the user for the sequential simulation of the well-known problem of the dinner philosophers. For instance, the class *Fork* may look like as follows:

```
class Fork {
   boolean is_busy;
   int PhilosopherPID;
   int PID;
public Fork(int ForkPID){
     is_busy = false;
     PhilosopherPID = 0; PID = ForkPID;
   }
public boolean IsBusy() {
     return is_busy;
   }
public void Get(int PhilPID) {
     is_busy = true;
     PhilosopherPID = PhilPID;
     System.out.println("Fork " + PID +": GET");
   }
public void Put(int PhilPID) {
     if (PhilosopherPID == PhilPID) {
        is_busy = false;  PhilosopherPID = 0;
        System.out.println("Fork " + PID + ": PUT");
     } else {
        System.out.println("Fork " + PID +
           ": Put() is failed by Philosopher" + PhilPID );
     }
   }
}
```

Then the user may specify the above classes in the RMI Specification Language. All public function members could be described. As this example demonstrates, the class *Fork* has three "methods". Methods *Get()* and *Put()* are defined as void functions, therefore they do not return any applied value, but the client will wait for the termination of the above "methods" since it called *Get()* or *Put()* in the client's code. The description of the *Fork* and *Philosopher* classes in the RMI Specification Language is as follows:

```
class Fork
   data
      boolean is_busy;
      int PhilosopherPID;
   method
         // this function is optional (unused by proxy)
      boolean function IsBusy();
         // it is synchronous
      procedure Get( int PhilosPID ) require not IsBusy();
         // it is synchronous
      procedure Put( int PhilosPID ) require IsBusy();
      constructor(int ForkPID);
      asynchronous  destructor();
end

class Philosopher
   method
      asynchronous procedure Live( in shared Fork left_fork,
                                   in shared Fork right_fork);
      constructor();
      asynchronous  destructor();
end
```

After the execution of the Server Generator, the user will obtain a package for the *SharedFork* and *SharedPhilosopher* classes, the client and server Java methods for the above classes. Each class defines a *Synchronizer* that becomes the "body" of its shared class. The generation of the *Synchronizer* method for the shared class *SharedFork* is also shown in the following example.

```
//******************************************
// This is shared class SharedFork
// (created by server generator)

class SharedFork extends SharedObject {
   protected Fork nonsharedclass;
private void SerGenSI_1_IsBusy (RMI_Request request) {
     // SerGenSI_1_IsBusy() implementation
   }
private void SerGenSI_2_Get (RMI_Request request,
                                Parameter param) {
     // SerGenSI_2_Get() implementation
   }
private void SerGenSI_3_Put (RMI_Request request,
                                Parameter param) {
     // SerGenSI_3_Put() implementation
   }
public boolean IsBusy() {
```

```
        // IsBusy() implementation
    }
public void Get(int PhilPID) { // Synchronous Procedure 'Get'
        //    Creation of parameters array
        Parameter parameters[ ] = new Parameter[1];
        //    Creation and filling out
        //       the structure for first parameter
        parameters[0] = new Parameter(new INTdescriptor,
                                      PhilPID));
        //    Remote invocation of procedure 'Get'
        //    with parameters array 'parameters'
        Receipt receipt = RemoteInvoke("SharedFork::Get",
                                      parameters);
        //    Waiting for procedure termination
        //    because 'Get' is synchronous
        GetResult( receipt );
    } // end of Get()
public void Put(int PhilPID) {
        // Put() implementation here
    }
public finalize() {
        // its implementation here
    }
public SharedFork(boolean proxy, String object_name,
                  int ForkPID) {
        // constructor implementation here
    }
public void  Synchronizer(String Classname) {
// This method will be performed only for class 'SharedFork'
    if( !Classname.equals("SharedFork") ) return;

    RMI_Request current_request;
    // Get all requests and put them in request queue
    while( true /* Forever. Break by request "finalize". */) {
       int ParametersNumber = 0;
       //    Get first request
       current_request =
          (RMI_Request)RequestQueue().firstElement();
       RequestQueue().removeElementAt(0);
       //    Checking of parameters number
       if(current_request.parameters == null) ParametersNumber = 0;
       else ParametersNumber = current_request.parameters.length;

       // Matching request with synchronous procedure 'Get'
       if((current_request.method_name.equals("SharedFork.Get"))
```

```
          &&( ParametersNumber == 1 )) {
      Parameter CDCS_SerGen_p1 =
                      current_request.parameters[0];
      INTdescriptor ObjectDataType1 = new INTdescriptor();

      // Checking of parameter type for correspondence
         with server
      if( (CDCS_SerGen_p1.TypeDescriptor())== ObjectDataType1 )
      if( /* Precondition */ (! nonsharedclass.IsBusy()) ) {
         // Call to server-side interface for 'Get'
         SerGenSI_2_Get(current_request, CDCS_SerGen_p1);
      } else { // Precondition is not satisfied
         // Suspend request
         RequestQueue().addElement(current_request);
      }
   }
   //   Matching request for other methods
   // ... and then
   if( RequestQueue().isEmpty() ) {
      GetRequests();
   } else {  NonBlockingGetRequests(); }
  } // while( true )
} // end of Synchronizer()
} // end of class SharedFork
```

When the queue of pending request is empty, then the Synchronizer tries to accept a message from the IPC channels in blocking mode, otherwise it tries to accept it using the function *NonBlockingGetRequest*.

The initial destination of a class instance is defined by a special file "config" that includes relationships between the run-time class names and host/ports of the CDCS agent application. The target CDCS agent is responsible for creating new instances of CDCS shared classes.

5 Conclusions

As mentioned above, the Java environment [1] and the concurrent C++-based systems[4, 5, 6, 7, 8], with the exception of ABC++[3], are primarily thread-based packages and have not attempted to exploit the object-oriented facilities of Java and C++ for distributed concurrency creation and control. These limitations can include limiting the number of inheritance levels to one, explicitly managing threads through the use of start routines, and managing synchronization and mutual exclusion through the use of explicit mechanisms to wait for an event and to signal events.

The use of a conception of distributed memory as in [3] imposes serious limitations that follow in its implementation on a network of homogeneous processors.

CDCS doesn't suffer from this drawback. Indeed, the allocation of objects in different address spaces and its communication through a proxy object makes it possible to implement CDCS on top of the standard UNIX RPC protocol (XDR) using TCP/IP on a network of heterogeneous UNIX hosts.

Another important limitation of systems such as ABC++ is that the user must rewrite C++ headers because users are required to declare as *virtual* all methods of an active object that are invokable by other active objects. The drawback of ABC++ is that it is not desirable to change the "interfaces" of classes even during their parallelization.

When using CDCS, the usual Java and C++ classes can be reused without any interface redesign. It delivers a way to generate all "interface" Java and C++ network communication units for shared objects automatically from nonconcurrent ones. The programmer can manage synchronization, remote exception handling and temporal restriction imposed on the interaction of the concurrent (shared) objects. Additionally, the CDCS approach doesn't restrict the number of public member functions in a shared class (as in [3]).

The interaction of CDCS objects (class instances) is implemented on the basis of remote method invocations (RMIs) and supports run-time type identification of the object that is passed to another shared object as an argument of the RMI. One of prime advantages of CDCS is automated parallelization of existing Java and C++ code in a straighforward and safe way.

Another advantage is a more simple and effective schema of communication for distributed objects than the one in the well-known OLE and CORBA approaches [11]. This is because CORBA and OLE are oriented toward flexible integration of existing applications rather then toward high-performance computing.

In addition to importing native C++ code into Java applications, those applications could directly interact with pure C++ applications by using the common RMI Specification Language and the RMI network protocol inside CDCS. As mentionned before, CDCS generates network units for both languages from the same specifications. This frees the developer from the necessity to reimplement existing C++ application in the Java language. Instead, the user may integrate classes written in different languages.

The development of distributed applications using CDCS is computer supported at all stages, transparent from the user's point of view, and requires minimal changes of source Java and C++ applications.

References

1. Ritchey, T.: Programming with Java! New Riders Publishing, Indianapolis, Indiana. (1995)
2. Vel'bitsky, I., Yershov, S., Futo, I. CDCS: computer assistance for development of object-oriented distributed applications. Proceedings of WOON'96 International Conf. in Object-Oriented Technology. St. Petersburg, June 20-21 (1996)

3. Arjomandi, E., O'Farrell W., Kalas, I., Koblents, G., Elger, F., Gao, G. ABC++: Concurrency by inheritance in C++. IBM System Journal **34** No.1 (1995) 120–137
4. Bershad, B., Lazowska, E., Levy, H. PRESTO: A System for Object-Oriented Parallel Programming. Software – Practice and Experience **18** No.8 (1988) 713–732
5. Burh, P., Ditchfield, G., Stroobosscher, R., Younger, B., Zarnke, C. uC++: Concurrency in the Object-Oriented Language C++. Software – Practice and Experience **22** No.2 (1992) 137–172
6. Chartterjee, A., Khanna, A., Hung, Y. ES-Kit: An Object-Oriented Distributed System. Software – Practice and Experience **21** No.6 (1991) 525–539
7. Gehani, N., Roome, W. Concurrent Programming with Class(es). Software – Practice and Experience **18** No.12 (1988) 1157–1177
8. Assenmacher, H., Breitbach, T., Buhler, P., Hunsch, V., Schwarz R. PANDA: Supporting Distributed Programming in C++. Proceedings of ECOOP'93 – Object Oriented Programming, Lecture Notes in Computer Science, Springer Verlag, Berlin (1993) 361–383
9. Meyer, B. Object-Oriented Software Construction. Prentice-Hall, New York. (1988)
10. Stroustroup, B. The C++ Programming Language (2nd Edition). Addison-Wesley Publishing Co., Reading, MA. (1991)
11. Jutkin, A. Object technologies in distributed systems. SUUG Open Systems Journal No.3 (1995) 6–11

A Messaging Architecture for Distributed Objects in Oberon

Daniel Scherer

Computer Engineering and Networks Lab (TIK)
Swiss Federal Institute of Technology (ETH) Zurich
CH-8092 Zurich, Switzerland
+41 1 632 7050
scherer@tik.ee.ethz.ch

Abstract. A distributed messaging architecture built on top of current Oberon System 3 implementations is designed and implemented. It is aimed at supporting a CORBA-inspired object request broker architecture for distributed objects. The emphasis is on compatibility with System 3 messaging without requiring modifications of existing systems. Some Oberon-specific issues are identified which require workarounds in the solution, and proposals are also made for improved distributed messaging support in future systems. The implemented solution is presented in detail and uses a precompiler for message-specific communications procedure generation without restricting runtime flexibility for message types.

Keywords: Messages, Distributed Objects, Oberon System 3, CORBA.

1 Introduction and Motivation

The benefits of distributed objects as provided by CORBA and similar technologies [4, 12], together with the emerging component technologies [1], are being recognized more and more, as they allow large applications to be distributed and split up into smaller manageable and extensible components, and as they provide abstraction from heterogeneity (platforms, programming languages) and location of persistent objects. While in Oberon the abstraction from language and different systems may be of lesser concern, object-oriented programming conveniently allows the communication required by distributed systems to be inserted transparently in method calls (see e.g. [3]), therefore distributed objects are an appropriate choice to create larger distributed systems also in Oberon.

In our DIPS (Distributed Integrated Process Services) project (part of the GIPSY [11, 15] project), we are designing and implementing a framework for distributed software engineering environments. A single-user (i.e. non-distributed) prototype allowing graphical definition and enactment of software development processes was already operational at an earlier project stage, implemented in *Oberon System 3* [5, 19] due to its advantages for rapid construction of a protoype system. Since the project thereafter focussed on cooperative software engineering, a distributed prototype was to be built in order to allow distributed operation on multiple workstations. As its underlying concept, an architecture of *distributed objects* was chosen and designed, as detailed in [15], which provides optimal support for heterogeneous objects, scalability and composability. Thus, the question was whether and how the existing prototype could be extended for distributed operation (in order to use the existing parts of the prototype), and more specifically in this paper, how to implement distributed objects in Oberon System 3 - originally designed as a single-user system - , and with the Oberon [18] language (not Oberon-2, as type-bound procedures were not supported at the time by some compilers used on different platforms). In this paper we demonstrate that we have found a satisfactory solution.

Distributed objects (often residing on different hosts) communicate by exchanging *messages* containing requests and responses, whereby the hosts involved may assume different roles (client and server) per operation. An object request broker (ORB) architecture for distributed objects (also known as object bus) therefore is based on an architecture of distributed messaging, and the implementation of such a messaging architecture in Oberon is the main focus of the paper.

1.1 Overview of Paper

The paper first discusses general design considerations which include design objectives and ORB-specific requirements. The emphasis is on showing how a *distributed messaging architecture* can be implemented on top of current Oberon System 3 implementations, i.e. without requiring changes to the system. A number of Oberon-specific issues are therefore identified which require workarounds in the implementation, and some proposals for a more seamless integration of distributed messaging support in future Oberon systems are also provided. An implemented portable solution compatible with current Oberon System 3 implementations and System 3 messaging is presented in detail. However, a description also of a complete ORB based on this is beyond the scope of this paper. The results are summarized in the conclusions.

2 Design Considerations

The implementation of a messaging architecture suitable for an ORB is studied. It could be used as a basis for implementing a simple ORB, possibly with a gateway to CORBA-compliant ORBs, or on the longer run, to implement a more comprehensive CORBA-compliant ORB [4] - once an Oberon language mapping exists in OMG's CORBA specifications.

Only ORB specifics relevant to the messaging architecture are discussed here, in particular request execution semantics. Other issues are to be studied in the ORB's design, e.g. the object model, object references, object and proxy creation and destruction, etc. For now, objects and proxies are assumed to be System 3 objects, and an object's reference is assumed to consist simply of a tuple of the object's name and its 32-bit Internet address (stored in a LONGINT), where it is stored persistently.

2.1 Design Objectives and Requirements

The adaptation of software for distributed operation should be as simple as possible. This goal is supported by using Oberon System 3's existing extensible persistent object and messaging architecture [5, 9] and extending it for distributed operation. System 3's module Objects defines a basic message type (ObjMsg), and a basic object type (Object) containing a procedure variable (handle) of type Handler = PROCEDURE (obj: Object; VAR M: ObjMsg), whose dynamically-assigned procedure handles all messages sent to the object, possibly by forwarding them to other handlers.

In System 3, all message types are extensions of the basic ObjMsg. In the same way, a new basic message type suitable for distributed operation is introduced, and all potentially distributable message types are required to be extensions of that one, which is not more restrictive than before. Compatibility with System 3 messaging is assured by defining the basic distributed message type as an extension of ObjMsg. Only extensions of more specialized built-in message types are hereby excluded from distributed operation, but any user-defined message type derived from ObjMsg can be defined as a distributed message by instead basing it on the new distributed type. It is important that distributed messaging will not restrict this generality.

Furthermore, many issues discussed here may also be applied to *Oberon V4*; as the built-in object and message types are not as general-purpose as in System 3, user-defined basic types could be used.

The distributed messaging architecture should be compatible with current System 3 implementations without requiring any changes to the system or language, as this would require prohibitive efforts and more importantly, it would diminish acceptance by potential users, therefore a major challenge is to find out how distributed operation can be added to the system - originally designed for single-user operation - without modifying it. The dependance on platform-specific issues of a particular System 3 implementation should also be as small as possible, i.e. portability is a major concern, as we are using System 3 (Gadgets Version 1.5) on four different platforms: MacOberon, PowerMac Oberon, SPARC-Oberon for SunOS 4 and SPARC-Oberon for SunOS 5.

In summary, the goal is to implement a messaging architecture for an ORB that provides high degrees of:

- compatibility with Oberon System 3 messaging;
- compatibility with current Oberon System 3 implementations;
- portability among Oberon System 3 implementations on different platforms.

2.2 Execution Semantics

The design of a messaging architecture is influenced substantially by the required execution semantics to be provided for ORB operations. Inspired by CORBA [4] as well as by Oberon specifics, four desired styles of execution can be distinguished:

- *synchronous operation:* send a request and perform a blocking wait for a response (similar to CORBA's "at-most-once synchronous operation");

- *asynchronous operation:* send a request and return immediately, without expecting a reply (similar to CORBA's "best-effort operation");

- *asynchronous operation with response:* send a request and return immediately, then perform non-blocking poll or blocking wait for a response (similar to CORBA's "at-most-once deferred-synchronous operation", followed by non-blocking or blocking call of "get_response");

- *deferred-synchronous operation:* send a request and return immediately, then perform non-blocking poll for a response; when the response has come, continue further requests in synchronous operation. This combination, used for multiple requests, may seem contrived, but it proves useful in the context of Oberon systems, as they do not provide preemptive multitasking: An initial message can be sent to synchronize two hosts without blocking the client (sender) if the server is not ready (as it cannot be interrupted), thereafter further messages may be exchanged synchronously without requiring costly re-synchronization or polling operations.

2.3 Oberon Issues

Specific properties of both the Oberon language and system influence the design and implementation and require that the following eight issues be considered:

1. *No task preemption:* The system provides single-process non-preemptive multitasking, i.e. tasks cannot be interrupted. In order not to modify the system, this assumes that a server services requests during a background task, and it has to be taken into account that it may not be scheduled immediately when a request arrives.

2. *No blocking of host system:* In those implementations where Oberon is hosted on another operating system, it has to be assured that in the case of synchronous operation, only Oberon should be blocked, and not the host system, otherwise the machine may deadlock[1].

3. *No coroutines:* Multiple outstanding responses to asynchronous requests could be handled elegantly by using a different stack for every request, i.e. with coroutines. However, due to their absence in the system, a more explicit solution will be required to hold a task's data while it waits for a response.

---

[1] For example, when running Oberon on a Macintosh and at the same time running an X-Window client on that machine that provides the display for another Oberon running on a SPARC, the dual communication channels (messaging from one Oberon to the other, and display from the SPARC to the Macintosh) will lead to deadlock.

4. *Determine message type:* A message's type needs to be determined at runtime in order to be able to re-instantiate it on the receiving host. The language does not portably support this, and module Types provides only a partial solution, but it was not available on all platforms and it has been found to be too platform-specific; another solution is required. Here, it would be beneficial if the language provided a portable way of retrieving a record's or pointer's type at runtime (the IS type test only tests for a type specified already at compile-time) and of using this information to instantiate a new pointer of that type at runtime (NEW(v) only allocates a pointer for a type specified already at compile-time).

5. *Message preservation:* Asynchronous operation requires an immediate return after issuing a request, i.e. since blocking is not permitted, the message may need to be stored temporarily until the network or receiving host is ready for physical transmission. However, the message is typically a local variable (whose type is an extension of the basic message's record type), i.e. it exists only on the stack and is lost on return from the caller. The message cannot be preserved by an assignment to a variable of its base type, as the language's semantics specify that the extended record fields are hereby lost (since their size is not known at the time the variable is allocated), except in the case of a variable parameter (whose size is only determined at call time when its dynamic type is known) - as is required to implement message handlers. Therefore, a message-specific pointer type for the message must be newly allocated (i.e. on the heap) and the original message contents copied into it. This also assures that a dynamic number of messages may be preserved, which is required in order to be able to hold them in a queue of messages to be sent. Note that pointer types are only required for those message copies that are physically transmitted over the network, while for efficiency reasons local (non-distributed) messages are preferably only record types. In the case where the original message is already a heap-based object, the allocation of a new pointer type could be avoided, if the language provided a possibility of portably deriving a pointer from a heap-allocated record (i.e. without SYSTEM.ADR), since only the referenced (with ^) record of such a message is known in a handle.

6. *Determine message size:* Besides being able to copy a message to the heap, its size (in bytes in its network representation) needs to be determined at runtime (it may contain dynamic fields such as lists) and transmitted to the receiving host in advance, in order to allow message-specific read operations on the network only to be performed when it is assured that enough data is available (otherwise the read operations would block, assuming a simple network transport read implementation).

7. *Message linearization:* Transmitting a message over the network occurs sequentially, therefore its record fields must be linearized. Since the fields may contain platform-specific representations of data types, information about their types is required in order to perform the correct conversion operations. As has been noted in various places [8, 17], it would be advantageous for these purposes if a record's type tag were extended to hold this information.

8. *Non-portable parts:* All inherently non-portable (platform-dependant) parts should be well separated from the portable ones and implemented in modules with common interfaces on all platforms. There are three non-portable issues:

- the lower network layers (in OSI reference model [16] terminology) up to (including) the transport protocol (since they were not provided as standard in the system - more recent systems now provide networking);

- conversion (mapping) of platform-specific representations of Oberon data types to a standard network representation (linearization or marshalling);

- object finalization (will be used to remove loaded (instantiated) objects from an ORB's list of loaded objects when removed from the heap by the garbage collector).

3 Implemented Solution

3.1 Architecture

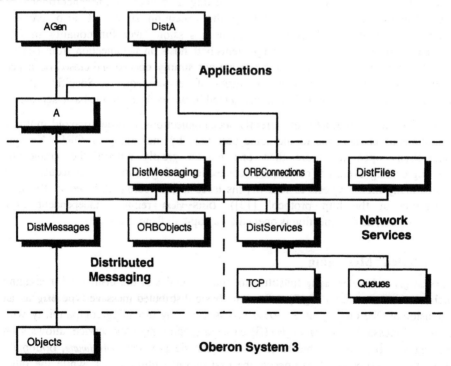

Fig.1: Excerpt of the Messaging Architecture's Module Hierarchy

A solution has been designed and implemented which provides a distributed messaging architecture suitable for an ORB, satisfying the three objectives listed in section 2.1, supporting the four execution styles shown in section 2.2, and which takes the eight Oberon-specific issues identified in section 2.3 into account. It already incorporates some preliminary aspects of an ORB design in order to provide an application for messaging, although the main focus is on the messaging architecture.

The implementation's module hierarchy is illustrated in fig.1 (an arrow from X to Y indicates Y imports X; direct imports reachable through indirect ones are omitted). It consists of *Network Services, Distributed Messaging* and any number of *Applications*.

Network Services

As common network transport protocol, we chose the widespread TCP (similarly, TCP has been chosen in CORBA [4] to support the mandatory interoperability protocol), as System 3 did not provide networking (newer System 3 releases now include networking, some of which use our TCP implementations [14]). It is implemented in module *TCP* which also provides data type conversion.

DistServices provides basic extensible communication services and protocols for clients and servers, running as state machines in Oberon background tasks, taking into account non-preemption e.g. by using long timeouts and by ensuring that only data is read that is physically available to avoid blocking. It supports both synchronous and asynchronous operation, as required by the execution styles. It also provides connection dialog control (corresponding to a session layer functionality in OSI reference model terminology) which prevents both hosts on a connection from issuing a request simultaneously (if connections are not simply opened and closed on a per-request basis). *Queues* handles FIFO queues of service requests. Specific network services such as file transmission (implemented in *DistFiles*) extend the basic services.

ORBConnections manages a list of currently open connections, in order to avoid multiple simultaneous connections to the same peer host by messaging or ORB. Keeping connections open for more than one request greatly reduces the connection opening/closing overhead (but requires connection dialog control), as a request often causes many more requests to follow (this issue is also being addressed in the next generation of the http protocol [13]). DistServices remains independent from ORBConnections, as a connection is opened by an up-call from DistServices.

Distributed Messaging

DistMessages and DistMessaging constitute the main modules of the distributed messaging architecture. *DistMessages* (fig.2) defines the basic distributed message type *Msg* as an extension of Oberon System 3's *Objects.ObjMsg*, thereby providing compatibility with System 3 messaging. *DistMessaging* (fig.3), as a specific network service, allows such messages to be sent to objects on other hosts via procedure *DistHandle*, optionally requesting a response. This supports the first two execution styles, while the other two are currently under construction and not detailed here. DistMessages and DistMessaging, while closely related, have been separated into two modules in order that modules defining potentially distributable messages but which themselves use their messages only locally need only import DistMessages and remain independent of

DistMessaging and all its network modules (the number of directly or indirectly imported modules has been found to be seriously restricted on some Oberon systems).

ORBObjects manages a list of all currently loaded (instantiated) objects on a host in order to ensure consistency, i.e. that multiple requests to an object are all routed to the same instantiation, and also ensuring that neither an object is loaded using several different names nor that different objects are loaded using the same name. Incoming messages may be routed to such objects from DistMessaging.

```
DEFINITION DistMessages;

    IMPORT Objects;

    TYPE
        MsgPtr = POINTER TO Msg;
        Msg = RECORD (Objects.ObjMsg)
            Read: PROCEDURE (VAR M: Objects.ObjMsg);
            Write: PROCEDURE (VAR M: Objects.ObjMsg);
            Copy: PROCEDURE (VAR M0, M1: Objects.ObjMsg);
            Len: PROCEDURE (VAR M: Objects.ObjMsg): INTEGER;
            type: ARRAY 64 OF CHAR;
        END ;

        PtrMsgPtr = POINTER TO PtrMsg;
        PtrMsg = RECORD (Msg)
            ptr: PtrMsgPtr;
        END ;

END DistMessages.
```

Fig.2: Simplified Interface of Module DistMessages

```
DEFINITION DistMessaging;

    IMPORT Objects, DistMessages, TCP;

    VAR
        NewMsg: DistMessages.MsgPtr;
        ObjHandle: PROCEDURE (objName: ARRAY OF CHAR; VAR M: Objects.ObjMsg);
        msgC-: TCP.Connection;

    PROCEDURE DistHandle (destAdr: LONGINT; destObj: ARRAY OF CHAR;
        VAR M: Objects.ObjMsg; answer: BOOLEAN; VAR res: INTEGER);

END DistMessaging.
```

Fig.3: Simplified Interface of Module DistMessaging

Application

While the prime application will be an ORB, the messaging architecture is more general-purpose, and an example of how distributed messaging may be used (without an ORB) is the following. Module *A* defines and implements some object and message types for local (non-distributed) operation, but some messages are potentially distributable and are therefore defined as extensions of DistMessages.Msg. In order to later adapt A's objects for distributed operation without modifying A, a new module *DistA* is implemented to provide new handles (message dispatchers) for distributed objects. Some objects will now only be proxies whose handles pass on the messages to their original copies on other hosts, via DistMessaging.DistHandle. At a later stage, when a complete ORB will be built, this message-routing functionality (as well as object and proxy creation) is to be integrated into the ORB itself, thereby eliminating the need for separate modules such as DistA.

As is detailed in the next section, a *precompiler* called *GenDistMessages* is used to automatically generate a communications module for a specific message type, which provides the message-specific procedures for message instantiation (type determination), message copying, message length determination, message sending and message receiving (data type conversion). In the example of module A, module *AGen* has been automatically generated by the GenDistMessages precompiler out of information from module A.

An alternative to generating message-specific modules would be to use only *dynamic message fields* in messages, similar to dynamic attributes in System 3. An object would be defined for every data type to be used in message fields, together with its object-specific procedures for instantiation and linearization. While representing a possible solution, this restriction of message field types would not provide the same level of compatibility with System 3 messaging as the implemented solution.

3.2 Message-Specific Communications Module Generation

As has been explained in the Oberon-specific issues (section 2.3), necessary type information about messages to support linearization and re-instantiation is not available at runtime. The only portable approach is therefore to access this information at compile-time to create a message-specific support module. Due to the dynamic loading and linking possibilites of Oberon systems, no runtime flexibility is compromised in this way: the specific support module procedures are accessed automatically via an Oberon command. The message-specific modules are *generated automatically by the GenDistMessages precompiler*, therefore the cost of requiring these modules is relatively small.

The creation of this precompiler also required comparatively little efforts. It has been written as an extensible attribute grammar (EAG) [10] specification, as an extension to an existing Oberon frontend EAG specification, and generated with our CHIPS compiler-compiler (Components for Highly Integrated Process Support, part of the GIPSY [11] project). Due to the extensibility of EAG specifications, the extension of the Oberon frontend specification to create the precompiler was rather straightforward.

The GenDistMessages precompiler finds the relevant message types in an Oberon module, and generates the required communications procedures as Oberon source code, creating a module whose name is the original module's name with "Gen" appended. Only globally defined message types which are direct or indirect extensions of DistMessages.Msg, and which are exported and marked with the comment "(* Dist *)" are handled, with any number of record fields, but only the exported ones are handled. The fields may be of any of the eight basic Oberon types (BOOLEAN, CHAR, SHORTINT, INTEGER, LONGINT, REAL, LONGREAL, SET) as well as ARRAY integer OF CHAR. A dynamic list of LONGINT is also currently supported, and more types can be added as required. Support for more generic extensible types may be provided in future - problems such as the linearization of circular data structures are however not treated.

Per handled message type, six procedures are generated: One procedure each is generated to *read* and to *write* the (exported) message fields from/to a TCP connection (temporarily supplied in a global variable in DistMessaging to avoid using TCP in the basic message type), using the relevant TCP procedures to provide the platfrom-dependent data type conversion. A procedure to *copy* the message fields from one instance to another, and a procedure to calculate its *length* at runtime (which may vary if dynamic data structures are used) are generated. A fifth procedure, a command, provides message *initialization*, assigning the previous four procedures to corresponding method fields (procedure variables) defined in DistMessages.Msg. The sixth procedure is a *command to instantiate a new message* (also calling the initialization procedure). In this way, after message instantiation with its command via an up-call (e.g. from module DistMessaging), its other message-specific procedures are available as method fields in the message and are called from module DistMessaging during message transmission (respectively a message instantiated otherwise may be initialized for distribution using the initialization command).

BGen (fig.6) is an example module: It has been generated automatically by the GenDistMessages precompiler out of module B (fig.5) which defines BMsg extending AMsg defined in module A (fig.4), illustrating message extensibility: the relevant procedures of AMsg (here in the separate module AGen, not shown) are called by those of BMsg where necessary.

```
MODULE A;

    IMPORT DistMessages;

    TYPE
        AMsg* = RECORD
            (DistMessages.Msg) (* Dist *)
            i*: INTEGER;
        END;

END A.
```

Fig.4: Module A

```
MODULE B;

    IMPORT A;

    TYPE
        BMsg* = RECORD
            (A.AMsg) (* Dist *)
            n*: LONGINT;
        END;

END B.
```

Fig.5: Module B

```
MODULE BGen;

(* Generated by GenDistMessages *)

    IMPORT Objects, TCP, DM := DistMessaging, B, AGen;

    TYPE
        BMsgPtr* = POINTER TO B.BMsg;

    PROCEDURE ReadBMsg*(VAR M: Objects.ObjMsg);
    BEGIN
```

```
      WITH M: B.BMsg DO
        AGen.ReadAMsg(M);
        TCP.ReadLInt(DM.msgC, M.n);
      END;
    END ReadBMsg;

    PROCEDURE WriteBMsg*(VAR M: Objects.ObjMsg);
    BEGIN
      WITH M: B.BMsg DO
        AGen.WriteAMsg(M);
        TCP.WriteLInt(DM.msgC, M.n);
      END;
    END WriteBMsg;

    PROCEDURE CopyBMsg*(VAR M0, M1: Objects.ObjMsg);
    BEGIN
      WITH M0: B.BMsg DO
        WITH M1: B.BMsg DO
          AGen.CopyAMsg(M0, M1);
          M1.n := M0.n;
        END;
      END;
    END CopyBMsg;

    PROCEDURE LenBMsg*(VAR M: Objects.ObjMsg): INTEGER;
    BEGIN
      WITH M: B.BMsg DO
        RETURN AGen.LenAMsg(M) + 4
      END;
    END LenBMsg;

    PROCEDURE InitBMsg*;
    BEGIN
      DM.NewMsg.Read := ReadBMsg;
      DM.NewMsg.Write := WriteBMsg;
      DM.NewMsg.Copy := CopyBMsg;
      DM.NewMsg.Len := LenBMsg;
      COPY("B.BMsg", DM.NewMsg.type);
    END InitBMsg;

    PROCEDURE NewBMsg*;
    VAR M: BMsgPtr;
    BEGIN
      NEW(M);
      DM.NewMsg := M;
      InitBMsg;
    END NewBMsg;

END BGen.
```

Fig.6: Automatically Generated Module BGen

3.3 Messaging Operation

A description of a messaging operation illustrates the dynamic interaction of issues described statically in sections 3.1 and 3.2, in particular usage of the specific message fields in DistMessages.Msg. A message M is sent from an object X to an object Y (on different hosts), in a manner compatible with System 3 messaging: Y is represented by a proxy YP on X's host, and X calls YP.handle(YP, M) as usual, the only precondition is that the message's type must have been assigned (as a string) to its M.type field beforehand. X's host is in the client role for this operation, Y's host is in the server role. The operation runs as follows (illustrated in fig.7 for request and response):

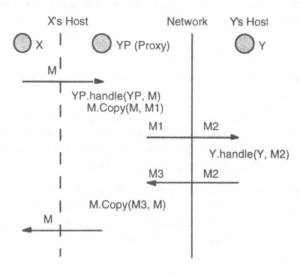

Fig.7: Messaging Operation (Request and Response)

Client: X calls YP.handle(YP, M). If YP is a distributed object, it has a handle that checks for distributed messages. If M is one, and YP's address (e.g. in a dynamic attribute) refers to a different machine, YP is actually only a proxy on the client and it calls DistMessaging.DistHandle with M and Y's address and name. DistHandle then allocates a copy M1 of M on the heap as a pointer type (in order to be able to insert it in a message queue for sending, as M is only on the stack) as follows: Its M.type field is used to determine its generator command to allocate the new message M1, then M.Copy(M, M1) is called to copy all fields (which are accessible due to WITH type guards). For asynchronous operation, control is returned and sending is performed by a background task only when the connection is available (to avoid blocking), while for synchronous operation, a blocking send is performed immediately. For the third and fourth execution styles, outstanding responses to asynchronous requests will be handled by storing the notifier procedure - to be called (with parameters) when the response arrives - in a data structure referenced by the message (not yet implemented). Upon sending, the length (calling M1.Len), M1.type, the object's name, and the fields (calling M1.Write) are sent.

In our DIPS environment, some messages may also be created dynamically (through a command), as not all message types are determined at compile-time of message-sending procedures. In this case, M is already a dynamic object (pointer type) on the heap, and an *optimization* is to not copy the message but to use the original one (if it is known not to be modified). The message must be of type *DistMessages.PtrMsg*, with a pointer to itself in M.ptr (as the pointer cannot be portably derived from the record afterwards), used as above (i.e. inserted in the message send queue).

Server: A server background task receives M1's length, to determine how many bytes to wait for, its type, to determine its generator command to allocate the new message M2 (also initializing its methods), the object's name, and calls M2.Read to receive its fields. Then DistMessages.ObjHandle is called with the object's name and M2 (referenced with ^). This either finds the object Y in the server's list of loaded objects (in ORBObjects), or loads it, and finally calls Y.handle(Y, M2).

If an answer is required, M2 (modified by Y) is inserted in the return queue to the client, to be sent back to X the same way.

Client: For a synchronous response, the client performs a blocking wait in DistHandle, so when the response arrives, DistHandle's variable parameter M is still of the correct dynamic type, so the fields from the response message M3 can be copied back to M using M.Copy(M3, M), and control is returned from DistHandle.

For an asynchronous response, a specified up-call procedure will be called (to be implemented). A numbering scheme for messages is also planned in order to support *recursive* operation, e.g. a request may cause another request to be sent back before the response is sent, but care must then be taken to avoid deadlocks.

4 Conclusions

The successfully implemented solution demonstrates that it is possible to provide a distributed messaging architecture on top of current Oberon systems without requiring system modifications. This could provide a basis for a full ORB implemenation for distributed Oberon objects, as will be used in our DIPS project, and on the longer run possibly even for a CORBA-compliant one. Since the importance of distributed objects will undoubtedly increase in future, the availability of distributed objects in Oberon may provide additional attractiveness to Oberon systems.

While there have been some efforts to extend various Oberon systems for distributed operation, e.g. some in [2] or the recent [7], the main distinctions of this work are that no changes of existing systems are required, that compatibility with Oberon System 3 messaging is provided, and that it is aimed at supporting general-purpose distributed objects. Also, only a lean messaging system is proposed here and not a full remote procedure call or network objects (e.g. [3]) implementation - as in non-distributed Oberon systems, it is up to the object's handles to interpret incoming messages as method calls; however, an ORB can be added on top of our proposed system. While the presented solution may seem complicated and costly, it was necessary to use workarounds for the Oberon issues detailed in section 2.3, in order not to compromise compatibility and portability, i.e. in order not to require changes to Oberon System 3. While the original Oberon system was specifically designed for single-workstation operation, future system revisions may include some proposals of section 2.3 in order to provide improved built-in support for distributed objects. In this respect, the proposed Active Objects [6] (Oberon language extension) seem a highly interesting concept as they provide amongst others preemptive priority scheduling (addressing our most important issue) and object-local activity control (eliminating the need for coroutines or a workaround).

An elegant way of providing the message-specific operations without compromising runtime flexibility has been found with the EAG-specified GenDistMessages precompiler (created with our CHIPS compiler-compiler) that automatically generates the necessary procedures at a negligible cost.

Acknowledgements

I would like to thank the other members of the GIPSY project team, Tobias Murer and Andreas Würtz, for their support, and the anonymous referees for some helpful comments. The GIPSY project has been funded in part by the Swiss Priority Programme (SPP) Informatics Research of the Swiss National Science Foundation.

References

[1] Adler, R. M. Emerging Standards for Component Software. *IEEE Computer,* March 1995, 68-77.

[2] Advances in Modular Languages - *Proc. JMLC (Joint Modular Languages Conference),* Ulm, 1994.

[3] Birrell, A. D., Nelson, G., Owicki, S., Wobber, E. P. Network Objects. *Software Practice and Experience,* 25(S4), December 1995, 87-130. Also appeared as Digital Systems Research Center (SRC) Research Report 115, available at <ftp: //gatekeeper.dec.com/pub/DEC/SRC/research-reports/SRC-115.ps.Z>.

[4] Common Object Request Broker Architecture and Specification (CORBA) V2.0, Object Management Group. Available at <http://www.omg.org/docs/ptc/96-03-04.pdf>, 1996.

[5] Gutknecht, J. Oberon System 3: Vision of a Future Software Technology. *Software-Concepts and Tools,* 15, 1994, 45-54. Also: Oberon System 3 home page, <http: //www-cs.inf.ethz.ch/Oberon/System3.html>, 1996.

[6] Gutknecht, J. Do the Fish Really Need Remote Control? A Proposal for Self-Active Objects in Oberon. *Proc. JMLC (Joint Modular Languages Conference),* Linz, 1997.

[7] Hof, M. Partially Distributed Objects. *Proc. ECOOP-96 (European Conference on Object-Oriented Programming) Workshop WS9: Putting Distributed Objects to Work.* Available at <http://oberon.ssw.uni-linz.ac.at/Projects/DistrObjects.html>, 1996.

[8] Knasmüller, Markus. Adding Persistence to the Oberon-System (Project Oberon-D). Institut für Informatik (Systemsoftware), Johannes Kepler Universität Linz, Report 6, January 1996.

[9] Marais, J.L. Towards End-User Objects: The Gadgets User Interface System. *Advances in Modular Languages - Proc. JMLC (Joint Modular Languages Conference),* Ulm, 1994, 407-420.

[10] Marti, R., Murer, T. Extensible Attribute Grammars. *TIK Report No. 6,* Computer Engineering and Networks Laboratory, ETH Zürich, December 1992.

[11] Murer, T., Würtz, A., Scherer, D., Schweizer, D. GIPSY: Generating Integrated Process support Systems - Project Overview. *TIK Report No. 22,* Computer Engineering and Networks Laboratory, ETH Zürich, December 1996, available at <http://www.tik.ee.ethz.ch/Publications/TIK-Reports/TIK-Reports.html>. Also: Project GIPSY home page (with subprojects CHIPS and DIPS), <http: //www.tik.ee.ethz.ch/~gipsy/>, 1996.

[12] Orfali, R., Harkey, D., Edwards, J. The Essential Distributed Objects Survival Guide. Wiley, 1996.

[13] Overview of Hypertext Transfer Protocol-Next Generation (HTTP-NG). <http: //www.w3.org/pub/WWW/Protocols/HTTP-NG/Overview.html>, 1996.

[14] Scherer, D. TCP/IP for MacOberon and PowerMac Oberon. *The Oberon User Group, Newsletter Number 3,* Institute for Computer Systems, ETH Zurich, December 1994.

[15] Scherer, D., Murer, T., Würtz, A. Designing the Distributed Architecture DIPS for Cooperative Software Engineering. *Proc. HICSS-30 (30th Hawaii International Conference on System Sciences),* January 1997.

[16] Tanenbaum, A.W. Computer Networks, 2nd ed. Prentice-Hall, 1989.

[17] Templ, J. Metaprogramming in Oberon. Diss. ETH Zürich No. 10655, 1994.

[18] Wirth, N. The programming language Oberon. *Software-Practice and Experience,* 18(7), 1988, 671-690.

[19] Wirth, N., Gutknecht, J. Project Oberon: The Design of an Operating System and Compiler. Addison-Wesley, ACM Press, 1992.

Just-in-Time Stub Generation

Markus Hof

Department of Computer Science (System Software)
Johannes Kepler University Linz, Austria
hof@ssw.uni-linz.ac.at

Abstract. In distributed object systems, one generates local surrogate objects to achieve transparent remote method invocations. These surrogates intercept method invocations, transfer the invocations to the actual (remote) object, and invoke the respective method by using so-called stub code. We describe a method which automatically generates surrogate and stub code. The actual generation is delayed until run time, which allows late adaptations to current needs and restrictions. Objects using this mechanism are not necessarily derived from a common base class.

1 Introduction

Today's highly interconnected systems put more and more emphasis on the exploitation of the advantages inherent to a network, i.e. increased fault tolerance, better availability, and easier scalability. However, network systems have their disadvantages as well, and it is not easy to actually exploit their advantages. Independent failure modes, which have to be handled when dealing with several computers, increase the complexity of software development. Additionally, networked systems are often heterogeneous and highly dynamic. The configuration of available computation resources may change on a moments notice. To cope with these problems different approaches have been proposed. A common approach is to put part of the additional complexity into the object system, i.e., to hide it from the developer, by extending the notion of objects and classes.

The purpose of the work described in this paper is to add support for distributed objects to the Oberon system [Rei92]. In particular, distributed objects should support the implementation of distributed models (in the sense of the MVC paradigm [KrP88]), i.e., they should support the adaptation of existing Oberon applications (ease the transition of existing MVC applications) to a distributed environment. To ease this transformation we proclaim automatic just-in-time generation of surrogate and stub code. Generating stub code not in advance, but only on demand, allows the system to adapt the generated stub and surrogate code to current circumstances (e.g., recent changes in the network topology). Additionally, delaying code generation as long as possible allows one to distribute objects, which are not aware of the network and the notion of distributed objects.

1.1 Overview

A client sees an object as a reference into memory, some data fields, and a set of type bound procedures (methods). An application does not have to distinguish between local and remote objects (see Figure 1). Different access methods are handled transparently by the distributed object system.

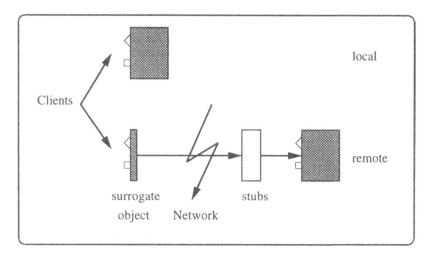

Figure 1: View on objects as seen by clients

The application has transparent access to all objects regardless of their actual location. Oberon's strict type checking is still enforced and run-time type information is still available. For every accessed remote object the system automatically generates a so called *surrogate object*. A surrogate object is the local representative (placeholder) of an object located on another site. It offers exactly the same interface as its associated actual object, but redirects incoming requests to the actual object. The request (object ID, invoked method, and actual parameters) is transformed (marshalled) to a byte stream which is sent from the surrogate to the stub. This stream includes all information needed to reconstruct the receiver object, the called method, and the actual parameters. This mechanism is similar to the RPC mechanism [BiNe84, Tan95], except that a receiver object is passed along with each new invocation.

For every method there is a surrogate part and a stub part, as each method has its own individual interface (signature). The surrogate part

- offers the same interface as the actual method,
- transforms the incoming data into a byte stream,
- transfers the stream to the corresponding stub code,
- waits for the result,
- and returns the resulting data to the client.

The respective stub

- receives a byte stream,
- reconstructs the streamed parameters,
- calls the method of the actual object, while handing on the reconstructed parameters,
- converts the results into a byte stream,
- and sends the stream back to the surrogate.

In order to put records and even complex data structures into a byte stream, the stub and surrogate code uses a so-called *linearizer*. Linearizers convert arbitrary data structures into machine-independent byte streams and vice versa.

1.2 Just-In-Time Stub Generation

Generation of stub and surrogate code can be highly automated. The common approach, e.g. chosen in CORBA [COR95] or Network Objects [BiN94], is to generate stub and surrogate (also called skeleton code) statically, in advance, previous to the compilation of the client code. We delay the generation as long as possible and generate the needed code dynamically on demand. The advantages of dynamic code generation over static code generation are:

- Using dynamic code generation, different variants of surrogates and stubs can be generated depending on current needs of the application (e.g., parameters could either be transformed using deep copy or shallow copy).
- If surrogates and stubs are only generated at run time they need no space on the disk.
- Statically generated stub code is no longer portable and has to be generated for each new platform.

2 Implementation

The implementation consists of two parts. First, the generic marshaller, which is responsible for the linearization of parameters, and second, the stub and surrogate generator. This paper mostly elaborates on the second part, but gives a quick overview over the marshalling mechanism.

The generated code actually works as a framework. The stub and surrogate code itself does not contain any dependencies on distribution, but acts only as a general-purpose redirection mechanism. Distributed objects is just one possible application of this scheme. Other applications might be a method invocation logging facility.

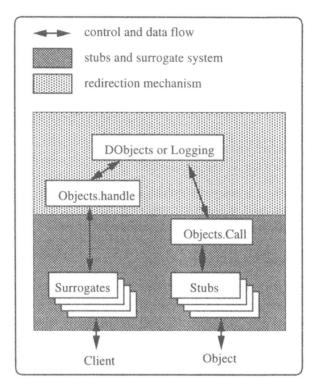

Figure 2: Overview of redirection mechanism

When a surrogate method is invoked, it transforms its parameters to a byte stream and passes this stream to the currently installed redirection mechanism in *Objects.handle* (up-call) (see Figure 2). The redirection mechanism may transfer the stream over a network, log the method invocation, or do anything else. If the stream is transferred over the network, the receiving site passes it to a procedure called *Objects.Call* which is part of the stub system. *Objects.Call* reads the method identifier from the stream and invokes the appropriate stub, which then calls the actual method. *Objects.Call* can invoke arbitrary stubs, as they all have the same interface.

The installed redirection mechanism is completely hidden from the client and from the implementation of the invoked object. Therefore, one can freely swap between different mechanisms invalidating neither the client's nor the object's implementation.

2.1 Marshalling

The marshalling mechanism consists of a manual part and an automatic part. For the manual part, the programmer has to write a marshaller for every structured type used as a parameter or receiver type. This marshaller is activated whenever an instance of this type is marshalled or unmarshalled. It has to decide which instance variables are written to or read from the stream.

The automatic part of the marshalling mechanism takes care of the inter-record dependencies. It stores information about inter-record dependencies together with the actual record data as stored by the individual marshallers. This information allows the restoration of arbitrary data structures (trees, circular lists, ...).

All data stored to a stream is automatically converted into a well-defined byte- and bit-ordering, i.e. the resulting stream is platform independent. Data read from a stream is automatically converted back to the local processor specific ordering.

2.1.1 Manual Marshallers

A marshaller consists of a sequence of calls to the linearizer for each record field to be read or written. The mechanism is completely orthogonal with respect to writing and reading, i.e. the same calls are executed while reading from or writing to the linearizer. Therefore we only need one marshaller per type (see Figure 3), which is used for writing to, as well as for reading from a stream. The linearizer offers calls for every basic Oberon type, e.g. INTEGER, BOOLEAN, PROCEDURE, ...

```
TYPE
   MyPtr = POINTER TO MyPtrDesc;
   MyPtrDesc = RECORD
      i: INTEGER;
      r: REAL
   END;

PROCEDURE Marshall (lin: Linearizer.Linearizer; o: SYSTEM.PTR);
VAR obj: MyPtr;
BEGIN
   obj := SYSTEM.VAL (MyPtr, o);
   lin.Integer (obj.i);
   lin.Real (obj.r)
END Marshall;
```

Figure 3: Example marshaller for type *MyPtr*

Special considerations:

- A marshaller for a given type *T* does not have to care about possible base types of *T*. They are handled automatically and the correct run-time type is restored.
- For special data structures it is possible to distinguish between reading and writing, e.g. when marshalling a reference to a font (see Figure 4), one may only write the name of the font instead of the complete font information:

```
TYPE
    MyPtr = POINTER TO MyPtrDesc;
    MyPtrDesc = RECORD
        f: Fonts.Font
    END;

PROCEDURE Marshall (lin: Linearizer.Linearizer; o: SYSTEM.PTR);
VAR obj: MyPtr;
BEGIN
    obj := SYSTEM.VAL (MyPtr, o);
    IF lin.writing THEN lin.String (obj.f.name)
    ELSE lin.String (name); obj.f := Fonts.Font (name)
    END
END Marshall;
```

Figure 4: Marshaller distinguishing read and write

- When storing or retrieving pointers, a marshaller has two possibilities. It may either perform a deep copy or a shallow copy (see Figure 5). A deep copy of an object *x* duplicates object *x* onto the stream. Objects referenced by *x* are handled as defined in the marshaller handling x. An independent copy of *x* is generated, whenever the byte stream is unmarshalled. This may be slow and quite space consuming. A shallow copy of object *x* puts only the object identifier of *x* onto the byte stream. This is fast and needs just a few bytes. However, the program, which unmarshalls the stream, has to cope with incoming object identities and create a suitable surrogate object.

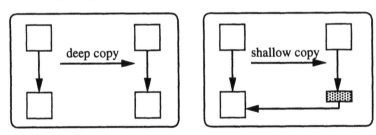

Figure 5: Deep versus shallow copy

2.1.2 Automatic Marshalling

If a parameter represents a data structure (e.g., a list or a graph), the whole data structure is saved and restored automatically. Object identities are saved onto the stream, i.e., references to the same object will still reference the same object after the data structure has been restored. The linearizer achieves this by putting each object onto the stream only once. If an object is referenced for the first time, its run-time type and data is written into the stream. If the same object is referenced again, the linearizer stores only an identifier, which allows the restoring process to identify the actual - previously restored - object. This allows marshalling of arbitrary data structures, as well as reducing the size of the resulting byte stream.

2.2 Just-In-Time Stub Generation

Stub and surrogate code are generated on demand, i.e., if either an external object is requested or a local object is made public. The code is generated, loaded, and discarded as necessary. This allows late adaptation to current needs and to recent restrictions.

Our system offers two choices when implementing a new class. First, one may choose for each method, wether it is executed locally on the surrogate object, or wether the request is forwarded to the actual object. Second, one may influence the mode in which parameters are passed.

Our stub generator needs three different kinds of information:

- Which methods should be executed on the surrogate object and which on the actual object. This information has to be supplied by the developer.
- Each parameter with a pointer type is - by default - passed by making a deep copy. However, in order to achieve a shallow copy, it is possible to change this behaviour for individual parameters. This information has to be supplied by the developer.
- The complete interface of the object's type. Our current stub generator uses the corresponding source file as input. However, using existing metaprogramming facilities which offer the complete reference information [Tem94, StMö96] of all types, would allow us to distribute objects without making the corresponding source code public.

The stub generation is platform independent. It only requires an Oberon compiler using the portable front-end OP2 [Cre90].

As an example let's look at the following type definition (Figure 6):

```
TYPE
  MyPtr = POINTER TO MyPtrDesc;
  MyPtrDesc = RECORD
    i: INTEGER;
    PROCEDURE (obj: MyPtr) Method (VAR i: INTEGER; p: MyPtr)
  END;
```

Figure 6: Example type definition

The stub generator will generate two Oberon procedures (surrogate method and stub procedure) (see Figure 7). As one can see, both stub and surrogate code, mainly linearize and restore parameters (see Figure 7). The surrogate code makes an up-call to *Objects.handle* in order to redirect the method invocation. It passes as parameters the receiver object, the streamed actual parameters, and a method identifier. The method identifier is a unique constant value, which identifies the invoked method. This constant is generated automatically by the stub generator.

```
PROCEDURE (obj: MyPtr) Method (p: MyPtr) : INTEGER;
VAR lin: Linearizers.Linearizer; s: Linearizers.Stream; retVal: INTEGER;
BEGIN
   lin := Linearizers.NewWriter ();
   lin.Ptr (p);
   s := lin.Stream ();
   s := Objects.handle (obj, s, xxx); (*  xxx is a method identifier *)
   lin := Linearizers.NewReader (s);
   lin.Integer (retVal);
   RETURN retVal
END Method;

PROCEDURE Stub (o: SYS.PTR; VAR data: Linearizers.Stream);
VAR lin: Linearizers.Linearizer; obj, p: MyPtr; retVal: INTEGER;
BEGIN
   obj := SYS.VAL (MyPtr, o);
   lin := Linearizers.NewReader (data);
   lin.Ptr (p);
   retVal := obj.Method (p);
   lin := Linearizers.NewWriter ();
   lin.Integer (retVal);
   data := lin.Stream ()
END Stub;
```

Figure 7: Generated stub and surrogate code

Actually, the shown source code (see Figure 7) is never generated in this form. The generator directly creates an abstract syntax tree, as it is created by OP2 [Cre90]. This syntax tree is then translated to code by the compiler back end. Generating the syntax tree instead of human readable source code is simpler and faster, since no scanner and parser has to be used during code generation.

Recent work [FrKi96, Java95] shows advantages of just-in-time compilation (e.g., platform independence). However, delaying not only the actual code generation, but also allowing late parameterization has some additional advantages:

- The stub generator is sufficiently fast and runs only once per type. There is no significant speed penalty when using delayed code generation. The generated stub and surrogate code remain valid for the lifetime of their respective type.
- The stub generator is small and simple (approximately 400 lines of source code).
- The generator is system independent, i.e., it runs on every computer equipped with an OP2 Oberon compiler.
- The stubs and surrogates are platform independent, since the actual coding into machine instructions is done at run-time.
- Since there are no persistent files (interface definition, stub sources, stub object files, ...) there are no version conflicts.

- The development of clients is independent of the stub generator (no stub headers have to be included).
- It is possible to adapt stub and surrogate code at run-time.

3 Related Work

Other stub generators require the source code generation to be done before the application is developed. The application includes information about the stubs and the surrogate objects (e.g., using include files in the CORBA C++ mapping [COR95]).

We don't build a new system with a new language, as e.g. Emerald [JuLe88], but emphasize the reuse of existing systems. Similar to the network objects [BiN94] we primarily try to keep our system simple without discriminating its generality. The main difference between our system and other systems is that we delay stub generation until run time. Contrary to the network objects we support parameters of type PROCEDURE, i.e. one may initiate up-calls on remote systems.

4 Conclusions

Our system offers a simple, fast and flexible redirection mechanism for method invocations. It is intended for supporting distributed objects with transparent remote method invocations. However, the mechanism is more general and can be used to implement other applications, e.g. logging of method invocations.

By delaying stub generation until run-time, we achieve a higher degree of flexibility than similar systems, which force the programmer to generate stub and surrogate code before the actual application is developed.

Some important points have not yet been addressed in our distributed object system. Currently, we work on the implementation of distributed garbage collection. Additionally, the Oberon language has, unfortunately, no exception handling. We therefore have difficulties to offer an elegant solution for handling exceptions due to the redirection of the method invocation, e.g. broken connections. Currently we handle these problems using a state associated with each surrogate object, which indicates earlier failures.

5 References

[BiN94] Birrell A., Nelson G., Owicki S., Wobber E.: Network Objects. SRC Research Report 115, 1994

[BiNe84] Birrell A., Nelson B.: Implementing Remote Procedure Calls. ACM Transactions on Computer Systems, vol. 2, Feb. 1984

[COR95] The Common Object Request Broker: Architecture and Specification. OMG, Revision 2.0, July 1995

[Cre90] Crelier R.: OP2: A Portable Oberon Compiler. Institut für Computersysteme, Report 125 Februar 1990, ETH Zürich

[FrKi96] Franz M., Kistler T.: Slim Binaries. University of California Irvine, Technical Report 96-24

[Java95] The Java Virtual Machine Specification. Sun Microsystems, Release 1.0, August 1995

[JuLe88] Jul E., Levy H., Hutchinson N., Black A.: Fine-grained mobility in the Emerald system. ACM Transactions on Computer Systems, 6(1):109-133, 1988

[KrP88] Krasner G., Pope S.: A Cookbook for Using the MVC User Interface Paradigm in Smalltalk. Journal of Object Oriented Programming Aug./Sep. 1988

[Rei92] Reiser M., Wirth N.: Programming in Oberon - Steps beyond Pascal and Modula-2. Addison-Wesley 1992

[StMö96] Steindl C., Mössenböck H.: Metaprogramming Facilities in Oberon for Windows an Power Macintosh. University of Linz, Department for Systemsoftware, Report 8, July 1996

[Tan95] Tanenbaum A.: Distributed Operating Systems. Prentice Hall 1995

[Tem94] Templ J.: Metaprogramming in Oberon. PhD thesis, Swiss Federal Institute of Technology (ETH Zürich), 1994, Number 10655

Do the Fish Really Need Remote Control?
A Proposal for Self-Active Objects in Oberon

Jürg Gutknecht, ETH Zürich

Abstract

Based on the language Oberon we propose a unified framework for concurrent, object-oriented programming. Inspired by simulation, the idea is to regard objects as processes in contrast with the more common approach treating processes as objects. More concretely, our framework extends the original Oberon language by four new concepts: (a) Object-centered access protection, (b) object-local activity control, (c) system-guarded assertions and (d) preemptive priority scheduling. (a) and (b) are expressed syntactically by upgraded record types, (c) by a passivation/activation mechanism and (d) by a priority option. None of the conventional facilities like semaphores, locks, critical regions, signals, channels, rendez-vous, forks etc. are primitive constructs in our framework. Currently, an implementation of a compiler, a corresponding runtime kernel and a non-blocking local server exists for native Intel architectures.

Keywords: Object Oriented Programming, Active Objects, Concurrency, Multiprogramming, Oberon.

1 Introduction

The technology of object-oriented software construction is a manifestation of the remarkable level that has been reached in this area in terms of abstraction, modularity, extensibility and reusability. However, at least in practically available systems, the conceptual combination of objects with processes has been neglected. Merely re-acting to messages, objects are typically passive and remote controlled by concept. This is regrettable in several respects, primarily in view of the desire for a high degree of coherence in programs on one hand and for most possible self-containedness of objects on the other hand. This latter aspect is of particular importance in connection with portable end-user objects that are now available, for example, via Internet in the form of "plug-ins" and "applets".

2 Processes and Objects

From a conventional point of view, the basic ingredients of a program are *processes* and *objects*, coupled by the obvious *operating-on* relation. Correspondingly, software research has pursued the conceptual development of processes and objects separately and has paid little attention to their integration or even their unification. In an object-oriented environment, multiprocess functionality is commonly provided in the form of a separate hierarchy of process classes, thereby emphasizing separation rather than unification. Smalltalk and Java [1] are prominent representatives of this kind. Due to its non-symmetric rules of inheritance among the two kinds of objects (active and passive), Synchronous C++ [2] is a further example of a separating architecture.

A different and somehow dual approach is taken by simulation programming. Rather than treating processes as objects, simulation programming treats objects as processes. Simulated objects often show a hybrid nature expressing itself in a continuous alternation of active and passive phases. For example, a simulated device takes an active role when operating and a passive role when being serviced, and a customer in a shopping center can be considered active when browsing around the shops and passive while waiting in a queue for check-out.

The two views, conventional and simulation, are substantially different. The essential point is that, in the conventional case, objects are basically passive in the sense that they are completely controlled by remote processes via message passing in contrast to the case of simulation, where objects are self-controlling their activity in principle or, in short, are *self-active*. We prefer the simulation view because it is more general (passive objects can be regarded as active objects with an empty active phase) and because it leads to more coherent mappings from given specifications to programs.

A trivial but entertaining example is the well-known animation of an underwater world (often used as a screen-saver) that mimics a random population of fish with some greedy sharks among them. Most naturally, the life-story of every single fish is defined intrinsically by some type-specific control-program that operates on its internal state: Ordinary fish move peacefully unless they are caught by a shark. Should this case occur, they change to a skeleton and sink down to the ground. Sharks are harmless unless they are hungry. When they are, they snatch any fish crossing their path coincidentally. We shall take up this example again in Section 4 when we present a sketch of a corresponding Oberon program.

3 A Unified Framework

Inspired by simulation programming in general and by the Simula language family [3] (the very origin of object-oriented programming) in particular, we have experimented with modelling self-active objects on the Oberon language and environment [4], [5]. The result is a unified framework for concurrent, object-oriented programming. It can briefly be summarized in terms of four new concepts on the level of individual objects that, together, constitute the core of our framework: (a) Protected access, (b) local activity control, (c) guarded assertions and (d) preemptive priority scheduling. (a) and (b) support the *competitive* aspects of concurrency, (b), (c) and (d) its *collaborative* aspects.

These concepts are integrated smoothly into the Oberon language by an upgrade of record types and the addition of one keyword and one built-in procedure.

We now present our unified framework in three steps: (a) Introduction of the new language constructs, (b) explanation of the new object concepts and (c) illustration of their combination by two comprehensive program examples from different areas.

Upgraded Record Types

Record types are used in Oberon as a model for object classes. A record type can be viewed as a production pattern for object instances. The two kinds of components of a record type are data variables and procedure variables. They are mapped at creation time to the new object's state variables and its (instance-specific) methods respectively.

New types can be derived from an existing base-type by extension of the set of components. Such derived types inherit the base-type's structure and therefore correspond to subclasses in object-oriented terminology.

Like modules, record types define a static scope. It is now natural to use this scope for the specification and implementation of local functionality, in particular for (a) *controlled access* to local data and (b) implementation of local activities, i.e. of *intrinsic behavior*. For this purpose, we upgrade Oberon record types by (a) optional procedure entries for controlled access and (b) an optional record body for the implementation of intrinsic behavior.

A further syntactical upgrade concerns an *option specification clause* for statement blocks, i.e. sequences of statements delimited by BEGIN ... END brackets. In original Oberon, statement blocks are scheduled unconditionally and uniformly as sub-routines of the (one and only) system process. In our new multi-process environment, however, different possible scheduling options exist as, for example, exclusive access, separate thread of control and special priority. Accordingly, the syntax now allows a list of runtime options and directives to be specified within a pair of curly braces immediately following the BEGIN keyword of a statement block.

Example:

```
TYPE
  Object = RECORD (Object0) (* derived from base-type Object0 *)
    VAR
      t: T; (* state variables *)
      h: H; (* instance-specific methods *)

    PROCEDURE P (t: T); (* procedure entry for controlled access *)
    BEGIN { optionlist } (* option specification clause *)
```

```
... (* statement sequence *)
END P;

BEGIN (* record body implementing intrinsic behavior *)
  { optionlist } (* option specification clause *)
  ... (* statement sequence *)
END Object;
```

Remarks:

(1.) Procedure entry implementations are inherited in type-extensions unless they are overridden by a new implementation (under the same name and with the same parameter list). Within the scope of the new implementation, the original version can be identified by adding a "↑" to its name. This notation is borrowed from Oberon-2 [6], where it is used for a similar purpose.

(2.) Within the scope of a record type, (unqualified) names of its variables and procedures always refer to components of the current object. The current object as a whole is denoted in the record scope by the new keyword SELF.

(3.) The section keyword VAR and the repetition of the record type's name after the keyword END are optionally allowed as a concession to syntactical conformity with the module construct.

Of course, such far-reaching conformity of object types and modules on the syntactical level should reflect itself on the semantic level. It is therefore justified to clarify the semantical relationship between (upgraded) record types and modules.

Upgraded Record Types versus Modules

We first remember that, by definition, an Oberon module is a set of logically connected ingredients like type-declarations, variables, procedures and body. Partitioning this set in two, type-declarations and complement, the module can be regarded as a (possibly empty) collection of explicit type-declarations and an implicit (upgraded) record type that we call *module type*.

Module types are anonymous and cannot be referred to explicitly, that is they cannot be extended, nor can instances be created explicitly. The one and only instance of a module type is created automatically at loading time: The module itself. However, apart from the anonymity of their type, modules are like any other object and are therefore treated as such consequently by our unified framework. In particular, whenever we refer to object in general, modules are included. Modules as objects are beneficially used to model system-wide resources and services.

It is noteworthy that the presented upgrade of record types significantly increases the language's uniformity and "orthogonality", so that it appears to programmers and compiler-writers as a removed restriction much rather than as extension.

After this formal introduction of syntactic constructs, we are now prepared to focus on their use for the construction of the desired unified framework.

Access Protection

Independent of any self-activity, an object is still an ob-ject and can therefore be used as a *resource*. Only in the simplest of all scenarios, if the object is passive and under exclusive possession of some specific process, no access control is needed. In all other cases, multiple processes may potentially compete for the use of the object, so that some kind of access protection is indispensible. For this reason, we introduce two protective options EXCLUSIVE and SHARED for procedure entries.

We postulate *mutual exclusion* among the processes requiring service from an object via any procedure entry marked EXCLUSIVE. This means that, for every single instance of an object type, one process at most is allowed to be active in the set of its procedures marked EXCLUSIVE at any time. In other words, every process entering this set *locks* the object for the time of its active presence.

The option SHARED refers to a weaker form of access protection. Procedure entries with this option can be shared by an arbitrary number of processes as long as no process is active in an EXCLUSIVE entry. The SHARED option is typically used for *read-only* access.

Procedure entries neither specified as EXCLUSIVE nor as SHARED are unprotected and can be entered unconditionally. They are assumed to implement their own access control.

Example:

```
TYPE
  Object = RECORD
    VAR t: T;

    PROCEDURE P (t: T);
    BEGIN { EXCLUSIVE } ... (* mutually exclusive access*)
    END P;

    PROCEDURE Q (): T;
    BEGIN { SHARED } ... (* shared access *)
    END Q;

    PROCEDURE R (): T;
    BEGIN ... (* unprotected *)
    END R;

  END Object;
```

For any given instance x of type *Object*, multiple processes are allowed to enter x.Q simultaneously. However, if any process enters x.P, mutual exclusion is required and no other process is allowed to enter either x.P or x.Q as long as the first process is still active in x.P. Any process may enter x.R at all times.

Local Activity Control

An object is rarely a pure resource that is used by remote processes only. Typically, the object itself develops some kind of *intrinsic behavior*. We already know that the intrinsic behavior of an object is expressed by its body part, running as a separate and local *thread of control*. In detail, several aspects have to be considered carefully.

A first question arises in connection with initialization. A special mechanism is required because an object must normally be initialized consistently by external parameters before its local process can start. For this purpose, an *initializer* can be distinguished among the procedure entries in the object type by an "&" tag. The way of parameter specification at creation time depends on the kind of the object's type. In the cases of pointer-based types and static types, the actual parameters of the initializer are simply added to the NEW statement's parameter list and to the type specification respectively. For module objects no parameters are allowed.

In the case of extending types several bodies along the base-type chain may exist. By definition, the *total behavior* of an object is the *parallel composition* of these bodies. Objects without a body along their base-type chain or objects whose bodies have been terminated are invariantly passive.

The creation of a general object is thus an atomic three-step action:

Create object = { allocate memory block; call initializer and pass parameters; create and start a separate process for each body in the base-type chain }.

In concluding this section we note that the above introduced protective options EXCLUSIVE and SHARED for procedure entries are applicable in principle to object bodies as well. However, most local processes should not block their object permanently and, therefore, run in unprotected mode. Unprotected local processes access their object's shared data via the official protected interface - as any remote process does.

Example:

```
TYPE
  Object0 = POINTER TO ObjDesc0;
  ObjDesc0 = RECORD (* base-type *)
  BEGIN
    (* local thread of control,
    implementing base part of intrinsic behavior,
    running concurrently with local threads in extending types,
    unprotected *)

    ...
  END ObjDesc0;

  Object = POINTER TO ObjDesc;
  ObjDesc = RECORD (ObjDesc0) (* derived from base-type ObjDesc0 *)
```

```
VAR
  t: T; (* state variables *)
  h: H; (* instance-specific methods *)

PROCEDURE P (t: T); (* procedure entry for controlled access *)
BEGIN { EXCLUSIVE } ... (* statement sequence *)
END P;

PROCEDURE& Init (t: T; h: H); (* tagged as initializer *)
BEGIN ... (* statement sequence, automatically called at creation time *) ...
END Init;

BEGIN
  (* local thread of control,
  implementing extended part of intrinsic behavior,
  running concurrently with local threads in base type,
  unprotected *)
  ...
END ObjDesc;

VAR x: Object;
BEGIN ... NEW(x, myT, myH); ... (* creation of pointer-based object *)
END

VAR X: ObjDesc(myT, myH); (* creation of static object *)
```

Guarded Assertions

Assertions are an important concept in programming. They are typically used at critical points in a program as a safeguard against erroneous continuation. Let us imagine the guard as a universal demon behind the scenes. In a single-process environment where assertions in a given program state are invariantly valid or invalid, the guard simply either lets through or aborts. In a multiprogram, however, the validity of a given assertion may be changed by partner processes and the guard's task is getting more intricate. Instead of just aborting a process in case of an invalid assertion, the guard should rather suspend this process, watch the assertion and resume the process at a later time when the assertion is valid.

We have adapted the concept of assertions to active objects. In this context, suspending an object's process amounts to *passivating* the object, that is to diminishing or to freeze its activity. The built-in operation PASSIVATE serves exactly this purpose. More precisely, the effect of calling PASSIVATE with condition parameter c within object (or module) scope S is

PASSIVATE(c) =
  { suspend current process; unlock S; await c; lock S; resume process }.

The difficult part to implement in the run-time system is *await c* that, of course, must run concurrently with the partner processes. A straightforward solution for the frequent case of c *local* to S is checking c as a side-effect of unlocking S.

Note that this implementation is efficient in terms of context-switches, because no context-switch is needed for the evaluation of the condition. Also useful are global *stable conditions* that are not falsified by peer processes. Such conditions can easily be watched by some periodic system process. A separate report [7] in detail discusses an implementation of self-active objects for the Intel architecture.

Preemptive Priority Scheduling

Regarded on a somewhat lower level of abstraction, the topic of guarded assertions is nothing but the topic of synchronous process scheduling in a different clothing, tailored to our framework of self-active objects. The purpose of this section is a brief discussion of the complementary topic of *asynchronous scheduling* that, within our framework, is based on (a) a priority scheme and (b) time-slicing.

There is only one syntactical feature for the support of implicit scheduling, namely an optional *priority* option: PRIORITY(level). Possible priority levels are non-negative integers, where 0 is lowest priority. When a priority option is omitted, priority level 0 is ssumed.

The essential rule guarantees that no process of any given priority is allowed to progress as long as any process of a higher priority is able to progress (i.e. active and not blocked by some lock of mutual exclusion). This rule implies potential preemption of any process of a priority level lower than the maximum. In particular note this corollary: A precondition for an object to be reactivated in a certain scope is the absence of any higher priority objects that are active in the same scope.

Time-slicing is a processor-sharing scheduling strategy that concedes a time-slice of a certain length to each process before suspending it again in favor of another process. While the use of explicit assertions is far preferable to asynchronous preemption in most cases, time slicing can sometimes be justified to allow a group of independent (and perhaps never-ending) processes to progress simultaneously. In such situations, the option TIMESHARED should be included in the body of an object type as a hint to the runtime system. Note that the implementations of preemptive priority scheduling and time-slicing are very similar. The only difference is that, after suspension of a time-sliced process at the end of a slice, the set of candidates for resumption may include processes on the same priority level.

4 Series of Program Examples

Selective Lister: A Case of Structure Conflict

This first example is a member of a class of problems that have been used to show the benefits of coroutines for the design of seemingly ordinary uniprograms (one process only). The task is the generation of several lists from one input stream of typed items, so that each item goes to one or more lists, according to its type, and each page of each list is headed by a title.

More concretely, the following program produces two lists *List1* and *List2*, where all items of type 1 and type 2 go to *List1* and *List2* respectively and all other items go to both lists. Lists are active objects. They use a one-element buffer for structural decoupling and resolution of the structure conflict. Their type is roughly defined as

```
TYPE
  List = POINTER TO ListDesc;
  ListDesc = RECORD
    VAR buf, x: Item; line: INTEGER;

    PROCEDURE Enter (x: Item);
    BEGIN { EXCLUSIVE } PASSIVATE(buf = NIL); buf := x
    END Enter;

    PROCEDURE Get (VAR x: Item);
    BEGIN { EXCLUSIVE } PASSIVATE(buf # NIL); x := buf; buf := NIL
    END Get;

    PROCEDURE& Init (listName: ARRAY OF CHAR);
    BEGIN buf := NIL
    END Init;

  BEGIN Get(x);
    WHILE type of x # 0 DO PrintTitle;
      line := 0;
      REPEAT PrintItem(x); INC(line); Get(x)
      UNTIL (type of x = 0) OR (line = MaxLine);
      ShowPage
    END
  END ListDesc;
```

The relevant part of the list generator then looks like this:

```
NEW(L1, "List1"); NEW(L2, "List2");
REPEAT Read(x);
  IF type of x = 1 THEN L1.Enter(x)
    ELSIF type of x = 2 THEN L2.Enter(x)
    ELSE L1.Enter(x); L2.Enter(x)
  END
UNTIL type of x = 0
```

Underwater World: A Real-Time Animation

Our second example is the animation of an underwater world, referred to in the title of this article and at the beginning. It is a caricature of a real-time program. Participating objects are (ordinary) fish and sharks. Both kinds of object basically move uniformly and straight with a certain probability of changing direction a little every once in a while. When hungry, sharks catch any fish that happens to cross their way. If they do not succeed, they finally starve. Starved or caught fishes sink down to the ground as skeletons.

On one hand, module *Underwater World* provides two types *Fish* and *Shark*. They essentially represent moving objects with some generic behavior determining their life-story. On the other hand, the module stands for the entire population of fish. Together with the functionality for finding a victim, it is therefore a complex resource object itself that is readily used by sharks.

Notice that types *Fish* and *Shark* are derived from a purely passive base type *Object* that implements general objects in a two-dimensional space together with functionality for (a) moving to a new position within a given (incremental) amount of time and (b) deciding about vicinity to a given area. We emphasize that any "active" reuse of a type whose designer has not taken specific precaution would not be possible in combination with a separating framework based on some root class of active objects as, for example, *Threads* in Java [1].

We should also point out the formal similarity of this real-time example and typical simulation examples. Both use a *Hold* statement for the description of an invariant phase. However, while simulation typically refers to some notion of *virtual* time, *Hold* in the current case refers to *real* time and is provided by the base type *Kernel. Object*.

```
TYPE
  (* passive base object *)
  Object = POINTER TO ObjDesc;
  ObjDesc = RECORD (Kernel.ObjDesc)
    VAR prev, next: Object; X, Y: INTEGER;

  PROCEDURE Move (dT: REAL; dX, dY: INTEGER);
    BEGIN { EXCLUSIVE } Hold(dT); X := X + dX; Y := Y + dY
    END Move;

    PROCEDURE IsClose (X0, Y0: INTEGER): BOOLEAN;
    BEGIN { SHARED } (* decide about vicinity and return result *)
    END IsClose;

    PROCEDURE& Init (X0, Y0: INTEGER);
    BEGIN X := X0; Y := Y0
    END Init;

  END ObjDesc;

  (* active objects *)
  FishDesc = RECORD (ObjDesc)
    VAR dX, dY: INTEGER;
  BEGIN
    LOOP
      (* calculate next step dX, dY in current direction *)
      Move(dT, dX, dY);
      IF next = NIL (* caught *)THEN EXIT END
```

```
    END;
    LOOP
      (* calculate next step dX, dY in sinking direction *)
      Move(dT, dX, dY)
      IF Y <= 0 THEN EXIT END
    END
  END FishDesc;


  SharkDesc = RECORD(ObjDesc)
    VAR dX, dY: INTEGER; obj: Object;
  BEGIN
    LOOP
      (* calculate next step dX, dY in current direction *)
      Move(dT, dX, dY);
      IF (* hungry *)THEN FindVictim(X, Y, obj);
        IF obj IS Fish THEN (* at it *)
          ELSIF (* starved *)THEN EXIT
        END
      END
    END;
    LOOP
      (* calculate next step dX, dY in sinking direction *)
      Move(dT, dX, dY);
      IF Y <= 0 THEN EXIT END
    END
  END SharkDesc;

(* fish population *)
VAR pop: Object;

PROCEDURE Include (pop, obj: Object);
BEGIN { EXCLUSIVE }
  obj.prev := pop; obj.next := pop.next;
  pop.next.prev := obj; pop.next := obj
END Include;

PROCEDURE Exclude (obj: Object);
BEGIN { EXCLUSIVE }
  obj.next.prev := obj.prev; obj.prev.next := obj.next;
  obj.prev := NIL; obj.next := NIL
END Exclude;

PROCEDURE FindVictim (X, Y: INTEGER; VAR obj: Object);
BEGIN { EXCLUSIVE } obj := pop.next;
  WHILE (obj IS Fish) & ~obj.IsClose(X, Y) DO obj := obj.next END;
  IF obj IS Fish THEN Exclude(obj) END
END FindVictim;
```

5 Conclusion and Outlook

The framework presented, that is the set of new concepts together with the corresponding language constructs, shows several attractive properties, distinguishing it from existing and more pragmatic solutions. Most important, the framework is (a) unified, (b) complete and (c) minimal. (a) and (b) can be paraphrased as providing sufficient expressive power for a natural formulation of every possible object-oriented program, every possible process-oriented program (multiprogram, concurrent program) and every combination thereof. (c) means that none of the concepts can be removed without sacrificing property (b).

Our unified framework suggests a programming style that formally resembles simulation programming. However, it is more general thanks to the institution of guarded assertions that allows any kind of genuine concurrency, including parallelism modelled on a multiprocessor architecture.

With the condition-based guarded assertions, the usual self-administration of peer processes (typically implemented by mutual signalling) is replaced in our framework by a systemwide scheduler. A similar (but less rigorous) step has been taken by Ada95 with guarded entries [8]. We believe that the trend to delegate responsibilities from individual participants to the operating system is equally beneficial in the area of multiprocessing as it was in the area of memory management and garbage collection.

Interestingly, the delegation of responsibilities to the operating system has the very desirable side effect of a move of lower-level mechanisms to behind the scenes. In fact, none of the low-level institutions like semaphores and forks traditionally used for multiprogramming are part of the unified framework in their raw form but are, possibly, used as implementation tools behind the scenes. Nevertheless, the framework is expressive enough to support constructs like *locks* etc. for fine-grained access protection on demand.

It is perhaps desirable to briefly compare our Active Oberon framework with Java's thread system. We already mentioned that Java is a representative of the "separating" culture that roots "active" classes in a base class called *Threads*. This is different from our approach in the sense that Java subordinates concurrency to inheritance by concept, while we clearly aim at a decoupling of "orthogonal" combination of objects and threads from inheritance. Java class designers need to specifically design "runnable" objects as such and, in particular, they cannot reuse passive classes by inheritance. However, this problem could be healed practically by preventively deriving every potentially "runnable" Java class from class Threads.

One significant difference still remains. Unlike our object bodies, Java threads are not composable along subclass chains, because they are represented in the form of a method. Parallel composition of behavior is sometimes structurally desirable, as the following archetypal example of objects driven by a *consumer-producer* scheme shows. Assuming the existence of some generic base type producing a buffered stream of tokens, we can construct any specific processor of such a stream simply by composing this base type with a subtype that contributes to the object's total behavior by an application-specific consumer process.

Two potential advantages of Active Oberon over Java are its assertion-based concept of synchronous process scheduling and the SHARED option for controlled access that essentially represents a built-in version of the *readers-and-writers* paradigm.

We have implemented our framework on the base of a version of the OP2 Oberon compiler and on the native Oberon kernel for the Intel architecture. The current implementation of the runtime kernel is primarily designed and used for a versatile and non-blocking local Oberon server that has been in successful use since July 1996. A next and more refined version of a runtime system (in terms of stack management and scheduling strategy) that is in addition able to make beneficial use of multiple physical processors is currently under development.

Acknowledgement

A successful implementation is always a final legitimation of a design. Rarely, however, is an implementation so demanding and its quality of such paramount importance as in the case of a programming framework. In this sense, my special respect and thanks go to the implementation team consisting of Andreas Disteli (runtime kernel and server) and Patrick Reali (compiler). Their expertise and continuous feedback substantially contributed to the advanced state of the project. The implementors themselves could not have succeeded without the sound and professional basis that was laid earlier by Pieter Muller (native Intel kernel) and the development team of the Oberon OP2 compiler. I no less greatfully acknowledge their work. My best thanks may further reach the audience of an early talk that I gave on the subject at DEC SRC, Palo Alto, and that resulted in a stimulating discussion and in some most valuable suggestions. Last but not least, I thank Martin Reiser and the referees for their apt comments.

References

[1] J. Gosling, F. Yellin, The Java Team,
The Java Application Programming Interface, Volume 1, Addison-Wesley, 1996.

[2] A. Divin, G. Caal, C. Petitpierre,
Active Objects: A Paradigm for Communications and Event Driven Systems, Proceedings GLOBECOM'94.

[3] K. Nygaard, O.-J. Dahl, Simula 67,
History of Programming Languages (R.W. Wexelblat, ed.), Addison-Wesley, 1981.

[4] N. Wirth, The Programming Language Oberon,
Software – Practice and Experience, 18(7), 671-690.

[5] N. Wirth, J. Gutknecht, Project Oberon,
Addison-Wesley, 1992.

[6] H. Mössenböck, N. Wirth, The Programming Language Oberon-2, Structured Programming, 12, 179-95.

[7] A. Disteli, P. Reali, Combining Oberon with Active Objects, Proceedings of the JMLC, Linz, Austria, 1997.

[8] J.G.P. Barnes, Programming in Ada,
Addison-Wesley, 1994.

Combining Oberon with Active Objects

Andreas R. Disteli
Patrik Reali

Institut für Computersysteme, ETH Zürich

Abstract. Multitasking is a topic on which many discussions have been held. There are different opinions about its need. Our own operating system, Oberon, was originally designed as a single user and single process system. While developing server systems and simulation kits we came to the conclusion that we need some notion of slim and easy to use process. We then decided to start a new project comprising the design of a new kernel and a new compiler for the support of concurrent execution of several processes on different priority levels with an appropriate protection mechanism preventing processes from inadmissible access to each other. The idea of active objects, simultaneously representing processes and containing both their action and their data, was the base for the 'Active–Oberon' project. Active objects are independent processes scheduled by the system. The management of the memory including stack allocation devolves on the new kernel. This takes much responsibility away from the programmer and makes the system safer.
The goal of this paper is to present the implementation of the 'Active–Oberon' project whose concepts are described in detail in [Gut96b].

Keywords: Object Oriented Programming, Active Objects, Concurrency,
             Multiprogramming, Operating Systems, Oberon

1. Introduction

The Oberon system is a single user and a single process operating system [Rei91] [WG92]. Although very small, it is a very powerful system which is sufficient for almost all applications. As long as only one person is working with an Oberon based computer, the single process system with its central loop is powerful enough. So, there is no explicit need for multitasking. In spite of this fact, the Oberon system allows multitasking, but in a very coarse way. As described in [WG92], it is possible to install tasks into the main processing loop. Alternating with the system tasks, i. e. keyboard and mouse handlers which are also part of the central loop, they are executed as a whole, without any scheduling opportunity. A task has to run from the beginning to the end of the current action and it cannot be interrupted by any other usertask or systemtask. It is obvious that this can result in remarkable delays for interactive system tasks. E. g. a task calculating some complex expression can block the whole system during its execution unless it is programmed as a state machine, executing a small piece of code operating on some globally saved state. For systems like a server, which offer a variety of different services, sometimes time consuming, this tasking system is unsatisfactory. Besides that, inverted programming of a state machine is much less natural than programming a process in a linear way.

Another point is that a task is represented as a procedure in a module. Data which are used in the next execution period of the task have to be global in order not to get lost. This means that there is no persistent local environment for a task. Also two tasks using the same environment, i. e. the same global data, would cause race conditions. It would be much more elegant to have an object which (a) can keep its data local for its whole lifetime,

(b) knows all about its behaviour and (c) could even appear in more than one instance at the same time.

For these reasons we launched the 'Active–Oberon' project with the aim to include multitasking into the existing Oberon system, allowing the programmer to write lightweight processes in a straightforward and secure way without taking care of scheduling. Scheduling should not burden the programmer but be part of the operating system. For example, even when lots of time consuming background processes are running, the user should get immediate control over the interactive part of the system without even noticing the background actions.

In our system we only use lightweight processes (threads) that have their own stack but share their global address space with the other processes in the system.

All these considerations lead us to the following requirements:

– the old Oberon tasks are eliminated
– there are active objects simultaneously containing data and action (process)
– the system controls the scheduling
– the user has only a restricted control over scheduling
– there are different priority levels for the processes
– the objects can be access–protected against one another
– as much management as possible should be done by the system instead of the user

The concepts of active objects and the Active Oberon language description can be found in detail in [Gut96b].

Respecting the Oberon philosophy we tried to keep the changes to a minimum. Case studies show that this approach is sufficient for a variety of applications (see chapter 4).

The embedding of these new concepts into the existing system required major changes at two places. The first one is the kernel which has to manage process scheduling and the second one is the compiler which has to support the new language features. Chapter 2 will first discuss the runtime environment and the kernel while chapter 3 will then focus on the compiler.

2. Runtime Environment

The whole runtime environment is concentrated in one module of the inner core, the kernel. It is based on the native Oberon port for PCs [Mul96]. Having complete control over the machine means that we can fully concentrate on the actual problems without having to take care of restrictions set by a foreign operating system.

The original kernel is responsible for memory management (allocating and collecting memory), interrupt handling and initialization of the system. The new kernel in addition contains the protection mechanism for processes, their management and their scheduling. Due to these new responsibilities we also had to change the memory organisation. The use of a different addressing technique was a crucial decision for the new memory management.

2.1 Organisation of the Memory

Every process needs its own stack for the local data and procedure activation frames. Normally the maximum stack size cannot be determined at compile time. In simple cases only the compiler can compute the needed stack size, if there are neither open array parameters nor recursion nor procedure variables. In all other cases the size is known at runtime only. In our old coroutine model [Gut] every coroutine was assigned a fixed–size stack at start time. The programmer had to make an estimate about the size the coroutine would need during its runtime. As there was no check against the stack boundary this insecurity often lead to an inpredictable behaviour of the system if the stack underflew. Another important restriction is that the stack must be contiguous if we do not want any additional tests, register setup or block relocation.

So we had to find a technique that allows us to create stack blocks at runtime as soon as the stack runs out. The new block should further be contiguous to the old stack and each lightweight process should independently be able to reduce or increase its stacksize during runtime.

Just focussing on stacks until now, we must not forget the heap. We did not intend to divide the main memory into predefined heap and stack blocks. The main memory should be treated like a general resource for both types of memory blocks.

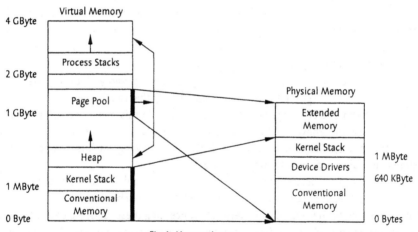

Fig. 1: Memory Layout

We found the solution in virtual addressing supported by the underlying hardware [Int91]. Each virtual address is translated into a physical address at runtime. This allows a memory block to look contiguous from the view of virtual addresses but is in fact split up into several blocks in different locations in physical memory. Or the other way round: we can allocate an arbitrary block in physical memory and simply adjust the mapping so that the new block is adjacent to the old stack address resp. the old heap address. This fits exactly our requirements mentioned above.

The only restrictions we have to deal with are the range of the virtual address space of 4GByte (given by the 32 bit architecture of the processor) and of course the amount of physical memory. It would be possible to extend the amount of memory by using disk swapping, but in the current implementation we did without it.

The whole memory is divided into pages, each 4 KByte in size. The granularity of the pages is given by the hardware and cannot be changed. Figure 1 shows the memory layout for our system. The whole physical memory is mapped to virtual addresses starting at 1 GByte. All free pages are linked together in the so-called page pool. Whenever a new page is needed, it is taken out of this page pool and its virtual address is adjusted so that the stack as well as the heap remains a contiguous memory block in the virtual address space.

Virtual addresses of the process stacks start at 2 GByte. This allows us to use the upper 2 GByte address space for the stack management. Assuming a maximum size of 128 KByte per stack this results in 16'384 possible processes as each process has exactly one stack. If every process needs only the minimum of stack space the system needs 64 MByte only for the stacks. We could think of a smaller stack limit in favor of more processes, but the coarse granularity of the memory blocks and the resulting memory requirements justifies the chosen stack size. A remark about waste of memory is still justified here. A page granularity of 1 KByte would be much more adequate for our purpose. Many processes do not need 4 KByte of stack memory. On the other hand, there would be more stack faults for stack consuming processes. Fortunately the hardware design made the decision for us.

The conventional memory (the first MByte) is mapped directly, i. e. the virtual addresses are the same as the physical addresses, this allowing easier access to hardware data and memory mapped I/O.

2.2 Organisation of the stacks

For each instance of a process, the new kernel allocates a memory block of a fixed size, i. e. the minimum size is given by the page size. Using the capabilities of the underlying hardware we can detect a page fault (stack underflow) in this memory block and can react on it. On every underflow we allocate a new memory block for the stack and append it to the existing one(s). This mechanism of a dynamically growing stack is new to the Oberon system which always dealt with fixed sized stacks.

Another approach for determining the needed stack size would be to insert a stack checking mechanism in the compiler [Die94]. But this results in a much more complex compiler and slower code due to the stack check overhead. Concerning these facts, we decided to use the hardware support of virtual addressing and keep the generated code and the compiler small and fast to achieve best performance regarding compile time and code size.

As mentioned above, a lot of processes do not even need 4 KByte of stack. As this is the minimum size we can get we could think of using this space for other purposes, too. Since each process has at least one stack block allocated at start time we use this block for storing process relevant information. At the beginning of each stack there is a reserved area shown in figure 2. On every process switch (see below) we store the current process state in this area. This includes both the state of the CPU and, if needed, the FPU. Furthermore, we defined a small area reserved for the operating system which is used in connection with process switch and a stack setup for a termination routine (see below).

Due to the fact that every process has its own stack, we also had to make changes in the garbage collector. Besides traversing the heap it has to traverse now all the process stacks and check them for pointer references. In the original system the garbage collector was only called at the end of a command and made no stack traversal at all. Now, the garbage collector is a process of its own and garbage collection on the stack has become an absolute need.

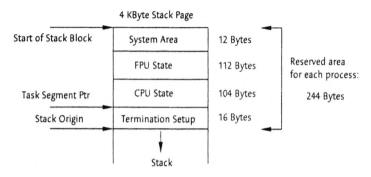

Fig. 2: Stack Block

2.3 Protection Mechanism

There are no explicit commands in the language for protecting and unprotecting an object from uncontrolled access. Both of these operations are done implicitly by the operating system. In the following we also use the terms *locking* and *unlocking* for protecting and unprotecting.

Whenever processes intend to write to some shared data, they need protection against each other. As long as a process is in a critical section (a section in which the working process must have exclusive access to the data) a second process must wait until the first one leaves this section.

Two processes can also be in the same critical section as long as they only read the data and do not modify it. A third process that wants to write data (*writer process*) would then have to wait until the two *reader processes* have finished, while another reader process could enter. It is obvious that reading and writing processes must exclude each other.

We use monitors [Hoa75] as a base for our implementation and added the readers/writers concept [Bac93].

In our system every object consists of a set of exclusive, shared and/or unprotected entrypoints. Entrypoints can either be module procedures in case the object to be entered is a module, or typebound procedures in case of an instance of an object. For detailed information about the dualism between modules and types see [Gut96b]. Each time a process enters an object or a module through an *exclusive* entrypoint, it tries to lock the referred object. If unlocked, the process enters the object and simultaneously locks it (Fig. 3.1). The same process may obviously enter an object recursively. This must be like that, otherwise a protected entry could not be called from within another protected entry in the same object. Note that it is under responsibility of the object to keep track of (a) which process entered and (b) the number of times the process entered (Fig. 3.2). An object locked by another process cannot let pass any new one trying to enter. In this case the new one is passivated by the operating system (see below: process management) and has to wait until the object will be unlocked (Fig. 3.3).

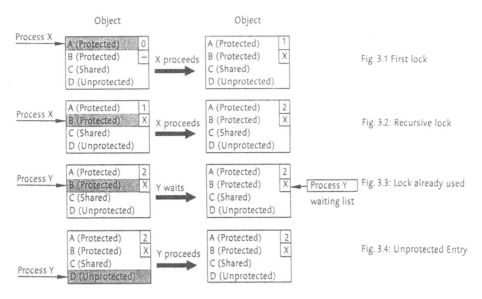

Fig. 3: Locks

Shared entrypoints work in a similar way. The difference is that as long as there are no writer processes trying to enter via some protected entry, reader processes can enter the object simultaneously via shared entries. An arriving writer process forces queueing of further reader processes until the writer has finished. The writer gets control as soon as all the readers already in the object have left. This guarantees that writer processes will get control as soon as possible and the data will be up to date for further reads.

On leaving a protected entry the operating system checks whether another process is waiting for the released object. If there is one, it will be activated, acquires the lock and gets control depending on its priority.

Unprotected entries do not check either for locks on entry or for waiting processes on exit (Fig. 3.4).

While a process is inside a critical section, it can occur that the process has to wait for a certain condition to become true. As mentioned above, the runtime environment then takes the process out of the *active queue*. If the lock would be kept while waiting for the condition, no other process could enter this object, although the condition can only become true through a call to another guarded entry of this object. This would lead to a deadlock: a process, waiting for a condition, keeps locking the entered object and no other process can enter this object and change the condition. For this obvious reason we have to unlock the object while waiting. It is the responsibility of the process to remember the object it has to relock when it gets reactivated.

2.4 Process Management
Every process is in one of four different states. A newly created process has its state set to *active* and is inserted into a queue which holds all active processes. Similarly to this 'active queue' there are also queues for the other states, namely queues for *passive, waiting* and

terminated processes. These queues are global to the system and contain only processes whose change of state depends on a global action, e. g. evaluation of a global condition or reactivation after an unconditional passivate (see below).

In addition there are queues local to the object. Conditions containing data local to the object can only be changed by another procedure call also local to the same object. Local conditions are therefore kept in a queue belonging to each object. Processes waiting for entry to an object are kept in another local queue. These local queues reduce search expenditure during runtime and promote locality and object orientation.

An active object can be passivated in two ways: unconditionally (using the *PASSIVATE* command), or waiting for a condition to become true *(PASSIVATE(condition))*. In the first case it has to be reactivated by a explicit call of ACTIVATE. We use this form whenever we do not know the exact condition of reactivation so that a different process needs to react. In the second case the operating system checks the condition and, if the condition is false, changes the state to 'waiting', i. e. it moves the object from the 'active queue' to the 'waiting queue'. Depending on the locality of the used data in the condition, the object is either inserted into the local queue and the reevaluation of the condition is done on the exit of a protected entry of this object, or it is in the global queue and the evaluation is done by a system task runnung on each timer interrupt. The reevaluation can be forced in both cases with an explicit call of ACTIVATE, but reactivation will only take place when the condition is true.

When reactivating an unconditionally passivated object (by calling ACTIVATE(you)), two cases can occur, leading to different transitions. If the reactivated object is allowed to enter the previously released object it is inserted back in the 'active queue'. If not, the reactivated process changes to the local waiting queue. As soon as the previously released object becomes free again, the waiting process relocks it and moves to the 'active queue'.

In a system with several processes there will normally be more than one process waiting for a locked object and also more than one process which can change back to active because the condition is true. In these cases the process with the highest priority gets control. If there are equal priorities and there is a process in the 'waiting queue', this process gets control first. The reason is that this process is already in the object (PASSIVATE(cond) is always called from within an object) while a process waiting for a lock is only about to enter the object. To guarantee fairness between processes, all queues are organized in first–in first–out order.

Terminating an object means removing it from the 'active queue' and inserting it into the 'terminate queue'. Its action is stopped but the object can still remain in the system as a passive object. The locks seized by the terminated object must be released, in order not to prevent other, still active processes from acquiring this lock. A terminated object cannot be reactivated, because the stack pages have been returned to the system. The terminate queue is checked periodically by the timer interrupt procedure. At this point all used stack and heap memory can be returned to the system. This means that a process can only terminate itself implicitly by reaching the end of its body. In particular there is no way to terminate a process remotely. Figure 4 shows all the possible transitions between the different queues:

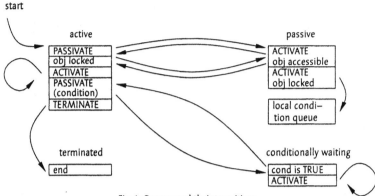

Fig. 4: Queues and their transitions

2.5 Process switch

The basic scheme of switching processes is simple. The state of the current process is stored on its stack. Then, the system selects the next process, restores its state and (re)starts its execution.

The underlying hardware provides different protection levels [Int91]. They must not be confused with our protection mechanism discussed above. Hardware protection simply means here controlled access to memory areas between system and user. All our processes run on the least privileged user level, i. e. they cannot use the privileged instructions. During a normal use of the system this does not matter. But when changing from one process to another, we exactly need some of these instructions. So, either we have to do expensive system calls to change the level of operation or we have to use a more privileged level for the user code. Both solutions are bad. Again we found a solution in the hardware support. The processor supports a special task switching mechanism. This allows us to store the whole CPU state and restore a new one by one instruction available at user level. Normally, such complex instructions are very slow compared with simple instructions as e. g. 'MOV' and 'ADD' and could be done much faster by reprogramming them using simple instructions. But measurements showed that, although too much is done by this instruction for our purposes, it is still faster than reprogramming it. Also it simplifies a lot as we shall see later.

When the processor performs a task switch it uses a so-called task segment [Int91] for storing the state of the old process and restoring the state of a new one. Some fields of this task segment contain information that we do not need. But as the layout of this segment is given by the hardware we cannot change it.

The processor offers an easy way for switching from one task to another. As the task segment contains all relevant data of a task, it would be easiest to store the state of the old task and restore the state of the new one. It is possible to do this by just using a special form of the 'JMP' instruction and indicate to which task segment, resp. to which process, we want to jump. The processor then performs the whole task switch by storing the state of the old task and restoring the state of the new one. This sounds very easy. In fact, it is so, but of course some setups must be done behind the scenes. Each process needs its own task segment which is located in the reserved stack area (Referred as CPU state field in Fig. 2).

The descriptor for this segment additionally needs 8 bytes in a system table. Assuming that we do not have thousands of processes this is resonable. But this covers only the CPU. The FPU state is not saved by this procedure. Considering the amount of time needed for storing the FPU state and the fact that not all processes use the FPU lead to the following idea: The state of the FPU is only stored when another process is going to use it. For this we have to keep track of the last process which used the FPU. As soon as another process acesses the FPU we store the state into the FPU state field (Fig. 2) of the last process and reload the new state if there is one or init the FPU if there is none.

As can be seen here, switching from one process to another is quite simple and can be done very efficiently. With this technique we also do not have to care about privilege level restrictions of certain instructions, e. g. changing of segment limits, flushing page tables, etc.

2.6 Scheduler

Active objects can run in two modes. The first mode handles them in a timesliced way which means that there is no need of taking care of synchronous process switches by the programmer. The system takes over this task and schedules the active objects each time it gets control. Still, timeslicing does not exclude the use of synchronous control passing statements. The timesliced mode is indicated at the beginning of the active body with the keyword {TIMESLICED}. The second mode exclusively uses the synchronous passing statements ACTIVATE, PASSIVATE and PASSIVATE(condition). Between these statements control is not passed to any other active object unless there is one with a higher priority. Of course, an active object running on a higher priority level always preempts the current process and gets immediate control. The only exception is a low priority process locking an object that the high priority process wants to enter. In this case even the high priority process has to wait until the lock is given back.

The timer interrupt handler routine is sketched in the following pseudo code:

```
PROCEDURE TimerHandler;
BEGIN
    IF current PC is outside the kernel THEN      (* Kernel is a monitor module *)
        WHILE there are processes waiting in the Condition Queue DO
            IF condition is true THEN activate this process END
        END;
        Get next process from the 'active queue' depending on the priority;
        IF current process # next process THEN switch to next process    (* higher priority *)
            (* If there are only processes with the same priority, next equals current *)
        ELSIF current process runs timesliced THEN switch to next ready process    (* time slice is over *)
            (* there is always a ready process, as the system owns a 'idle' process *)
        END
    END
END TimerHandler;
```

This handler also makes clear that it can be very time consuming to evaluate all conditions at every timer interrupt.

For each condition the address of the code is known at compile time. Every time PASSIVATE(cond) is used this address and the corresponding object (SELF) are passed to the kernel which inserts these data into the (local or global) waiting queue. When evaluating a condition the system makes a call to the address of the condition and passes SELF as a parameter. The returned boolean value indicates whether the condition is true or not. No context switch is needed!

Another frequent situation is waiting until a certain time has elapsed. Statements of the form

time := system time + dt;   PASSIVATE(time < system time);

are legal but can be handled more elegantly and more efficiently. Obviously, again if there are many of these conditions, evaluation gets very inefficient. As an optimisation, we introduced a timer object which offers a procedure 'Hold(dt)'. This object handles all waiting processes in a way that only a few tests have to be made every timer tick. This increases the efficiency of the system remarkably. Figure 5 shows the basic idea behind the implementation of this approach: a list sorted by reactivation time. All processes with the same reaction time are linked together and can be activated as a whole when time is ready.

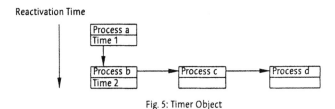

Fig. 5: Timer Object

3. The Active–Oberon Compiler

The Active–Oberon Compiler implementation is based on the OP2–Compiler [Cre91], a two pass compiler for the Oberon–2 language and generates code for Intel 80386 processors [Int91]. Because of differences in syntax and semantics Oberon–2 extensions have been discarded. The language implemented in the Active–Compiler is the Active–Oberon language [Gut96a] [Gut96b], a direct extension of the Oberon language [Wir88].

The relevant changes in Active–Oberon can be subdivided into three categories: (a) Syntax extensions to implement type bound procedures, (b) embedded protection and (c) embedded process management. The most important change of the compiler is the syntax extension. Perhaps surprisingly, it simplifies the parsing of the language a lot. Other changes have been made in the compiler to enhance code efficiency, in particular a facility for inline procedures has been introduced. Almost all the changes affect the parser, the back–end of the compiler remains nearly unchanged. Only five new system calls have been added.

3.1 Active Oberon Language Parsing

Instead of having three distinct syntax productions for modules, procedures and records, the Active–Oberon language unifies these productions in a single syntactical structure, here represented by the *DeclSeq* and the *Body* productions in EBNF notation:

```
$ Module      =   MODULE ["(" PROTECTED ")"] ident ";" [ImportList] DeclSeq Body ".".
$ ProcDecl    =   PROCEDURE {ProcTags} IdentDef [FormalPars] ";" DeclSeq Body.
$ RecType     =   RECORD ["(" Qualident ")"] DeclSeq Body.
```

```
$ DeclSeq        =    {CONST {ConstDecl ";" } | TYPE {TypeDecl ";"} | [VAR] {VarDecl ";"} |
                      ProcDecl ";" | ForwardDecl ";"}.
$ Body           =    [ BEGIN [ObjMode] StatementSeq | CODE {character} ]  END [Ident].
$ ObjMode        =    "{" ObjModeSpec { "," ObjModeSpec } "}".
$ ObjModeSpec    =    PARALLEL "(" ConstExpr ")" | EXCLUSIVE | SHARED | TIMESLICED.
```

The semantics of the different *ObjModeSpec* are described above and in [Gut96b]. The new syntax allows the implementation to have only one parsing procedure for modules, procedures and records. Still there are some checks to be done, because the language semantics are not completely orthogonal (e.g. active procedures make no sense). The following table resumes the actual implementation restrictions:

	Module	*Procedure*	*Record*
local vars/fields	yes	yes	yes
constants	yes	yes	yes
local types	yes	yes	no *
local procedures	yes	yes	yes
body	yes	yes	yes
protectable	yes	no	yes
active	yes	no	yes

(∗) Local record types are a temporary implementation restriction. Conceptually there is no reason for omitting them.

Procedures are not protectable but inherit the protection attributes from their context (i.e. the module or the object).

3.2 Code Patterns

In the Oberon System [Rei91] [WG92] the compiler and the system are bound very tightly and thus enable tight cooperation. This simplifies the compiler task by allowing assumptions about the runtime environment and therefore making possible the integration of run–time features (e.g. memory allocation) directly in the language semantics.

The interface between the compiler and the kernel is the object file. It contains the generated code, fixup information and the code itself.

The runtime environment is responsible for memory allocation and deallocation (via a garbage collector), data protection and process handling. These services are accessible by the compiler through system calls. In line with the Oberon philosophy, these services are integrated in the language in a transparent way and run–time system calls are automatically generated by the compiler. The number of system calls is kept to an absolute minimum. The Active Oberon kernel contains five new kinds of calls for providing the needed functionality to implement the added language semantics:

```
Kernel.Lock (SELF: PROTECTED);
Kernel.Unlock (SELF: PROTECTED);
Kernel.Start (body: PROCEDURE; priority: LONGINT; SELF: Kernel.ActiveObject);
Kernel.Passivate (condition: PROCEDURE(): BOOLEAN; contextPtr: LONGINT; SELF: Kernel.ActiveObject; global:
BOOLEAN);
Kernel.Activate (you: Kernel.ActiveObject);
```

The generation of code for processes and/or protection heavily relies on these new system calls, because these functions need substantial run–time support.

Object protection

When the code for a protected entry into an object is generated, the compiler automatically inserts the *Kernel.Lock* and *Kernel.Unlock* system calls. We optimized the average case by embedding part of the system call directly into the caller code and thus avoiding the expensive system call whenever possible. For example, the generated code for a call to the protected entry R is:

```
PROCEDURE R    enter
               IF SELF.lock = 0 THEN    (* not locked yet, normal case *)
                   SELF.count := -1; SELF.lock := Kernel.CurrentProcess
               ELSE
                   call Kernel.Lock (SELF)
               END;

               { code for x := 2 }

               IF SELF.count < -1 THEN
                   call Kernel.Unlock (SELF)
               ELSE
                   SELF.count := 0; SELF.lock := 0;
                   IF SELF.conditions # NIL THEN call Kernel.CheckConditions (SELF.conditions) END
               END;
               exit
```

The *Unlock* code pattern must again be inserted before every return statement. The variable *SELF* is always defined in every scope. Every type bound procedure has *SELF* as a hidden parameter. For example the call to R is:

```
active.R       push active
               call R
```

NEW

The code generated for object generation is more complex because the semantics of the *NEW* instruction have been extended. The *NEW* instruction implies three steps now: (1) allocate an object in the heap (2) initialise it (3) call the object body. NEW and the initializer build one atomic operation because the initialisation of a process must be done before the process is started (Configuring a running process may lead to race conditions). The compiler can now generate different code patterns for the *NEW* instruction: one for active objects and one for passive objects. The code generation routine for the *NEW* instruction is like this:

```
PROCEDURE GenNew (x: Node);    (* node x represents the NEW instruction *)
VAR obj: Node;
BEGIN
  obj := GetObject (x);
  GenNewRecSystemCall (obj, GetTypeDescriptor(obj));
  IF IsActive (obj) THEN AdjustActivePointer (obj) END;
  IF HasInitialiser (obj) THEN GenCall (FindInitialiser (obj), FetchInitParameters (x)) END;
  IF IsActive (obj) THEN GenStartSystemCall (FindBody (obj), FindPrio (obj))
  ELSE GenCall (FindBody (obj), NoParams) END
END GenNew;
```

The generated code can be best understood with the help of an example:

NEW (active, 1)   *Call Kernel.New (active)*
adjust pointer
Call active.Init (1)
Call Kernel.Start (active.body, 2, active)

The need for pointer adjusting is a consequence of the special memory layout of the active objects and our garbage collector implementation. Some compiler assumptions about the system organisation are hard–coded in the generated binary code. The memory layout used by the runtime environment to represent memory blocks and type descriptor structures are the most important assumptions in this context. The type descriptors contain information about the type of the record and the addresses of the type bound procedures (methods). This knowledge is used by the compiler to implement efficient type tests and entry calls to type–bound procedures without having to ask the runtime environment for this information.

The most relevant change in the memory organisation are process descriptors. Process–oriented information has to be stored somewhere in memory, and for efficiency reasons this data is stored at some fixed offsets relative to the object's base, making the retrieval of the needed data possible without any additional indirection or computation for memory access. Because positive offsets are already used for local instance data, negative offsets are used to store the process descriptor. The record tag (pointer to the type descriptor) now includes special information telling the garbage collector that this is an active object and that the original record tag is located below the process data. Duplication of the record tag is necessary because of our Mark-and-Sweep garbage collector.

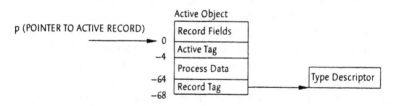

Fig. 6: Active Object Memory Layout

PASSIVATE

Another semantically complex instruction is passivate. A very simple implementation of passivate could be:

WHILE ~condition DO Kernel.PassControl END;

This implementation is very inefficient, because every single evaluation of the condition then requires a process switch. A much more efficient solution delegates the evaluation to the runtime environment thus avoiding a process switch. The condition in the PASSIVATE instruction is isolated in a procedure of type *PROCEDURE (): BOOLEAN* which is local to the procedure where PASSIVATE is called. The variables belonging to an outer scope are retrieved via static link, that is the linked list of all the procedure scopes. Access to local data without requiring a process switch is possible: the run–time environment pushes the pointer to the activation frame of the passivated procedure and then calls the condition

234

procedure. Therefore the condition procedure executes in the same context as the passivated procedure. For example, the type bound entry P is implemented as

```
hidden procedure @Guard1 (sl: StaticLink ): BOOLEAN
                enter
                return (sl.SELF.x # 1)

PROCEDURE P     enter
                call Kernel.Passivate (@Guard1, FP, SELF, FALSE)
                exit
```

The FP parameter is the current process frame pointer that will be used as a static link by the runtime environment to call the condition procedure. If a conditionless PASSIVATE is issued, no hidden local procedure needs to be generated, and a NIL pointer is passed to Kernel.Passivate. The fourth parameter (FALSE) is a hint to the runtime environment: the condition contains only local variables or fields and it needs to be reevaluated only when a protected entry of the same instance has been left. Note that this implementation is only possible if a 2–pass compiler is used, because the code for the condition has to be relocated.

ACTIVATE
The ACTIVATE instruction is mapped directly to the Kernel.Activate system call.

4. Conclusions
Considering the size of the compiled kernel we have succeded in combining active objects and Oberon in a very efficient and elegant way. In the 30 Kbytes of kernel code we find memory management, interrupt handling, the whole process management and the scheduler described above. Having now a small but very powerful toolkit, we had to write test applications for proving its correctness and robustness. In additions to small simulation programs which take full advantage of all the new facilities, we are currently working on a server version of the Oberon system. All the services, the operating system itself and the network are based on the model of active objects. A beta version is currently running. It offers different services like online teletext, a dictionary, a print server, a file server and simple FTP and WWW servers. It turned out that the minimum number of primitives we added to the original operation system is powerful enough to implement a whole server system and that the Oberon idea of 'making things as simple as possible, but not simpler' successfully applies once more.

5. Acknowledgements
We would like to thank here Pieter Muller who has implemented the one–process native Oberon Intel System that was the base for our project. He brought a lot of good ideas into our discussions and helped us understanding the details of a native Kernel. His knowledge about the dark sides of PC–Hardware was indispensable.
Our thanks also go to Erich Oswald who wrote the 'Figures' graphic editor that was used for the design of the several figures in this text.
We also would like to thank J. Gutknecht for his helpful comments on earlier versions of this paper.

6. References

[Bac93]   Jean Bacon;
          Concurrent Systems; An Integrated Approach to Operating Systems,
          Database, and Distributed Systems; Addison Wesley; 1993

[Cre91]   Régis Crelier;
          OP2: A Portable Oberon–2 Compiler;
          Proceedings of the 2nd International Modula–2 Conference,
          Loughborough, England, 58–67; 1991

[Die94]   Reinhard A. Dietrich;
          Dynamic Stacks for Lightweight Processses; Diplomarbeit ETHZ; 1994

[Gut96a] Jürg Gutknecht;
          Oberon, Gadgets and Some Archetypal Aspects of Persistent Objects,
          Information Sciences: An International Journal, 1996

[Gut96b] Jürg Gutknecht;
          Do the fish really need remote control?
          Proceedings of the JMLC, Linz, Austria; 1997

[Gut]   Jürg Gutknecht;
          Vorlesung: Simulation diskreter Systeme; ETH Zürich

[Hoa75]   C. A. R. Hoare;
          Monitors: An Operating System Structuring Concept;
          Communication of the ACM 18(2), 1975

[Int91]   Intel Corporation; 386 DX Microprocesssor Programmer's Reference Manual; 1991

[Mul96]   Refer to ftp://anonymous@ftp.inf.ethz.ch/pub/Oberon/System3/Native

[Rei91]   M. Reiser;
          The Oberon System: User Guide and Programmer's Manual;
          Addison–Wesley, 1991

[WG92]   Niklaus Wirth, Jürg Gutknecht;
          The Design of an Operating System and Compiler; ACM Press; 1992

[Wir88]   Niklaus Wirth;
          The Programming Language Oberon;
          Software – Practice and Experience 18(7): 671–690, July 1988

Using Real Time Constraints for Modularisation

Brian Kirk*, Libero Nigro**, Francesco Pupo**

Abstract. This paper advocates an object-oriented approach to the development of distributed real-time systems which clearly separates timing from functional concerns. It also describes a philosophy for modularising, and then designing systems, based on the localisation of timing constraints as one of prime criteria for partitioning. Active objects (i.e., actors) are adopted as the basic building blocks in-the-small. They are not aware of timing constraints nor of scheduling structures. Active objects are in charge of processing messages as they arrive. Message buffering and delivery is the responsibility of a control machine which hosts a reflective scheduler object. Timing constraints express, in general, patterns of multi-object, time-driven co-ordination and synchronisation. The resultant approach improves modularity and object reusability. The paper illustrates the application of the proposed concepts through real world examples.

Key words: distributed real time systems, object orientation, timing constraints in-the-large, modularisation

1   Introduction

A problem with the use of many existing languages for real-time is related to the management of functional and timing issues which often get mixed and intertwined into the same application code. All of this makes it difficult to develop and verify a new system or to adapt and extend a given system to changed requirements. In addition, timing constructs often depend on hidden and inflexible runtime mechanisms. A typical example is the Ada programming language. Though it has been designed for time-critical applications, it lacks the necessary features for distributed programming and offers a limited support to timing essentially through the *delay* construct. The only communication mechanism in Ada is *rendezvous*, which expresses the readyness of participating tasks to communicate, independently from timing. Asynchronous and non-blocking interprocess communication, which is common in distributed systems, is not supported. Moreover, the wakeup time of a task which invoked a delay operation is only a lower time bound, so complicating real-time specifications. Ada and its successor Ada95 depend on hidden runtime support which cannot be tuned to the application at hand. In other languages, which rely on a "system-centred" approach, real-time constructs depend ultimately on the features of an underlying time-sliced operating-system kernel. Here the developer can be concerned with overcoming tricky scheduling control through priority, which tends to make timing behaviour unpredictable.

This paper reports on a research project whose aim is an object-oriented development of distributed real-time systems. A distinguishing feature of our

---

* Robinson Associates, S. Mary's Street, Painswick, Glos., GL6 6QG, UK, Email: b.kirk@robinsons.co.uk

** Dipartimento di Elettronica, Informatica e Sistemistica, Università della Calabria, I-87036 Rende (CS) - Italy, Email: {l.nigro | f.pupo}@unical.it

project is an application of the separation of concerns principle, which allows functional and timing aspects of a real-time system to be dealt with separately [26]. The approach is mainly driven by modularisation of timing constraints. It is under experimentation using DART [11, 15], a modified version of the Actor model [1]. DART has been designed to favour *timing predictability*. Functional issues are decentralised into a set of autonomous reactive objects, which are characterised by their message interface. Objects are triggered into execution as a consequence of incoming messages. Messages are handled locally according to an object lifecycle, i.e., a finite state machine. Objects are not aware of *why* and *when* they are activated by messages. Rather, these issues are delegated into the definition of a *control machine* where a combination of event-driven and time-driven paradigms of message handling can be applied. A control machine is characterised by a set of *timing control clauses* which directly affect message scheduling. Messages can be scheduled according to a timeline in order to be dispatched at the "right time". The control machine can be customised in order to fulfil the application needs. Different control machines of a distributed real-time system can be required to synchronise their execution in order to implement timing constraints at the system level, e.g., a "simultaneous" execution of selected messages. In these cases, the use of a predictable interconnection network such as CAN [5] can help implementing such operations like a real-time barrier synchronisation [22] by preallocating priority of messages for transmission.

A major benefit of the adopted approach is object reusability. Objects can be used in the context of distinct applications with possibly different timing requirements. Verification of the timing properties can be tackled by system simulation [3] or animation and analysis of a modelled system using formal tools like high-level Petri nets [8, 16].

Our work has been influenced by the previous work by Ren, Agha and Saito [20, 21], who developed RTsynchronizers to provide a declarative specification of coordination and timing constraints of groups of actors. RTsynchronizers allow to specify quantitative constraints, adequate for hard real-time systems. Moreover, the work on the HyperReal project by Tisato, Nigro et al. [7, 17], who isolated the time dimension as a fundamental paradigm upon which the event-driven one can be simulated, has contributed to the time management framework described in this paper.

Section 2 introduces the basic concept of modularisation by timing constraints of distributed real-time systems. The discussion makes a reference to the experience gained during the development of a recent real life and complex project. Section 3 reviews the basics of the DART framework used in the implementation. A DART extension with a control model which enhances modularisation is then presented. Section 4 describes the handling of timing constraints in-the-large. The timing management of a simple control system is exemplified in Section 5. Section 6 discusses implementation issues of the proposed timing model. In addition, a particular hardware/software organisation which helps fulfilling very hard timing constraints is illustrated. Finally, the conclusions are presented together with an indication of further work.

2 Modularisation

It is only possible to analyse design and build large complex systems by using modularisation. This involves breaking down the substance, complexity and interaction into component parts which are intellectually manageable and can also be joined together by well defined interfaces [2, 18]. There are three prime criteria for modularisation these are manageability, functional cohesion and localisation of timing constraints. For real-time systems, which must provide guaranteed behaviours within defined time constraints, it is generally the time constraints that ultimately determine the system partitioning.

System modularisation can occur at a number of levels

- *product level* - typically one system with several variants that can be configured for sale and use
- *subsystem level* - typically a physically separate part of the system, such as an engine or gearbox in a car
- *subsystem of a subsystem level* - typically an integrated smaller subsystem, such as a digital signal processor in a speech recognition subsystem of a PC
- *real world interface hardware* - which connects the system to the external environment and real time

The "real-timeness" of each level depends on the real world application. Table 1 shows an example from a recent tin can production line automation project.

Level	Response required	Comment
Product flow rate Metal sheets	1 large metal sheet every 6 seconds	Continuous cutting into can sized pieces
Tin cans	20 cans per second	Continuous production of cans
Subsystem co-ordination	100 events per second	To co-ordinate the making of each can
Sub-subsystem co-ordination	10,000 events per second	To assess quality of welding per can

Table 1. Typical real-time response levels

2.1 Modularising the system

The main criteria here is usually the product being designed. Typically products must be sold in various combinations but always making a system. In the tin can example the products were a metal sheet slitter, a can maker, a can coating oven and a weld quality monitor. Each of these could be sold as separate products (a system) or together in various combination (still one system).

This can also be viewed as modularisation by time constraints, in this case of when units are operated in production (sometimes alone, sometimes together) and of the timing of the data and control interactions between the separate products.

The result of product modularisation is inevitably a set of products containing subsystems, the criteria being

- the purpose of the product (functional cohesion)
- physical distribution of the implementation (localisation and simple interfaces)
- the timing constraints within the subsystems (tight) and between them (loose)

In practice the Marketing people decide the product modularisation and the subsystem modularisation is then designed by system engineers. For the tin can production machines standard processor nodes were used to implement each subsystem. Using the DART design framework (see later in this paper) this has been easily achieved using Motorola 68332 processors and a CAN network [11].

2.2 Modularising the subsystem

At this level the timing constraints could not always be met using the typical DART model due to limitations of scheduler response, processor throughput and CAN network delays (they all reached their time limit at about 1,000 events per second). One subsytem had a very severe timing constraint, this involved processing over 10,000 events per second. The solution was to design "recursively" using a sub-subsystem to reduce the external information to less than 100 events per second so that a conventional subsystem could be used (see Figure 1). In

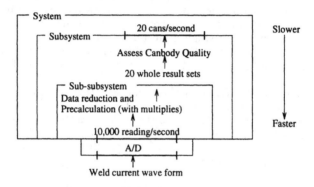

Fig. 1. Recursive subsystem modularisation

fact this was achieved by using another board with the same type of processor but dedicated only to data reduction and calculation of power profiles. A DSP could have been used but would have been more complex and costly. The system wide metaphor of using actors and sending messages between them is preserved. The time critical work being done by a single actor implemented partially in hardware and partially in software (see a later section for details).

3 The DART model

DART [11, 15] represents a modified version of the Actor model [1] suited to the construction of real-time applications. It centres on active objects modelled as finite state machines which evolve according to a *life cycle* [23]. Into each state selected laws and policies apply. Object life cycles directly control synchronisation. Active objects are at rest until a message arrives which triggers a state transition and then the execution of an action. Action execution cannot be pre-empted nor suspended. As in the Actor model, three basic operations are available:

- *new*, for the creation of a new actor as an instance of a class. The data component of an actor includes as attributes a set of acquaintances, i.e., the known actors (including itself) to which messages can be transmitted
- *send*, for transmitting an asynchronous message to a destination actor. The message can carry data values only. The sender continues immediately after the send operation
- *become*, for changing the current object state. Each state defines a specific behaviour represented by a particular action associated to it and the possible

state transitions corresponding to each expected message. The processing of an unexpected message can be postponed by proper designing the object lifecycle or by storing the message into private data.

Modifications to the Actor model were introduced for ensuring real-time behaviour. Each object no longer has an internal thread. Rather, concurrency is provided by a scheduler object (more details later in this paper) which transparently buffers all the exchanged messages among the actors residing on a same physical processor, and delivers them according to a selected control strategy. Concurrency relies on a light-weight mechanism: *action interleaving*, which costs a method invocation in an object-oriented language. Atomic action execution allows for a deterministic computation of message processing time. Only one message processing can be in progress within an actor at any instant in time. Instead of associating a single mail queue to every actor, a few message queues (e.g., one) are handled by the scheduler. The existence of a customisable scheduler avoids dependencies from the policies and mechanisms of an operating system.

As in the Shlaer-Mellor OOA method [23], a notion of time can directly be supported by DART through timer objects. A timer captures a time interval (fire time) and a timeout message. An active timer delivers its timeout event to the relevant target actor, at the fire time. Before firing, a timer can be reset. The use of timers allows for timed reactivation of actors. However, timer management suffers of the following weaknesses:

- it is a subject of programming in-the-small, in the sense that timer setting and resetting operations must be dealt with during object lifecycle design
- it isn't a natural or easy way to express and implement timing constraints in general hard real time systems
- it ignores the fact that much real time co-operation is peer to peer in nature.

As a consequence, a different viewpoint is adopted in this paper which favours a definition and application of timing constraints in-the-large, i.e., out of object lifecycles.

3.1 System level architecture

At the system level a DART application consists of a collection of subsystems/processors, linked one to another with a deterministic interconnection network (e.g., a Token bus, Token ring, CAN bus ...). A subsystem hosts a group of actors which are orchestrated by a control machine. Each object is referenced by a unique object identifier (*oid*). An oid determines a physical processor and the belonging subsystem. The structure of a typical control machine is portrayed in Figure 2. It is composed of

- a *local clock*, which contains a "real" time reference clock for all the actors in a subsystem
- a *plan* (or *calendar* or *agenda*), which arranges message invocations along a timeline
- a *scheduler* (or *planner* or *synchronizer*), which filters message transmissions, applies to them a set of timing control clauses and schedules them on the plan. The scheduler is actually split into two objects: the *input filter* (iFilter) and the *output filter* (oFilter). iFilter is responsible of scheduling "just sent messages"; oFilter is mainly devoted to verifying timing violations at the dispatch time of a message;

– a *controller* which provides the basic control engine which repeatedly selects (*selector* block) from the plan the next message to be dispatched, and delivers it (*dispatcher* block) to its receiver actor.

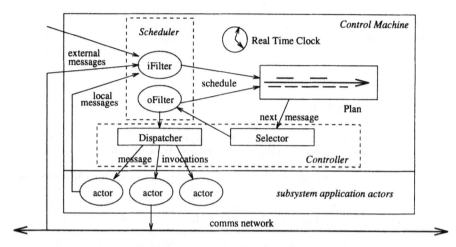

Fig. 2. The structure of a control machine

At its heart, the control machine is naturally event-driven. Asynchronous messages are received either from the external environment or from within a subsystem, and are processed by the relevant actors. A message processing can give rise to further messages and so on. From this point of view, the message plan of the control machine can ultimately reduce to a FIFO queue. The event-driven paradigm is well suited to usual concurrent actor-based applications.

The time-driven paradigm, on the other hand, adds the possibility of scheduling messages to occur at certain due times. A common interpretation relies on a pre-scheduled plan of messages which are dispatched on a regular, cyclic basis: it is the *cyclic executive* of most hard real time systems [13]. The external environment is polled periodically through a set of input sensors, each one with its associated frequency. The environment is maintained stable by actuators operated synchronously. A basic time frame is firstly identified, possibly by a preliminary harmonisation of the polling frequencies. Then a major cycle consisting of one or more minor cycles is structured at the design time which controls the evolution of the real time system.

More in general, a DART control machine can embody a combination of event-driven and time-driven components. The chosen approach in this paper, proposed also in [20-22], retains the basic event-driven character of the actor-based computational model and superimpose to it a time-driven paradigm. Timing constraints are embedded as control clauses or filters [4] of the scheduler. This way the application actors are not conscious of timing issues and can be designed according to functional issues only thus improving modularity and reusability.

A possible organisation of the message plan consists of a set of partial ordered time windows of message invocations. A message invocation specifies a message msg, its destined actor and two pieces of timing information: t_{min} and t_{max}. It is intended that msg cannot be dispatched before t_{min} and should be delivered before t_{max} to avoid a timing violation. The selector component can choose the next message invocation on the basis, for example, of a *Earliest Deadline*

First strategy. For a real-time system served by such a plan to be schedulable it must be ensured that at each selection step a deterministic choice of a message invocation can always be guaranteed.

Generally speaking, a DART system requires both local and global coordination and control. A selected subsystem can behave as a master control machine, where the operator, through a friendly and asynchronous Graphical User Interface (GUI), can issue configuration or monitoring commands. A limited set of system-wide control messages, directly recognised by the control machines, can be introduced in order to support configuration and monitoring operations and the implementation of inter-subsystems synchronisation and timing constraints.

3.2 Programming issues

DART programming in-the-small has been implemented in popular object oriented languages like C++ [15], Oberon-2 [11] and Java [9] with the aid of a few base classes. Actor classes are programmed as a direct or indirect extensions of a base Actor class. Messages are programmed as extensions of a base Message class. In Java, an actor class and its related message classes are conveniently organised into a same package. Each actor class is equipped with a message handler [19] which dynamically determines the type of an incoming message and processes it according to object attributes and message parameters. The programming style is simple yet effective. No modification to the syntax of the host language is required. DART dependency on hardware details is limited to synchronous I/O operations confined within *terminator objects* at the interface with the controlled environment (see section 7.2 for more details). Programming in-the-large is under experimentation using CAN bus [10, 11], Token ring in the presence of TLI transport layer software [6] and PVM [9]. A system-wide "language" of network messages [11, 12] is used which is transparently translated from (respectively into) the message format of the sending (respectively destination) subsystem address space.

4   Timing constraints at the subsystem level

A key factor of the control machine concept is a customising of its behaviour in order to fulfil application dependent timing constraints. A timing constraint normally specifies a time interval between the occurrences of a group of causally connected messages. The most common case is a message which periodically awakes an object in order to perform something (e.g., polling a condition of the external environment). Another case is when a message is expected to occur within a deadline since the occurrence of another message. A violation of the timing constraint can require a recovery action to be carried out. In this section, a procedural specification of timing constraints will be exemplified using Java syntax for simplicity. The following operations are assumed:

- msg.*cause()*, which returns the identity of a message msg' whose processing caused the transmission of the message msg
- msg.*iTime()*, which returns the time at which the message msg was dispatched
- *schedule*(msg, t_{min}, t_{max}), which schedules on the control machine plan the message msg with the associated time window $[t_{min}..t_{max}]$
- *now()*, which returns the current value of local clock.

It should be noted that for the *iTime* function to be applicable to an incoming external message, a notion of a global time must be provided. It is often possible for the local clocks of a distributed system to be assumed closely synchronised one with another and the local clock skew bounded by a limited time value [24, 25]. The general structure of an input/output real-time filter is outlined in Figure 3. It is assumed that at the construction time, a filter be initialised by

```
class RTFilter extends Actor {
   local data and constructors
   public void handler(Message m){
      switch(currentstatus)
         {case status1: if(pattern) apply timing constraint relevant to pattern,
                                    possibly changing current status
                        else if( ... ) ...
                        else //default message processing
                        break;
             case status2: ... }; // switch
      }; // handler
}; // RTFilter
```

Fig. 3. General structure of an RT filter

all the relevant subsystem data such as the frequency of a periodic message, an exception handler actor dealing with a timing violation and so forth. The handler method verifies timing constraints and applies the associated scheduling actions. It collects many independent RTsynchronizers in the sense of [20-22].

It is interesting to note that a filter is itself an actor, devoted to managing timing constraints through the operations *cause, iTime, schedule* and *now*. Filter states are useful for implementing nested time clauses.

A timing constraint is identified by a given *pattern*. A pattern is made up of a yet to be processed message plus, in general, a boolean expression involving message parameters and local data of the filter. If the pattern is satisfied, the corresponding timing constraint is applied, possibly executing a scheduling action. The following examples give a flavor of the expression of timing constraints.

4.1 Periodic message

The time clause is associated with an actor (e.g., modelling a sensor) which has a repetitive message (e.g., ReadCO for reading the environment CO level). After being processed, the message is sent again to the actor itself. Periodicity of the message is ensured externally to the actor in the handler method of the iFilter:

```
if(m instanceof ReadCO && m.cause() == m)
   schedule(m, m.cause().iTime() + P, m.cause().iTime() + P);
```

where P is the message period, which is data local to the iFilter.

4.2 Exception handling of a timing violation

A message m1 is required to be processed within a time limit t1. Would t1 be missed, a message m2 directed to an exception handler actor must be scheduled to occur at a time t2 after t1.

```
if(m instanceof M1 && m.iTime() > t1)
    schedule(m2, t1 + t2, t1 + t2);
```

There are two points worth noting in this example: (i) message m1 is captured at its invocation time by an output filter; (ii) message m2 is already known to the filter, i.e., it is a pending message waiting to possibly be scheduled. Should the missing event never occur, message m2 would continue to remain pending.

4.3   Time-bounded buffer

This is a variation of the classical producer/consumer communicating through an unbounded buffer. A timing requirement is set such that a product cannot be held in the buffer for longer than a given interval T. The time clause applies to two corresponding messages: a producer *put* and a consumer *get*. An informal expression of the timing constraint is shown in the following:

```
if(get and put are two pending and corresponding messages) {
    schedule(put, now(), now());
    schedule(get, now(), now() + T);}
```

Such a time clause preserves pre-existing code of producer and consumer which are unaware of the timing constraint.

4.4   Deadline on all the interface messages of an actor

A real-time actor exists in one of several *operating modes*. One mode, e.g., High-Speed, requires all its incoming messages to be invoked with a deadline Thigh-Speed. This timing constraint can be expressed thus:

```
if(m.target instanceof RTActor &&
    ((RTActor)m.target).mode==RTActor.HighSpeed)
    schedule(m, now(), now() + ThighSpeed);
```

4.5   Default time clause

If a message is not captured by an explicit time clause the policy might be to process it "as soon as possible". To achieve this behaviour, it is sufficient to program a default alternative of the handler method of a filter so as to enforce an immediate release of the message, thus:

```
schedule(m, now(), now());
```

If a weak time constraint is required, it can be achieved by:

```
schedule(m, now(), infinite);
```

4.6   Informal semantics of time clauses

A fundamental concern of the time clauses is related to the adoption of the *safe progress, unsafe wait* principle [21]. By this it is meant that a filter normally releases a message for scheduling if it does not cause a violation of any constraints in the future. This condition enables the system to make progress. On the other hand, a filter can be in a position to retain a message if more information is necessary to decide about message release. Consider again, as an example, the time-bounded buffer. The capture of a put forces the input filter to wait for the next get message to arrive before making a schedule of both put and get. Indeed, without information about the consume process timing, the scheduling of the put could be hazardous. Similarly, the arrival of a get without a put would cause it to wait. In order to correctly apply the timing constraint, the filter is required to buffer temporarily unpaired put or get messages and to retrieve corresponding put and get messages at the application of the time clause.

4.7 Filter programming and reflection

Filter development is an example of a reflective architecture [14]. Indeed, reflection is a model where an object can manipulate a causally connected description (i.e., meta-object) of itself. A change in the meta-object results in a change of implementation or behaviour of the object. In the case of the control machine organisation, the application of timing constraints to *just sent messages* has the effect of changing the plan of messages to be dispatched which in turn affect actor behaviours.

5 Timing constraints at the system level

Consider the possibility of constraining two or more actors allocated upon different processors to execute "simultaneously", i.e., with a negligible difference in time, two related messages. An example could be that of passing a glass between the two hands of a robot. The *release* message of one hand should be executed simultaneously with a *grab* message of the other hand. Another example could be that of operating in parallel a set of input/output devices (sensors, actuators, and so forth) distributed on different processors, e.g., the various sensors need to perform a coordinated read operation. Such timing constraints involve the cooperation among a set of participating control machines, i.e., an *interaction policy* or system level protocol which can be achieved on the basis of a set of control messages transparent to the application actors. An example implementation of system level timing constraints centres on synchronized local clocks and a *real-time barrier synchronization* operation [22].

6 An example

This section exemplifies the handling of timing constraints of a simple dye industrial process control system [20]. There is a sensor set including three sensors: a liquid level sensor, a temperature sensor and a pressure sensor, which are responsible for reading the dyeing liquid level, temperature and pressure respectively. These sensors also interact with the devices which are relevant to their functionality. A dye valve controls the incoming dye liquid; a drain valve controls the out-going dye liquid. Finally, there exist a heater controller and a pressure controller. The system operation is basically cyclic but disrupted by exceptions. Preparation of the dye liquid is under control of a timer. The following timing constraints must be met.

1. As soon as the dyeing liquid reaches level L, the temperature reaches value H, and the pressure reaches P, the timer starts timing
2. After T time units, the timer signals that the dyeing process is done
3. The dyeing liquid has to be drained out through the drain valve within D time units after the timer sends out the finishing signal

4. For safety reasons, the temperature and the pressure in the tank have to be reduced to room temperature and room pressure, respectively, before the dyeing water can be allowed do drain out
5. The timer periodically (with period p) reports its time
6. All three sensors periodically read their data with period p1
7. When sensor quantities do not satisfy the requirements, the corresponding devices are signalled to make an adjustment within t time units.

6.1 A DART solution

In the following a simple DART solution is sketched with a single subsystem. Some preliminary hints about functional aspects are given to help clarify timing management.

Functional aspects The following actor classes are identified:

- *DyeingMachine*, which represents the dyeing process control system. It is signalled by sensor readings and interacts with output devices to tell them if the associated physical quantity must be increased or decreased. It also starts timer and commands valve operations
- *Dye* and *Drain*, which are associated to the two valves
- *SensorL*, *SensorH* and *SensorP*, respectively associated to the liquid, temperature and pressure sensors
- *Heater* and *Pressure*, respectively associated to the heater and pressure controllers.

The DyeingMachine has the Init, SigL, SigH, SigP, Operate, TimeElapsed, Empty and Restart message classes. A sensor understands the Init and ReadX messages. A sensor signals the read value to the dyeingMachine through the invocation of an associated SigX message. The Timer class admits four messages: Init, Start, Alarm and ReportT. The Heater expects the messages Init, Heat and Cool. The Pressure actor handles the Init, IncreasePressure and DecreasePressure messages. A message Init initialises an actor by transmitting to it necessary initialisation data. To help clarify timing management, some message causal relationships are summarised in the Figure 4.

- DyeingMachine.operate.cause()==(DyeingMachine.sigL(level) ‖ DyeingMachine.sigH(temp) ‖ DyeingMachine.sigP(pres)) && (level==L && temp==H && pres==P)
- Timer.start.cause()==DyeingMachine.operate
- Timer.alarm.cause()==Timer.start
- DyeingMachine.timeElapsed.cause()==Timer.alarm
- DyeingMachine.empty.cause()== (DyeingMachine.sigH(temp) ‖ DyeingMachine.sigP(pres)) && (temp==roomtemperature && pres==roompressure)
- DyeingMachine.restart.cause()==DyeingMachine.sigL(level) && level==0

Fig. 4. Some message causal relationships

Timing aspects Figure 5 and 6 show respectively an input and output filter implementing the time clauses of the Dyeing Machine control process. For simplicity, the recovery action to be taken when the emptying process does not end within its deadline is left unspecified.

```
package actor;
class InputFilter extends Actor{
  private long T, p, p1, t;
  InputFilter(long T,      // time required for preparing the dyeing water
              long p,      // timer report time period
              long p1,     // sensor reading period
              long t)      // device adjust time
  {this.T=T; this.p=p; this.p1=p1; this.t=t;}
  public void handler(Message m) { //periodic message timing constraints
    if((m instanceof sensorL.ReadL || m instanceof sensorH.ReadH ||
       m instanceof sensorP.ReadP) && m.cause()==m)
      ControlMachine.schedule(m, m.cause().iTime()+p1, m.cause().iTime()+p1);
    else if(m instanceof timer.ReportT && m.cause()==m)
      ControlMachine.schedule(m, m.cause().iTime()+p, m.cause().iTime()+p);
    else // reaction timing constraints
    if(m instanceof heater.Cool || m instanceof heater.Heat ||
       m instanceof pressure.IncreasePressure || m instanceof pressure.DecreasePressure)
      ControlMachine.schedule(m, ControlMachine.now(), ControlMachine.now()+t);
    else // operational timing constraints
    if(m instanceof timer.Alarm)
      ControlMachine.schedule(m, m.cause().iTime()+T, m.cause().iTime()+T);
    else // default time clause
      ControlMachine.schedule(m, ControlMachine.now(), ControlMachine.now());
  };//handler
};//InputFilter
```

Fig. 5. An input filter for the Dye Control System

```
package actor;
class OutputFilter extends Actor{
  private long D;
  private dyeingMachine.TimeElapsed timeElapsed;
  OutputFilter(long D){this.D=D;} //deadline before which the dyeing liquid must be drained out
  public void handler(Message m) {
    if(m instanceof dyeingMachine.TimeElapsed) timeElapsed=(dyeingMachine.TimeElapsed)m;
    else if(m instanceof dyeingMachine.SigL && ((dyeingMachine.SigL)m).level==0) {
        if(m.iTime() > timeElapsed.iTime()+D) recovery action; }
  };//handler
};//OutputFilter
```

Fig. 6. An output filter for the Dye Control System

7 Implementation notes

DART actors and control machine can easily and efficiently be implemented in Java. A flavour of control machine implementation is suggested in the next subsection. After that, a hardware/software achievement of a terminator actor for the sub-subsystem modularisation is described.

7.1 Control machine implementation

The *actor* package contains all the basic classes supporting actor programming, the control machine and timing concepts: Actor, Message, various lists of Messages, ControlMachine, ... The Message base class is reproduced in Figure 7. Methods *cause()* and *iTime()* have package visibility. They are designed to be used in a filter actor which is supposed to be defined in the context of the actor

```
package actor;
public class Message {
   Actor target;
   private long tmin, tmax, _iTime;
   private Message _cause;
   Message cause()
   {return this._cause;}
   long iTime()
   {return this._iTime;}
};//Message
```

Fig. 7. Message base class

```
package actor;
public class ControlMachine {
   list_of_messages plan;
   final long infinite = ... ; ...
   public void controller
   (Actor iFilter, Actor oFilter) {...}
   static schedule
   (Message m, long tmin, long tmax) {...}
   public static long now() {...}
};//ControlMachine
```

Fig. 8. An excerpt of the ControlMachine class

package. ControlMachine is a public class whose definition is sketched in Figure 8. A fundamental method is *controller()* which hides the selector and dispatcher components of Figure 2. Controller performs an endless loop at each iteration of which the operations in Figure 9 are carried out. At step 5. the dispatch message can be made null by a recovery action triggered by a timing violation. The set of just sent messages is built by basic send operation and is held into a (package visible) static list of messages of the Actor class. The now() static method is achieved on the basis of an underlying clock system, i.e., a library time function. In Java, the System.currentTimeMillis() method can be used.

1. the _cause attribute of each just sent message is set with the last dispatched message
2. the *iFilter.handler()* method is invoked on every just sent message for achieving its scheduling on the plan
3. the next dispatch message is selected, possibly waiting for the selection process to complete
4. the _iTime attribute of the dispatch message is set to *now()*
5. the *oFilter.handler()* method is invoked with the dispatch message
6. the dispatch message, if there are any, is delivered to its target actor by invoking *dispatch_message.target.handler(dispatch_message)*

Fig. 9. Controller basic actions

7.2 Crossing the real-time hardware barrier

When the time constraints of a subsystem can't be handled through normal scheduler provisions, as it was in a particular subsystem of the tin can project, a sub-subsystem modularisation can be employed with the aid of a special terminator actor implemented as the bridge between the real-time hardware and the other actors in the subsystem. The challenge for this actor is to have two interfaces: one to the hardware, another to the software actors. First we observe that in our model an actor simply receives a message from another actor via a scheduler, the actor then interprets the message to produce behaviour and possibly sends some more messages. Next we observe that to obtain communication and synchronisation with the external environment processors have an interrupt facility. This makes it possible for hardware signal from the real world to alter the flow of program execution of the processor. A practical solution is to have the terminator object working continuously with only the interrupt as the scheduler. The actor behaviour is provided partly in hardware (e.g., to gather external data) and partly in software (to process it into a message and then send it). A typical example of reading data synchronously, pre-processing it and then sending it is shown in Figure 10. The basic idea is to partition the terminator actor work between hardware and software in the following steps:

1. Initialise software and hardware
2. Prepare the interrupt system to continue processing after the hardware behaviour is done
3. Transfer processing to the hardware
4. Do the hardware processing
5. Transfer processing to the software ("the interrupt")
6. Process the data and possibly send a message.

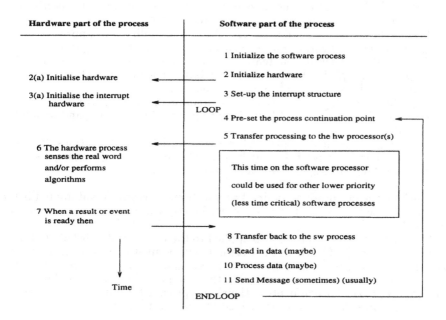

Fig. 10. Bridging the hardware/software barrier

Terminator actor behaviour is within LOOP ENDLOOP in Figure 10. It is a single "thread of control" which resides alternatively in the software then the hardware. Note that the interrupt just signals the continuation of the actor processing and behaviour. In effect the actor life-force is alternatively provided by a hardware (processor) engine or a software (non processor) engine. This is in contrast to the way in which low level ("system") programmers use interrupts, usually as the initiation of some activity rather than its continuation. Note also that the timing and synchronisation of the overall process is separately determined by the real world real-time part by means of the interrupt mechanism. Even so, the actor is activated and can send messages and receive them.

8   Conclusion

This paper proposes timing constraints in-the-large as a clean paradigm to modularise a distributed real-time system. The paradigm is embedded within the DART architecture [11, 15]. The following are some key points of the resultant approach:

- two development levels are supported: the *conceptual level*, where a collection of actors are allowed to cooperate peer-to-peer; the *control machine level*, where timing constraints are arbitrated
- timing constraints are embodied into filter actors which transparently apply them and regulate message scheduling
- filter behaviours directly reflect on a selected group of application actors
- filters can be extended in order to refine timing constraints related to a group of application actors
- the same timing constraints can be reused when extension actors are introduced which conform to the same message interface and provide, for instance, a different implementation of the message services
- besides improving modularity and object reusability, the approach makes it easier the verification phases which can be conducted separately on the functional and then on the temporal properties of a system. The possibility of exploiting high-level Petri nets [8] for animation and simulation of a DART system has been described in a recent paper [16]
- to make the timing behaviour of the system predictable the network for communicating messages must have deterministic delivery times, and preferably priorities
- the design approach is suitable for a wide variety of applications, it is also adaptable to use any of the widely available programming languages such as Modula-2, Oberon-2, C, C++ and Java.

A whole tin can production line has now been successfully automated based on the proposed concepts, involving over 25 co-operating subsystems connected via a CAN.

The methodology has been also applied to the building of a distributed measurement system [6, 9], where the external environment is sensed through complex measurement instruments, uniformly modelled by actors. Here modularity has been further enhanced by allowing the test procedure, the standard interface linking physical instruments to their conceptual actor images, and the actual kind of instrument objects to be defined at configuration time.

The current direction of research covers

- continued evaluation of the methodology with industrial case studies in CAN networks
- developing interaction policies for timing constraints at the system-level
- giving a better support for the analysis phase through formal tools.

Acknowledgement

The authors are grateful to Francesco Tisato for commenting a preliminary draft of this paper.

References

1. G Agha: Actors: A model for concurrent computation in distributed systems, MIT Press, 1986.
2. C Alexander: Notes on the synthesis of form, Harward University Press, 1964.
3. R Beraldi, L Nigro: Distributed simulation of large PCS networks using a Time Warp mechanism, Proc. of Eurosim 96 HPCN Conf., Delft, The Netherlands (to appear).
4. L Bergmans, M Aksit: Composing synchronisation and real-time constraints, J. of Parallel and Distributed Computing, September issue, 1996.
5. CAN, A serial bus - not just for vehicles, CIA, CAN in Automation, Am Weichselgarten 26, D-91058, Erlangen, Germany.
6. P Daponte, D Grimaldi, L Nigro, F Pupo: Distributed measurement systems: an object oriented architecture and a case study, to appear on Computer Standards and Interfaces.
7. F De Paoli, F Tisato: Architectural abstractions and time modeling in HyperReal, Proc. of EUROMICRO Workshop on Real Time Systems, pp. 222-226, Odense (Denmark), June 1995.
8. C Ghezzi, D Mandrioli, S Morasca, M Pezzè: A unified high-level Petri net formalism for time-critical systems, IEEE Trans. on Software Engineering, 17(2), pp.160:172, February 1991.
9. D Grimaldi, L Nigro, F Pupo: Development issues of distributed measurement systems, Proc. of Imeko Measurement Conf., Budapest, 12-14 September, 1996.
10. B Kirk: Real time protocol design for control area networks, Proc. of Real-Time 95 Conf., Ostrava (Cz Rep.), 5-7 Sept., pp. 251-268, 1995.
11. B Kirk, L Nigro: Distributed architecture for real time, in Oberon-2, in Advances in Modular Languages, P. Shulthess (ed.), Universitatsverlag Ulm GmbH, Proc. of Joint Modular Languages Conference 1994, pp. 325-366.
12. Java Remote Method Invocation and Object Serialization, http://chatsubo.javasoft.com
13. C D Locke: Software architecture for hard real-time applications: cyclic executives versus fixed priority executives, The Journal of Real-Time Systems, 4(1):37-53, 1992.
14. P Maes: Concepts and experiments in computational reflection, Proc. of OOPSLA 87, pp. 147-155, ACM SIGPLAN Notices, 22(12).
15. L Nigro: A real time architecture based on Shlaer Mellor object lifecycles, J. of Object Oriented Programming, 8(1):20-31, 1995.
16. L Nigro, F Pupo: Modeling and analysing DART systems through high-level Petri nets, Springer-Verlag, LNCS 1091, pp. 420-439, 1996.
17. L Nigro, F Tisato: Timing as a programming-in-the- large issue, Microsystems and Microprocessors J., 20(4): 211-223, June 1996.
18. D L Parnas: On the criteria to be used in decomposing systems into modules, Comm. ACM, December, 1972.
19. M Reiser, N Wirth: Programming in Oberon, Addison Wesley, 1992.
20. S Ren, G Agha: RTsynchronizer: language support for real-time specifications in distributed systems, ACM SIGPLAN Notices, 30(11), 1995.
21. S Ren, G Agha, M Saito: A modular approach for programming distributed real-time systems, J. of Parallel and Distributed Computing, Special issue on Object-Oriented Real Time Systems, 1996 (to appear).
22. M Saito, G Agha: A modular approach to real-time synchronization, in Object-Oriented Real-Time Systems Workshop, pp. 13-22, San Antonio, Texas, October 1995, OOPS Messenger, ACM SIGPLAN.
23. S Shlaer, S J Mellor: Object lifecycles - Modelling the world in states, Yourdon Press 1992.
24. N Suri et al.: Synchronization issues in real-time systems, Proc. of IEEE, 82(1), pp.41-54, 1994.
25. K Turski: A Global time system for CAN networks, Proc. of ICC94, Int. CAN Conference, Am Weichselgarten 26, D-91058, Erlangen, Germany.
26. N Wirth: Toward a discipline of real-time programming, Comm. ACM, 20(8), 1977.

How Well Do Inheritance Mechanisms Support Inheritance Concepts?

M. Evered
J.L. Keedy
A. Schmolitzky
G. Menger

Abteilung Rechnerstrukturen, Universität Ulm, 89069 Ulm, Germany,
email: markev@informatik.uni-ulm.de

Abstract. Inheritance mechanisms are used to express many different programming concepts. In this paper we analyse these inheritance concepts to determine the requirements for an inheritance mechanism which is to support the concepts well. On the basis of this analysis we identify weaknesses in current mechanisms, particularly in the areas of modelling and signature modification and show how an inheritance mechanism can better fulfil the requirements while remaining type-safe.

1. Introduction

How good are the inheritance mechanisms of object-oriented languages? We can answer this question by examining how well the mechanisms support the concepts for which they are used. The main areas supported by inheritance are:

- modelling of application domains by hierarchies of object types
- software reuse
- polymorphism
- data abstraction through deferred operations

It can be seen that this represents a very wide range of areas and within each area a number of distinct concepts can be identified. Most common object-oriented languages contain a single relatively simple inheritance mechanism which is oriented towards the common aspects of these concepts rather than at supporting each of them as well as possible. This means, on the one hand, that a programmer is not well supported in distinguishing between and expressing the various concepts and, on the other hand, that a maintenance programmer may have difficulty in understanding the intention of the programmer in using the inheritance mechanism.

Wegner [Weg87] and LaLonde and Pugh [LP91] have listed a number of distinct concepts which are often regarded as inheritance. More recently, Meyer [Mey96] has categorised a number of different uses for inheritance and shown how they can be supported in Eiffel [Mey92]. In the next section we identify sixteen different concepts which can be (and have been) realised via inheritance. For each of these we investigate the requirements for an inheritance mechanism which is to provide good support for that concept.

In the third section we investigate the inheritance mechanisms of a number of object-oriented languages in the light of our requirements analysis. We show that some of the concepts are not well supported by any of the languages. We also show that some languages, by concentrating on a particular concept, have neglected good support for other concepts.

Finally, we present a number of proposals for improving the expressive power of inheritance mechanisms. In particular we show how the support for specialisation, behaviour extension and behaviour restriction can be improved without risk of dynamic type errors.

2. Inheritance Concepts

The concepts listed here can all be said to be inheritance concepts in the sense that they can be realised via an inheritance mechanism. For each of the concepts we investigate the requirements for an inheritance mechanism which is to support that concept well. The concepts overlap to some extent in their semantics but each has its own particular emphasis and aim.

2.1. Modelling Concepts

Specialisation

Specialisation is the aspect of modelling in which several possible variants of a general object type are identified and defined as (usually mutually exclusive) subtypes. In general, each specialised type has a restricted set of possible values, additional operations and specialised behaviour for the inherited operations. Most textbook examples of inheritance as a modelling mechanism assume this concept. Examples are the specialisation of 'person' into 'man' and 'woman', 'figure' into 'circle' and 'square' or 'integer' into '32-bit-integer' and '64-bit-integer'.

This concept can require:
- inheritance of operation signatures[1]
- additional postconditions and invariants for inherited signatures
- covariant modification of parameter types in inherited signatures
- additional parameters in inherited signatures
- multiple inheritance
- restrictions on multiple inheritance to support mutual exclusion.

The additional postconditions and invariants can help to specify formally the specialised behaviour of the subtype. Additional parameters may also be necessary in conjunction with the extended behaviour. This is especially true of constructors, since these may need parameters to set initial values of new data fields in objects of the subtype (e.g. the radius for a circle).

Covariant parameter modification is useful so that parameters to subtype operations can be more specialised than the parameters in the parent type. For example, the operation 'marries' may have a parameter of the type 'person' in 'person' but a parameter of the type 'man' in 'woman'. This corresponds to the 'type definition rule' of Eiffel.

Restrictions on multiple inheritance would be useful to prevent a new type being defined which inherits from both 'man' and 'woman'. This would make the intention of the inheritance clearer and help avoid errors in the modelling.

We explicitly do not list inheritance of operation implementations here. The modelling of type behaviour is independent of the implementation of that behaviour.

---

1 By signature we mean here an operation header with operation name, parameters and their types, pre- and postconditions and for functions the result type

The implementation for the subtype could be programmed using inheritance of some kind (see below) or it could be programmed 'from scratch'. From the modelling point of view this is irrelevant.

This kind of specialisation can be understood as 'incremental' specialisation in the sense that the subtype inherits everything from the parent type and is incremented by further operations and additional behaviour. This is the kind of specialisation usually given in inheritance examples but it is not the only kind to be found in application domains.

Decremental Specialisation

It is possible that a specialised subtype no longer fulfils all the behavioural specifications of the parent type. An example is a 'blind person' who has lost the 'seeing behaviour' normally associated with 'person's. We call this decremental specialisation. A further example is the type 'integer' as a subtype of 'real'. 'Integer' can inherit the operations and the semantics for 'add' and 'subtract' but 'divide' must be redefined and 'sine' and 'cosine' can not be inherited (as pure integer functions) at all.

This concept can be supported by a mechanism which allows:

- selective inheritance of operation signatures
- selective inheritance of postconditions and invariants for inherited signatures
- additional preconditions for inherited signatures.
- selective inheritance of parameters in inherited signatures
- restrictions on multiple inheritance to support mutual exclusion.

Selective inheritance allows the subtype to discard operations, parameters and behavioural specifications of the parent type. Additional preconditions similarly weaken the behavioural specification by guaranteeing the behaviour for fewer situations.

The relationships modelled by decremental specialisation can often be modelled by incremental specialisation if the inheritance hierarchy is modified. So, for example, the type 'person' could have two subtypes, 'seeing person' and 'blind person' but this is rather artificial and is contrary to the extendable approach in which classes know nothing of their descendants.

Dynamic Incremental Specialisation

By dynamic specialisation we mean specialising an already created object to become an object of a subtype of the type it previously had. The object then dynamically acquires the specialised operations and specialised semantics of the subtype. This is similar to the 'value inheritance' [Bee90] or 'object inheritance' [KA90] of object-oriented databases.

This is also in principle a type concept but is difficult to realise unless the implementation of the subtype is an extension of the implementation of the parent type. It is therefore helpful if the inheritance mechanism additionally allows:

- inheritance of data and operation implementations from an implementation of the parent type
- redefinition of operation implementations with access to the inherited implementation.

These allow the implementation of the subtype to inherit the data exactly as in the parent implementation and to extend the data and the operations as appropriate for the subtype.

Dynamic decremental specialisation is even more difficult since attribute values must possibly be discarded and dynamic type checking becomes essential. Only the incremental variety will be discussed further here.

Generalisation

Generalisation is the 'bottom-up' equivalent of the 'top-down' specialisation concept. Two independently-defined object types are examined to identify common properties. These properties are extracted and defined in an abstract parent type.

Multiple inheritance is particularly useful in this modelling concept since an object type can be similar to several other object types in different ways. The type 'terminal', for example, is similar to the type 'card_reader' in being a text input device and similar to the type 'printer' in being a text output device. Through generalisation 'terminal' and 'card_reader' can have the common parent type 'text_input' while 'terminal' and 'printer' have the common parent type 'text_output'.

This concept can be supported by the same mechanism as incremental specialisation or by a special mechanism for automatically extracting common signatures from a number of types to form a new parent type, as is possible in Trellis/Owl [Sch86].

Attribution

We denote as 'attribution' a particular form of (incremental) specialisation achieved via multiple inheritance. Here an object type is formed as an extension of a parent object type by combining the parent type with the 'attributes' inherited from an abstract 'attribute type'. In a library application, for example, a type 'book' could be combined with the (attribute) type 'loanable' to give the subtype 'loanable book'. The objects of the subtype inherit the 'book characteristics' and additionally have the 'loanable characteristics' (e.g. a due date). Generally it is intended that the subtype is substitutable for the parent type (i.e. that the inherited characteristics do not interfere with each other). This concept corresponds to the specification aspect of 'mixins' [DG87], particularly as generalised in [BC90].

The attribute types can be seen as adjectives which can not alone be instantiated to objects but which can be used to specialise many different nouns (object types).

Attribution can be supported by:
- inheritance of operation signatures
- multiple inheritance
- forbidding instantiation of the attribute type alone (for example by allowing types without constructors)

Components

Inheritance can be used in such a way that the parent type is seen as a *component* of the child type. For example, a common inheritance example is the type 'point' with an operation 'set_position'. A type 'circle' can be defined as a subtype of 'point' [CP89]. 'Circle' inherits 'set_position' with the meaning 'set position of centre', i.e. it inherits a 'point' as the component 'centre' (although the component is in this case not actually named).

This use of inheritance is unusual since it contradicts the 'is-a' relationship. It is not true that 'circle is a point'. (In fact some textbooks explicitly denote this as a misuse of inheritance.) Nevertheless, this concept can also be supported by :
- inheritance of operation signatures
- multiple inheritance (to inherit several different components)
- repeated inheritance [Mey88] (to inherit several components of the same type)

2.2. Design Concepts

Modularity

Modules are units which contain related definitions and restrict access to these definitions via some kind of export control. In a well modularised system each variable and operation definition is in the module 'where it belongs'. This concept is already supported to some extent in class-based languages without inheritance through the concept of classes or object types. For example, the operation 'set radius' can be defined as part of the object type 'circle' rather than being a stand-alone operation as would be the case in Pascal or C. The type 'circle' is in this sense a module.

Inheritance can be said to further enhance modularity by allowing operations shared by several types nevertheless to be 'where they belong'. For example, the operation 'move' is not something concerning circles alone and so should preferably be defined in the parent type 'figure'. The inheritance mechanism can then be used to export the operation to the subtypes. This requires only the inheritance of operation signatures.

Behaviour Extension

This concept is in principle the same as specialisation but the emphasis here is not on the modelling aspect of identifying the *possible* subtypes of an object type. Rather the aim is to define a *particular* new type whose behaviour represents a particular extension of the parent type tailored for some purpose.

For example, we may define the type 'queue' as a subtype of 'bag' with the extended semantics that items are inserted at a particular position (i.e. at the end) rather than arbitrarily. A further example is a 'taxi driver' as a subtype of 'person'. Unlike other 'person's the taxi driver has the additional 'behaviour' of becoming richer by driving (which could, for example, be expressed in a postcondition).

The requirements for this concept are:
- inheritance of operation signatures
- additional postconditions and invariants for inherited signatures
- additional parameters in inherited signatures

Behaviour Restriction

The behaviour of a subtype may be restricted so that it refuses to work normally (i.e. returns an error) in some situations which the parent type can handle. An example for behaviour restriction in this sense is the definition of a type 'set' which (unlike a mathematical set) returns an error if an item to be inserted is already in the set. This could be derived via behaviour restriction from a parent type 'collection' which allows arbitrary insertions.

Paradoxically, the behaviour restrictions are most often expressed as *additional* behaviour (i.e. checking for problems and returning an error code). In this case the concept can be supported by the same mechanism as behaviour extension. If the restrictions can be expressed as preconditions (as is possible for the 'set' example), behaviour restriction can also be supported by additional preconditions for inherited signatures.

Genericity

Genericity allows the definition of a general *type template* which can be used to create several different particular object types. For example, a 'set' template could be used as a basis for defining both an 'integer set' and a 'person set'. This can be seen as an inheritance concept since both sets 'inherit' the characteristics of a set but for different element types.

This can be achieved by defining an abstract parent type (e.g. 'set_element') containing exactly those characteristics required of the element type (e.g. comparison for equality) and defining 'person' as a subtype of 'set_element'. The template can then be defined as a 'set_of_set_element' and a 'set_of_person' can be derived as a subtype of this using:

- inheritance of operation signatures
- covariant modification of inherited parameter types

The modification of the parameter types is necessary so that the operations (e.g. 'insert') which have parameters of the type 'set_element' in 'set_of_set_element' can have parameters of the type 'person' in 'set_of_person'. This is an unusual and rather awkward use of inheritance but it demonstrates what can in principle be achieved.

Polymorphism

This is probably the concept most often associated with inheritance on the type level. A variable is allowed to refer to objects of different types at different times as long as the operations performed on the variable are defined for all the types referenced. This can be supported by defining the type of the variable as an abstract type which contains exactly the required operations. The referenced object types are defined as subtypes of this parent type, i.e. the polymorphism is realised as 'inclusion polymorphism' [CW85].

The requirements for supporting this concept with minimal restriction and without dynamic type errors (as realised in Trellis/Owl [Sch86]) are:

- inheritance of operation signatures
- contravariant modification of inherited input parameter types
- covariant modification of inherited output parameter types

Usually, however, it is intended that the objects referenced by the variable can not only perform the operations but that their behaviour is 'similar'. This can be supported by:

- inheritance of invariants and pre- and postconditions
- additional postconditions and invariants
- selective inheritance of preconditions

Importation

The concept of importing a list of related facilities can also be realised via inheritance. An example is the 'STD_FILES' class of Eiffel which contains the features 'input', 'output' and 'error'. An object type which is defined as inheriting from 'STD_FILES' can use these three standard files. This is the recommended way of obtaining access to general-purpose facilities in Eiffel [Mey88]. In this case, the inheritance relationship is not an 'is a' relationship nor even a 'has a' but rather a 'uses a'.

This form of importation can be supported by:

- inheritance of operation signatures
- multiple inheritance (to import from several classes)

since the subtype can then call its own (inherited) operations. In contrast to the use of inheritance we have listed under 'modularity' the operations are imported not by a subtype but by a *client* of some instance of the type.

2.3. Implementation Concepts

Data Abstraction

This concept is also called implementation abstraction or information hiding. The idea is to make a clear distinction between the behaviour of a type and an implementation of that behaviour. This allows the implementation to be modified or to be completely replaced by another implementation without affecting the rest of the system. It may even be desirable to have several different implementations of a single type (e.g. a 'small' implementation and a 'fast' implementation) in a single program.

This concept can be supported by:
- omission of operation implementations in the parent class
- inheritance of operation signatures

As Snyder has noted [Sny86], unrestricted use of data inherited from a parent class conflicts with information hiding since a child implementation 'knows' the details of its parent implementation and is therefore affected by changes to the parent. This problem can be avoided by forcing the new operations in the child to access the inherited implementation only through the (inherited) interface operations.

Subtype Implementation

This is the most common use of inheritance for code reuse. The parent class represents a type and an implementation for the type. The subclass represents a subtype of the parent type (in the sense of behaviour extension) and is implemented by inheriting and extending the implementation of the parent class.

The type aspect of the inheritance can be supported as for behaviour extension above. The implementation aspect can be supported by:
- inheritance of data and operation implementations
- redefinition of operation implementations with access to the inherited implementation.

Alternatively, the parent class can *force* the subclasses to include its operation implementations in redefined operations as with the 'inner' construct of Beta [Kri89].

Substitutability

It may be intended that a subtype extends a parent type only by adding new operations and that the semantics of the inherited operations are left completely unchanged. This means that an object of the subtype can be substituted for an object of the parent type without *any* effect on the system.

Although this is in principle a type concept it is listed here since, in the absence of complete formal type specifications, it can only be guaranteed by:
- inheritance of data and operation implementations
- forbidding the redefinition of inherited operation implementations

General Code Reuse

This is the most general concept for implementation inheritance. The aim is to construct an implementation by inheriting operation implementations arbitrarily from other implementations irrespective of the type hierarchy. This has been described as a 'shopping list' approach [Mey92]. In practice, the types may be related but not necessarily in the same way as the implementations.

An example is to implement a 'stack' by inheriting some of the operations of an existing 'deque' implementation (a queue with insertion and removal at both ends).

The type relationship is the other way around: the type 'deque' can be seen as a specialisation of 'stack' (with additional operations).

General code reuse can be supported by:

- selective inheritance of operation implementations
- redefinition of operation implementations with access to the inherited implementation.
- multiple inheritance
- decoupling the type inheritance hierarchy from the implementation inheritance hierarchy

3. Some Existing Inheritance Mechanisms

We now investigate a number of object-oriented languages in terms of their inheritance mechanisms and their support for the concepts listed above. In such an evaluation it is important to distinguish between recommendations for using the language (as demonstrated in informal language descriptions and examples) and the actual semantics of the mechanisms as realised in language implementations.

3.1. Smalltalk

The inheritance mechanism of Smalltalk-80 [GR89] is typical of common object-oriented languages in being a combination of the inheritance of operation signatures and the inheritance of data and operation implementations. The operation implementations may be redefined (with access to the inherited implementations). Covariant and contravariant modifications can be said to be allowed but not supported in Smalltalk since the parameters of methods have no type at all. For the same reason polymorphism is possible but not supported in a controlled way.

The Smalltalk mechanism provides good support for the concept of subtype implementation. Data abstraction can be supported by 'abstract supertypes' which include calls to methods implemented in their subclasses.

The combination of type and implementation ideas in the class construct can lead to problems in defining the inheritance hierarchy as discussed in [LTP86]. Specification and modelling concepts are poorly supported due to the lack of pre- and postconditions. Pure code reuse is poorly supported since neither multiple nor selective inheritance is possible and since the inheritance of method implementations is coupled to the class hierarchy.

3.2. Eiffel

In Eiffel [Mey92] as in Smalltalk, a single inheritance mechanism is used for the type hierarchy and for implementations. Eiffel classes may contain constraints in the form of invariants and method preconditions and postconditions. Eiffel supports multiple inheritance. The Eiffel inheritance mechanism can be described as signature inheritance (including constraints) together with inheritance of data and implementations. Method implementations can be redefined in a subclass and can be omitted in a superclass.

In fact not all constraints of a class are treated equally by the inheritance mechanism. If methods are not redefined, all invariants, preconditions and postconditions are inherited by the subclass. However, if methods are redefined, only the invariants of a superclass are inherited. The preconditions and postconditions are not inherited. It is recommended (but not enforced) that the preconditions listed for a redefined method be equal to or weaker than in the parent class and that the postconditions be equal to or stronger than in the parent class.

Nevertheless, Eiffel provides a mechanism for inheriting behaviour constraints and so supports the modelling concepts of specialisation, generalisation, attribution and components and the design concept of behaviour extension better than Smalltalk. Subtype implementation and code reuse are supported as in Smalltalk. Genericity is handled by a special mechanism rather than by inheritance [Mey86].

Data abstraction is supported in Eiffel by the definition of a 'deferred class' containing only deferred methods. The methods can then be implemented in different ways in different subclasses. In contrast to Smalltalk, the deferred class can provide not only the signatures of the operations but can also specify some aspects of type behaviour via invariants, preconditions and postconditions. There is, however, no guarantee that the pre- and postconditions will not be discarded in a subclass which provides an implementation.

Eiffel allows covariant modification of parameter types when methods are redefined. This is useful for supporting specialisation and some forms of behaviour restriction but can cause a problem with polymorphism as shown in [Coo89]. This (and a similar problem arising from generic classes) means that Eiffel requires special system-level type checking and unnecessary restrictions to support polymorphism in a type-safe way.

3.3. Trellis/Owl

Trellis/Owl distinguishes between subtyping and (implementation) inheritance. The former is defined to impose the minimum restriction on signature modification compatible with type-safe polymorphism. The latter is inheritance of code and operation implementations with the possibility of redefinition.

By providing type-safe rules for inheritance this language avoids the Eiffel problem mentioned above. This necessarily means, however, that certain kinds of specialisation can no longer be expressed even if no polymorphic use of the types occurs in a program.

Although a distinction is made between types and implementations in Trellis/Owl, the two hierarchies are nevertheless bound together in one mechanism. A method implementation can only be inherited from an implementation of a supertype. This restricts code reuse. In addition, a type can have only one implementation. Thus, ironically, data abstraction is in this sense not as well supported as in languages without the distinction between types and implementations.

Genericity is handled, as in Eiffel, by a special mechanism rather than by inheritance. Components, also, are handled by a special mechanism.

3.4. Summary

The languages listed here are typical in providing inheritance of operation signatures and of data and operation implementations with the possibility of redefinition. Some provide multiple inheritance. Eiffel also provides selective inheritance of preconditions, addition of postconditions and covariant modification of parameter types and consequently gives better support for specialisation, generalisation and behaviour extension.

The above examples show that optimal support for one concept may limit support for another of the concepts. Trellis/Owl, in guaranteeing type-safe polymorphism, imposes restrictions on the use of inheritance for the modelling concepts and for behaviour restriction.

Some of the requirements listed in section 2 are not supported by any of the common object-oriented languages. These will be examined in the next section.

4. Improving Support for Inheritance Concepts

4.1. Reducing the Number of Concepts to Support

One method of improving the support of inheritance mechanisms for inheritance concepts is to reduce the number of concepts which a mechanism must support. There can be two reasons for removing a concept from the list of inheritance concepts to be supported in a language:

- realisation of the concept by a mechanism other than inheritance
- removal of the concept from the language

A number of the concepts listed in section 2 can be and have been realised by other mechanisms than inheritance. These include components, modularity, importation, genericity and data abstraction

Indeed it has been argued that these concepts are much more clearly supported by other mechanisms. Liskov [Lis87] has argued against the use of inheritance for data abstraction. Szyperski [Szy92] has argued against the use of classes as modules. Components and importation unnecessarily confuse the 'has-a' and the 'uses-a' relationships with the 'is-a' relationship. Meyer [Mey86] has argued for a separate mechanism for genericity.

It may, of course, be argued that a language with fewer concepts is easier to understand and it is certainly true that it is easier to implement. We hold the view, however, that good support for software engineering concepts is more important than reducing the number of language mechanisms at all costs.

In any language design it must be decided which concepts are to be supported at all. This is a trade-off between expressive power on the one hand and language complexity and implementation difficulties on the other. One concept which may well be excluded because of implementation difficulties is dynamic specialisation. It can be argued that this concept is necessary for object-oriented database systems or artificial intelligence systems but not for ordinary object-oriented programming languages. We will not further discuss dynamic specialisation here but it should be noted that in a persistent programming language this and other concepts from database systems must be considered.

4.2. Separating Type and Implementation Concepts

Another method of improving support for inheritance concepts is to supply more than one mechanism for the different kinds of inheritance. In particular, the separation of type hierarchies and implementation hierarchies has received increasing attention in recent years [CHC90], [Por92], [BR95]. This follows from the requirement that code reuse be independent of type relationships. It also follows from separating data abstraction from inheritance and replacing the class concept by the concept of an abstract type with several possible implementations. The language Java [Sun95] allows (but does not enforce) this separation by providing 'interface types' which are organised in a hierarchy independent of the class hierarchy.

The separation also helps to resolve the question of whether and where multiple inheritance is required. It could be that multiple inheritance is desired for code reuse but not for types. On the other hand, if multiple inheritance is desired for type relationships then it is also required for code reuse in order to support the concept of subtype implementation. Thus, in avoiding the complications of multiple implementation inheritance, Java sacrifices optimal support for one important inheritance concept.

4.3. What is still missing?

Assuming that the concepts listed in section 4.1 are excluded and that type and implementation inheritance are separated as in section 4.2, we can list the remaining inheritance requirements not adequately covered by typical inheritance mechanisms. These are:

- selective inheritance of operation signatures
- addition of parameters
- selective inheritance of parameters
- addition of preconditions
- selective inheritance of postconditions
- restrictions on multiple inheritance to express mutual exclusion
- types without constructors for abstract 'attribute types'
- restrictions on redefinition
- selective inheritance of operation implementations

A comparison with section 2 shows that the absence of these aspects in inheritance mechanisms leads to weakened support for incremental and decremental specialisation, generalisation, attribution, behaviour extension and restriction, subtype implementation, substitutability and general code reuse

These remaining requirements can be discussed under the headings of modelling, signature modification and code reuse.

4.4. Support for Modelling

Support for the modelling aspect of inheritance could be improved by providing:

- less restricted modification of signatures
- a method for expressing mutual exclusion of subtypes
- a distinction between object types and attribute types

The first point will be discussed below. The second point could be supported by a mechanism for (optionally) naming the criteria by which types are specialised. For example:

```
object type male refines person by sex ... end male
object type female refines person by sex ... end female
object type child refines person by maturity ... end child
object type adult refines person by maturity ... end adult
```

It would then be legal to define a type 'girl' as inheriting from 'female' and 'child' but it would not be legal to define a type inheriting from both 'male' and 'female'. If multiple inheritance can be called 'and-inheritance' in the sense that a girl is a female *and* a child then this mechanism would also support 'or-inheritance' in the sense that a person can be either a male *or* a female[2].

A distinction between object types and attribute types would make clearer which types represent instantiable objects (nouns) and which types represent abstract attributes (adjectives) which are themselves not instantiable but which can be combined with many different object types to give new object types. For example:

---

2   We use the terms 'and'-inheritance and 'or'-inheritance differently to [LTP86].

```
object type book
  constructor new
  enquiry title : string
  ...
end

attribute type loanable
  enquiry date_due : date
  ...
end

object type library_book isa loanable book
  ...
end
```

Object types would have constructors and at least one implementation. Attribute types would have no constructors and need not (but can) have an implementation. (The implementation for 'date_due' could be provided in a 'from scratch' implementation of 'library_book' in accordance with the separation of type and implementation hierarchies).

Attribute types are a clear indication of the usefulness of multiple inheritance for type inheritance as well as for implementation inheritance.

4.5. Support for Signature Modification

Some kinds of signature modification are already allowed in Eiffel and Trellis/Owl. It is, of course, no accident that these are all modifications which preserve the number of parameters and make the subtype operation more general in their input (with the exception of covariant input parameters in Eiffel) and more restricted in their output. This is to preserve type-safe polymorphism. Other kinds of modification can, however, be very useful and are not necessarily 'type-dangerous'.

In particular, two situations exist in which more extensive modifications are useful, clear and safe:

1. when the operation is a 'type operation' such as a constructor and not an operation on an instance
2. when the parent type is used only for modelling or consistency

A constructor is in effect a call to a particular type to create a new instance of that type and is therefore never polymorphic. No dynamic type error can occur where it is statically clear which type is being called. This is very fortunate since, as stated above, it can be very useful to add further parameters to a constructor in a subtype.

An example of the second situation is an abstract type 'integer' with two descendants 'int' and 'longint' which have 32 and 64 bits respectively. The operations on integers are to be described in 'integer' but only 'int' or 'longint' are to be used in declarations. A particularly useful kind of covariance is the use of a reserved word **mytype** meaning the type of the type definition in which it occurs or to which it has been inherited. The 'integer' example could then look like this:

```
conceptual type integer
  proc add(in i:mytype)
  ...
end

object type int isa concrete integer end
object type longint isa concrete integer end
```

The reserved word **conceptual** means here that the type 'integer' may be used only for inheritance and not for declarations. The 'add' operation of 'int' would then have a parameter with the type 'int' and the 'add' operation of 'longint' would have a parameter with the type 'longint'. Since there are no variables of type 'integer' in a program, the covariant modification of the input parameter type from 'integer' to 'int' (or 'longint') can cause no problems.

The 'conceptual' tag could also be attached to individual operations rather than the entire type with the meaning that these operations can have more extensive signature modifications but may not be called (polymorphically) on the parent type. For example:

```
object type collection
  func number_of_elements : int
  func contains(in e : element) : boolean
  conceptual proc insert(in e : element)
  ...
end

object type duplicate_rejecting_set isa concrete collection
  proc insert(in e : element) : boolean
    pre not self.contains(e)
  ...
end
```

The operation 'insert' is marked as 'conceptual' and can therefore be modified in a way not compatible with type-safe polymorphism (in this case the addition of a precondition). Nevertheless, the type 'collection' can be used in declarations and polymorphic calls to 'number_of_elements' are allowed. The reserved word **concrete** means that inherited conceptual operations are no longer conceptual in the subtype.

Given the above extensions to an inheritance mechanism we can safely allow the following modifications to all constructors, to conceptual operations and to all operations of conceptual types:

- removal of the operation completely
- addition of parameters
- covariant modification of input parameter types
- addition of preconditions
- selective inheritance of parameters
- selective inheritance of postconditions
- contravariant modification of output parameter types

A particular language may not in fact allow all of these but they present no problem in principle. We consider the first four to be the most important.

In fact no extra syntax is really necessary to allow these modifications. The compiler could check which operations are used polymorphically in a program and then check that these are not modified in a way which could lead to a type error. We think it is much clearer, however, if the mechanism is made explicit.

4.6. Support for Code Reuse

Only two of the requirements from section 2 now remain unfulfilled. Both are concerned with implementation inheritance rather than type inheritance. They are:

- restrictions on redefinition to ensure strict substitutability
- selective inheritance of operation implementations to support general code reuse

The first of these could be realised simply by a further reserved word attached to an operation implementation with the meaning that the operation must be inherited by a sub-implementation and that it may not be redefined. This is equivalent to the 'final' modifier of Java if (as is the case in that language) all operation implementations *must* be inherited.

The second requirement is in principle no problem once implementation inheritance has been separated from type interfaces. In practice, however, it remains to be seen whether such a 'shopping list' approach to developing an implementation is really viable. We feel it should be supported until the question is resolved by experience.

5. Conclusion

The many different concepts supported by inheritance mechanisms have widely varying and sometimes contradictory requirements. By catering for the requirements which most concepts have in common, object-oriented languages usually fail to support any of them as well as possible. By concentrating on one concept, languages can neglect the requirements of other concepts. As a consequence, programmers and system designers are not well supported in formulating the type and implementation relationships as they wish.

We have shown that this situation can be improved by:
- realising some of the concepts by a mechanism other than inheritance
- distinguishing clearly between type relationships and code reuse
- providing some simple extensions to mechanisms for type inheritance

In particular we have argued for:
- support for expressing the mutual exclusion of subtypes
- distinguishing between abstract attribute types and 'genuine' object types
- more flexible signature modifications to support extensions and restrictions

We have shown that it is possible to allow more extensive signature modifications in a way which is both useful and type-safe.

We are currently implementing a new object-oriented language which includes these proposals and have used them extensively in constructing a library hierarchy of collection types. Our impression is that the increase in language complexity is more than outweighed by the advantages in clarity and expressive power.

References

[BR95]   Baumgartner, G. & Russo, V.F. (1995) "Signatures: A Language Extension for Improving Type Abstraction and Subtype Polymorphism in C++", Software - Practice and Experience, 25(8), pp. 863-889.

[Bee90] Beeri, C. (1990) "A Formal Approach to Object-Oriented Databases", Data and Knowledge Engineering, 5, 4, pp. 353-382.

[BC90]   Bracha, G. & Cook, W. (1990) "Mixin-based Inheritance", OOPSLA '90 Proceedings.

[CW85]   Cardelli, L. & Wegner, P. (1985) "On understanding types, data abstractions and polymorphism", ACM Computing Surveys, 17,4, pp. 471-522.

[CP89]   Cook, W. & Palsberg, J. (1989) "A Denotational Semantics of Inheritance and its Correctness", OOPSLA '89 Proceedings.

[Coo89]   Cook, W.R. (1989) "A Proposal for Making Eiffel Type-Safe",
            ECOOP '89 Proceedings.

[CHC90]   Cook, W.R., Hill, W.L. & Canning, P.S. (1990) "Inheritance is not
            Subtyping", Proceedings 17th ACM Symposium on Principles of
            Programming Languages.

[DG87]   DeMichiel, L. & Gabriel, R. (1987) "The Common Lisp Object
            System", ECOOP '87 Proceedings, pp.151-170.

[GR89]   Goldberg, A. & Robson, D. (1989) "Smalltalk-80: the language",
            Addison-Wesley Series in Computer Science.

[Kri89]   Kristensen, B.B., et.al. (1989) "The Beta Programming Language - a
            Scandinavian Approach to Object-Oriented Programming", OOPSLA
            '89 Tutorial Notes.

[KA90]   Khoshafian, S. & Abnous, R. (1990) "Object Orientation", Wiley,
            New York.

[LTP86]   LaLonde, W., Thomas, D. & Pugh, J. (1986) "An Exemplar-Based
            Smalltalk", OOPSLA '86 Proceedings.

[LP91]   LaLonde, W. & Pugh, J. (1991) "Subclassing ≠ Subtyping ≠ Is-a",
            Journal of Object-Oriented Programming, 3/91, pp. 57-62.

[Lis87]   Liskov, B. (1987) "Data Abstraction and Hierarchy", OOPSLA '87
            Addendum to the Proceedings.

[Mey86]   Meyer, B. (1986) "Genericity versus Inheritance", OOPSLA '86
            Proceedings.

[Mey88]   Meyer, B. (1988) "Object-Oriented Software Construction",
            International Series in Computer Science, Prentice-Hall, Englewood
            Cliffs.

[Mey92]   Meyer, B. (1992) "Eiffel: The Language", Prentice-Hall, New York.

[Mey96]   Meyer, B. (1996) "The many faces of inheritance: A taxonomy of
            taxonomy", IEEE Computer, May, 1996, pp. 105-108.

[Por92]   Porter, III, H.H. (1992) "Separating the Subtype Hierarchy from the
            Inheritance of Implementation", Journal of Object-Oriented
            Programming, 4, 9.

[Sch86]   Schaffert, C. et. al. (1986) "An Introduction to Trellis/Owl", OOPSLA
            '86 Proceedings.

[Sny86]   Snyder, A. (1986) "Encapsulation and Inheritance in Object-Oriented
            Programming Languages", OOPSLA '86 Proceedings, pp. 38-45

[Sun95]   Sun Microsystems, Inc. (1995) "The Java Language Specification",
            Version 1.0 Beta.

[Szy92]   Szyperski, C. (1992) "Import is Not Inheritance. Why We Need Both:
            Modules and Classes", Proceedings ECOOP '92, LNCS 615, Springer
            Verlag.

[Weg87]   Wegner, P. (1987) "Dimensions of Object-Based Language Design",
            OOPSLA '87 Proceedings, pp. 168-182

Inheriting Synchronization Protocols via Sound Enrichment Rules

František Plášil[1,2], Daniel Mikušík[1]

[1]*Charles University, Faculty of Mathematics and Physics,*
Department of Software Engineering
Malostranské náměstí 25, 118 00 Prague 1, Czech Republic
e-mail: {plasil, mikusik}@nenya.ms.mff.cuni.cz

[2]*Institute of Computer Science, Czech Academy of Sciences*
Pod vodárenskou věží, 180 00 Prague, Czech Republic
e-mail: plasil@uivt.cas.cz

Abstract. This paper introduces a method for inheriting PROCOL-like synchronization protocols to control access to objects. A synchronization mechanism should allow for incremental changes to the synchronization code through inheritance. To our knowledge, among the few existing synchronization mechanisms supporting such incremental modifications there is none based on the protocol paradigm. We present the novel concept of enrichable protocols which can be incrementally modified via, in principle, context-sensitive enrichment rules. With the intention to reflect the intuitive requirement that the synchronization policy associated with a base class should not be turned "upside-down" in subclasses, we derive the sound enrichment relation concept. To make it practically useful, we provide an algorithm for testing the relation; the algorithm is based on the mapping claim proven in the paper.

1 Introduction

1.1 Synchronization in Concurrent OO Languages

In procedural programming languages supporting concurrency, a need for synchronization tools based on the ADT abstraction was recognized in the early seventies (e.g. monitors [Hoa74], path expressions [CH74]). With the spreading of OO languages, a lot of effort was devoted to combining concurrency with the OO paradigm leading to the notion of Object-Oriented Concurrent Programming Languages (OOCPL). Of all the options they offer, we will limit ourselves to passive objects visited by multiple threads (potential concurrent invocation of an object's methods). Numerous synchronization mechanisms for this purpose have been designed during past decades.

Most of the existing mechanisms are based on the idea to represent an object's synchronization state and its history by the object's attributes and the state of the processing of the object's synchronization code. In a more acceptable case, such a mechanism separates strictly the "synchronization" and "sequential" attributes, and/or also the synchronization and sequential codes. This also provides a significantly better level of modularity. The type of a synchronization attribute may be at a high level of abstraction, like enabled-sets [TS89] or a reference to an object of the behavior class type [Atk90], or may be at a low level of abstraction, e.g. an integer or enumeration type. The state of the processing of an object's synchronization code is captured by the underlying implementation. However, parts of the state may be accessible in the synchronization code, for example, as scheduling predicates or synchronization counters. Naturally, the form of the synchronization code must comply with the operations defined for the types of synchronization attributes used in a particular object. These operations are evaluated as reactions to specific events, typically arriving of a method's execution request, finishing of the execution etc., or are even explicitly called in the sequential code of the object's methods. In general, there are many different notations for expressing synchronization code. To the representative ones belong guards (in a number of variants, e.g. [MWY90], [Ada94], [BLR94], [Fro92], synchronizers [MY93]), protocols (Path expressions [CH74], PROCOL [BL91], [Flo95]), enabled-sets, mediators [GC86], and generic synchronization policies [CMH95].

The expressive power of a synchronization mechanism is usually judged only informally by implementing several well-known synchronization policies. More objective criteria are provided by Bloom in [Blo79]: A synchronization mechanism has a good expressive power if it has access to the following six types of information: the name of the invoked operation, the relative arrival time of invocation, the actual parameters of the invocations, the synchronization state of the object, instance variables, and the history (of finished invocations).

First articulated in ([MWY90],[MY93]), one of the key issues of tying the OO paradigm and concurrency is the difficulty of combining inheritance and synchronization. The issue is closely related to the inheritance anomaly problem; for a detailed discussion we refer the reader to [MY93], [Mes93], [KL95], [CMH95]. In this paper, supporting McHale's opinion [CMH95] that the problem is intrinsic to inheritance rather than being a conflict between synchronization and inheritance, we follow his suggestion to tackle the problem by designing a new inheritance model or alternative ways to reuse code, rather than designing a new synchronization mechanism.

During inheritance, the synchronization code should be subject to incremental changes to reflect incremental modifications in synchronization policy. However, there are very few synchronization mechanisms which allow such incremental changes. Enabled-sets, Sos/Esp [CMH95], and activation conditions in Guide [BLR94] are representative examples. To our knowledge, as for the protocol-based synchronization mechanisms, little effort has been devoted to incremental modification of protocols during inheritance. In our view, a protocol-based synchronization mechanism is very powerful, particularly with respect to providing information on synchronization status and history. Even though we understand that to achieve what [CMH95] calls "degrade gracefully" (or to avoid "creeping featurism" [CMH95]), the protocol idea has to be combined with some other synchronization tools, e.g. event handlers (actions) and synchronization variables [CMH95], we believe that the protocol paradigm is worth cultivation as it provides a remarkable ease of expression of many of the standard synchronization policies.

1.2 Sound Incremental Modification of Inherited Synchronization Policies

Another important issue is the quality of incremental modification of synchronization policies during inheritance. Instinctively, such a change should not be "upside-down"; for example, while operating upon a particular object O, to replace the requirement of sequential execution of methods O.A and O.B by allowing their parallel execution is intuitively wrong. On contrary, to add a new method C and require O.C to be executed in a particular order with O.A and O.B is intuitively appropriate. In the rest of the paper, we refer to such an intuitively appropriate modification as *sound* modification.

The key issue is how to check the soundness of an incremental modification. To our knowledge, the only attitude in reflecting the idea of soundness is the requirement of strengthening guards (e.g. activation conditions in Guide, synchronization constrains in [Fro92]). Naturally, this approach is limiting as it fails, for example, in the case of very simple history sensitivity: O.C is to be executed after O.A and, in a subclass, O.C is to be executed after O.A or O.B where B is a new method of the subclass. It is apparent that "ORing" of guards would work in cases like this. In our view, the policy of strengthening guards can be interpreted as an effort to find an analogy with the policy of controlled modification of a redefined method's precondition and postcondition in Eiffel [Mey92] (strengthening postconditions, weakening preconditions in subclasses).

1.3 The Goal of the Paper

The goal of the paper is to introduce a mechanism for the inheritance of protocols controlling access to objects; such a mechanism should reflect the idea of incremental changes to synchronization code during inheritance. An additional goal is to make the presented mechanism limited only to "sound" modifications of the synchronization policy associated with a given object. Finally, the designed mechanism should be language-neutral, so that it could be used in different host environments, including, for example, a CORBA environment.

1.4 Structure of the Paper

The rest of the paper is organized as follows: In Section 2, we introduce our variant of PROCOL-like protocols and define the concept of *enrichable protocol*. Then, the concepts of protocol enrichment, based on *enrichment rules* and *the sound enrichment* relation, are introduced in Section 3. Also, a practically useful algorithm for testing the sound enrichment relation is presented in this section. A way of employing enrichment rules for expressing the incremental modification of protocols through inheritance in an Eiffel-like language is presented in Section 4. For illustration, our solutions to the gget and get2 classical inheritance anomaly examples [MY93] are provided in Section 5. In the conclusion (Section 6), we summarize and discuss the main advantages and disadvantages of our approach.

2 Protocols

2.1 Protocols in PROCOL

In PROCOL, the synchronization of class methods is taken outside the code of methods. In a class, the synchronization is defined in a syntactically separated construct (protocol part) by means of protocols; protocols are based upon path expressions. For example, if placed into class b_buf with the methods put, get, and init_b_buf, the protocol

```
init_b_buf;
((in<out+SIZE)put+(in>out+1)get )*
```

would define that b_buf's method init_b_buf is to be called first; then, alternatively (operator +), put or get can be called an unlimited number of times (operator *). An alternative can be chosen only if the boolean expression preceding it, its guard, is true. Thus, e.g., after init_b_buf is finished, calls of get would be delayed until in>out+1. For the complete b_buf definition including the protocol part, see the Section 5 (note there that the protocol part concentrates all the synchronization code of a class).

2.2 Enrichable Protocols

With the aim to make protocols subject to inheritance, we define "enrichable protocol" allowing for its incremental modification based upon enrichment rules (Section 3). An *enrichable protocol* (*protocol* for short) is syntactically defined by the context-free grammar $G=\{N,T,P,A\}$:

$N=\{A, B, C, D, E, F, M\}$
$T=\{+, ;, |, *, \wedge, (,), a, b, ..., z, 0, 1, ..., 9\}$
$P=\{$

$A \rightarrow A+B$,	$A \rightarrow B$,	
$B \rightarrow B;C$;	$B \rightarrow C$;	
$C \rightarrow C|D$;	$C \rightarrow D$;	
$D \rightarrow E^*$,	$D \rightarrow E^\wedge$,	$D \rightarrow E$,
$E \rightarrow M$,	$E \rightarrow (A)$	
$M \rightarrow Method\_Identifier$		

$\}$

For simplicity we have omitted obvious rewriting rules for Method_Identifier. In the following text we will use currier-typed method identifiers, i.e. a, m, put1. Basically, a protocol is an infix-written expression with the operator priority: + (lowest), ; , | , * , ∧ (highest). The semantics of operations + (alternative), ; (sequencing), * (repetition via sequencing: $p^*=(p;p;...;p)$) is the same as in PROCOL. However, our operation | (potential parallel execution) is modified: it allows for both operands to be protocols (only simple protocols, i.e. those not containing the | operator, are defined as operands of | in PROCOL). In addition, we introduce the new operation ∧ (potential reentrant execution: $p^\wedge = (p|p|...|p)$) to allow a protocol to be executed by a finite number of threads in parallel. As a special case, $m^\wedge$ defines the method m to be reentrant. By definition, the operations satisfy the following axioms (p, q, r are protocols):

$$
\begin{array}{llll}
p|q & = & q|p \\
p|(q|r) & = & (p|q)|r \\
p+q & = & q+p \\
p+(q+r) & = & (p+q)+r \\
r;(p+q) & = & r;p+r;q
\end{array}
\qquad
\begin{array}{llll}
r|(p+q) & = & r|p+r|q \\
p^\wedge|p & = & p^\wedge \\
p^\wedge+p & = & p^\wedge \\
p^*;p & = & p^* \\
p+p & = & p
\end{array}
$$

We assume that every protocol is associated with unambiguously determined *protocol tree* (operational tree), i.e. the tree of which all the leafs are method identifiers and other nodes are operators. For simplicity, we have omitted guards (allowed in PROCOL) from G. A way of employing guards in our protocols is informally discussed in Section 4.

3 Protocol Enrichment

Our approach to protocol inheritance is based upon the *enrichment rule* concept (Section 3.1). Enrichment rules are employed in the incremental modification of protocols (Section 3.3). With the intention to eliminate overly general modification of protocols during inheritance and thus to reflect the idea of sound modification mentioned in Section 1.2, we define the *sound enrichment* relation (Section 3.1). A practical algorithm for testing sound enrichment is provided in Section 3.2.

3.1 Enrichment Rule, Sound Enrichment Relation

An *enrichment rule* has the form

protocol_p -> protocol_q

The rule means that the protocol protocol_p is to be replaced by the protocol protocol_q. Moreover, to capture the idea of sound modification of protocols, we assume that protocol_p s_enrich protocol_q , i.e. protocol_q is a sound enrichment of the protocol_p. The sound enrichment relation is formally defined as follows:

Let p and q be protocols and tree_p and tree_q be the protocol trees of p and q. We say that q is a *sound enrichment* of p (denoted as p s_enrich q) if tree_q can be constructed from tree_p by a finite repetition of the following 3 actions (*enrichment step*. see also Figure 1):

1. Cut a (whole) subtree subtree_p (with a node R in its root) from tree_p.
2. Construct a protocol tree subst_tree containing subtree_p.
3. Modify tree_p by appending subst_tree to the edge which R was cut from ; i.e. put subst_tree into the original position of subtree_p in tree_p (the enrichment step).

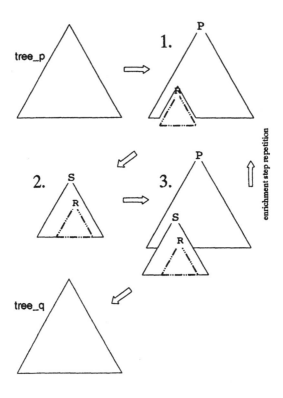

Fig. 1. Sound enrichment

Informally, "sound" means that some subexpressions in protocol_p are enhanced but kept in protocol_q (moved in the protocol tree of protocol_p in such a way that the original ordering of operations in protocol_p is preserved).

Inspired by the Eiffel requirement of strengthening a method's postcondition and weakening of the method's precondition when redefining the method in a subclass, we believe that also the "flavor" of the superclass's protocol should be preserved; e.g. if two methods can be run in parallel in a class, the same should be true in its subclass, if two methods are to be run in a particular sequence in a class, the order should be preserved in its subclass, etc. The sound enrichment relation is the framework for expressing the idea in an exact way. Table 1. illustrates the concept of sound enrichment on several examples. Indeed, the s_enrich relation excludes intuitively incorrect cases of protocol redefinition, e.g. calling the same methods in a different order (Table 1, fourth row), eliminating some members of parallel execution (third row), eliminating a member from an alternative execution (second row), replacing the synchronizing operation upon the method (first row).

correct	incorrect
a +b s_enrich a + b + c	a + b s_enrich a ; b + c
a + b + c s_enrich a + b + c + d	a + b + c s_enrich a + b
a l b s_enrich (a ; m) l b	a l b s_enrich a ; m l b
a ; b s_enrich a ; b	a ; b s_enrich b ; a

Table 1. Sound enrichment relation in examples

3.2 Verifying Sound Enrichment

The above definition of the sound enrichment relation does not, however, provide a way to effectively test for sound enrichment. The following algorithm had to be developed in order to do this. It tests whether Prot_1 s_enrich Prot_2 holds for any given protocols Prot_1 and Prot_2 (the input to the algorithm are the corresponding protocol trees Prot_tree1, Prot_tree2).

```
int Match(Prot_tree1, Prot_tree2)
            //returns 1 if Prot1 s_enrich Prot2; otherwise returns 0
{
List_of_nodes search_list;
if empty(Prot_tree1) return 1;
            // empty protocol is s_enriched by any protocol
if empty(Prot_tree2) return 0;
            // empty protocol can not be sound enrichment of non-empty protocol
T = find_first(root(Prot_tree1), Prot_tree2, &search_list);
            // it creates the search_list of all the nodes of Prot_tree2 that are labelled
            // equally as the root(Prot_tree1) is; it returns (and removes) the first node
            // from the list or NULL if search_list was empty
while (T<>NULL) {
    if ( Match(root(Prot_tree1)->Left_subtree), T->Left_subtree)
        && Match(root(Prot_tree1)->Right_subtree, T->Right_subtree) )
        return 1;
            // Protocols corresponding to the left and right subtrees of Prot_tree1 are
            // in s_enrich relation with protocols that correspond to the left and right
            // subtrees of T, respectively. If root(Prot_tree1) or T are unary operators
            // (*, ^), their right subtrees are considered empty
    else
        T = find_next(&search_list);
            // returns (and removes) the next node from search_list or NULL
};
return 0;
            // no more matches found
};
```

Intuitively, the algorithm looks for a mapping f from Prot_tree1 into Prot_tree2, such that for any pair of corresponding nodes a, b=f(a) their properties "being in the left subtree" or "being in the right subtree" are preserved. Note that in case of an unary operation the right subtree is considered empty.

The claim below has to be proven to show that the algorithm complies with the sound enrichment definition. In the claim, we use the following conventions. Let T be a protocol tree and let U be a node of the tree T (U∈T). By U_L (resp. U_R) we denote the left (resp. the right) subtree of the node U, (not including the node U). Further, ~ denotes the following equivalence: U ~ V iff$_{def}$ U and V represent the same method identifier or the same operator (+, ;, |, *, ^).

Claim (Mapping Claim):

   p s_enrich q

   iff

there exists a mapping f such that:

     a) f is a one-to-one mapping from tree_p into tree_q
         where tree_p (resp. tree_q) is the protocol tree of p (resp. q)
     b) f(V) ~ V for every node V ∈ tree_p
     c) $U ∈ V_X \Rightarrow f(U) ∈ f(V)_X$ for every U, V ∈ tree_p, and X ∈ {L, R}

Sketch of a proof:

Left to right implication: The definition of f is simple; it just maps nodes from tree_p onto "itself" in tree_q, as by step (2) of s_enrich definition, subtree_p is contained in subst_tree. That is why f is one-to-one mapping (a)) and f(V) ~ V (b)). The property c) is satisfied as by step (3) of the s_enrich definition subst_tree was appended to the same edge that subtree_p was cut from.

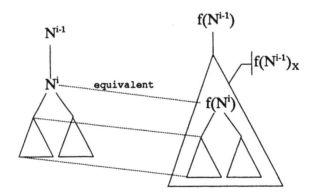

Fig. 2. Replacing N_L by $f(N)_L$

Right to left implication: If for given protocol trees tree_p (of a depth d) and tree_q there exists a mapping f with the properties a) - c), we can construct tree_q from tree_p by the following algorithm (see also Fig 2.):

```
for (i=d-1, i--, i>=0) {
    for every node N of depth i {
        cut off N_L and replace it by f(N)_L
        cut off N_R and replace it by f(N)_R
    }
}
```

As can be shown by induction, every execution of the inner cycle applies steps (1)-(3) of the s_enrich definition upon both the left and the right subtrees of N. Thus, after the outer cycle is finished, tree_p has been transformed into tree_q and the corresponding protocols p and q are in the sound enrichment relation.

□

3.3   Employing Enrichment Rules in Incremental Modification of Protocols

In this section, we present the *rule application algorithm* as a way of employing enrichment rules for incremental modification of protocols during inheritance.

To illustrate the principle of applying enrichment rules, consider that the protocol put;(put + get) defines the synchronization in the class buf; in its subclass xbuf, the synchronization is to be defined by the protocol put;(put;x + get). Instead of stating the protocol explicitly in xbuf, we employ protocol inheritance by providing the enrichment rule

put+get -> put;x + get

in xbuf. The inheritance mechanism applies the rule on the superclass protocol constructing as the result the protocol put ; (put ; x + get) which will define the synchronization in xbuf.

More formally, let p -> q be a rule, tree_p resp. tree_q be the protocol tree corresponding to p resp. q, and original_protocol be a protocol. Application of the rule p -> q upon original_protocol is defined by the following algorithm (*the rule application algorithm*):

Step 1 -   Create the protocol tree T of the original_protocol. Mark all its nodes as "unmodified".

Step 2 -   While an "unmodified" occurrence of tree_p is found in T, repeat steps 2a, 2b.

    Step 2a - An occurrence of tree_p is found; the corresponding subtree of T is cut off.

    Step 2b - Into the emptied space, the right side of the enrichment rule is appended (T is modified). The appended part of T is marked as "modified" (to prevent recursive replacements).

Step 3 - T defines the final_protocol.

□

Figure 3 illustrates the algorithm. Thus, the rule application algorithm modifies an *original protocol* into a *final protocol.*

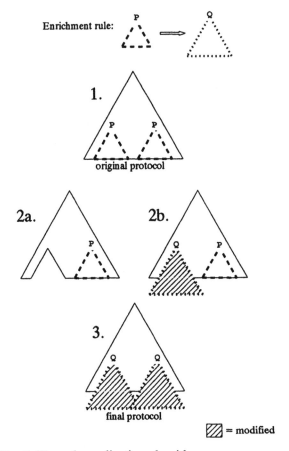

Fig. 3. The rule application algorithm

4 Using the Idea in an Eiffel-like Language

To describe the idea in more detail using Eiffel-like syntactical sugar, consider the following class C that inherits classes A, B... The access to C's methods is coordinated by the protocol constructed by application of the enrichment rules present in C's protocol part:

```
class C is
   inherit A;
   inherit B;
     . . .
   feature
      at1C:att1C;          -- attributes
      M1C is .... end;     -- methods
      M2C is .... end;
   protocol                -- protocol part
      from A               -- enriching A'sprotocol
         sub_p_exprA1 ->  enriched_sub_p_exprA1;
         sub_p_exprA2 ->  enriched_sub_p_exprA2;
           . . .
      from B               -- enriching B's protocol
         sub_p_exprB1 ->  enriched_sub_p_exprB1;
         sub_p_exprB2 ->  enriched_sub_p_exprB2;
           . . .
      from
         . . .
   invariant ...
end;    -- C
```

Using the rule application algorithm, the rules listed in a **from** X clause are applied on the protocol of the superclass X sequentially in the order they are listed in the **from** X clause. For example, the protocol of A (prot_A for short) is enriched as follows: A subtree corresponding to sub_p_exprA1 is identified in the tree of prot_A. Then the subtree is replaced by the subtree corresponding to the enriched_sub_p_exprA1. This is repeated until no other subtree corresponding to sub_p_exprA1 is present in the not yet modified part of the tree of prot_A; then, the second rule is applied, i.e. a subtree of sub_p_exprA2 is to be localized in the already modified tree of prot_A, etc.

In the case of multiple inheritance, the resulting protocol is constructed from the enriched protocols of all the superclasses by connecting them with the operation | (in principle the ancestors' methods are independent and therefore executable in parallel). For simplicity, we exclude the case of repeated inheritance.

Even though, in Sections 2 and 3, we supposed for simplicity no guards in protocols, there is a simple way of combining guards during protocol inheritance, namely by "ANDing" them; the following examples illustrate the idea:

original protocol:	`[G1]get+anything;[G2]get`
rule:	`get->[G3](get;xget)`
final protocol:	`([G1&G3](get;xget))+anything;` `([G2&G3](get;xget))`
original protocol:	`[G1]get+anything;[G2]get`
rule:	`get -> (get;[G3]xget)`
final protocol:	`[G1](get;[G3]xget)+anything;` `[G2](get;[G3]xget)`

where & denotes the logical "and" and by convention `[G1][G3]` = `[G1&G3]`. Note that we do not allow a guard on the left hand side of a rule.

5 Examples

In this section, we present our solution to the `gget` and `get2` classical inheritance anomaly examples [MY93]. Our version of the class b_buff looks as follows:

```
class b_buf
  creation
    init_b_buf
  feature
    in, out: integer;
    buf: array[item_type];

    init_b_buf is do in:=0; out:=0; end;
    put is do in:=in + 1; ... end;
    get is do out:=out + 1; ... end;
  protocol
    from ANY
      ->init_b_buf;([in<out+SIZE]put + [in>out+1]get )*;

end;     --b_buf
```

Notice the empty left-hand side of the enrichment rule - it defines the "base" protocol. It can be used only in a class for which all predecessors have empty protocol parts. The following class `gb_buf2` jointly presents the solution to the `get2` and `gget` problems [MY93].

```
class gb_buf2
  inherit
    b_buf
  feature
    gget is do out:=out + 1; ... end;     -- callable after
                                          -- put only
    get2 is do out:=out + 2; ... end;     -- gets 2 elements
  protocol
    from g_get
      put  -> (put+(put;[in>out+1]gget));
      get  -> (get+[in>out+2]get2);
end;     --gb_buf2
```

6   Conclusion, Related and Future Work

In this paper, we have defined the novel concept of enrichable protocols. A benefit of an enrichable protocol is that it can be inherited, and at the same time, be subject to incremental modification during the inheritance. The way it is modified is specified by means of, in principle, context-sensitive enrichment rules. Thus an enrichable protocol allows reuse of the synchronization code; in this way the need for potential rewriting of the entire protocol "by hand" in a subclass is avoided.

Moreover, to capture the intuitive notion of sound modification, we have introduced the concept of a sound enrichment relation. Sound enrichment ensures that the synchronization policy is "enriched", not turned "upside-down" in a subclass. Sound enrichment is based on the idea of enhancing subtrees in the given protocol tree. To make the concept practically useful, we presented an algorithm which tests for sound enrichment relations. Based on the mapping claim (Section 3.2), the algorithm looks for a one-to-one mapping between the left and right sides of an enrichment rule to verify that it satisfies the sound enrichment relation.

An important issue is combining protocols with guards. As we do not expect guards on the left hand side of a rule, the only way to modify guards is by "ANDing" them. This, in general, makes the resulting guard in a subclass more restrictive. In related work, e.g. ([Fro92], [BLR94]), the strengthening of guards approach does not fit well when synchronization attributes capturing the invocation history are used within guards (see e.g. the gget example in [MY93]); it is usually necessary to rewrite the synchronization code from scratch. However, if our protocol inheritance is used, such a problem is avoided in cases when the history can be captured by the expressive power of protocol. Even though our protocol inheritance works in the get2 (division of state) example [MY93], as presented in Section 5, the division of state problem is not generally solved by the protocol mechanism. Just imagine having get2 in the base class and trying to introduce get in a subclass; in this case, the state "empty_or_one" is to be divided which cannot be achieved by strengthening a guard. This is also related to the context sensitivity of enrichment rules discussed next.

The context sensitivity of enrichment rules has a shortcoming - we need a context in the protocol of a base class to be able to enrich it in a subclass. Introduction of a new method which does not relate to the methods currently present in the protocol is not possible. We may, however, require the base class to contain a "nucleus construct" allowing for future enrichments; this can be viewed as an analogy with generic classes and abstract methods. For example, the protocol [G1]a + [G2]b + dummy can be enriched by dummy->dummy+[G3]c. Without the dummy method, enrichment would not be possible as guards are not allowed on the left side of a rule.

As for future work, we intend to investigate whether the protocol concept can be combined with the generic synchronization policy (GSP) concept [CMH95]. We are going to explore the idea that a combination of GSP's in one object could be modelled by the parallel tracing of multiple protocols. For example, ReaderWriter({A,B},C) and Mutex({A,B,C}) could be modelled by, say, $((A+B)^\wedge+C)^*$ partrace $(A + B + C)^*$. Further, a more thorough study needs to be done to analyze the limitations of sound enrichment. At the same time, we intend to analyze in more detail the behavior of enrichable protocols with respect to inheritance anomaly.

The protocol concept is to be viewed more as a paradigm rather than as a specific synchronization mechanism. It is "open" in the sense that we do not specify the kind of information that guards can access. To create a concrete synchronization mechanism, the protocol concept might be combined with, for example, event handlers, scheduling predicates [MWBD92], etc. In a distributed environment, a protocol can be applied to control access to a server object, and, at the client side, to control the issuing of external requests.

A simple prototype implementation of enrichable protocols was designed [Mik96] with the intention to integrate enrichable protocols with the CORBA environment; the implementation is based on ideas very close to the dynamic protocol checking we found later in [Flo95]. Currently, an experimental implementation of protocol-based concurrency control in a CORBA environment is being realized as a part of the TOCOOS project [KPT96].

Acknowledgements: We are grateful to Martin Plátek for valuable comments on the text. A significant credit belongs to Michal Gróf who came up with the idea of "proper" modification of protocols which preserves the original "flavor" of protocols as mentioned in Section 3 and contributed to publications [PG94] and [PG95]. Finally, the authors are grateful to Adam Dingle for proofreading the text.

References:

[Ada94] Programming Language Ada. Language and Standard Libraries. Draft Version 5.0. IR-MA-1363-4, Ada 9X Mapping/Revision Team, Intermetrics, Inc., 733 Concord Avenue, Cambridge, Massachusetts 02138 (ANSI/ISO DIS 8652 Draft International Standard, June 1994

[Ame87] America, P.: Inheritance and Subtyping in a Parallel Object-Oriented Language. In: Proceedings of ECOOP'87, Springer LNCS 276, pp 234-242, 1987

[Ame90] America, P., van der Linden,F.: A Parallel Object-Oriented Language with Inheritance and Subtyping. In: Proceedings of OOPSLA'90, ACM SIGPLAN Notices, Vol.25, Oct.1990

[Ame91] America,P.: Designing an Object-Oriented Programming language with Behavioral Subtyping. In: Proceedings of the Workshop on Foundations of Object-Oriented Languages, Springer LNCS 489, pp 60-90, 1991

[Atk90] Atkinson, C.: An Object-Oriented Language for Software Reuse and Distribution. PhD thesis, Department of Computing, Imperial College of Science, Technology and Medicine, University of London, February 1990

[BL91] van den Bos J., Laffra C.: PROCOL - A concurrent object-oriented language with protocols delegation and constraints, Acta Informatica 28:511-538(1991)

[Blo79] Bloom, T. Evaluating Synchronization Mechanisms. In Seventh International ACM Symposium on Operating System Principles, pages 24-32, 1979.

[BLR94] Balter, R., Lacourte, S., Riveill, M.: The Guide Language, The Computer Journal, vol.37, Dec.94, pp.519-530

[CH74] Campbell, R.H., Habermann, A.N.: The specification of process synchronization by path expression (Springer LNCS, Vol. 16, 1974, pp. 89-102).

[CMH95] McHale, C.: Synchronization in Concurrent, Object-oriented Languages: Expressive Power, Genericity and Inheritance, PhD Thesis, (http://www.dsg.cs.tcd.ie/) October 1994

[Fer95] Ferenczi, S.: Guarded Methods vs. Inheritance Anomaly. Inheritance Anomaly Solved by nested Guarded Method Calls. ACM SIGPLAN Notices, Vol.30, No.2, Feb. 1995

[Flo95] Florijn, G.: Object Protocols as Functional Parsers, ECOOP'95, Springer LNCS 952, pages 351-373, August 1995

[Fro92] Frolund, S.: Inheritance of synchronization constraints in concurrent object-oriented programming languages. In O. Lehrmann Madsen, editor, Proc. ECOOP'92, pages 185-196. Springer LNCS 615, 1992.

[GC86] Grass, J.E., Campbell, R.H.: Mediators: A synchronization mechanism. Proceedings of the 6th International Conference on Distributed Systems (ICDCS), Cambridge, pp 468-477, IEEE 1986

[Hoa74] Hoare, C.A.R.: Monitors: An Operating System Structuring Concept. Communications of the ACM, 17(10):pages 549-557, October 1974

[KL89] Kafura, D.G., Lee, K.H.: Inheritance in actor based concurrent object-oriented languages. In: Proceedings of ECOOP'89, pages 131-145. Cambridge University Press, 1989

[KL90] Kafura, D.G., Lee, K.H.: ACT++: Building a Concurrent C++ with Actors. JOOP May/June 1990, pages 25-37

[KPT96] Kleindienst, J., Plášil, F., Tůma, P.: Lessons Learned from Implementing the CORBA Persistent Object Service, Proceedings of OOPSLA'96, ACM SIGPLAN Notices, pages 150-167, Vol. 31, Number 10, October 1996

[Mes93] Meseguer, J.: Solving the Inheritance Anomaly in Concurrent Object-Oriented Programming. Proceedings of ECOOP'93, LNCS, Springer July 1993

[Mey92] Meyer, B.: Eiffel: the language, Prantice Hall, 1992

[Mik96] Mikušík, D.: Implementing Protocols with Inheritance and Enrichment Rules, TR 96-3, Department of Software Engineering, Faculty of Mathematics and Physics, Charles University, available at http://www.uivt.cas.cz/~kleindie/

[MTY93] Matsuoka, S., Taura, K., Yonezawa, A.: Highly Efficient and encapsulated Re-use of Synchronization Code in Concurrent Object-Oriented languages. Proceedings of OOPSLA'93, pages 109-126, ACM 1993

[MWBD92] McHale, C., Walsh, B., Baker, S., Donnelly, A.: Evaluating Synchronization Mechanisms: The Inheritance Matrix. TR TCD-CS-92-18, Department of CS, Trinity College, Dublin. July1992

[MWY90] Matsuoka, S., Wakita, K., Yonezawa, A.: Synchronization Constrains with Inheritance: What is not possible - so what is? TR 10, Department of Information Science, University of Tokyo, 1990 (ftp: is.s.u-tokyo.ac.jp)

[MY93] Matsuoka, S., Yonezawa, A.: Analysis of Inheritance Anomaly in Object-Oriented Concurrent Programming Languages. In: Agha, G., Wegner, P., Yonezava, A., editors: Research Directions in Object-Based Concurrency, MIT Press, 1993

[Neu91] Neusius, Ch.: Synchronizing Actions. In: Proc. ECOOP'91, LNCS 512, 1991, pp.118-132

[NP90] Nierstrasz, O., Papathomas, M.: Viewing Objects as Paterns of Communicating Agents. In: ECOOP/OOPSLA'90 Proceedings, ACM, 1990

[Pap89] Papathomas, M.: Concurrency issues in object-oriented languages. In: Tsichritzis, D., editor: Object Oriented Development, Chapter 12, pp 207-245. Université de Genève, 1989

[PG94] Plášil, F., Gróf, M.: An Approach to Overcoming the Inheritance Anomaly, SOFSEM '94 conference, Czech Society for Computer Science, 1994

[PG95] Plášil, F., Gróf, M.: An Overcoming of Inheritance Anomaly, Département Informatique I.N.T., EVRY, France, TR n° 95-05-02

[Riv94] Riveill, M.: Synchronizing Shared Objects. Bull-IMAG/Systèmes, 1994 (ftp: imag.fr)

[Roset89] Tomlinson, Ch., Kim, W., Scheevel, M., Singh, V., Will, B., Agha, G.: Rosette: An Object-oriented Concurrent Systems Architecture. SIGPLAN Notices, Vol.24, No.4, 1989

[TS89] Tomlinson, Ch., Singh, V.: Inheritance and Synchronization with Enabled Sets. In: OOPSLA'89 Conference on Object-Oriented Programming, pages 103-112. ACM, 1989

Reflection in Oberon

Christoph Steindl

Department of Computer Science (System Software)
Johannes Kepler University Linz, Austria
steindl@ssw.uni-linz.ac.at

Abstract. We introduce metaprogramming facilities into the Oberon V4 system. Metaprogramming means that a module can access the structure of other modules (i.e., procedures, types, run-time data) at run time. We discuss how type safety can be enforced in an environment with strong typing. Finally we show how metaprogramming can be used to implement an easy-to-use database interface and conclude with a comparison with other metaprogramming systems for statically-typed programming languages.

1 Introduction

In programs we distinguish between the *data level* and the *program level*. Variables are at the data level and can be accessed by the statements of a program. Modules, types and procedures are at the program level. They serve to structure a program but they are usually not viewed as data. Sometimes, however, programs want to inspect the components of other programs at the program level, for example, in order to answer the following questions:

1. What are the field names of a record type T declared in module M?
2. Which procedures are currently active (e.g., when a run-time trap occurs)? What are the names, types and values of their variables?
3. Does the caller of the currently executing procedure have a variable named "x", and if so, what is its type and value?

Questions like these are considered to be on a *meta level*. They treat modules, types, and procedures as data. They have to know the structure of this "data" in order to access (or modify) their contents. If a programming system supports questions of this kind we call it a *metaprogramming system*. If programs can ask these question also about themselves we call such a system *reflective*.

The notions of metaprogramming and reflection are common and widely used in programming languages like Lisp ([McCar60], [Smi82]) and Smalltalk ([GR83]). In Lisp all programs are treated as data. It is possible to inspect their structure and even to dynamically build new programs (higher order functions) that can be executed. In Smalltalk types are represented as classes and procedures as methods of these classes. The structure of a class is described in a metaclass of which the class is an instance. The metaclass information can again be accessed and even modified. Many other languages allow metaprogramming in a similar way (e.g., Self [US87], CLOS [Att89], or BETA [MMN93]).

The original Oberon system [WiGu89] is a modular operating system based on the general-purpose programming language Oberon. It offered only a limited degree of metaprogramming. It provided a module *Modules* which allowed programmers - among other things - to inspect information about all loaded modules. Later a module *Types* was added, which provided basic information about record types. However, *Types* was not documented in the books about Oberon ([Rei91], [WiGu92]). In his dissertation ([Tem94]), J. Templ implemented an experimental version of Oberon for Sun workstations, which treated modules, procedures, and record types as data allowing full access to their components.

Metaprogramming and reflection are not widely used in statically typed programming languages, although their use might be beneficial, too. One reason is the need for special language constructs to express the access to meta-level information. The code accessing meta-level information must be type-checked at compile time although it will have to work with arbitrary (yet unknown) types and modules.

We introduce support for metaprogramming and reflection into the Oberon system not via new language constructs, but via a new library. Together with the compiler and the dynamic loading facility of the Oberon system it is possible to construct program fragments at run time, to dynamically load and execute them.

In the next section, we provide background about metaprogramming and reflection. In section 3 we introduce our support for metaprogramming and reflection. In section 4 we present applications that make use of the new facilities. In section 5 we compare our approach with other systems, and present our conclusions in section 6.

2 Background

In this section we explain the controversy between a rigid, but safe type system and a system that allows for metaprogramming. We explain what we understand under introspective, invocational, and intercepting capabilities of a metaprogramming system. Furthermore we show to which amount meta-information is produced by standard Oberon compilers ([Cre90]).

2.1 Roles of the Type System

There is a controversy between a rigid type system and a system that allows for metaprogramming. The first sacrifices flexibility for increased safety, the latter increases flexibility.

The type system of a language plays three roles ([Ste+93]):

- it shall facilitate data modelling,
- it shall help detect and avoid errors in programs at compile time, and
- it shall allow efficiency in code generation.

Static type checking verifies type assertions prior to a program's execution. Strong typing is a little weaker in that it only requires that all programming entities be typed before use and that all use be consistent with the type system. Strong typing ensures that a certain class of errors is cleanly detected and static typing improves efficiency by removing type checks from run-time code. The goal of most type systems is to make checking as static and thus as efficient as possible. However, some type checking cannot be performed statically (especially with object-oriented programming languages). Some programs will be rejected by the type checker as being unsafe although they might execute without errors.

Oberon is a general-purpose programming language in the tradition of Pascal and Modula-2. Its most important features are block structure, modularity, separate compilation, static typing with strong type checking (also across module boundaries), and type extension with type-bound procedures.

Metaprogramming introduces much flexibility into a system: problems that have previously been unsolvable or hard to solve can now be easily solved (e.g., automatic persistence of objects). It allows programs that are more interpretative in their nature, programs that act on arbitrary other programs. Compiling such programs with static type-checking is apparently difficult, if not impossible.

Within a strongly-typed environment, code accessing meta-level information must pass type-checking. Nevertheless meta-programs may have to work with arbitrary types and programs. A generic mechanism must be at hand to access all possible kinds of types and programs (even those that will be created some time in the future).

2.2 Introspective, Invocational, and Intercepting Capabilities

The metaprogramming system should provide introspective, invocational, and intercepting capabilities ([Bra95]).

Introspection allows a program to look into itself, to inspect other programs, and to obtain information about the current run-time state. It does not allow the program to perform any changes.

Invocational capabilities allow a program to explicitly call functionality that is normally hidden in the run-time system, e.g. creation of new objects, dynamic loading, linking, and unloading of compiled code.

Intercepting capabilities allow a running program to change the behaviour of language primitives at run time, e.g., object creation and destruction, method dispatch, and access to simple attributes.

2.3 Reference Information

To implement these capabilities, information that is contained in the symbol table during compilation must be accessible at run time. It must be possible to get information about the type of an object, about its fields, and it must be possible to get information about the parameters and local variables of procedures.

The compiler ([Cre90]) used in many Oberon environments generates an object file and a symbol file out of an Oberon source file using the symbol files of imported modules in order to get type information about imported items and to detect changes to the interface of the imported modules. Furthermore a reference file is generated containing information about the types and procedures defined in the module. The reference file does not exist as an own file but is appended to the object file, which reduces the overall number of files. When a module is loaded, its data and code are loaded into memory, the type descriptors for the types defined in the module are built and the reference information contained in the reference section of the object file is loaded into memory as well.

The structure and contents of the reference section can be considered as a simplified or linearized symbol table. Therefore it contains information about the fields of record types, information about local variables and parameters of procedures, and information about global data. An EBNF grammar describing the contents of the reference section can be found in [StM96].

3 Module Ref

We opted not to extend the programming language Oberon to facilitate metaprogramming but to extend the Oberon system by a new module which supports metaprogramming.

Module *Ref* can be used to obtain information about the procedures, record types, and variables of a module. For example, it is possible to access the names, types and components of these items at run time. For variables it is also possible to read and write their values.

3.1 Riders

All information is accessible via *riders*. A rider is a cursor that iterates over sequences of variables, procedures, types, or other items. The general pattern for using a rider r is

```
Ref.Open ... (..., r);
WHILE r.mode # Ref.End DO
  ...
  r.Next
END
```

At any time the rider contains information about the item on which it is positioned. A rider can be opened on data (global variables, local variables, heap) or on a module's list of its procedures or record types (see Table 1).

Program data is organised hierarchically, e.g., the stack is a sequence of stack frames, which are sequences of variables, which may be sequences of record fields and so on. Table 2 shows the organisation of data.

Table 1. Opening Riders

global variables	OpenVars(module, r)	sets r to the first global variable of the module *module*
local variables	OpenStack(info, r)	sets r to the topmost stack frame
heap	OpenPtr(p, r)	sets r to the first record field or array element to which *p* refers
procedures	OpenProcs(module, r) OpenProc(pc, r)	sets r to the first procedure of the module *module*, or to the procedure containing *pc*
record types	OpenTypes(module, r)	sets r to the first record type of the module

Table 2. Organisation of Data

Stack	= {Frame}.	*accessible via OpenStack*
Frame	= {Variable}.	
Variable	= simpleVar | RecordVar | ArrayVar.	
RecordVar	= {Field}.	
ArrayVar	= {Elem}.	
Field	= Variable.	
Elem	= Variable.	
Globals	= {Variable}.	*accessible via OpenVars*
PointerBase	= RecordVar | ArrayVar.	*accessible via OpenPtr*
Procedure	= {Proc}.	*accessible via OpenProcs*
Proc	= {Variable}.	*and via OpenProc*
Types	= {RecordType}.	*accessible via OpenTypes*
RecordType	= {Field}.	

When a rider is positioned on a composite item it is possible to zoom into this item and iterate over its elements. For example, to iterate over the variables of the second frame on the stack (i.e., the variables of the caller of the currently active procedure) one does the following:

```
Ref.OpenStack(NIL, r);   (* r is on the frame of currently active procedure *)
r.Next;                  (* r is on the caller's frame *)
r.Zoom(r)                (* r is on the first variable of the caller's frame *)
```

DEFINITION **Ref**;

IMPORT SYSTEM, Types;

CONST
  (* *item forms* *)
  None = 0; **Byte** = 1; **Bool** = 2; **Char** = 3; **SInt** = 4; **Int** = 5; **LInt** = 6;
  Real = 7; **LReal** = 8; **Set** = 9; **String** = 10; **NilTyp** = 11; **NoTyp** = 12;
  Pointer = 13; **Procedure** = 14; **Array** = 15; **Record** = 16; **DynArr** = 17;
  (* *item modes* *)
  End = 0; **Var** = 1; **VarPar** = 2; **Elem** = 3; **Fld** = 4; **Frame** = 5;
  Proc = 6; **Type** = 7;

TYPE
  ProcVar = PROCEDURE;

  Rider = RECORD
    name: ARRAY 32 OF CHAR;
    mode: SHORTINT; (* *End .. Type* *)
    form: SHORTINT;
    idx, off, len: LONGINT;
    mod: ARRAY 32 OF CHAR;
    level: SHORTINT;

    PROCEDURE (VAR r: Rider) **Next**;
    PROCEDURE (VAR r: Rider) **Zoom** (VAR sub: Rider);
    PROCEDURE (VAR r: Rider) **Adr** (): LONGINT;
    PROCEDURE (VAR r: Rider) **Type** (): Types.Type;
    PROCEDURE (VAR r: Rider) **SetTo** (idx: LONGINT);

    PROCEDURE (VAR r: Rider) **Read** (VAR ch: CHAR);
    PROCEDURE (VAR r: Rider) **ReadInt** (VAR i: INTEGER);
    PROCEDURE (VAR r: Rider) **ReadProc** (VAR p: ProcVar);
    PROCEDURE (VAR r: Rider) **ReadPtr** (VAR p: SYSTEM.PTR);
    PROCEDURE (VAR r: Rider) **ReadString** (VAR str: ARRAY OF CHAR);
    ...
    PROCEDURE (VAR r: Rider) **Write** (ch: CHAR);
    PROCEDURE (VAR r: Rider) **WriteInt** (i: INTEGER);
    PROCEDURE (VAR r: Rider) **WriteProc** (p: ProcVar);
    PROCEDURE (VAR r: Rider) **WritePtr** (p: SYSTEM.PTR);
    PROCEDURE (VAR r: Rider) **WriteString** (str: ARRAY OF CHAR);
    ...
  END ;

  ExceptionInfo = ...; (* *machine state: system dependent* *)

  PROCEDURE **OpenVars** (mod: ARRAY OF CHAR; VAR r: Rider);
  PROCEDURE **OpenStack** (inf: ExceptionInfo; VAR r: Rider);
  PROCEDURE **OpenPtr** (p: SYSTEM.PTR; VAR r: Rider);
  PROCEDURE **OpenProcs** (mod: ARRAY OF CHAR; VAR r: Rider);
  PROCEDURE **OpenTypes** (mod: ARRAY OF CHAR; VAR r: Rider);
  PROCEDURE **PC** (mod, name: ARRAY OF CHAR): LONGINT;
  PROCEDURE **OpenProc** (pc: LONGINT; VAR r: Rider);
END Ref.

Operations

- *OpenVars(mod, r)* sets the rider *r* to the first global variable of module *mod*.
- *OpenStack(inf, r)*. If *inf* = NIL the rider *r* is set to the stack frame of the
  procedure that called *OpenStack*. If *inf* # NIL, it describes the machine state
  at the time of a run-time exception (trap); the rider *r* is set to the stack

frame of the procedure in which the trap occurred.

- *OpenPtr(p, r)* sets the rider *r* to the first field of the record pointed to by *p*.
- *OpenProcs(mod, r)* sets the rider *r* to the first procedure of module *mod*.
- *OpenTypes(mod, r)* sets the rider *r* to the first record type of module *mod*.
- pc := *PC(mod, name)* returns the absolute start address of the procedure *name* declared in module *mod*.
- *OpenProc(pc, r)* sets the rider *r* to the procedure that contains the (absolute) program counter value *pc*.
- *r.Next* advances the rider *r* to the next item (variable, array element, record field, stack frame, procedure, or record type). If *r* was already positioned on the last item, *r.mode* is set to *End*.
- *a := r.Adr()* returns the address of the current item (variable, parameter, record field, or array element).
- *t := r.Type()* returns the type of the current item if this item is of a record type, otherwise the result is undefined.
- *r.Zoom(sub)*. If *r* is positioned on a composite item, a new rider *sub* is set to the first component of the composite according to Table 3.
- *r.SetTo(i)*. If *r* is positioned on an element of an array (*r.mode = Elem*), it is set to the *i*-th element of that array. If it is positioned on the fields of a record type *T* (*r.mode = Fld*), it is set to the first field of the *i*-th extension level of *T*.
- *r.ReadX*. If *r.mode* IN { *Var, VarPar, Fld, Elem*} and if *r* (or the rider from which it was zoomed) was opened with *OpenVars*, *OpenStack* or *OpenPtr*, the value of the current item can be read with the *ReadX* procedure that matches the *form* of the item (i.e., *r.ReadInt* if *r.form = Int*).
- *r.WriteX*. If *r.mode* IN { *Var, VarPar, Fld, Elem*} and if *r* (or the rider from which it was zoomed) was opened with *OpenVars*, *OpenStack* or *OpenPtr*, the value of the current item can be written with the *WriteX* procedure that matches the *form* of the item.

Table 3. Zooming into Riders

r.mode	r.form	sub.mode
Var, VarPar, Elem, Fld	Record, Pointer to Record	Fld
Var, VarPar, Elem, Fld	Array, DynArr, Pointer to Array or DynArr	Elem
Type	—	Fld
Proc, Frame	—	Var or VarPar

4 Applications

We have implemented the following tools using module *Ref*:

- a post-mortem debugger that is invoked when another program terminates with a trap. Its responsibility is to show the machine state in a human-readable form. We show all variables in the same window and expand structured variables "in place". A mechanism for "zooming" into structures was already available in the Oberon system in the form of fold elements [MöKo96]. We extended the fold elements so that they now include also relevant reference information.

- showing the global variables of a module: As in the original Oberon system, the command System.State opens a viewer displaying the global variables of the specified module with the possibility to zoom into structured variables.
- a heap inspector which displays a bitmap that represents the heap. All blocks of a desired type are coloured red. By clicking on a block, the information contained in the block is displayed. Furthermore information about the number and sizes of objects, the memory space occupied by objects of a specified type, etc. is displayed.
- a general output module which can be used to facilitate simple output.
- a database interface.

In the following we will explain the usage of the database interface in more detail (see also [Ste96b]).

4.1 A Database Interface

Databases allow users to perform queries on the stored data. Some databases even allow queries to be executed from within a program. That means that the programming language has to be extended so that query statements can be expressed or that a preprocessor must be used to specify the query in a preprocessor language.

Using module *Ref*, one can specify such queries as strings and pass them to a procedure that analyses the strings and executes the statements described by them. For example, one can write

conn.Prepare("CREATE TABLE Persons FOR Person")

without needing a language extension nor a preprocessor. We implemented a module *ESQL* [Ste96a] that provides access to ODBC databases [ODBC94].

DEFINITION **ESQL**;

CONST
  (* *return codes* *)
  InvHandle = -2; **Error** = -1; **Success** = 0;
  SuccessWithInfo = 1; **NoDataFound** = 100;

TYPE
  Connection = POINTER TO ConnectionD;
  ConnectionD = RECORD
    ret: INTEGER; (* *return code of last operation* *)
    PROCEDURE (c: Connection) **Prepare** (sqlStr: ARRAY OF CHAR): Statement;
  END ;
  Statement = POINTER TO StatementD;
  StatementD = RECORD
    ret: INTEGER; (* *return code of last operation* *)
    conn-: Connection; (* *the connection on which the statement is executed* *)

```
PROCEDURE (s: Statement) Execute;
PROCEDURE (s: Statement) Fetch (): BOOLEAN;
PROCEDURE (s: Statement) IsNull (name: ARRAY OF CHAR): BOOLEAN;
PROCEDURE (s: Statement) SetNull (name: ARRAY OF CHAR);
END ;

PROCEDURE Open (source, user, passwd: ARRAY OF CHAR): Connection;

END ESQL.
```

Types

- *Connection* represents a communication channel between the application and the database. Requests are issued and responses are returned via this connection. *ret* indicates the success of the last operation.
- *Statement* represents an SQL statement that has been prepared for execution via connection *conn*. *ret* indicates the success of the last operation.

Operations

- *conn := Open(source, user, password)* opens a connection to the database with the given user identification and password.
- *stat := conn.Prepare(s)* prepares an SQL statement (specified by the string *s*) for execution.
- *stat.Execute* executes the previously prepared SQL statement.
- *done := stat.Fetch()*. If the execution of an SQL statement results in a table (i.e., a sequence of records), *Fetch* retrieves one row of the table (i.e., one record of this sequence) at a time and stores it in the variable(s) specified in the statement. If there are no more rows to retrieve, *done* becomes FALSE.
- *b := stat.IsNull(n)* returns TRUE if the variable specified by the name *n* contains a null value. Null values are special values which indicate that the value is not valid or present. As this cannot be expressed by a legal value in programming languages (e.g., 0 for integer variables, or "" for string variables), *IsNull* is necessary to check for the validity of a value.
- *stat.SetNull(n)* makes the variable specified by the name *n* contain a null value.

4.2   Embedded SQL and Oberon

For data transfer between the database and the application, SQL statements use ordinary Oberon variables. In order to distinguish these variables from names that are used within the database (e.g. names of tables and columns), they are preceded by a colon. In the SQL statement

"SELECT firstName FROM Persons WHERE age > :minAge INTO :name"

minAge and *name* are Oberon variables. *minAge* is an input variable, and *name* is an output variable.

Variables can be either scalar or of a record type. When record variables are specified, they are implicitly expanded to their fields. The statement
"SELECT * FROM Persons INTO :person"
is therefore equivalent to
"SELECT * FROM Persons INTO :person.firstName, :person.lastName, :person.age".

We declare the type *Person* that will be used to represent persons. After opening the connection, we create a table for the persons that we will insert later on. The table will consist of as many columns (with appropriate types) as there are fields in the record type *Person*. The record type can be qualified with the module in which the type is declared.

```
TYPE
    Person = RECORD
        firstName, lastName: ARRAY 32 OF CHAR; age: INTEGER
    END ;

VAR
    conn: ESQL.Connection; stat: ESQL.Statement;

BEGIN
    conn := ESQL.Open(source, user, password);
    stat := conn.Prepare("CREATE TABLE Persons FOR Person");
    stat.Execute
END
```

In order to insert data into the table, we prepare an INSERT statement in which we specify the variables containing the values to be inserted (*firstName, lastName, age*). These variables are preceded by a colon (which distinguishes them from database identifiers for tables and columns). Then we assign values to the variables and consider null values (i.e., values that should remain undefined). When we finally execute the statement the values from the variables are taken and transferred into the database. Note that the statement - once it has been prepared - can be executed several times with different values.

```
PROCEDURE Insert;
    VAR firstName, lastName: ARRAY 32 OF CHAR; age: INTEGER;
BEGIN
    In.Open;
    stat :=
        conn.Prepare("INSERT INTO Persons VALUES (:firstName, :lastName, :age)");
    REPEAT
        In.Name(firstName); In.Name(lastName); In.Int(age);
        IF firstName = "NULL" THEN stat.SetNull("firstName") END ;
        IF lastName = "NULL" THEN stat.SetNull("lastName") END ;
        IF In.Done THEN stat.Execute END
    UNTIL ~In.Done
END Insert;
```

In order to retrieve all persons older than *minAge* we can use the following procedure *Select*. After preparing the SELECT statement and assigning values to the input variables (in this case *minAge*), we execute the statement and fetch the resulting data row by row. As the table is defined for the type *Person*, every row is a record of type *Person*. If we were only interested in the columns *firstName* and *lastName*, we could use a SELECT statement like "SELECT firstName, lastName FROM Persons WHERE age >= :minAge INTO :person.firstName, :person.lastName".

```
PROCEDURE Select;
  VAR person: Person; minAge: INTEGER;
BEGIN
  stat := conn.Prepare
    ("SELECT * FROM Persons WHERE age >= :minAge INTO :person");
  In.Open; In.Int(minAge);
  stat.Execute;
  WHILE stat.Fetch() DO
    Out.Ln; Out.String(person.firstName); Out.Char(" ");
    Out.String(person.lastName); Out.String(", ");
    IF stat.IsNull("person.age") THEN Out.String("NULL")
    ELSE Out.Int(person.age, 0)
    END
  END
END SelectAll;
```

Implementation. The analysis of the SQL commands is implemented using module *Ref*. Any variable preceded by a colon is looked up in the local scope of the procedure that issued the SQL statement (the local scope contains the local variables, as well as the parameters of the procedure). The addresses of such variables are then passed to the database driver. When processing a "CREATE TABLE" statement, the variables' types are used to generate the expanded SQL statement with a column for each scalar variable (with type and name).

A minor restriction is that the variables specified in an SQL statement must exist when the statement is actually executed. Local variables go out of scope when the procedure returns. Therefore it is not possible to use local variables in an SQL statement and execute the statement at a moment where these variables do no longer exist.

5 Comparison

We support introspective capabilities to a high degree. Via the standard modules *Modules* and *Types*, information about loaded modules and their type descriptors is available. For a description of these modules see [StM96]. We also provide access to global variables of modules, to variables and parameters of procedures, to the currently active procedures, and to the fields of record types. When a rider is positioned and the value over which the rider is positioned shall be read, run-time checks are performed. Therefore we do not lose type safety, but ensure type safety at run time. Up to now, we do not restrict access to the exported interface of the modules but we provide access to all available items, e.g. we allow access to non-exported global variables, likewise we allow access to local variables of procedures. The motivation behind this was to extend the scope of applications (e.g., also to post-mortem debuggers, etc.) which need access to more than only exported variables.

Invocational capabilities are supported by the standard Oberon system to a large degree. New objects can be created via module *Types*, modules can be loaded on demand via module *Modules* (they are automatically linked to the already loaded modules), and modules that are not needed any more can be freed explicitly. A running program can also invoke the compiler to generate new object code, which can then be loaded. The linking loader checks whether the version of the module that shall be loaded is consistent with the versions of the modules that are already loaded. We do not provide a generic mechanism for the invocation of procedures, i.e. it is not possible to call arbitrary procedures. Nevertheless it is possible to read procedure variables via a rider (e.g., *r.ReadProc(p)*). If the parameter list of the procedure is known at compile time, this procedure variable p can be type-cast to a procedure variable of the proper type (e.g., *handler := SYSTEM.VAL(Display.Handler, p)*) and the procedure can then be invoked via this procedure variable where the compiler handles the parameter passing (e.g., *handler(f, msg)*). We admit that this is a major restriction, but accept it for the sake of simplicity.

Intercepting capabilities are not fully supported up to now. It is possible to position a rider over data and update the values of the data. Scalar variables, as well as procedure variables and pointer variables can be updated. Run-time checks enforce type compatibility of the value and the memory location that shall be updated. It is not possible to install callback procedures that are called if an object of a given type is created. Up to now patching the method table is also not supported, as this is considered dangerous. It is also not possible, to be notified of access to simple attributes of a record.

There is no run-time overhead if metaprogramming and reflection are not used. Only when meta-information is needed, it is looked up. But even this lookup is very efficient, since the reference information is kept in memory and there is no disk access.

The main source of inspiration for our support for metaprogramming was the dissertation of J. Templ [Tem94]. He implemented a version of the Oberon System with better support for metaprogramming than our extension to the Oberon System. In his metaprogramming protocol he provides generic access to objects in a way similar to ours (actually we provide access to objects in a way similar to his approach). His work inspired us to use iterators to access arbitrary data structures. We unified the iterators to one type (*Rider*) which serves as a *Rider*, *ArrayRider*, *RecordRider*, or *ActivationRider* in his terminology. We also unified the way how the iterators are opened by the *Zoom* operation. Therefore we think to provide a more orthogonal approach but with some restrictions that did not exist in his system. In particular he provides a mechanism to control procedure activations. Arbitrary procedure objects can be evaluated with arbitrary parameters (*PROCEDURE Eval (proc: Procedure; VAR par: Parameters)*). Therefore it is necessary to tag procedures (like ordinary objects in Oberon are tagged, i.e., each object has a reference to its type descriptor). Every procedure has its own parameter record with the procedure specific parameters. Access to these parameters is available via *GetParams(p, params)*. *OpenParams(paramRider, params)* can then be used to iterate over the parameters and set the input parameters accordingly. Finally *Call(proc, params)* calls the procedure *proc* with the parameters *params*. He also introduces the notion of *active procedures*, i.e. procedures which have a message handler installed in order to react to messages sent to them. A generic message handler would simply evaluate the procedure object with the parameters of the message, but more specific message handlers can filter messages, can access and modify parameters before and after the evaluation.

The metaprogramming support in Oberon/F [Pou95] apparently also stems from the dissertation of J. Templ. In contrast to our approach, Oberon/F restricts access to public information, i.e. it does not allow access to non-exported items of a module. They guarantee safety because their metaprogramming support does not allow to change data which is not exported as modifiable. It only allows to do with a module what could also be done by a normal client module - but in a more dynamic way. It allows inspection and modification of data depending on run-time decisions, without static import of the inspected or modified module. In Oberon/F it is not possible to implement a post-mortem debugger building on the metaprogramming support as it is not possible to access the procedure activation stack. Furthermore it is not possible to inspect the variables of procedures or the types defined by a module. As far as we know, Oberon/F only provides access to global data with the possibility to zoom into the data structures at run time.

The meta-level architecture for the BETA language ([Bra95], [MMN93]) uses language extensions so that the compiler can type-check code that exploits the meta-information. But in order to perform the really interesting tasks like automatic persistence of objects, unconstrained attribute references are necessary which cannot be type-checked at compile time. The introspective capabilities seem to be quite powerful and comparable to the capabilities provided by our system. The invocational capabilities include replacement of code objects. We did not support this (which could be done by patching the method table of type descriptors), as we consider this to be dangerous. All the other aspects of invocational capabilities of the BETA meta-level architecture are equally covered by our system. The intercepting capabilities are more powerful than in our system. It is possible to register a callback procedure to trace instantiation of objects of a given type. Tracing of garbage collected objects is also possible. This is supported in our system by the mechanism of finalization (see [Tem94] for more details), where an object can register a procedure that will be called if the object is about to being garbage collected. Furthermore method dispatch and simple attribute access can be intercepted. We did not include this into our metaprogramming system as we consider patching the method table dangerous and because intercepting access to simple attributes can only be done at a high cost. Nevertheless work is going on in the area of safe and transparent remote method invocation (see [Hof96] for details).

CLOS [Kiz+91] includes a comprehensive meta-level interface, which allows the meta-level programmer to inspect and change several primitives of the basic programming language, including redefinition of slot access, multiple inheritance semantics, and replacement of meta-classes. We do not reach the same expressive power as CLOS, but we found many applications where our support for metaprogramming was sufficient.

C++ [Str94] has the concept of pointers to members which are basically offsets of attributes within objects. These pointers to members can be applied to objects to get the value of the member they are declared to point to. However, access to run-time type information is only rudimentary supported via the dynamic_cast and typeid; garbage collection is only rarely used in C++ environments. Therefore we do not consider C++ to encourage reflection.

6 Conclusions

We designed and implemented support for metaprogramming and reflection for the interactive environment of the Oberon system. We made use of dynamic linking and loading, of run-time invocation of the compiler and of the reference information that is generated by the compiler. Our system does not incur any run-time overhead, but still provides for powerful metaprogramming. As there are already tools for profiling, the need for additional intercepting capabilities (interception of method invocation) is not as big as in other systems. Other problems like type-orthogonal persistence ([Kna96]) and distributed object systems ([Hof96]) are currently solved at the department, partly based on the metaprogramming system.

As metaprogramming systems are still rare for strongly-typed systems, we believe that we can contribute that the concepts of metaprogramming are spread among the undergraduate students that have to use our version of the Oberon system in programming courses. We hope that some of them will recognise and exploit the possibilities of metaprogramming and reflection.

Acknowledgements

We wish to thank J. Templ and H. Mössenböck and all other members of the department for fruitful discussions and hints. Further thanks go to the anonymous referees that supplied interesting comments.

References

[Att89] G. Attardi et al.: Metalevel Programming in CLOS. Proceedings of the ECOOP'89 conference. Cambridge University Press, 1989.

[Bra95] S. Brandt, R.W. Schmidt: The Design of a Meta-Level Architecture for the BETA Language.

[Cre90] R. Crelier: OP2 - A portable Oberon compiler. Computer Science Report 125, ETH Zurich, 1990.

[GR83] A. Goldberg, D. Robson: Smalltalk-80, the language and its implementation. Addison-Wesley, 1983.

[Hof96] M. Hof: Connecting Oberon. Johannes Kepler University Linz, System Software, Technical Report 7, April 1996.

[Kiz+91] G. Kiczales, J. Rivieres, D. Bobrow: The Art of the Metaobject Protocol. MIT Press, 1991.

[Kna96] M. Knasmüller: Adding Persistence to the Oberon System. Johannes Kepler University Linz, System Software, Technical Report 6, January 1996.

[McCar60] J. McCarthy: Recursive functions of symbolic expressions and their computation by a machine. Communications of the ACM 3 (4), 1960, 184-195.

[MMN93] O. Lehrmann-Madsen, B. Moller-Pedersen, K. Nygaard: Object-Oriented Programming in the BETA Programming Language. Addison-Wesley, 1993.

[MöKo96] H. Mössenböck, K. Koskimies: Active Text for Structuring and Understanding Source Code. To appear in Software - Practice and Experience, 1996.

[ODBC94] Microsoft Open Database Connectivity Software Development Kit Version 2.0, Microsoft Press, 1994.

[Pou95] D. Pountain. *The Oberon/F System*, Byte, January 1995.

[Rei91] M. Reiser: The Oberon System. User Guide and Programmer's Manual. Addison-Wesley, 1991.

[Smi82] B. C. Smith: Reflection and Semantics in a Procedural Language. PhD thesis, M.I.T., 1982.

[Ste96a] C. Steindl: Entwurf und Implementierung einer Stücklistenverwaltung mittels einer Client/Server-Datenbank. Diploma thesis, University Linz, 1996.

[Ste96b] C. Steindl: Accessing ODBC Databases from Oberon Programs. Johannes Kepler University Linz, System Software, Technical Report 9, Dezember 1996.

[StM96] C. Steindl, H. Mössenböck: Metaprogramming Facilities in Oberon for Windows and Power Macintosh. Johannes Kepler University Linz, System Software, Technical Report 8, July 1996.

[Ste+93] D. Stemple, R. Morrison, G.N.C. Kirby, R.C.H. Connor: Integrating Reflection, Strong Typing and Static Checking Proc. 16th Australian Computer Science Conference, Brisbane, Australia (1993), pp. 83-92.

[Str94] M.A. Ellis, B. Stroustrup: The Annotated C++ Reference Manual. AT&T Bell Laboratories, Murray Hill, New Jersey, 1994.

[Tem94] J. Templ: Metaprogramming in Oberon. Dissertation, ETH Zurich, 1994.

[US87] D. Ungar, R. B. Smith: SELF: The Power of Simplicity. Proceedings of the OOPSLA'87 conference, Orlando, SIGPLAN Notices 22 (12), 1987.

[WiGu89] N. Wirth, J. Gutknecht: The Oberon System. Software-Practice and Experience, 19(9), 1989, 857-893.

[WiGu92] N. Wirth, J. Gutknecht: Project Oberon - The design of an operating system and compiler. Addison-Wesley, 1992.

Developing a Full Life Cycle Language

Alonso J. Peralta, Pere Botella and Joan Serras

Department of Software, Universitat Politècnica de Catalunya
Pau Gargallo 5, 08028 Barcelona, Spain
E-mail: peralta@lsi.upc.es, botella@lsi.upc.es, serras@lsi.upc.es

Abstract. An Eiffel-based language is presented which can be used throughout the full life cycle offering interoperability between different analysis and design methodologies and their corresponding notations and the CASE tools supporting them. This direct support from beginning to end obviates the need to translate between different stages and activities and provides systems with a seamless transition.

1 Introduction

This paper summarizes a Ph.D. thesis[1] describing a full life cycle language, for use with the entire range of tasks involved in the specification, design, implementation and documentation of object-oriented systems. Far from replacing the graphical notations of OOAD methodologies, this language provides them with internal support, as well as a link to the user. Although partial aspects of the language proposed are supported by some CASE tools, not all of these support the same functionality, nor do they understand it in the same way. This would make the distinction between what can be described and what cannot permanently dependent on each CASE tool constructor. A language supporting the full life cycle and serving as the substrate of the CASE tools would guarantee that we could always describe all our needs, either graphically with the tool itself or textually with the language proposed here.

A total of 16 notations for analysis and design methodologies were studied in depth in order to gain a precise picture of their descriptive capabilities and find recurring features among them: Objectory (or OOSE) ([Ja92]), Shlaer/Mellor ([Sh88], [Sh91]), Booch ([Bo91], [Bo93]), Coad/Yourdon ([Co91a], [Co91b], [Co93]), Martin/Odell ([Ma92], [Ma94], [Ma93]), Fusion ([Cl94]), Syntropy ([Ck94]), Hood ([Ro92]), Bon ([Wa94]), OMT ([Ru91]), Moses ([He94a]), RDD ([Wi90]), Kiss ([Kr94]), ADM4 ([Fi93]), SOMA ([Gr94b]) and UML ([BRJ96]). The results of this analysis were used as criteria for the design of our full life cycle language, which was therefore required to cope with relations between objects, describe their dynamic behaviour

---

[1] The necessary space limitation does not allow us to include the full BNF grammar and examples more extended. Refer to [Pe96a] and [Pe96b] for a complete description.

(through states and transitions), group them in supraclass constructs (clusters), allow description of usecases, and upgrade the ability of the chosen object-oriented language to specify and document.

The option of creating a completely new language for these purposes was discarded, for two main reasons. Firstly, the inertia of the computer market would inevitably prove to be a barrier to its implantation. Secondly, because of the significant matching between OO programming and analysis/design concepts, pure object-oriented (OO) languages can be extended without any of the problems associated with other types of languages, such as C, Pascal or COBOL. The seamless transition resulting from the common task of all activities (analysis, design, programming in pure OO languages) which consists in identifying and defining objects and their relations guarantees the non-existence of contradictions.

Of the eight OO languages considered (C++, Eiffel, Object Pascal, Objective-C, OO-COBOL, Sather, Simula and Smalltalk), Eiffel [Me92] was chosen as most suitable, as is fully explained in [Pe96b]. It is strictly independent of procedural concepts, and is the only one of these languages to have formal aspects. Furthermore, on a more market-conscious level, it is easier to use and more widespread than most of the others, except for C++ and Smalltalk. The resulting language, an extended version of Eiffel, is called Eiffel+. We have called this new language Eiffel+, for the purpose of the project (Eiffel is a registered name of NICE) and a compiler translating Eiffel+ to Eiffel has been built.

The description we will carry out will be extending Eiffel's syntax and we assume a familiarity with Eiffel.

2 Description

2.1 Relations

Relations between objects are a constant in OO methodologies, since domain structure must be addressed. With regard to analysis, there are three main categories of relations, referred to as aggregation, association and use, each with its own subcategories. For example, the first can be divided into Component-Integral Object, Material-Object, Part/Portion-Object, Place-Area, Member-Bunch and Member-Partnership ([Od94a]). This range of relations must be fully within the descriptive capabilities of the target language. Furthermore, an indication must be given as to how these relations can be converted into client-server type relations, the only non-inheritance relation supported by OO programming languages. In this regard, the templates employed by many OO-CASE tools allow the description of the relations separated from the participating classes ([Pe94]). These templates are used to automatically generate code to implement the relation. Other authors have recently given support also to interactions as first-class citizens ([Do95]).

Static charts are used universally to model relations, but the treatment is quite different for the user and the designer-programmer. For the former, the most important factor is the faithful representation of the domain according to the various categories and subcategories mentioned above. Although the semantics of these types varies greatly, the difference is seldom significant for the user. The task of the designer-programmer, on the other hand, is profoundly affected by these same differences. The accuracy of the conversion into a client-server relation depends on the clarity of the analyst's intentions. The tasks the designer-programmer is required to cover fall into eight areas:

1. Add attributes to related members
2. Add methods to related members
3. Describe the objects created by the relation
4. Delegate services to members
5. Make related members visible
6. Implement the cardinality of members
7. Specify constraints on the relation in the subcategories concerned
8. Locate identifiers for persistence or access purposes

The problem we are faced with is that no formal definition generally accepted exists to describe a given relation with complete accuracy. It can only be implemented without ambiguity by extending its semantics textually, thus involving the analyst. Our proposal provides the analyst with the means to construct an exact description of all the various categories of relations employed. Using BNF syntax, the entity *relation* can be described as follows:

```
RELATION_DECLARATION: relation RELATION_NAME [FORMAL_GENERICS]
                      CLASS_DECLARATIONS
                      end [-- end relation RELATION_NAME]
RELATION_NAME         : identifier
FORMAL_GENERICS       : "["FORMAL_GENERIC_LIST"]"
FORMAL_GENERIC_LIST   : {FORMAL_GENERIC","...}
FORMAL_GENERIC        : FORMAL_GENERIC_NAME [CONSTRAINT]
                      | routine FORMAL_ROUTINE_IDENTIFIER
FORMAL_GENERIC_NAME   : identifier
CONSTRAINT            : "->" CLASS_TYPE
FORMAL_ROUTINE_IDENTIFIER: identifier

RELATION _DEFINITION: relation RELATION_NAME is
                         RELATION_NAME [REAL_GENERICS]
REAL_GENERICS         : "["REAL_GENERIC_LIST "]"
REAL_GENERIC_LIST     : {REAL_GENERIC ";"....}
REAL_GENERIC          : REALGENERIC_TYPE
                      | REAL_GENERIC_PROCEDURE
REAL_GENERIC_TYPE     : FORMAL_GENERIC_NAME ":"
                        REAL_GENERIC_MEMBERS
```

```
REAL_GENERIC_MEMBERS: {REAL_GENERIC_NAME","....}
REAL_GENERIC_PROCEDURE: routine FORMAL_ROUTINE_IDENTIFIER ":"
                        REAL_GENERIC_MEMBERS
```

This description features two distinct parts: declaration and definition. The former is a template for an abstract relation, and as such provides the means to augment classes and convert them into client-server relations. The latter instantiates the relation, working from the basis of the declaration to meet the specific requirements of individual cases.

The process is considerably simplified at this point by introducing a catalogue of declarations enabling us to allocate relations according to inevitably recurrent types and so concentrate on the second, specific step. This idea is closely linked to that of the patterns referred to in recent investigations ([Ga94]), which we have used to compile a library of declarations.

For the sake of simplicity, the issue of inheritance among relations is not dealt with here, although the proposed language takes full account of it.

2.2 States

A full life cycle language must include the means to express the state of an object, as this is taken into consideration in most OO methodologies because of the information it provides regarding the dynamic behaviour of the objects and, consequently, the system as a whole. We have developed a textual notation to support the widespread graphical one developed by [Ha87] and supported by most methodologists. The notion of using a dynamic model extension to introduce state inheritance and objects can also be found in ([So95)].

The object's behavior is univocal when the object is in a state. Therefore, states describe the dynamic behavior of an object. They specify which is the object's behavior when the object is in each of the states in question. That is to say, a state describes how the same object reacts before different or similar stimuli according to the state in which the object is.

An object can go through different states. By this we mean that the object, during its life-cycle, can be in different states. However, it can be in only one state at a given time. The change of state is brought about by the stimuli it reacts to.

Objects can be in any one of three temporal classes of state: initial (that in which the object is created), transitional (those that lead to subsequent states, though the intervention of a propitious event) and final (those that do not).Those final states which are related to a destructor action are called terminal.

The state of an object is an unambiguous indication of its dynamic behaviour when confronted with certain events occurring in the system. The action caused by these events (which may affect more than one object) may bring about a change in the object's state, but at any given moment a given object is in one and only one state. Actions are expressed as code or methods, which are supplied with a name and a set of parameters.

Events may originate either inside or outside the system, i.e., they can occur as a response to an internal stimulus or they can be activated by the user or some other real-world agent. In addition, they may be simple (giving rise to no secondary events) or compound (causing a chain reaction of consequent events). Real-world events are usually of the latter sort.

A transition is the change of state. If a given object is in a state, then a certain change of state or transition can be brought about by the occurrence of an acceptable event for this state. However, there may be events which do not cause a transition, that is they remain in the same state at the end of the action.

Also encompassed by the language but not included here for reasons of space is the ability to describe nested states, orthogonal states and state inheritance.

Eiffel+ accounts for states as follows:

```
STATE_DECLARATION     : state MACHINE_STATES_DEF
MACHINE_STATES_DEF    : MACHINE_STATES
                      | MACHINE_STATES_LIST
MACHINE_STATES_LIST   : machine identifier MACHINE_STATES
                      | MACHINE_STATES_LIST machine identifier
                        MACHINE_STATES
MACHINE_STATES        : BLOC_STATES_LIST ALLOW_CLAUSE
BLOC_STATES_LIST      : BLOC_STATES
                      | BLOC_STATES_LIST BLOC_STATES
BLOC_STATES           : STATES_QUALIFIER STATES_LIST
STATES_QUALIFIER      :
                      | initial
                      | transit
                      | final
STATES_LIST           : STATE_ITEM
                      | STATE_LIST ";" STATE_ITEM
STATE_ITEM            : STATE_DEF CREATE_CLAUSE_OPT
                                  EVENT_STATEMENT_OPT
STATE_DEF             : identifier
                      | identifier ":" EXPRESSION
                      | identifier nest to MACHINE_STATES end
EVENT_STATEMENT_OPT   :
                      | EVENT_STATEMENT
EVENT_STATEMENT       : event EVENT_ACTION_LIST
```

```
EVENT_ACTION_LIST      : EVENT_ACTION_CLAUSE
                       | EVENT_ACTION_LIST ";"EVENT_ACTION_CLAUSE
EVENT_ACTION_CLAUSE : EVENT_ACTION TRANSITION_STATEMENT_OPT
EVENT_ACTION           : identifier
                       | routine
                       | call
TRANSITION_STATEMENT_OPT:
                       | TRANSITION_STATEMENT
TRANSITION_STATEMENT: transition to DESTINATION_BLOC
DESTINATION_BLOC       : STATE_NAME
                       | DESTINATION_WITH_GUARDS "," STATE_NAME
                         when EXPRESSION
ALLOW_CLAUSE           : allow EVENT_LIST";"
EVENT_LIST             : identifier
                       | EVENT_LIST "," identifier
CREATE_CLAUSE_OPT      :
                       | CREATE_CLAUSE
CREATE_CLAUSE          : created by identifier
```

2.3 Clusters

It was thought appropriate to include clusters as a feature of our full life cycle
language, in common with some existing OO languages, such as Ada (package),
Modula-3, Modula-90 and TurboPascal (Unit), but not others: Eiffel (with the
exception of LACE), C++, Sather, Simula and Smalltalk.

Clusters are supraclass language entities, a higher level of encapsulation, thus
coinciding with the concept of subsystem, covering smaller, more specific entities
such as definitions and declarations of objects and relations, definitions of routines,
and indeed other clusters. Not only do they facilitate the handling of large systems by
containing groups of entities treated as a single unit, but they can also cope with
traversal routines that fit poorly into classes. Moreover, clusters improve the
performance of libraries, narrowing down the search to the area concerned, a property
related to the concept of the kit ([Be93]), and used to construct domains. However,
each member of a cluster must at all times share a logical, coherent concept with all
the others, in accordance with the function of the cluster in the system as a whole.

Each cluster must first declare the relations it has with other clusters in the system, or
with a library of clusters. Clusters may be related by inheritance, importing or use. In
the first case, the offspring initially inherits the totality of its entities from the parent,
and the task of declaring consists of stating which of the parent's entities are redefined
or renamed in the offspring. The key word *export* changes the visibility of the
entities. The second type of relation between clusters concerns the possibility of
importing entities from a supply cluster. In this way, elements of interest can be
donated piecemeal, without indiscriminate wholesale integration. Finally, relations

may be categorized according to use; a cluster server supplies a client cluster with definitions and declarations of the entities concerned.

Routines can be used to initialize the cluster's objects or any other applicable operation. Such a routine is defined in much the same way as other routines, except that its name must directly follow the key word in the definition of the cluster.

The declaration and definition of the main part of the cluster amounts to the definition of the objects, classes, relations and routines contained within it. The cluster may end with a declaration of its invariant.

The following is the description of clusters that features in our language:

```
CLUSTER            : cluster identifier
                     INHERIT_CLAUSE
                     IMPORT_CLAUSE
                     USE_CLAUSE
                     CREATION_CLAUSE
                     FEATURE_BLOCS
                     INVARIANT_CLAUSE
                     end
INHERIT_CLAUSE     : [inherit LIST_OF_CLUSTERS
                     [rename identifier as identifier]
                     [redefine LIST_OF_IDENTIFIERS] ]
IMPORT_CLAUSE      : [import LIST_OF_ENTITIES from identifier]
USE_CLAUSE         : [use LIST_OF_CLUSTERS
                     [rename identifier as identifier] ]
CREATION_CLAUSE    : creation LIST_OF_ROUTINES
FEATURE_BLOCS      : {FEATURE_BLOC,......}
FEATURE_BLOC       : feature CLIENTS
                     USE_CLAUSE
                     FEATURE_DECLARATION_LIST
INVARIANT_CLAUSE : [invariant  ASSERTION]
```

2.4 Usecases

At the requirements or analysis stages of an OO system it is necessary to be able to describe the functionality or set of requisites which it must support. This functionality, must be accurately described in terms of the objects and methods involved and the sequence of the messages sent between objects.

Unlike structured methodologies, OO methodologies cannot describe functionalities by means of data flow diagrams. Instead, they use another concept that has been given a variety of names: walk-through ([Wi90]), event trace diagram ([Ru91]), interaction diagram ([Ja92], [Bo93]), message trace diagram and object message diagram ([BRJ96]). The application of these diagrams results in what has been called a usecase ([Ja92]) or scenario ([Wi90], [Ru91], [Bo93]).

Eiffel+ includes usecases and interaction diagrams ([Ja92]) to allow the description of the functionality of a system.

Interaction diagrams show the three steps taken by the system to solve a particular functionality in a particular usecase: identification of objects, identification of the methods or responsibilities of each object, and identification of messages passing between objects. They are also useful for ascertaining how responsibilities should be distributed, and to test the static diagram design. Usecases, for their part, serve to determine functionality and communication to and from the system, and provide the pattern to follow when writing the user manual (a parallel that means that we can produce highly adaptable skeleton user manuals matching parameterized usecases). For the purposes of Eiffel+, the word *usecase* embraces both concepts, and as such covers the following fields: specification of the functionality of the system, specification of external agents (referred to as actors), and detailed description of the objects, routines and messages involved in the functionality.

Usecases also serve to test a system developed in Eiffel+. The objects necessary for a given usecase must be seen to be present, the routines for its execution must be correctly declared, and the messages used must be in the right order. Furthermore, any parts of the complete system which the usecases do not use are detected and the user (analyst) is informed.

Usecases may be related to one another either by use or by extension ([Ja92]), both types being included in Eiffel+. In Eiffel+ we can specify the extensions to the usecases by making use of the use relation plus a conditional expression by which if the probe condition is verified the extending usecase (the usecase that extends) is executed.

Usecases are analogous to relations, classes and clusters in that they can be parameterized or inherited, thus opening up new possibilities. Prototypical architectures (batch, real-time, reactive, etc.) interact with the user in their own particular way ([Ru91]), a description of which can be provided by parameterized or inherited usecases.

The Eiffel+ description of usecases is reproduced below. As previously, the issues of inheritance and parameterization are omitted here.

```
USECASE : usecase identifier is
            actor LIST_OF_ACTORS
            [class LIST_OF_CLASSES]
            [cluster LIST_OF_CLUSTERS]
            [usecase LIST_OF_USECASES]
        do
```

```
      ACTOR_IDENTIFIER ":" STRING_ACTION
      USECASE_BODY
      SYSTEM_REACTION_STRING ":" ACTOR_IDENTIFIER
end
```

```
USECASE_BODY      : LIST_OF_ACTIONS
LIST_OF_ACTIONS : {ACTION, ....}
ACTION            : REFERENCE ROUTINE_BODY end
                  | usecase_identifier
REFERENCE         : class_identifier.method_identifier
                  | cluster_identifier.method_identifier
```

Note the following reference to other usecases, which creates the options of lumping or exploding usecases as necessary.

2.5 Specification

The beginning of a software development process is associated with the specification of the routines to be employed. The implementation is a lengthy and difficult task, and frequently carried out in an incremental cycle.

Depending on the stage of development reached, routines can be implemented, deferred, pending or specified; all four are considered by Eiffel+, whereas Eiffel itself only recognizes the first two.

An analyst may appreciate that a routine is necessary but is unable to specify it until later on in the process. In the same way we declare that a method is deferred, we may also declare that a method is pending. This type of declaration has been used previously in specification by [Lh94], the difference being that the compiler allows the incomplete class to be compiled and executed, issuing an exception in the event of an attempt to access it.

We also find frequently the situation in which a routine is specified, without being coded in an early phase, by means of either text, pseudo-code (*structured English*) or formal specification.

The first of these three methods is clearly unsatisfactory, since the vagueness of human language is at the root of most problems of communication.

The second is suitable for many situations, including descriptions of processes for programmers by analysts, as its recognition by a large number of CASE tools testifies. It also allows incremental development in such a form that the programmer may code parts of a method and test them before the complete implementation is finished. For the sake of flexibility, it seems advisable to use incomplete coding (i.e., the full Eiffel range with open-ended instructions such as *initialize_local_variables* where appropriate). In this way the routine can be made more or less specific at the discretion of the analyst. His work and that of the programmer are perfectly demarcated, the latter only being required to perform the incremental coding of the incomplete ends. A class with unfinished routines may be compiled and executed, but any attempt to access them will result in an exception being registered.

Thirdly and lastly, formal specification is an area in which Eiffel has made considerable headway. In addition, Eiffel+ imports three new clauses from other languages:

1. The clause *modify* "list of variables" specifies which attributes each routine may modified.

2. Parameters may be declared *in, out* or *inout*. The first type starts non void, finishes unmodified and is evaluated with deep equality, the second finishes non void, and the third is non void at both the beginning and the end.

3. The fact that Eiffel allows references to routines can be exploited to bypass its inability to support quantifiers, by means of simulation. Predefined library iterators with deferred routines facilitate this task, although they have the drawback that the deferred routines cannot be defined *in situ* (in the assertion). Moreover, functions inserted into a class in order to simulate a quantifier will be gratuitously passed on to any subclasses it may have. Eiffel+ features *manifest functions* as an aid to the incorporation of quantifiers. They enable the user to instantiate the deferred class directly, by manifesting the deferred routine (i.e., the operation, accessed by means of iteration, in the example below).

```
ensure
!!ArrayIterator[Floodgate].make(floodgates).iteration
where operation is
do
    Result := not (floodgates.item(i).opened)
end
```

2.6 Documentation

Individual computing centres can produce their own customized documentation corresponding to each major entity in Eiffel+ by use of templates. To this end, the structure of each template must be defined and compiled, using a purpose-built utility. This will require all programmes using the language to comply to the structure of the templates. The various types of templates (attribute, class, cluster, relation, state and routine) are described in extended BNF, terminal symbols being expressed by key words. The analyst accesses the Eiffel+ source and outputs it by means of a scripting language. The following is an example of a template description.

```
template routine :
                    "Description:" text
                    "Visibility:" (Private|Public|Protected)
                    "Class:" (Yes|No)
                    "Restrictions:" text
                    end
```

3 Other Analysis and Design Languages

The only experiences bearing direct comparison with the development of Eiffel+ are OOSDL ([Fi93]) and ODL ([Ch93]).

OOSDL or Object-Oriented Specification and Design Language is a strongly typed, quasi-formal language developed from ADA ([Aj83]) with contributions from DRAGOON ([At91[) and Eiffel. However, it is non-executable, and features almost 100 reserved words. At the analysis stage it is limited to a graphical notation with 15 diagrams, ruling out the possibility of transferral to other methodologies.

ODL or Object Design Language also has its own graphical notation (Object Analysis Notation or OAN), plus an intermediate language for the design stage. As with OOSDL, execution is through a programming language, and the necessary translation is easy but not automatic. Moreover, the concepts of relation, transition, cluster and usecase are not included.

4 Conclusions

In OO the division between programming and other software activities is blurry and depends largely on the language constructor, and is therefore far from well defined. Furthermore, if we do not use a full life cycle language, that is a software development language, the analysis or design stages require specific descriptions which will inevitably result in redefinition at the following stage, with all the additional work and possibilities of error that this involves, unless it is done with a full life cycle language. Clearly, then, it is desirable to use the same language at all the stages of software development, thus creating a truly seamless transition and effectively ensuring interoperability between methodologies and their supporting CASE tools.

Naturalness in the description is important at each stage, and it should be the responsibility of the compiler to relocate descriptions in order to construct a programme that can be executed. In addition, all descriptions, of whatsoever type, and documentation should be reused for increased productivity, testing purposes, and cross-checking to guarantee consistency.

This paper describes the core of a Ph.D. thesis which includes case studies and a compiler translating Eiffel+ to Eiffel ([Pe96b]). Real experiences are in process of development.

References

Aj83   Ada Joint Program Office (1983)
        Reference Manual for the Ada Programming Language; United States Department of Defense

At91   Atkinson C. (1991)
        Object-Oriented Reuse, Concurrency and Distribution; Addison Wesley

Bo91   Booch G. (1991)
        Object-Oriented Design with Applications; Benjamin-Cummings

Bo93   Booch, G (1993)
        Object-oriented Analysis and Design with Applications, 2nd Ed., Benjamin Cummings

BRJ96   Booch, Rumbaugh, Jacobson (1996)
        The Unified Method, Ver. 0.9, Rational

Ch93   de Champeaux D, Lea D., Faure P. (1993)
        Object-Oriented System Development; Addison-Wesley

Ck94   Cook S, Daniels J (1994)
        Designing Object Systems. Object-Oriented Modelling with Syntropy, Prentice Hall

Cl94   Coleman D. et al. (1994)
        Object-Oriented Development: The Fusion Method, Prentice-Hall

Co91a   Coad P., Yourdon E. (1991)
        Object-Oriented Analysis 2nd Edition; Prentice Hall

Co91b   Coad P., Yourdon E. (1991)
        Object-Oriented Design; Prentice Hall

Co93   Coad P., Nicola J. (1993)
        Object-Oriented Programming; Prentice Hall

Do95   Dodani, Velazquez (1995)
        Supporting Interactions as First-Class Citizens in OO Methodologies, ROAD Vol. 2 No. 4, Nov.-Dec. 1995

Fi93   Firesmith D. (1993)
        Object-Oriented Requirements Analysis and Logical Design, A Software Enginerring Approach; Wiley

Ga94   Gamma E., Helm R., Johnson R., Vlissides J. (1994)
        Design Patterns: Elements of Object-Oriented Software Architecture; Addison-Wesley

Gr94b   Graham I. (1994)
        Migrating to Object Technology; Addison-Wesley

Ha87   Harel D. (1987)
        Statecharts: avisual formalism for complex systems, Science of Computer Programming 8:231-274

He94a   Henderson-Sellers B., Edwards J. (1994)
        Booktwo of Object-Oriented Knowledge: The Working Object; Prentice-Hall

Ja92	Jacobson I. et al. (1992)
	Object-Oriented Software Engineering: A Use Case Driven Approach, 4th Ed. Addison-Wesley
Kr94	Kristen G. (1994)
	Object Orientation, The Kiss Method, From Information Architecture to Information System; Addison-Wesley
Lh94	Lano K., Haughton H. (1994)
	Object-Oriented Specification Case Studies; Prentice Hall
Ma92	Martin J, Odell J. (1992),
	Object-Oriented Analysis and Design, Prentice Hall
Ma93	Martin J (1993),
	Principles of Object-Oriented Analysis and Design, Prentice-Hall
Ma94	Martin J, Odell J. (1994),
	Object-Oriented Methods: A Foundation, Prentice Hall
Me88	Meyer B (1988),
	Object-Oriented Software Construction, Prentice Hall
Me92a	Meyer B. (1992)
	Eiffel: The Language"; Prentice-Hall
Od94a	Odell J. (1994)
	Six diferent kinds of composition; Journal of Object-Oriented Programming. V. 5 No. 8
Pe94	Peralta, A, (1994)
	Making the Transition from ADTs to Objects in Undergraduate Software Engineering: a CASE-based Approach, 1994 Joint Modular Language Conference
Pe96a	Peralta A., Serras J. (1996)
	Extending Eiffel as a Full Life-cycle Language, UPC Report LSI-96-45-R
Pe96b	Peralta A (1996)
	Eiffel+: A Software Development Language for Objecte-Oriented Systems, Ph.D Thesis, draft version, URL: http://www-lsi.upc.es/www
Ro92	Robinson P. (1992)
	Hierarchical Object-Oriented Design; Prentice Hall
Ru91	Rumbaugh J. et al. (1991)
	Object-Oriented Modeling and Design, Prentice-Hall
Sh88	Shlaer S, Mellor S.J. (1988),
	Object-Oriented Systems Analysis: Modelling the World in Data, Yourdon Press
Sh91	Shlaer S, Mellor S.J. (1991),
	Object LIfecycles: Modelling the World in States, Yourdon Press
So95	Sourrouville, Lecorude (1995)
	A Dynamic Model Extension to Integrate State Inheritance and Objects, ROAD Vol. 2 No. 2, July-August 1995
Wa94	Walden K., Nerson JM (1994)
	Seamless Object-Oriented Software Architecture; Prentice Hall
Wi90	Wirfs-Brock RJ, Wilkerson B., Wiener L. (1990)
	Designing Object-Oriented Software; Prentice Hall

Scalable Modules in Generic Modula–2

Cornelis Pronk[1] and Richard J. Sutcliffe[2]

[1] c.pronk@twi.tudelft.nl
Faculty of Technical Mathematics and Informatics,
Delft University of Technology,
PObox 356, 2600AJ, Delft, The Netherlands
[2] rsutc@twu.ca
Faculty of Natural and Applied Sciences,
Trinity Western University,
7600 Glover Rd., Langley, BC, Canada
British Columbia, Canada

Abstract. It is conventional wisdom that modules are not scalable in the same sense as functions and classes. That is, while calls to many functions can be assembled as a single function, and the addition of new facilities to a class (in a subclass) forms a new class, a collection of modules is not a module. Standard Generic Modula–2, however, introduces an original technique of refining generic modules as local modules that does provide a means of combining into a single new module the refinements of one or more existing generic modules, possibly with the addition of new facilities.

1 Introduction

This paper will summarize the basic syntax and facilities of Generic Modula–2 as described in the Committee Draft (CD) of the proposed International Standard for Generic Modula–2. In addition, this paper will show how one of the facilities of Generic Modula–2, namely, the ability to refine generic modules as local modules, can be used as a novel module composition mechanism.

Section 2 will contain a brief discussion of the need for generic facilities in modern programming languages. In section 3 we will describe the syntax and semantics of the generic extensions to Modula–2. In section 4 we will describe the new module composition mechanism. Finally, section 5 will provide a conclusion.

2 Rationale

Programmers often face the situation where data must be handled within a structure in a manner that is dependent on the structure, but independent of the data stored in those structures. Since it may well be the case that more than one (almost identical) instance of such structures (e.g. linked lists) is required to contain different types of data, it is desirable to write the code for the manipulation of such structures only once and in a manner independent of any possible contents, -that is, in a generic fashion. In like manner, it may be necessary to code procedures and functions (such as sorts) that operate on data stored in structures already recognized by the base language (such as an array.) Such manipulations (apart from, say, the specific means of doing comparison) are also independent of the data type of the structure elements. In conventional languages this was commonly done using pointers and passing a reference or address parameter, but such solutions are contrary to the spirit of programming in modular languages because they do not allow for strong type checking of the parameters. Generic programming facilities to meet this need exist in Ada, Modula-3, and C++.

2.1 History

Initial discussions of generic programming methods in Modula-2 were held at the first meeting of WG13 in Nottingham in 1987 [10]. Following discussion papers circulated to WG13 in 1994, and a round of voting that saw a draft of the proposals approved in 1995, comments were discussed and responded to [12] at the Oxford meeting of WG13 in the summer of 1996 and a new committee draft with some revisions was circulated through ISO that summer [11] for a further round of voting.

Readers interested in the development of ISO/IEC 10514-1 (the base standard) [1] and other extensions to Modula-2 are referred to [4] and [7].

2.2 Generic and OO Modula-2

Because of the decision of WG13 not to use the module as the basis for object classes, and because the rules for refinement of generic separate modules are applied before translating a Modula-2 program with unaltered base standard syntax and semantics, the provisions of standard Generic Modula-2 are orthogonal to the provisions of the draft standard on object oriented Modula-2, with the single exception that "GENERIC" becomes a keyword and is not available as an identifier to programs.

It is not the intention that Generic Modula-2 facilities compete with those of the OO proposal that is also circulating at this moment [13]. WG13 encourages the use of both generic and OO facilities, whether separately or in concert with one another, and believes that the use of both together can promote good programming style.

The primary use of the generic mechanism will be in the construction of frameworks or templates of reusable code for classical ADTs such as lists, and for the coding of generic techniques such as sorting, where, in both cases the target type will no longer have to be specified ahead of time.

Generic modules are not value based objects; they are templates (not unlike those of C++) for the development of abstract data types (e.g. lists) and techniques for manipulating abstract data types (e.g. sorts) where both are free of the constraint of having to represent the specific types at the outset.

2.3 Implementation

The proposed standard will not enforce any particular compilation mechanism for generics. As the implementation of the generic mechanism is not the main subject of this paper we will restrain ourselves here to mentioning that the result of refinement should be an ISO/IEC 10514-1 conforming program and therefore be compilable by any compiler conforming to the base standard.

R. Sutcliffe has already implemented and tested Standard Generic Modula-2 using a preprocessor and renaming approach. This does not give quite the correct syntax, but is adequate to determine that all aspects of the extensions described in this paper do work correctly.

3 Description of the Language

For a detailed description of the proposed Standard Generic Modula–2 see [11]. What will be provided here is a less detailed summary.

3.1 Syntax and Semantics

Standard Generic Modula–2 is identical to the ISO Standard Modula–2 described in [1] with the addition of:

- Generic definition and implementation modules. These modules have formal value parameters that are either constants or types;
- The concept of refining a generic separate module with respect to specific constants and types;
- Refining definition and implementation modules. These modules provide the actual parameters corresponding to the formal parameters of the generic separate modules from which they refine;
- The new reserved word GENERIC to identify generic separate modules;
- A new use of the reserved word TYPE as though it were also a standard identifier in generic separate module parameter lists; (avoids thinking up a new pervasive name that is merely a synonym for TYPE)
- The ability to refine a generic separate module as a local module;
- The concept of a refinement as the effective end product (the entire module, or some entity it contains) of the process of refining a generic separate module.

There are no new library modules defined for Standard Generic Modula–2 at the present time, though this does not preclude such work at a later date.

One now has the following concrete syntax for working with separate modules:

```
compilation module = program module
                   | definition module
                   | implementation module
```

```
| generic definition module
| generic implementation module
| refining definition module
| refining implementation module ;

generic definition module =
        "GENERIC", "DEFINITION", "MODULE", module identifier,
        [formal module parameters], semicolon,
        import lists, definitions,
        "END", module identifier, period ;
```

As this brief summary (and the following example) illustrate, the concept is somewhat similar to the generic capabilities of Modula–3 and C++. As in both of those languages, the new facilities of Generic Modula–2 are static. As in Modula–3, (and unlike Ada) genericity is achieved by parameterizing modules only. Unlike Modula–3, the parameters are types and constants, rather than interface (module) names, and refinement is not confined to the generation of separate (library) modules.

3.2   Refining as Separate Modules

The generic separate modules are written in a conventional way, but have formal parameters specifying local names for types and/or constants that will be supplied when the module is refined. For instance, to have generic queues that could be refined for specific data types and lengths, one could write:

```
GENERIC DEFINITION MODULE Queues
                (itemType : TYPE; maxSize : CARDINAL);

TYPE
  Queue;    (* details in implementation *)
  ActionProc = PROCEDURE (itemType);

PROCEDURE Init (VAR q : Queue);
PROCEDURE Destroy (VAR q : Queue);
PROCEDURE Full (q : Queue) : BOOLEAN;
PROCEDURE Empty (q : Queue) : BOOLEAN;
PROCEDURE Enqueue (q : Queue; item : itemType);
PROCEDURE Serve (q : Queue; VAR item : itemType);
PROCEDURE Traverse (q : Queue; Proc : ActionProc);

END Queues.
```

The implementation part of this separate module is written in a similar way. In order to guarantee the integrity of the implied contract with clients that is presented in the definition part, the implementation is required to have the same parameters.

```
GENERIC IMPLEMENTATION MODULE Queues
               (itemType : TYPE; maxSize : CARDINAL);

TYPE
   Queue      (* details here *) ;

(* provide code *)
END Queues.
```

Inside the generic implementation module all code is written in terms of entities of the formal type **itemType**, and, where applicable, the formal constant names as well. Such constants may include procedures of a type defined in the definition part, and this allows one to pass, for instance, a comparison procedure acting on formal items to a generic sorting module.

To refine this generic separate module as a separate module one provides two more compilation units, the refining separate definition and implementation modules. A refining module cannot have a protection expression, additional imports, or declarations of its own in addition to the ones it refines from its generic counterpart. Neither can it have a body of its own.

If one wanted queues of student records for instance, one would first encapsulate any non-pervasive data types in a separate module and decide on the length of the queue (say, 100) then write the refining module parts with these actual parameters. A pervasive data type name could be passed as a parameter without any qualifying module name.

```
DEFINITION MODULE StudentQueues = Queues (Students.SRecord, 100);
END StudentQueues.

IMPLEMENTATION MODULE StudentQueues =
                               Queues (Students.SRecord, 100);
END StudentQueues.
```

The effect of translating a refining module is the same as constructing and then translating a module obtained from the (definition or implementation) module of the generic separate module that it refines from but with the results of evaluating the actual parameters of the refining module substituted for the formal parameters of the generic separate module that is being refined. The resulting refinement is a (definition or implementation) module in the sense of the base language, and the translation that is done following refinement employs only the rules of the base language.

3.3   A Bit of Rationale

It should be noted that at various stages of the discussions in WG13, proposals were advanced to make refinement dynamic. Conventional wisdom as expressed by the majority of WG13 members was that moving refinement (and therefore memory allocation) to run time would create inefficient code, and be too difficult to implement. All such proposals were therefore rejected by the committee as being overly complex.

The simplicity of the syntax of the current proposal does, however, just move some complexity to the code level. For instance, if one is working with recursive routines operating on matrices of reals or complexes, many sizes of matrix may be required at run time and a different instance of the code may need to be present for each size and data type in a standard generic solution. Suggested workarounds include (a) find an OO approach to the solution or (b) implement arrays themselves as dynamic types. Similar comments apply to data structures such as trees, stacks, or queues. The amount of duplication of code is not so great as for the case of matrices, but the current approach will probably use a copy of the entire code for every type of data to be contained within such a structure (or, to be manipulated by, say, a generic sorting routine.)

3.4 Refining as a Local Module

The module composition mechanism, the main subject of this paper, is based upon the (unique to Generic Modula–2) facility that allows one to refine generic separate modules as local modules.

The refining module may be local to some other module. In this case of course it can not have (nor does it need) both a definition part and an implementation part. Rather, as a local module referring to a name in the outer scope (imported) it refines only the generic implementation module, but that in turn depends on the prior existence of the generic definition module. This refining local module may also have an export list (qualified or not) that specifies the items to be available (post refinement) in the surrounding scope. Because these exports may be qualified, two refinements (under different names) of the same generic separate module could both be made in one scope without causing a name clash. Because these exports may be unqualified, they may serve within an implementation module as the declarations of items defined in a definition module.

The syntax is:

```
refining local module declaration =
        "MODULE", module identifier, equals,
        generic separate module identifier,
        [actual module parameters], semicolon,
        [export list],
        "END", module identifier ;
```

and the module **Queues** can be refined locally in one or both of the following ways:

```
MODULE Program;
IMPORT Queues, Students, Faculty;

MODULE StudentQueues = Queues (Students.SRecord, 100);
```

```
EXPORT Queue, Init, Destroy, Full, Empty, Enqueue, Serve,
                                              Traverse;

END StudentQueues.

MODULE FacultyQueues = Queues (Faculty.FRecord, 10);
EXPORT QUALIFIED Queue, Init, Destroy, Full, Empty, Enqueue,
                                            Serve, Traverse;

END FacultyQueues.

(* code to use these structures *)
END Program.
```

It should be noted that, although the name of the generic separate module has to be imported (to allow the local refining module to see it), any reference in the enclosing module to that generic name other than for refinement is an error.

Because refinement is not itself a declaration but a command to the preprocessor or translator, actual parameters in the refining module are similar to the parameters of a procedure, in that they need only be visible in the surrounding scope to be used in this way. They need not be "imported" into the refining module as they would if a module were being declared here.

4 The Composition of Modules

In the examples of local refinement above, no new facilities were added. However, this may also be done. Perhaps the most interesting way is to define new separate modules (whether Generic or not) that use some or all of the functionality developed in existing generic separate modules but with some changes or additions.

Suppose, for instance, one wished to develop a new separate module to define and implement priority queues, using as a partial base the generic separate module **Queues** illustrated above. The definition might be altered as follows:

```
GENERIC DEFINITION MODULE PriorityQueues
     (itemType : TYPE; maxSize : CARDINAL, Compare : CompareProc);


TYPE
  PQueue;   (* details in implementation *)
  ActionProc = PROCEDURE (itemType);
  CompareResults = (less, equal, greater);
  CompareProc = PROCEDURE (itemType, itemType) : CompareResults;

PROCEDURE Init (VAR q : PQueue);
PROCEDURE Destroy (VAR q : PQueue);
PROCEDURE Full (q : PQueue) : BOOLEAN;
PROCEDURE Empty (q : PQueue) : BOOLEAN;
```

```
PROCEDURE Enqueue (q : PQueue; item : itemType);
PROCEDURE Serve (q : PQueue; VAR item : itemType);
PROCEDURE Traverse (q : PQueue; Proc : ActionProc);

END PriorityQueues.
```

In this version, refinement requires a procedure parameter that provides the functionality of determining the relative priority of two items of the type to be enqueued (presumably by examining some field of the data,) so that a new item can be placed in the proper place in the queue. When the implementation part is written, most of the procedures in the original generic implementation part can be retained by exporting them in the refinement. The **Enqueue** procedure will, however, have to be changed. Portions of the implementation would look like:

```
GENERIC IMPLEMENTATION MODULE PriorityQueues
      (itemType : TYPE; maxSize : CARDINAL; Compare : CompareProc);

IMPORT Queues;
TYPE
  PQueue = Queues.Queue;
MODULE LocalQueues = Queues (itemType, maxSize);
                                  (* pass along parameters. *)
EXPORT Queue, Init, Destroy, Full, Empty, Serve, Traverse;
END LocalQueues;

PROCEDURE Enqueue (q : PQueue; item : itemType);
(* code to place a data item in position by doing comparisons
   as needed *)
END Enqueue;
END PriorityQueues.
```

It should be observed that since a local refinement is performed on the implementation part of the generic separate module, the details of the data type **PQueue** itself are available in the new module for its use and therefore it is possible to replace the procedure **Enqueue** in this way. Semantically, this should not be thought of as a relaxation of the rules for opaque types, but rather as the inclusion of what can be regarded as a copy of the (refined) code (that is, with the appropriate parameter substitutions made) in the implementation module. For clients of refinements of this new module, the type **PQueue** is of course exported opaquely by the refinements of the definition part of the module.

In addition, because the refined implementation can export into the scope of the refinement only those items named in the generic separate definition module, any other items in the implementation can not be made available in the scope of the refinement for use there and remain strictly private.

Should it be also be thought desirable to refine a separate module specified as to the data type and size, it would be a simple matter to define the appropriate type in a separate module, import from this in the new definition part, and then refine fully in the implementation part, thus:

```
DEFINITION MODULE StudentPriorityQueues;

FROM Students IMPORT
  Student;
TYPE
  PQueue;    (* details in implementation *)
  ActionProc = PROCEDURE (CHAR);

PROCEDURE Init (VAR q : PQueue);
PROCEDURE Destroy (VAR q : PQueue);
PROCEDURE Full (q : PQueue) : BOOLEAN;
PROCEDURE Empty (q : PQueue) : BOOLEAN;
PROCEDURE Enqueue (q : PQueue; item : Student);
PROCEDURE Serve (q : PQueue; VAR item : Student);
PROCEDURE Traverse (q : PQueue; Proc : ActionProc);

END StudentPriorityQueues.

IMPLEMENTATION MODULE StudentPriorityQueues;

IMPORT Queues;
FROM Students IMPORT
  Student, CompareStudent;

TYPE
  PQueue = Queues.Queue;
MODULE LocalQueues = Queues (Student, maxSize );
EXPORT Queue, Init, Destroy, Full, Empty, Serve, Traverse;
END LocalQueues;

PROCEDURE Enqueue (q : PQueue; item : Student);
(* code to place a data item in position by doing comparisons
   as needed *)
END Enqueue;
END StudentPriorityQueues.
```

In this version, the functionality associated with the data type **Student** and that associated with the generic separate module **Queues** is combined (and extended as above) into a single refined module with a standard client interface.

It should be noted in passing that the new definition part of the refined module must be produced in full in such cases, because the base standard does not permit a definition module to contain a local module, and hence it cannot itself contain a refining local module acting on the definition part of the original generic separate module. This is one reason why the refinement of generic modules as local modules is defined to be the refinement of the implementation part of the generic separate module.

It is also important to note that a refining definition module is not itself a declaration, but should be regarded as a command to either a preprocessor or the translator (as the case may be) to produce a refined declaration from the generic separate module. Likewise, a refining implementation module has no code, but should be regarded as a command to produce refined code from a generic separate implementation module.

4.1 A Bit of Rationale

This example, and the earlier suggestion for generic sorting routines illustrate the expected use of the new Generic Modula–2 facilities. Generic Modula–2 does not obviate the need for OO techniques, but it does provide an original means to promote code modularization and reusability. The means now exists to use modules to abstract in a scalable fashion both the framework for classical ADTs and many standard algorithms for data manipulation.

The partial refinement of a generic separate module allows the programmer to add facilities to or restrict facilities from an existing generic separate module when producing either a new separate module (generic or not) or a refinement in a program module.

4.2 Comparing with other languages

The mechanism proposed here is of less complexity than similar mechanisms used in Ada [2] and C++ [5, 9]; the mechanism is of similar complexity to the mechanism used in Modula-3 [3, 6, 8]. Comparing the mechanisms is not straightforward however, because in the latter languages the mechanisms have been integrated with the base language, whereas it is an add-on for Modula-2. In Ada, Modula-3 and Modula-2 the generic entities coincide with the separate compilation entities. In C++ the generic entities are 'template classes' and 'template functions'. The allowed kinds of generic parameters are more diverse: Ada allows types, constants, subprograms and variables, whereas Modula-2 and C++ only allow types and constants (which includes procedure constants in Modula-2). Modula-3 allows only the names of interfaces to be parameters to generic modules.

5 Conclusion

The proposed Standard Generic Modula–2 is a novel but very slight extension (by a single keyword and some syntax) of ISO Standard Modula–2. For this modest investment one obtains all the functionality of the static generic facilities already present in such languages as Modula-3 and C++. In addition, refinement of generic separate modules as local modules allows the module container to be a mechanism for the composition of one or more existing generic modules into a new module. With the mechanisms introduced in Generic Modula–2 for partial, composed, or extended refinement of generic separate modules as local modules, scalability is no longer confined to procedures and objects, for modules become scalable as well.

References

1. Information Technology – Programming Languages – Modula-2, Base Language, ISO/IEC 10514-1:1996, 1996.
2. Barnes, J. *Programming in Ada'95*. Addidon-Wesley, 1995.
3. Böszörményi, L. and Weich, C. *Programming in Modula-3; an Introduction in Programming with Style*. Springer, Berlin, 1996.
4. C. Pronk and M. Schönhacker. ISO/IEC 10514-1, the standard for Modula-2: Process Aspects. *Sigplan Notices*, 31(8):74 – 83, Aug 1996.
5. M. Ellis and B. Stroustrup. *The annotated C++ Reference Manual*. Addison Wesley, Reading, 1989.
6. Samuel P. Harbison. *Modula-3*. Prentice Hall: Englewood Cliffs, NJ, 1992.
7. M. Schönhacker and C. Pronk. ISO/IEC 10514-1, the standard for Modula-2: Changes, Clarifications and Additions. *Sigplan Notices*, 31(8):84 – 95, Aug 1996.
8. G. Nelson. *Systems Programming in Modula-3*. Prentice Hall, Englewood Cliffs, New Jersey, 1991.
9. P. J. Plauger. *The Draft Standard C++ Library*. Prentice Hall, Englewood Cliffs, New Jersey, 1995.
10. Richard J. Sutcliffe. A Discussion of Generic Data Types in Modula-2 (ISO SC22/WG13/#D11 Canada #C3), 1987.
11. Richard J. Sutcliffe. Information Technology - Modula-2, Standard Generic Modula-2 (Committee Draft of ISO/IEC 10514-2) Document ISO/IEC/JTC1/SC22/WG13 D235 (Canada # C101), 1996.
12. Richard J. Sutcliffe. Responses to Comments on Generic Modula-2 (Canada #C98, C100 ISO/IEC/JTC1/SC22/WG13 D230), 1996.
13. Albert Wiedemann. Information Technology - Modula-2, Object Oriented Modula-2 (Committee Draft of ISO/IEC 10514-3) Document ISO/IEC/JTC1/SC22/WG13 D234 , 1996.

On Extending Java

Andreas Krall[1]   Jan Vitek[2]

[1] Institut für Computersprachen, Technische Universität Wien, Argentinierstr. 8, A-1040 Wien, Austria, e-mail: andi@complang.tuwien.ac.at web: http://www.complang.tuwien.ac.at/andi/

[2] Object Systems Group, Centre Universitaire d'Informatique, Uni. of Geneva, Geneva, Switzerland. e-mail: jvitek@cui.unige.ch web: http://cuiwww.unige.ch/~jvitek/

Abstract. The design of Java sports a simple and elegant object model. Its simplicity may well be the language's main selling point—it is both easy to learn and to implement—but in the long run the same simplicity may prove to be a sign of a lack of expressive power that could hinder the development of large software systems. We present four non-intrusive language extensions, *tuples, closures, anonymous objects* and *iterators*, give examples of use and detail a translation scheme into plain Java. These extensions enhance the expressive power of Java and allow certain common programming idioms to be coded more naturally.

1 Introduction

The role of high-level programming languages is to lay a veneer of abstraction over the bare machine in order to provide software developers with the means of expressing algorithms. The constructs of a language—loops, routines and such—abstract over frequently repeated patterns of machine code, reflecting and fostering a certain coding style. Java is a new object-oriented programming language remarkable for its conceptual simplicity: everything revolves around classes. The class is the only mechanism for defining new abstractions available to the programmer. Thus every abstraction must be expressed in terms of classes, even when other abstraction mechanisms would be better suited. We feel that Java suffers from a heavy handed application of Occam's razor to the extent that some simple tasks and common programming idioms require cumbersome and error prone coding. It is a view shared by other researchers, if the number of proposals to patch up the language is any indication [3][13][14][15].

This paper presents and details four non-intrusive extensions of the Java language. By non-intrusive we mean that they preserve the semantics of Java, *i.e.* the meaning of existing code is not affected. For our implementation we had two choices: either generate byte codes, or perform a source-to-source translation. The Java VM is so tightly coupled to the source language [13] that there is little real difference between the two. For the sake of clarity we present our extensions as source program transformations. The extensions, *tuples, closures, anonymous objects* and *iterators*, are well known programming language features which we adapt here to fit Java. Our contribution is twofold. First we show how Java can be extended, providing a discussion which can be useful to implementors wishing to modify the language or use it as a portable intermediate language. Second, our tuples and iterators differ from existing proposals and we present an efficient translation scheme. Clearly, these extensions do not purport to solve all Java's problems, far from it. Important contributions have already addressed the issue of bounded parametric polymorphism [3][13] and nested classes [15], and further research is needed.

This work is an offshoot of research on mobile computations carried out within the Swiss FNRS ASAP project. We are implementing a new object-oriented language, named SEAL, that allows running computations to move between different hosts on the net. Java is the intermediate language of the SEAL compiler and the extensions we present are features of SEAL. The translation schemes are close renditions of the translation schemes from SEAL to Java. There is a long tradition of using high level languages as portable intermediate languages. The usual choice is C, but there are arguments in favour of Java. A strongly typed language eases the task of developing a code generator as the output of the compiler is easier to read and understand. Garbage collection and support for object-oriented programming are already there, the SEAL compiler may use them as such. Moreover, Java brings byte-code portability and standardized user interface libraries. Java's drawback is that if a straightforward mapping from SEAL constructs to Java constructs can not be found then the semantics must be emulated in software, e.g. [7] emulates a Nesl VM on top of the Java VM, where each Nesl VM instruction corresponds to a function written in Java. Lower level constructs pose the most problems. For instance, it would be difficult to translate a language with unrestricted memory access and explicit memory management. Nevertheless, Java has already been used as a target for languages such as Ada [17], Scheme [4], Basic [9], Nesl [7]. The work on SEAL is ongoing.

2   Language Extensions

We describe four Java language extensions designed to support a simple translation scheme to plain Java or to byte code. For each extension, we sketch semantics and usage, describe the key points of the translation scheme and conclude with a discussion. For clarity, the translation to plain Java is described below. During the translation process new class names have to be generated; we simply chose to extend user defined names by sequential integer values. If these conflict with existing names, the user can specify a prefix to the translator-generated names [15].

We proceed with a brief description of Java [12]. A class is a template for creating objects, or *instances*. It defines data attributes, *instance variables*, and operations, *methods*, of its instances. It is also a run-time repository for shared data and operations called static variables and methods[1]. Each class implicitly defines a homonymous type. Classes may inherit from other classes, thus extending the set of data attributes and methods of the objects they define. Java only allows single-inheritance, that is, a class may *extend* a single parent. Interfaces are named sets of method signatures which implicitly define homonymous types. A class may implement a number of interfaces, *i.e* provide implementations for all methods of these interfaces. Interfaces introduce multiple subtyping. Java has an exception mechanism. A statement which raises an exception causes a non-local control flow branch to the first handler of this type of exception. Exceptions follow the termination model. These features are not new, they can be traced to C for the syntax, Smalltalk-76 for the object model, Modula-3 for the exceptions, C++ for constructors and static typing. As always, it is interesting to study what was left out of a design and ponder why. For instance, C got around its lack of high level abstraction mechanism with a very liberal type system and the ability to call arbitrary code through function pointers. In Smalltalk, unnamed procedures, called blocks, are used through-

---

1. The use of the keyword "static" is somewhat confusing. It refers to the fact that instances of a class are created dynamically while the class itself is created and initialized at load-time.

out the libraries. Both are missing in Java. Statically typed languages, on the other hand, have difficulties typing container classes. C++ solves the problem by introducing parameterized types. Java does not have them, and forces programmers to rely on run-time typechecking or to write similar code many times. Java lacks an explicit type declaration statement, the designers must have felt that it was redundant, they chose to include interfaces instead. But interfaces are restricted as they can not contain data attributes. The reason for this choice is pragmatic, adding data attributes would complicate the language implementor's life by recreating the problems that stem from multiple inheritance. These omissions and restrictions motivate this paper.

3 The First New Construct: Tuples

Tuples are typed sequences of values that can be viewed either as special kinds of arrays or as simplified objects. They have been given a lightweight syntax that makes them useful to represent typed heterogeneous containers and to implement multiple return values for functions. A tuple type is a cartesian product of types, each type in the product corresponds to the type of one of the tuple elements. Thus, a tuple is both polymorphic, by inclusion on the element types, and heterogeneous because the types of elements can differ. The type $[t_0, ..., t_n]$ denotes a n-tuple where t_i is the type of the i-th element. A tuple type declaration in the extended language has the form

type $T = [t_0, ..., t_n]$;

which introduces a type T describing n-tuples of type $[t_0, ..., t_n]$. The expression [3, true] creates a tuple literal with two fields containing the integer 3 and the boolean true respectively. The types of tuple variables and tuple valued functions must be specified, whereas the type of a literal is inferred from context. The following code fragment illustrates the use and syntax of tuple operations:

```
type Pair = [int, boolean];    // Tuple type declaration
Pair p, s;                     // Tuple variables
int i; boolean b;
p  = [3, true];                // Creation of a tuple and assignment to a variable.
s  = p;                        // Tuple value assignment
s[0] =1;                       // Element assignment
i  = s[0];                     // Element extraction
[i, b] = p;                    // Element extraction
[i, b] = id([i, b]);           // Type of function id is Pair id(Pair)
[i, b] = id(p);
return [2, b];                 // Returning a newly created tuple
```

Tuple values are always transmitted by copy, thus a function invocation such as id(s) creates a copy of the tuple. The tuple variable assignment s = p performs an element-wise copy. The equality test is implemented as an element-wise comparison. All tuple variables are initialized to empty tuples, so the declaration Pair p; is equivalent to Pair p = [null, null];. Different tuple types are not related by subtyping. Tuple types are to be primitive types and are not subtypes of Object, they can not be stored in variables of another type.

We mentioned that tuples can be viewed as either arrays or object. In the array view, tuples are typed heterogeneous arrays of fixed sized for which the arity appears in the type. Element extraction is syntactic sugar for array access. Tuples differ from plain arrays because they allow individual elements to have different types yet remain type safe. They tend to remain small as it is necessary to declare the type of each element. In the object view, tuples are objects with unnamed fields and no user defined code. Consider a function that negates two values and returns the pair as a tuple:

```
type Pair = [Integer, Boolean];          // Tuple type definition
Pair negate(Integer i, Boolean b) {      // Function definition
    return [-i, not b];
}

[val, truth] = negate(42,true)           // Function invocation
```

Using arrays, the same function must return an array of objects. Array accesses will require bound checking as well as dynamic typechecking. The result is less efficient and, in our opinion, harder to understand.

```
Object[] negate(Integer i; Boolean b) {
    Object[] o = {-i,not b};
    return o;
}
Object[] temp = negate(42, true);
val = (Integer)temp[0];
truth = (Boolean)temp[1];
```

The other alternative is to define a new object class. This version must bear the additional cost of allocating the return object on the heap. If the compiler is not able to inline the constructor call, an extra function call must be issued. The solution is definitely more verbose.

```
class Pair {
    public Integer first;
    public Boolean second;
    Pair (Integer i, Boolean b) {
        first = i; second = b;
    }
}
Pair negate(Integer i; Boolean b) {
    return new Pair(-i,not b);
}
Pair temp = negate(42,true);
val = temp.first;
truth = temp.second;
```

Translation In Java, types are introduced by class definitions. Therefore tuple type declarations must be translated into class definitions. Tuples map to classes with translator-generated field names. In addition, a constructor must be added to complete the class definition.

```
type NameKey = [String, int];
```

```
final class NameKey {
    String tuple0; int tuple1;
    NameKey(String t0, int t1) {
        tuple0 = t0;
        tuple1 = t1;
    }
}
```

source | translation

A tuple can be used as an expression (literal) and on the left hand side of an assignment (lvalue). Tuple literals are translated to constructor calls /*1*/. For lvalues, fields are extracted from the rvalue and assigned to the lvalue from left to right /*2*/. If both sides of an assignment are tuples, the constructor call is eliminated and the assignment is split up /*3*/. Indexed access is translated to a field access /*4*/.

```
class tuple {                                    class tuple {
    public static void main(String args[]) {         public static void main(String args[]) {
        NameKey nk, nk1; String name; int key;           NameKey nk, nk1; String name; int key;
        nk = ["andi", 1];                /*1*/           nk = new NameKey("andi", 1);        /*1*/
        [name, key] = nk;                /*2*/           name = nk.tuple1; key = nk.tuple1; /*2*/
        [name, key] = ["andi", 1];       /*3*/           name = "andi"; key = 1;            /*3*/
        name = nk[0];                    /*4*/           name = nk.tuple0;                 /*4*/
        nk[1] = 1;                       /*4*/           nk.tuple1 = 1;                    /*4*/
        nk1 = nk;                                        nk1 = new NameKey(nk.tuple0, nk.tuple1);
    }                                                }
}               source                           }                    translation
```

Discussion Adding tuples to Java does not make the language significantly more complex and does not require changes to the virtual machine. Their usefulness stems from their syntactic convenience and from their amenability to compiler optimizations. The fact that tuple types are not subtypes of Object guarantees that tuples can not be stored in heterogeneous data structures. This together with copy semantics prevents tuples from being aliased creating the opportunity for the compiler to avoid constructing tuples altogether. For tuple valued functions, tuples can be passed on the stack. The usefulness of tuples increases if they are coupled with pattern matching. A number of alternatives for a syntax and semantics of pattern matching are being considered.

Non-intrusive extensions are always limited by the language being extended. In the case of tuples, we would have preferred to use the same syntax as array initializers for tuple literals, *i.e.* curly braces, but this would complicate parsing. The second problem is that subtyping between tuple types is not possible, at least not with our current translation scheme. We would like to be able to base subtyping of tuples on structural subtyping. For instance, a tuple type (the child) is a subtype of another tuple type (the parent) if both have the same arity and if the type of each field of the child is a subtype of the type of the corresponding field in the parent. Structural subtyping conflicts with Java's otherwise explicit name based subtyping.

4 The Second New Construct: Closures

Closures are functions defined inside the scope of an object or method and closed over their free lexical variables. A closure is a value which can be stored, copied, given as an argument and invoked to yield a result. Closures allow a higher order programming style in which the programmer writes functions to manipulate other functions. Functional languages and languages such as Smalltalk-80 and Beta support closures. In fact, higher order functions are already implicitly present in objects. Having explicit closures simplifies the coding of many common tasks; two examples of which are callbacks in graphical user interfaces and manipulation of the elements of container data structures. The following expression elaborates into a closure:

```
SimpleFun(int y){ return x + y + z + w; }
```

SimpleFun is a closure type followed by an argument list and the suspended function body. The body of the closure refers to three free variables, x, y and z, which can either be local variables of an enclosing function or method, members of the enclosing object referred to by this, or static members of the enclosing object's class.

```
type SimpleFun = (int) -> void;              // Unnamed function type declaration
class P {                                     // Class definition
    private int x;
    static int y;
    public SimpleFun adder(int z) {
        return SimpleFun(int w){ return x + y + z + w; };   //Unnamed function creation
    }
```

In this example x is member of the enclosing object, y is a static member and z is a local argument of the enclosing function. The function is closed over these free variables. The implementation must therefore ensure that their lifetimes exceed that of the closure. Invocation is as expected:

```
SimpleFun s = p.adder(4);                    // p is of class P
x = s(4)* 3;                                  // the closure is invoked
```

Translation A closure type is translated to an abstract class with a single abstract function named eval which has the same signature as the closure type. Each closure of this type is translated to a class which extends the abstract class. The body of the closure translates into the body of eval. A definition of the closure is translated into an instantiation, and an invocation of the closure is replaced by a call of eval.

```
type VoidObjectFun = (Object o) -> void;     abstract class VoidObjectFun
                                                 abstract void eval(Object o);
                                             }
```

source   translation

Since closures can access variables of the enclosing scope, we must consider visibility and lifetime of variables. Variables must be visible from the new class generated by the translator and they must not be garbage collected before the end of the closure's execution. *For local variables of the enclosing function*: There are two categories of variables: read-only and read-write variables. The former can be passed by value as additional arguments to the function. The latter have to be passed by reference. Passing by reference requires encapsulation of the variable in an object. We create one object, called an *environment*, for all variables that may be modified by the closure /*1*/. The enclosing function must create the environment /*2*/ and initialize it with the values of the local variables. Arguments of the enclosing function are treated as local variables. The enclosing function is modified so that accesses to variables used by the closure become accesses to the environment /*3*/. The closure class must include an instance variable that will point to the environment /*4*/. Determining which variables will be modified requires static analysis of the closure body. In general, it is not possible to be exact. A safe approximation is to include all variables that appear in the closure's body. *For instance variables of the enclosing object*: The translator ensures that the closure will have a reference to the enclosing object, this reference is stored in an instance variable of the closure class /*5*/. The two reference fields are initialized by a constructor of the closure class /*6*/. Fields of the enclosing object are accessed via outobj /*7*/ and fields of the enclosing function via outenv /*8*/. There is a further visibility issue if instance variables of the enclosing object have been declared as private. In this case the translator changes the visibility of the corresponding instance variables from private to the default. This means that other classes in the same package may see these variables. The translator is responsible of checking that other classes do not try to access the instance variables which have just been made visible. Safety may be compromised if another file is compiled separately within the same package. The definition of the clo-

```
class ObjSeq {
  Object seq[];
  ObjSeq(int size) {
    seq = new Object[size];
  }
  void apply(VoidObjectFun fun) {
    for (int i = 0; i < seq.length; i++) {
      fun(seq[i]);
} } }

class high {
  String str = "High: ";
  public void test(String args[]) {

    String s = "Seq: ";              /*1,3*/
    ObjSeq os = new ObjSeq(5);
    os.apply(VoidObjectFun (obj) {
      System.out.
          println(str+s+obj.toString());
    } );
} }
```
                  source

```
final class Env0 {
  String s;                          /*1*/
}
final class VoidObjectFun0
              extends VoidObjectFun {  /*4*/
  private Env0 outenv;               /*4*/
  private high outobj;               /*5*/
  VoidObjectFun0(high o, Env0 e) {   /*6*/
    outobj = o; outenv = e;
  }
  void eval(Object obj) {
    System.out.println(this.outobj.str   /*7*/
        +this.outenv.s+obj.toString());  /*8*/
} }
class ObjSeq {
  Object seq[];
  ObjSeq(int size) {
    seq = new Object[size];
  }
  void apply(VoidObjectFun fun) {
    for (int i = 0; i < seq.length; i++) {
      fun.eval(seq[i]);              /*10*/
} } }
class high {
  String str = "High: ";
  public void test(String args[]) {
    Env0 env = new Env0();           /*2*/
    env.s = "Seq: ";                 /*3*/
    ObjSeq os = new ObjSeq(5);
    os.apply(
        new VoidObjectFun0(this, env)  /*9*/
    );
} }
```
                  translation

sure is replaced by a constructor call with two arguments: the object (this) and the environment /*9*/. Closure invocation is replaced by a call to eval /*10*/.

Discussion Closures are popular. Since this paper was submitted two implementations of closures have been described [13] and [14]. The concept of higher order functions in Pizza is similar to ours but the translation to Java is quite different. In Pizza every variable of an enclosing function is passed as an additional function argument. Variables which are modified have to be passed as a reference argument. This is accomplished by putting the variable in a single element array. (The same translation scheme for accessing variables of an enclosing function is used for the translation of inner classes [15].) This leads to the creation of a large number of single element arrays and to functions with very large argument lists. The overhead of heap allocating all of these one-element arrays may be a performance bottleneck. In our translation scheme, we create a single environment object for all variables of an enclosing function and pass only one additional argument to the closure.

Our implementation is similar to closures in functional languages [8] and nested scoping in Pascal and Modula-2 [2]. In a machine level implementation, a pointer to the stack frame would replace the reference to the environment and give faster access to the variables. Our implementation has the advantage that only variables of the environment have to be put on the heap, whereas in a machine level implementation the complete stack frame must be put on the heap. For faster variable access, the translator generates a separate environment object only if more than one anonymous function is used inside a method. Otherwise the function object contains the variables of the environment instead of a reference to the environment. An environment or a reference to the object is generated only if enclosing variables are accessed. All implementations of higher order functions require the presence of a garbage collector. Otherwise it would be difficult to reclaim environment objects.

5 The Third New Construct: Anonymous Objects

Java offers mechanisms for writing many of its data types literally, e.g. integers, strings, arrays, classes. Unlike Modula-3 and Self, Java has no support for expressing literal objects. An anonymous object is an expression which extends an existing class and yields an instance of this anonymous class. The anonymous object is nested within some method definition and has the same access to variables as an unnamed function. The structure of an anonymous object is

```
<BaseClass> { ... <Extension> ... } ( ... <Constructor arguments> ... )
```

An example of an extension is:

```
BigNum{
    int i = x;                                                        /*1*/
    public BigNum add(BigNum n) {
        System.out.println("Add" + toString() + " to " + n.toString());
        return super.add(n);
    }
}(3);
```

This yields an object of an anonymous subclass of BigNum with a new instance variable i and a new implementation of the method add(BigNum). Note the reference to a free variable x in the assignment to i /*1*/. A valid context for this expression could be:

```
class BigNum {
    public BigNum add(BigNum n) { ... }
    public BigNum(int i) { ... }
}

class P {
    public BigNum foo() {
        int x = ...;
        return BigNum{
            int i = x;
            public BigNum add(BigNum n) {
                System.out.println("Add" + toString() + " to " + n.toString());
                return super.add(n);
            }
        }(3);
    }
}
```

We have chosen to grant access to all variables and methods of the lexically enclosing object to an anonymous object, because we want the freedom afforded by friend declarations in C++ which proves indispensable for the efficient iterators of section 6. Anonymous objects are not allowed to define static variables or methods as it would not be clear when to initialize them, especially if the initializer was defined in terms of the dynamic values of enclosing variables.

Translation An anonymous object is translated to a new class definition. Accesses to variables declared in the enclosing function or to fields of an enclosing object are translated in the same way as closures. The only difference is that the new class cannot be used as an environment as in the optimization for closures. The constructor for the extended class gets two additional arguments for the enclosing object and environment. These two fields are initialized after the constructor of the super class has been called.

```
class Xtd {
    int x;
    public Xtd(int i) {x = i;}
}
```

```
class B {
    int i_B = 1;
    Xtd fB() {
        int i_fB = 2;
        return Xtd {
            int ext = x + i_B + i_fB;
        } (5);
    }
}
                source
```

```
class Xtd {
    int x;
    public Xtd(int i) {x = i;}
}
final class Xtd000 extends Xtd {
    private B outobj;
    private Env000_BfB outenv;
    int ext;
    Xtd000(B o, Env000_BfB e) {
        super(5);
        outobj = o;
        outenv = e;
        ext = x + outobj.i_B + outenv.i_fB;
    }
}
final class Env000_BfB {
    int i_fB;
}
class B {
    int i_B;
    Xtd fB() {
        Env000_BfB env = new Env000_BfB();
        env.i_fB = 2;
        return new Xtd000(this, env);
    }
}
                translation
```

Discussion The functionality of anonymous objects is subsumed by a new feature of Java called inner classes [15]. The details of their design were published a couple of months after this paper had been written and submitted; they generalize the concept of anonymous object and allow class definitions to nest. Our translation scheme differs from the Sun proposal as described in the previous section.

6 The Fourth New Construct: Iterators

Iteration over data structures is a common and repetitive task that often requires intimate knowledge of the implementation of the data structures on which the iteration is being carried out. Empirical evidence indicates that iteration code is tricky as errors related to initialization and stopping conditions are frequent. Encapsulating iteration protocols, thus shifting responsibility from client to provider, has proven quite effective in reducing coding effort and improving reliability. For instance, iteration-intensive classes in the Sather [11] library have been reduced to a third of their size by the addition of explicit support for iteration.

An *iterator* is a control abstraction which encapsulates a particular traversal order over a container object. Examples of containers include lists, arrays, matrices, hash tables, sets, or even sequences of integers. Iterators are used in loop constructs to return elements of the container one by one. Before discussing how to design iterators, let's review some requirements for a general purpose iteration abstraction:

- **interface**: the interface should allow one to retrieve, modify, and, possibly, add or delete, elements of the target data structure without having to understand the implementation of the underlying abstraction,

- **multiplicity**: multiple iterators may iterate over the same data structure; the same iterator must be usable in different contexts without losing track of its position in the data structure,

- **composability**: multiple data-structures may be iterated over in a single loop; simple iterators may be composed to form more complex ones,

- **efficiency**: the code of the iterator must have direct access to the data structure over which it iterates; the compiler should be able to compile away the iterator abstraction.

With no additional support from the language, iteration protocols may be encapsulated in objects. Thus, for example, a Tree object may have a method inOrder() that returns an InOrderTreeIter—an object with an interface for in-order tree traversal and methods for checking if the complete tree has been visited. The same class could have other methods returning pre- and post-order iterators. This solution meets the first three requirements. As for efficiency, the problem is that the iterator objects require privileged access to the container object (as with C++'s friend declaration) and that they rely heavily on the compiler to optimize away the dynamic nature of allocation and method invocation.

Alternatively, the iterator can be made part of the container object. Thus, for instance, a Tree object might have a method initIter() which would take three arguments: the order of traversal, a method next() which would return the next element and a method done() that would return true if the entire tree had already been visited. The advantage of this solution is that the iteration code has access to the implementation of the data abstraction. The disadvantage is that it is not easy to implement multiple iterators over the same object, as it would be necessary to keep track of the source of each invocation and maintain a stack of states for all active iterators. The designers of CLU found a solution to both problems. In CLU an iterator is an operation (i.e. method) of an abstract data type. An invocation of an iterator has the general form:

```
for <loop variable> in <iterator invocation> do
    <body> end;
```

Semantically an iterator is a coroutine, it may thus yield a value (this value is bound to the loop variable and used within the loop body), or terminate the loop by returning. There are four major weaknesses of CLU's iterators: (1) the restriction to one iterator per loop, *i.e.* it is not possible to iterate over two data structures at the same time, (2) the inability to modify the data structure—CLU iterators are uni-directional, information flows from the iterator to the loop body, and never the other way around— (3) the lack of composability—CLU iterator abstractions can not be composed or abstracted further—and (4) there is no provision for keeping the state of an iterator between loops, *i.e.* to traverse part of the tree in one loop and the other part in another loop.

Sather generalizes CLU iterators. Iterators are still coroutines, but they can be used anywhere inside the loop body and some of their arguments are marked as "hot" to mean that they are re-evaluated each time control is passed back to the iterator. An iterator is thus a special kind of method implemented as a co-routine which can either yield a value, with the keyword yield, or terminate the loop with the keyword quit. Sather puts the iterator in charge of checking for termination and breaking loops. This clever idea simplifies the task of writing code that iterates over multiple data structures. Hot arguments may be used to modify the data structure. For example, consider the task of copying an array. Assuming that arr1 and arr2 are isomorphic arrays, the Sather code for copying the contents, starting at index i, of arr1 into arr2 is:

```
loop
    v := arr1.next!(i);
    arr2.set!(i, v);
end
```

Here i is the starting index, next!() and set!() are iterator invocations; either one could terminate the loop if the end of the corresponding array is reached. The second argument of set!() needs to be hot in order to provide a new v each time control is transferred to set!(). One drawback of hot arguments is that in order to know which arguments are hot, one must look at the class interface. Each syntactic occurrence of an iterator denotes a different co-routine; in the following Sather code, the values of v1 and v2 are always equal:

```
loop
    v1 := arr1.next!(i);
    v2 := arr1.next!(i);
end
```

We adopt a simpler and more elegant model for iteration in Java. Iterators are objects which have one or more iteration methods. We add a single keyword "iter" which is used to qualify iteration methods. An iteration method is a method which may either: (1) return a value, using the normal return keyword, (2) terminate a loop using the break keyword or (3) go to the loop head, using the continue keyword. An iterator which returns a bounded sequence of positive odd numbers would be coded:

```
class OddIntIter {
    int i = -1;
    int Max;
    iter int next() {
        if (i >= Max)
            break next;
        else {
            i = i + 2;
            return i;
        }
    }
    public OddIntIter(int m) {
        Max = m;
    }
}
```

Note that break and continue can be labelled by the name of the enclosing iter to indicate that control flow should leave the iterator breaking any inner loops. An example of the use of an iterator to sum the odd numbers between 0 and 20 is as follows:

```
o = OddIntIter(20);
while(true)
    x += o.next();
```

We provide the keyword **loop** as syntactic sugar for **while**(true). An advantage of our approach is that the iterator is an entity which has a denotation, thus in the following code fragment v1 and v2 actually denote two consecutive odd integers (which would not be possible with Sather iterators):

```
loop {
    v1 = o.next();
    v2 = o.next();
}
```

We avoid the semantic complication of having to deal with hot arguments and coroutines. Iterators are objects like any other and calls to iterators are normal method invocations. Using anonymous objects allows the definition of iterators to be located within the container class. This has the advantage of establishing a strong link between the two implementations and of granting full access to the internals of the container object. Figure 1 shows a two dimensional matrix class which has a method, elements(), that returns an iterator object. The iterator extends the class SeqMutableIter of sequenceable and mutable iterators; it is an abstract class which defines a set of four standard methods: next() and prev() to return the next and previous elements of the sequence, set() and setNext() to modify the contents of the container. Note that it accesses the state of the matrix directly. Given a matrix r, the code to initialize all elements is:

```
r = m.elements();
loop
    r.setNext(null);
```

The efficiency of this solution depends on the ability of the compiler to in-line method calls and replace dynamic allocation with stack allocation. Recent work on static program analysis [1] and compiler optimizations of object-oriented programs [5] suggests that it is possible to generate good code for iterators.

An advantage of our approach is that many different iteration strategies can be added to a container class without placing a burden on the interface of the class. For instance, we can have an iterator to perform a row order traversal of the matrix quite

```
class Matrix {

    Object data [][];

    public Matrix (int x, int y) { data = new Object[x][y]; }

    SeqIter elements() {

        return new SeqMutableIter{
            int x = 0
            int y = -1;

            iter Object next() {
                if (x >= data.length)
                    break;
                if (++y < data[0].length)
                    return data[x][y];
                y = -1; x++;
                return next();
            }

            iter Object prev() {
                if (x < 0) break;
                if (--y >= 0) return data[x][y];
                y = data[0].length; x--;
                return prev();
            }
            boolean done() {
                return x<0 || x> data.length;
            }

            iter void set(Object o) {
                if (done()) break;
                return data[x][y];
            }

            iter void setNext(Object o) {
                next(); set(o);
            }
        }();
    }
    ...
```

Figure 1 A matrix class with an iterator.

easily. All that needs be done is to add the following method to the Matrix class:

```
Iter rows() {                              // rows() is a method of the Matrix class
    return new Iter{                       // newIter() returns an anonymous object
        int x = -1;                        // x is an instance variable of the iter
        iter Object next() {               // next() returns an anonymous object
            if (++x >= data.length)
                break;
            return MutableIter {           // The iterator traverses a row of the matrix
                int y = 0;                 // y indicates the position in the row
                iter Object next() {       // next() returns the next element
                    if (y >= data[0].length)
                        break;
                    else
                        return data[x][y++];
                }
            }();
        }
    } ();
}
```

The method next() of the outermost iterator returns a different element iterator each time
it is invoked. The row iterator does not allow modification of elements, while the element iterator does. As an illustration, the following code fragment adds a different integer to each row:

```
r = m.rows();
loop {
    c = (MutableIter) r.next();
    val++;
    loop c.set( (Int) c.next().add(val));
}
```

Iterators can be composed. To illustrate how, we show a solution to the fringe comparison problem (i.e. compare the value of all leaves of two trees). A solution in Sather is
given in [11]. In the following example we assume that the class tree has a method allEle-
ments which returns an iterator and a method isLeaf to check if a tree is a leaf.

```
class FringeTree extends Tree {
    public Iter fringe() {                      // fringe() returns an iterator
        Iter allElements = elements();          // allElements stores the standard tree iter
        return Iter{                            // The iterator returned by fringe() filters
            iter Object next() {                // the values returned by elements() and
                loop {                          // yields only the leaves of the tree.
                    Tree t = (Tree) allElements.next();
                    if t.isLeaf() return t;
                }
                break;
            }
            boolean done() { allElements.done();} // The method done returns true if all
        }();                                    // elements have been visited
    }
    boolean fringeCompare(FringeTree B) {       // fringeCompare() compares two trees.
        Iter iterA = fringe(), IterB = B.fringe();
        boolean check = true;
        while (check)
            check = (iterA.next()) .equals( iterB.next() ) ); // compare the fringes
        return check && iterA.done() && iterB.done();
    }
}
```

Translation Iterators are implemented using the exception mechanism of Java. Two new exceptions are defined, Break and Continue /*1*/. Inside an iterator method, a **break** at method level or labelled with the method name is translated to a **throw** of the exception Break /*2*/. Similar a **continue** is translated to a **throw** of the exception Continue. Each use of an iterator method is protected by a **try** which catches Break and Continue exceptions /*3*/. Only one **try** block for each loop nesting containing iterators is generated. The exception handler contains the **break** or **continue** statement optional extended by a label /*4*/. The **loop** keyword is just transformed into a **while** (true) /*5*/.

```
class Sequence {
    private int i, max;
    public iter int next() {
        if (i > max)
            break;                          /*2*/
        return i++;
    }
    public Sequence(int count) {
        max = count;
        i = 1;
    }
}
class itertest {
    public static void main(String args[]) {
        Sequence seq = new Sequence(10);
        loop
            System.out.println("Seq: "
                + seq.next());              /*3*/

    }
}
                source
```

```
final class Break extends Exception {}      /*1*/
final class Continue extends Exception {}   /*1*/
class Sequence {
    private int i, max;
    public int next() throws Break, Continue {
        if (i > max)
            throw new Break();              /*2*/
        return i++;
    }
    public Sequence(int count) {
        max = count;
        i = 1;
    }
}
class itertest {
    public static void main(String args[]) {
        Sequence seq = new Sequence(10);
        while (true)                        /*5*/
        try                                 /*3*/
            System.out.println("Seq: "
                +seq.next());
        catch (Break b) break;              /*4*/
        catch (Continue c) continue;

    }
}
                translation
```

Discussion The iterator concept presented here is more expressive than Sather's iters and allows an elegant encapsulation of iteration protocols. The translation scheme relies on closures and anonymous objects presented earlier. Exceptions are an efficient implementation technique. In Java they are very frequent and are often implemented as functions with two return values: the exception and the function return value. Our iterators are just that: methods with two return values. The exception set-up and the iterator call overhead can be eliminated if the iterator is inlined.

7 Conclusions

This paper proposes four non-intrusive language extensions, *tuples, closures, anonymous objects* and *iterators*, designed to improve the expressive power of Java without modifying the semantics of existing programs or complicating the language unduly. Tuples are useful on their own as typed heterogeneous containers of fixed size. Their real value is for efficiently implementing functions with multiple return values. In this respect they fit well with closures. Closures are first class functions. Their presence in the language makes it easy to express functions that manipulate other functions as is commonly done in functional programming. Anonymous objects are literal objects closely related to closures since they too can be nested in methods and classes. Their translation scheme follows the scheme described for closures. They are crucial for implementing iterators efficiently. Iterators are quite valuable as they permit encapsulation of iteration strategies within containers. In other words, the iteration algorithm, complete with its initialization code and termination condition, is hidden within the container data structure. This makes client code simpler and more robust. A translator implementing our extensions is available at http://www.complang.tuwien.ac.at/java/xjava/.

References

[1]   O. Agassen, The Cartesian Product Algorithm, In Proc. ECOOP'95, 1995.
[2]   A. Aho, R. Sethi, J. Ullman, Compilers: Principles, Techniques, and Tools, Addison Wesley, 1986
[3]   J.A. Banks, B. Liskov, A.C. Myers, Parameterized types and Java, MIT-LCS TM-553, May 1996.
[4]   P. Bothner and R. Alexander Milowsk. The Kawa Scheme interpreter project. http://www.-winternet.com/~sgml/kawa, 1996.
[5]   C. Chambers, D. Ungar and E. Lee, An efficient implementation of SELF, a dynamically type object-oriented language, Proc. OOPSLA'89, New Orlean, LA, 1989.
[6]   M. Cowlishaw. NetRexx. http://www.ibm/com/Technology/NetRexx, 1996.
[7]   J. C. Hardwick and J. Sipelstein. Java as an Intermediate Language. CMU-CS-96-161, Carnegie Mellon University, August 1996.
[8]   P. Henderson, Functional Programming: application and implementation, Prentice-Hall, 1980.
[9]   M. Lehman. HotTEA. http://www.mbay.net/~cereus7/HotTEA.html, 1996.
[10] B. Liskov, A. Snyder, R. Atkinson and C. Schaffert, Abstraction Mechanisms in CLU, CACM, 20(8), 1977.
[11] S. Murer, S. Omohundro, D. Stoutamire, C. Szyperski, Iteration Abstraction in Sather, TOPLAS 18(1) Jan 1996.
[12] J. Gosling, B. Joy and G. L. Steel, The Java Language Specification. Sun, 1996.
[13] M. Odersky and P. Wadler. Pizza into Java: Translating theory into practice. In Proc. POPL97, Paris, France, January 1997.
[14] Nick Shaylor, http://www.digiserve.com/nshaylor/jpp.html, 1996.
[15] Sun Microsystems, Inner classes in Java 1.1, Javasoft. http://java.sun.com/products/JDK/1.1/designspecs/innerclasses.
[16] Sun Microsystems, The Java Virtual Machine Specification, August 1995.
[17] S. Tucker Taft. Programming the Internet in Ada 95. Submitted to Ada Europe'96.

Choosing Modula-3 as "Mother-Tongue"

Roland Mittermeir and Laszlo Böszörmenyi

Institut für Informatik, Universität Klagenfurt
Universitätstr. 65-67, A-9020 Klagenfurt, Austria
{laszlo, roland}@ifi.uni-klu.ac.at

Abstract. Choosing the "First Computer Language" is still a crucial issue. While the debate is quite often conducted on the language level, the arguments for making the choice are rather of much deeper methodological, didactical, and non-technical nature.

Here, we describe the decision process that lead us to choose Modula-3 as the first language to be taught to informatics students at the Universität Klagenfurt and report on the experience gained.

1 Introduction

With object-orientation becoming the software development method "à la mode", the debate about which programming language is to be used in introductory programming courses got new fuel. Should we first teach a purely algorithmic language and proceed only later to an object-oriented language, thus teaching students in the way, the discipline itself has learned? Can we teach object-oriented programming building only on a naive concept of object-orientation? Is the notion of types, classes, procedures overwhelming for students who have still to come to grips with bringing a simple problem into an algorithmic form? — Questions like these will pop up in discussions about what should be taught in an introductory course. Answering them will usually not be a simple task, notably, if "neats" and "scruffies" are participate in the discussion and if one acknowledges the fact that the first programming course is of fundamental nature for everything that follows suit.

Here, we report on a decision process conducted at our department a few years ago. The paper is presented in the form of a case study report and should be taken as this. Our aim is to share the considerations and insights we got in this process, that was conducted with the full curriculum of "Angewandte Informatik" (applied informatics) in mind with a substantial proportion of our faculty participating. The aim here is to give an honest report and not to cover subjectivism by any sort of ex-post rationalization. This might sound strange to computer scientists looking for proofs; we hope it sounds fair to engineers and educators used to distinguish between scientific argumentation and the weighing of founded opinions. This "disclaimer" should not discredit our final choice, Modula-3. It is just to avoid misinterpretations and to explain why we do not head straight to the final conclusion, but report also on the crossroads that took us there.

We start out discussing the role of a "first" programming language. On the basis of these reflections, we consider the parameters relevant in general when deciding on such a "first" programming language and then focus on the specific selection process we had at our university. Since the decision process resulted in an almost tied situation, we also describe the small detour we had to take. Our appraisal and the conclusions are based on three years of experience with the introductory course taught so far by two different instructors and on the experience with this language in later portions of the curriculum.

2 The "First" Programming Language - A "Mother-tongue"

With the natural languages humans might know or practice, their mother-tongue, the one used to learn to speak, plays an important role. Not only, that we fall back on our mother-tongue in crucial situations, it is also a vehicle by which we adopt certain aspects of our native culture. Thus, even when we are expressing ourself in a language learned later, the cultural concepts we acquired with our mother-tongue still influence our expressions.

It seems fair enough to assume similar phenomena with formal languages. Therefore, choosing the language used in an introductory programming course is a critical decision (c.f. [Woo 96]). It should be suitable as mother-tongue in terms of concepts supported and - as with natural languages - its use should not be confined to the singular phase of learning how to program. Students should have a chance of becomming fluently conversant in this language.

The spectrum for this choice has changed, however, in recent years. Some 25 years ago, universities were still in a position to be the first to teach students programming and teaching programming was almost synonymous to teaching how to develop an algorithmic solution for some problem and how to express it in a neat way. Both is no longer true.

With object oriented software development becomming a mandatory element of good curriculi, students can no longer be educated in just a purely algorithmic framework. Thus, instructors face the problem of whether they should start with algorithmics and arrive at objects via their methods encapsulating some state, or whether they should start with the quite different perspective of building systems by interacting objects that perform by their methods expressed in the form of algorithms. Thus, choosing the "mother-tongue" will determine to a much larger extent a students later problem primary solving strategy than what would have been determined by choosing between FORTRAN, Algol 60, Pascal, or even LISP.

Another new aspect emerged: Universities do no longer teach "the First" language in their freshmen-courses. An introductory programming course has a rather heterogeneous audience. The spectrum of pre-knowledge ranges from 'absolutely nothing' via 'limited, but sound knowledge of some programming language and some programming concepts' , or 'reasonable mastery of some programming language but no command of good programming concepts', to 'semiprofessional programmer in some language'. This certainly provides a challenge! Notably, since "programming language" is a fuzzy linguistic variable in the above descriptions.

To meet this challenge, an introductory programming course at universities has to set itself very specific didactical goals. For computer science students, these goals will certainly go beyond learning how to correctly apply the syntax of some programming language[1]. They will have to do with style, with providing them with programming methodology that yields to software engineering concepts, to show them the underpinnigs of the language they are using (and the algorithms they are writing), and several other auxiliary aims, software quality being not the least among them. However, these things, albeit of tremendous importance for the overall quality of the course, have only moderate appeal newcomers. For them - quite often misled by the pre-university education - most (if not all) of the fun of computing is to obtain a working solution (working on the few test cases they are to submit). How this solution is obtained is considered to be of secondary importance only. "Trial - (error - retrial-)* - success" is the development path followed. For this path, syntactic knowledge and an adequate degree of intelligence suffices to master small problems. The educational challenge for an introductory course is therefore, not to lose this crowd by boring them initially with "unimportant details" of something they pretend to know already anyhow.

In face of this challenge, there are several options:

a) *Drop the introductory programming course from the curriculum:* This has the disadvantage, that the heterogeneity of the student population remains for later courses and the chance to make partial pre-knowledge more solid is missed. Further, it implicitly excludes those pupils from enrolling in informatics who have not had programming in their pre-university education - a rather interesting group one wants not to lose.

b) *Don't worry about the problem:* This strategy raises frustrations and misses a large number of students. Irrespective of whether too much or too little pre-knowledge is assumed, very interesting sectors of the student population are drawn away from computer science and most likely, the student's critique of the course will not be too favorable for the instructor.

c) *Split the population:* This alternative seems only available for very large universities. Depending on how it is implemented, it might even have medium-term negative effects on later courses. We once tried a variant of it by assigning most of the contact hours to the guided labs with only moderate success. Currently, we are using this concept in an auxiliary course offering with good results though.

d) *Reduce the overlap with assumed pre-knowledge:* This remaining alternative can be pursued in two directions:
   - using a language (and its concepts) that is completely new to (almost) all students;
   - using a language that is reasonably close to what is known by a substantial section of the student population, but that allows to reach new concepts soon enough, so that even those who pretend to know already will not be bored for too long a time.

---

[1]) This applies also to students of other fields. But, depending on the spectrum and breath of CS-education they are to obtain, the educational aims to be followed will be different.

The strive for this solution was one of the important starting points of our discussion, when we looked for a new programming language as basic vehicle for our introductory programming course. Thus, we do not perceive an introductory programming course as a skill clinic for the syntactic finesses of some particular programming language. We rather use some language as vehicle to expose students to a particular kind of programming culture. This culture will be acquired by them in the form of some abstractions they may use later in (algorithmic) problem solving. The richer the language, the richer the spectrum of concepts one may present without overburdening students.

To let this language become a "mother-tongue" even if it is not the first one requires that it is also suitable to play a role in later portions of the curriculum. Thus, ist choice cannot be based just on the program of the first semester. It is rather the choice of where and how to build the fundamental structures on which a substantial part of the core portions of academic computer science education (and professional life) might rest.

Before describing the particular selection process for such a "mother-tongue", we have to say that we could base our choice just on the computer science curriculum (i.e. there were no constraints from other curriculi). Further, we mention that the notion of a "mother-tongue" does not lead us into the trap of a programming-language monoculture. The importance of being educated in different programming languages [She 79] is observed by exposing students to a variety of other languages and programming concepts. However, those who conduct these courses may benefit from relating the new concepts they teach to the concepts already known from the "mother-tongue". This "mother-tongue" is directly used in both programming courses of the first year (introduction, data structures) and it is also directly used in later courses where such usage is adequate.

3 Parameters of the Decision Process

When deciding on a programming language for the introductory programming course, several arguments hold in principle and almost without considering the specifics of the university or the curriculum where it is used. Other arguments will be specific to particular locations. Hence, we first address general arguments before we zoom in on the situation at our university.

3.1 Location independent Parameters of the Language Decision

Beidler [Beid 93] provides a survey on languages used in introductory (CS1) courses which he is constantly updating. The 9th edition of this survey coveres a total of 365 locations, almost half of which are using Pascal (148), another 156 are using either Ada, Modula, or Scheme (about 50 entries for each of these languages). Taken together, these four languages make up for the large majority. After 28 C-courses and 8 courses each using C++ and Fortran one reaches already counts of 5 and below for languages considered apparently as exotic.

While some of these numbers might have changed over the last three years (certainly with benefits for C++, Oberon, and Smalltalk), the questionnaire as to what determined the choice might be enlightening. The criteria mentioned are:

- This was the only (best) language supported by the book we preferred;
- The language used for the Ph.D. work by the faculty teaching;
- We chose it, because other schools are using it;
- We were limited in the choice, since it is a service course;
- The course is concept driven and this language allows to emphasize concepts:
- It is more a training course than a CS course;
- The language is used in industry and therefore it should be used in CS1;
- Our choice was limited because of lack of good texts using the language we preferred;
- other.

The high emphasis on textbooks certainly induces conservatism and also serves as standardizing factor. The conservative touch can be also be infered from the summary list of the introductory chapter to [Woo 96], where the Woodman concludes that academics have been considering support for ADTs and OOP; availability of textboods, and the ease with which they can progress from Pascal to whatever is used as new choice as key arguments. In our decision process we placed relatively little emphasis on this aspect, but acknowledged that if there were severe deficits concerning texts, we would eventually have to write our own.

Since we all agreed that we want a "concept course", we placed an investigation of concepts first on our list of criteria. However, we also knew the trap of allowing concepts (or the instructors preferred subset of concepts) completely dominate the decision. Therefore, we tried to establish the following list of arguments:

- The language should be adequate to serve as primary language for several courses. Thus, students should have a chance to obtain the amount of proficiency necessary for calling this language not only the first one - which it might not be anyway - but really their "mother-tongue".
- There should be sufficient consensus in the department, such that other instructors will use this language at least as language of reference.
- The language should allow to teach the introductory course in such a way that it provides a real challenge even to those students who know already some programming concepts from prior education. But it must not pose insurmountable hurdles for those who are strict novices.
- The language should support a neat style of programming.
- The language should be suitable for including object-oriented concepts.
- If possible, it should be suitable for the development of larger student projects.
- If possible, it should have industrial relevance.
- The language and/or its environment should be easily accessible for students. Notably those who own their private PC should be able to develop lab assignments at home.
- We should not step back behind the language used up to this point (Modula-2).

Apparently, these arguments are neither operational nor free from contradictions. But they helped us to arrive at a set of languages (or concepts) to be evaluated in detail. Before discussing this, we want to mention some specifics of our curriculum though.

3.2 Klagenfurt-specific Background Information

Since our curriculum is called "Angewandte Informatik" (applied informatics), we feel obliged to (and our students are motivated to) have a degree of application orientation within the curriculum that goes beyond having compulsory business- and law classes. To structure the 1. Studienabschnitt (undergraduate portion on a 4 semester schedule) such that students might legitimately consider themselves as candidates for application programming after ist completion is one way to recognize this.It is clearly structured into course sequences. The software sequence contains SW1/Programming, SW2a&b/Data-Structures & Databases, SW3/Design and Test, SW4/Logical and Functional Programming. A related sequence in "Betriebsinformatik" covers the courses Introduction to Applied Informatics, Analysis and Conception of Information-Systems, Informatics in Business and Industry, and Development of Application Systems. At the end of these sequences, a Software Development lab provides a platform where students can apply their knowledge and skills in a comprehensive project that is to be solved by guided teams of three.

Besides the "mother-tonge", students learn also a database language, LISP and Prolog, as well as some language for developing typical commercial application software (formerly COBOL, now the application development languages of a widely used database management system). Later in the curriculum, students might learn further languages. But these, such as C/C++ for the operating systems course/lab, are not "taught". Students have to acquire them on their own with only moderate guidance by the teachers of the labs.

This context certainly played a role when we investigated, whether object-orientation suggests to replace Modula-2 as "mother-tongue". We felt motivated but not pressed for change, since we were quite satisfied withModula-2's role in a course that started at level-0 and covered after the basics recursion, the module concept, dynamic data structures, and natural binary search trees, as well as file-I/O. From the history of this course, it seems worth to mention, that the module concept was initially taught at the very end (some lab instructors wanted to exclude it from the first semester altogether) and progressively moved forward over the years. This lead to confidence, that students can grasp such concepts without problems as long as they are properly introduced. An argument that might also hold for object-orientation.

3.3 The Decision Process

On these premises, an open working group was established. It should develop a catalogue of criteria to be held against a set of candidate languages.This was not to mechanize the decision process but rather to structure it. The discussions of this task-force were partly face-to-face and partly via e-mail.

Initially, we were quite open about languages as well as operational criteria. In a sort of brainstorming, the following languages, each of which has at least an object-flavour, have been proposed:

- some conceptually clean *"paper-and-pencil-language"* (no further details) to help students avoid (or get rid of) a hacker-type programming style,
- *Smalltalk*, as a strictly object-oriented language,

- *LISP*, as an example of a conceptually clean language, new to almost all students and requiring a style of programming new to them,
- *Prolog*, with similar arguments as for LISP,
- *C++* (or even just *C*), for its industrial relevance,
- *Ada*, as a rich language that would not have the stigma of being "purely educational",
- *Eiffel*, with similar arguments and with the argument of being fully object-oriented,
- *Modula-2*, as reference point and as the conservative choice of postponing the decision,
- *Modula-3*, as its (not compatible) successor for its richness and cleanness,
- *Oberon-2*, as the clean minimal core of an object-oriented language, and
- *Pascal6*, as a typical PC-language that every student might have on its own PC.

In screening this list, we rejected the *"paper-and-pencil-languages"* with the argument, that neither the students nor our industrial environment would tolerate that a curriculum of "Angewandte" (applied !) Informatik starts by initially turning the back to the computer and all the tools it provides. We took this as a conscious "political" decision, well knowing the didactical merits such an approach might have had.

Likewise, we rejected *Smalltalk, LISP*, and *Prolog*. The arguments were again dominated by political considerations. We did not see broad enough a field of industrial usage in our environment (the decision was taken in spring '93). Further, we felt that starting with LISP or Prolog would give an AI-turn to the curriculum we considered inappropriate with respect our founding charter (connections with business administration). Moreover, we had seen the choice of any of these languages to require drastical restructuring of the whole curriculum, a revolution we were only prepared to perform when heavy arguments pressed for it. *C* was considered to be dominated by C++ and therefore also not further considered.

This left *Ada, C++, Eiffel, Modula-2, Modula-3, Oberon-2*, and *Pascal6* in the race to be held against the set of criteria established in the meantime.

This catalogue, which resulted after verbal and electronic discussions, had in its revised (finally agreed upon) form the following categories and subcategories:

- CONCEPTS TO BE TRANSFERRED TO STUDENTS ("vermittelbare Konzepte")
  - type concept (classical)
  - procedures
  - recursion
  - module concept
  - object-/class concept
  - genericity
  - parallelism

  - procedurality
  - non-procedurality

  - software development using existing libraries
  - "dirty features", low level constructs

  - a comfortable environment for software development

- LINGUISTIC ELEGANCE
  - conceptual cleanness
  - syntactic uniformity / simple syntax

- DIDACTICAL FEASIBILITY ("didaktische Umsetzbarkeit")
  - can we demonstrate and use all those language features, that were decisive in the selection process
    * in the introductory course
    * within the first year (introduction and data structures course)
    * within the mandatory program of the 1. Studienabschnitt (first two years)

- AVAILABILITY
  - in general
  - within the student population (inexpensive licenses)
  - on campus on PCs
  - (on campus) under Unix

- EASE OF ACQUISITION ("Erlernbarkeit")
  - for novices
  - for beginners that have already some programming experience, but not necessarily software engineering knowledge

- CHALLENGE
  - for novices
  - for beginners with pre-knowledge

- RELEVANCE
  - within the curriculum (suitability as "mother-tongue")
  - in industry

This catalogue is not free from contradictions. This was on purpose, since the contradictions (e.g. procedurality/non-procedurality) should show in the weighting process and thus allow to better position arguments. (Finally, we got the experience that making the contradictions explicit was sufficient to align opinions). Further, the catalogue helped to bring those, who never taught the introductory course, away from illusionary arguments about elegant features one would not have the time to explain and practice in an introductory course or even in the mandatory part of the first two years (1. Studienabschnitt). There was agreement, though, that nice features are important even when one would not reach them during the first semester. However, with "didactical feasibility" the evaluators were reminded that they should not argue for the unreachable.

"Dirty features" might be another point worth some explanation. It seems odd, to have this as positive criterion. However, the choice was justified on the ground, that a language which does not allow any of them would raise students in a too artificial environment. Thus, they would have motivational problems to understand some software engineering recommendations without having ever felt the problems resulting from their violation.

The category "linguistic elegance" was split into "conceptual cleanness" and "syntactic uniformity", the former refering to the inherent structure of the languages considered, the latter to how the syntax is presented (Testquestion: "If I have forgotten how to express something of which I know that it can be expressed in this language: Do I have to look it up, or can I obtain the solution by simple reasoning").

"Ease of acquisition" and "challenge" were categories provided with the intention to let people clearly voice their preferences. Is our concern rather to have students following the course as easily as possible, thus making it accessible even to beginners, or do we rather strive for challenging even those, who pretend to know already?

An argument that was voiced several times but not included into the catalogue in spite of its general importance was "support of persistency". We lost it, because we felt that anything beyond relatively simple sequential file I/O would be beyond what can and should be taught in the first semester, notably since students have a data base course right thereafter. File-I/O, however, would not have been a distinguishing criterion.

Participants weighed the individual categories according to their preferences and made these weights publicly available. Surprisingly, after the heated debates before, it turned out, that there were no serious divergencies in the weights. Thus, we dispensed of building aggregated weights and directly entered the discussion of the seven remaining languages.

4 The Choice

The relative agreement on the weighted categories allowed us to enter the discussion about the various languages again rather on an argumentative basis than on pseudo-rational numerical preference scales. To present this discussion, which certainly did not progress that linearly, a "knock-out" system seems to come the closest to what actually happened:

C++ had right from the beginning only a minority of supporters and lost its fan-club after the criteria discussion. The pro-arguments of industrial relevance were upheld but got adjusted by the question of whether C++ had really that large a constituency in comparison to C, which was no longer considered at this time. The role of C/C++ within the curriculum was not considered as serious pro-argument. It got balanced by the benefits of showing students, that they have to be capable of learning a new language (almost) on their own. The actual killing argument, however, was - surprisingly - not on the conceptual but on the didactical level. The group, notably the C++ supporters saw severe problems in having students yet unexperienced to adequately debug C(++) programs. It was felt that there are better ways to invest the time students would waste in debugging their C++ assignments.

Pascal(6) slipped off the platform of preferred languages without much debate. During all the discussion, there was not much enthusiasm for it. Going from Modula-2 to Pascal was considered a step back right from the beginning. The argument that many students might have it already installed on their PC was not considered to be sufficiently relevant. The nice environment of Turbo-Pascals was an argument with pros and cons. The pro-side was, that students are spoiled by it and anything less would earn critique; the con-side, however, hit into the same spot by claiming that it kindles a "hack-run-correctOneSingleError-rerun-...-rehack" - style of development which was not only not appreciated but which is going to consume a lot of time, notably with weaker students. The final and elegant argument to eliminate Pascal6 though was that it cannot be considered an object-oriented language in its concepts. The object-model it supports is rather superimposed and depends quite a lot on the discipline of the programmer.

Ada was dropped thereafterwithout much discussion[2]. It was doubted that during early semesters we could buy enough for the effort of switching from Modula-2 to Ada.

Having C++, Pascal 6, and Ada removed, it became somehow clear that we did not want to stick to **Modula-2**. It was dropped in honour for the benefits promised by the remaining candidates, Oberon-2, Modula-3, and Eiffel, all three of which have a conceptually clean, albeit different concept to support objects. The final decision among this triplet was difficult.

4.1 Why not Oberon-2?

One of us had already teaching experience in Modula-3 in an advanced course and could report that students had no problems at all with its differences to Modula-2 (which surely would have hold also for Oberon-2). Further, he had made in-depth comparisons between Modula-3 and Oberon-2 [Bös 92]. These experiences and careful examination of the two languages left an edge for Modula-3. Not least in the line of arguments was that we anticipated Modula-3, by being more explicit about module interfaces, to allow students better understand the concept of interfaces, module interconnection, and programming in the large.

In Oberon-2 no explicit interfaces are provided (in contrast to the "definition modules" of predecessor Modula-2). Exported identifiers are simply marked by some special characters ("*" for normal export and "-" for read-only export). The environment provides tools to extract interfaces (with or without comments) from a module. Surely, this approach is extremely simple to use and to implement in the compiler. It can be also well argumented against the definition modules of Modula-2. It has, however, at least two important drawbacks:

- Students are not forced to design their interfaces first. Instructors may insist on that, nevertheless, students will easily confuse the different levels of abstraction.

- One cannot have a module with different interfaces to different clients. This is, however, the key in solving a well-known and inherent problem of object-oriented systems. *Encapsulation* of objects is highly desirable, many authors consider it as a central feature of object-orientation. Clients, just using an object, should not know anything about its internal data structures. Building a subclass, however, or implementing management functions of an object-oriented system, often require some knowledge of the internals of a class. These two requirements are strictly contradictory. A reasonable solution lies in having modules with multiple "faces".

---

[2]) Some readers might consider this "silent drop" as unfair to Ada and its interesting concepts. But nevertheless, this is what has happened and it can be well explained by the fact that human choice is not a process of binary comparisons but a process of holding complete situations against each other.

Modula-3 supports this by allowing modules with several interfaces. It also allows to split the implementation of a large interface into several pieces (surely a much less important feature than the previous one).

4.2 Eiffel ?! - not really!

The comparison between *Modula-3* and *Eiffel* was similarly very difficult and resulted almost in a tie. However, in spite of the fact that one group in the department had a research commitment with respect to Modula-3, Eiffel had finally an edge for it. It was not grounded in arguments coming from the introductory course, but from later courses, where both, the concept of multiple inheritance and most of all, the notion of explicitly expressing assertions about portions of the program in the code were considered as key arguments. The fact that Eiffel was "a truly object-oriented language" was of course another argument. Hence, we had a "photofinish" with Eiffel declared winner!

With the selection process thus concluded, work started to redesign the introductory course on the basis of Eiffel. The situation seemed favourable, notably since new books on the language appeared at this time. All that it took was to make the course design with all the excitement about using a new, rich, clean, and truly object-oriented language. — And there, I (one of the authors) failed.

It was reasonably clear to me, what the first quarter of twelve course units should contain and it was relatively clear what the whole course sequence should contain. But at this time - not considering the didactical concepts presented in [Fer 92] - I could not see how to present and explain from a constructive perspective the very first object-oriented program expressed in Eiffel to novices, i.e. to students who do not yet know anything about procedures, about types, and about parameter passing. It seemed to me, while I was quite active in having the final decision turned in favour of Eiffel, that mastering this language would require too big a bite of knowledge for those who did not know anything about programming yet.

I went back, checking to how I would teach the course using Smalltalk. But this analogy did not work, because there, one would worry about objects and their methods, but not really about types and interfaces; this discussion can be postponed. I felt this cannot be done with using Eiffel. So I tried Modula-3 and figured, I can more or less teach the course as it has been taught before and still reach the new aims.

To reach object-oriented programming in Modula-3 just needs to put ample emphasis on the notion of types. If one presents types, starting in a sound way with the predefined ones, one can relate already without any pain, that a type is not just the description of static properties of a domain, a particular value, and the variable holding such a value. The difference between simple arithmetic operations on integers and reals as well as the different ranges of simple or extended numerical values suffices to get the concept across. Simple user defined types (subranges, enumerations) as concepts for extending the expressive repertoire are easy to grasp for a young programmer. On subranges even the concept of subtyping can be demonstrated. With the procedure-concept and with modules one comes back to this concept and can explain encapsulation for simple as well as for composite types. The power of encapsulation becomes clear when working with dynamic data structures. Finally, the notion of procedure-types and variables referring to procedures is helpful. When presented, it might be considered a nice gimmick by students. However, having it grasped, they got everything for comprehending objects. All that remains to be explained are a little bit of syntax and the notion of inheritance.

Thus, by means of a feasibility study, *Modula-3* finally made the race. We will now explain, how we are using it and report on our experience.

4.3 Modula-3: Appraisal and Experience

Having thus a decision reached, we had to consider supporting measures, such as
- what can we provide concerning an educational programming environment?
- what might be used as textbook?
- is the course as perceived not too steep for novices who are not only novices to programming but also to the whole of university life?

We solved the issues in the following way:

- *Environment:* L. Böszörmenyi and his students had already earlier performed a port of the Unix-based SRC Modula-3 compiler to PCs running under MS-DOS. This environment was further improved to have the stability needed for broad public usage by beginners. It remained relatively terse though. Since it is strictly public domain software, students can freely copy it to their private PCs. Both, its spartan nature and notably the relatively long compilation times (over 1 minute for an average program) led to complaints. However, we explained them away by pointing to the benefits of sound designs and desk-checks even for small programs.

- *Textbook:* At the time we started, only Nelson's [Nel 91] and Harbison's book [Har 92] were available. In the first course using Modula-3 at our university (an upper level course on parallelism), [Nel 91] was used. But it is apparently unsuitable for beginners. Hence, we initially used just the course-notes and fully developed example programs [Mit 93] with [Harb 92] recommended as additional source for the details[3,4]. Students could work reasonably well with this material, but reported at the end of the semester that they had difficulties with the text. To preempt this problem, one of us started to write a textbook for an introductory course based on Modula-3 [BöW 95]. Preprints of this book helped to fill the gap to some extent, as soon as they were available.

- *Coping with speed:* We knew that the course had an ambitious design — perhaps too ambitious for complete novices. To compensate for this, we have forseen an elective

---

[3]) Some special funding allows students to acquire selected textbooks on reduced rates. We put [Har 92] on this list. About two thirds of students have bought and used it.

[4]) We made also the Modula-3 report [Car 92] available so that students with adequate pre-knowledge could benefit from it. Without knowing details, we assume that this source was rarely consulted.

(SW0) for this clientele. The aim of SW0 was to homogenize the student population to the extent, that the SW1-teacher (introductory course) could go rather fast over the basics of predefined types (focusing on "theoretical" aspects) and over the fundamental control structures. SW0 was/is conducted as a lab run on an intensive schedule during the first two weeks of the semester. Its goal is to bring students to about the level of who learned Pascal in high school. Thus, participants should learn to bring verbally presented problems into a syntactically correct algorithmic form. It is taught in Modula-3, but instructors should not go beyond a "Pascal-subset" of this language and need not necessarily arrive at the concept of procedures. To refer students to this course, a self assessment test was developed.

Based on these supporting measures, the program/schedule of the real introductory course (SW1) is:

1. General introduction to software development, programming, programming languages, definition of formal languages, syntax definition and recursion in the syntax, finally presentation and explanation of a simple program;

2. Arithmetic expressions, assignments, predefined types;

3. Basic control structures and development strategies for algorithms/programs;

4. User defined simple types (enumeration, subrange) and how they are embedded into the type system of the language;

5. Structured types (focus on records and arrays) and their relation to control structures, nesting of structured types;

6. Algorithms in an unstructured data- and control-space: On the example of simple $O(n^2)$ sorting algorithms discussion of loop invariants and of the complexity of algorithms;

7. Structuring the data- and control-space: procedures, scopes, and parameter passing, reformulating the sorting routines of unit 6 by using procedures and functions;

8. Structuring of systems: the module concept, information hiding, revisiting the I/O module;

9. Dynamic data structures (their simulation in arrays, their realization by references), references within the type system, opaque types, data encapsulation on the example of linked lists;

10. Recursion as an algorithmic concept, its formulation and implementation, invariances and recursion in proofs;

11. Comprehensive example using quicksort on various sorting arguments as summary of the concepts presented so far; to pass the sorting criteria as parameter, procedure variables have been introduced;

12. Recursive data structures: lists revisited, natural binary search trees (traversal, insertion, deletion in their recursive and in their iterative form);

13. File I/O;

-----

14. Objects, classes, instances; information hiding and type concept revisited, inheritance and polymorphism.

This list of topics, but the last one is covered within the first semester. For object-orientation though, we "borrowed" so far the first week from the data structures course that follows suit and benefits directly from the discussion of sorting algorithms and algorithmic complexity.

Topics such as exception handling are only covered in the third semester (SW3), parallelism and unsafe programs only in the 2. Studienabschnitt.

4.4 Modula-3 in Later Courses

Modula-3 was used in two advanced courses (parallel systems, networks) before being introduced as introductory language. Students, who had Modula-2 as "mother tongue", needed only a short introduction into the basics of the language. After that we could concentrate on its advanced features resp. the environment, such as threads, exceptions and network objects. The students mastered relatively complex tasks - such as the implementation of a remote object server, providing a set of persistent objects to a number of remote clients. In the operating systems course the concepts for synchronization and communication of processes are demonstrated with the help of examples written in Modula-3. During the exercises, the students must implement some of these concepts in C. An important didactical by-product is that they may compare the expressive power of the two languages.

5 Conclusions

We presented the selection process followed when deciding on a new (object-oriented) language upon which to base the introductory programming course. From our experience, we might give the following recommendations for choosing a "mother-tongue":

- The language for the introductory course is no longer the first to be learned by many students. This will provide arguments for those favouring a concepts-course.
- We obtained positive results with treating the language used in the first course as a "mother-tongue". This however requires to consider the full context of the curriculum.
- To focus the arguments and highlight conflicting didactical goals, it helps to develop a relatively comprehensive set of criteria and to put weights to the individual subcategories. This will not mechanize the decision process but structure the discussion and help to avoid inconsistent argumentation or the dominance of someones favourite fad.

- It seems fair to students to acquire teaching experience in the programming language intended for the introductory course at advanced levels first.
- After having decided on "the best" language, didactical considerations might lead to reconsider the choice. If one considers pure novices, the language has to be teachable/accessible in small conceptual chunks.

Modula-3 has proved to be a proper choice for us as an introductory language:

- The basic concepts of structured programming can be taught as easy, as they were taught in Pascal or Modula-2.
- The advanced type system and the notion of interfaces allow us to prepare object-orientation and considerations for programming in the large in a sound way.
- Some advanced features of the language, such as exceptions and threads can be easily used in later courses.
- Its lingusitic elegance serves as a reference for the students opinion on other languages.
- The rich library of the SRC-implementation (available in source code) serves as a rich reference for interested advanced students.
- Last but not least, a personal measure: How many times do I have to apologize for the idiosyncrasies of the language. With Modula-3 rarely.

It might be noted that these recommendations are in no way "scientifically proven". They reflect the outgrow of our case-based experience after a process conducted in due dilligence having as broad a scope as possible in mind.

References

[Beid 93]   Beidler J.: "CS1 Languages Used — 9th ed"; electronic message in News Group <comp.edu> or by <beidler@cs.uofs.edu>.

[Bös 92]   Böszörmenyi L.: "A Comparison of Modula-3 and Oberon-2"; in: Mittermeir R. (ed.): "Shifting Paradigms in Software Engineering", Springer-Verlag, Wien, 1992, pp. 126 - 137.

[BöW 95]   Böszörmenyi L., Weich C.: "Programmieren mit Modula-3 - Eine Einführung in stilvolle Programmierung"; Springer Verlag, Berlin, 1995.

[Car 92]   Cardelli L. et al.: "Modula-3 Language Definition"; acm SigPlan Notices, Vol. 27/8, Aug 1992, pp. 15 - 42.

[Fer 92]   Ferchichi A.: "Teaching Programming via Specification, Execution and Modification of Reusable Components: An Integrated Approach"; in: Mittermeir R. (ed.): "Shifting Paradigms in Software Engineering", Springer-Verlag, Wien, 1992, pp. 238 - 249.

[Har 92]   Harbison S.P.: "Modula-3"; Prentice Hall, Englewood Cliffs, N.J. 1992.

[Mit 93]   Mittermeir R.: "Software-Technologie I: Algorithmen und Programmieren"; Vorlesungsunterlagen, Inst. f. Informatik, Univ. Klagenfurt, WS 1993.

[Nel 91]   Nelson G. (ed.): "Systems Programming with Modula-3"; Prentice Hall, Englewood Cliffs, N.J., 1991.

[She 79]   Sheppard S.B., Curtis B., Milliman P., Love T.: "Modern Coding Practices and Programmer Performance"; IEEE Computer, Vol. 12/12, Dec. 1979, pp. 41 - 49.

[Woo 96]   Woodman M. (ed.): "Programming Language Choice - Practice and Experience"; International Thomson Computer Press, 1996.

Generative Programming (GP) with C++

Ulrich W. Eisenecker

Fachhochschule Heidelberg, Fachbereich Informatik,
Bonhoefferstraße 1, D-69123 Heidelberg, Germany
eiseneck@pico.fh-heidelberg.de

Abstract: This paper gives a brief summary of generative programming (GP) and its main principles. To investigate GP and for implementing generators usually new languages are developed and deployed in research. But it seems not to be imperative to base work on new languages. Therefore the qualification of the multiparadigm language C++ will be examined. The effectiveness of C++ for GP as well as basic idioms and techniques are explored in more detail. This includes statically and dynamically configured systems, migrating from generic to generative programming, compositional use of templates, delaying code injection in statically configured systems, controlling virtualization of functions, interface extension and adding properties by inheriting from template parameters, and expressing constraints for template parameters of related classes.

Keywords: generative programming, object-orientation, reusability, C++, templates

1   Introduction

1.1   What is Generative Programming?

Generative programming (GP) is about designing and implementing software modules which can be combined to generate specialized and highly optimized systems fulfilling specific requirements. This resembles the aims of generic programming. In the remainder of this section I describe how generative programming differs sufficiently from other techniques to warrant coining a new term.

Genericity was introduced in languages like Ada many years ago. The main principle was to achieve a higher level of abstraction combined with improved reusability by writing routines which can be instantiated for different types. The work of Musser et al., especially the C++ Standard Template Library (STL) (e.g. [Mus94] and [Mus96]) is insofar remarkable, as they present generic algorithms which can be orthogonally combined with generic container representations. This is an important step but not a radical change in the point of view. Therefore this technique represents the leading edge of generic programming.

Much more can be done. Besides types, algorithms, and interfaces, software systems have general properties and behavior like persistence, error detection and treatment, running in parallel or not, and so on. And all these properties and behavior are necessary in many combinations to meet different sets of requirements. Additionally sometimes self-adaptiveness of systems even in conjunction with the ability to combine new components may be required. Compared to all these possible extensions the

STL as a result of the efforts of Musser et al. seems to be rather modest: even parameterization of error handling or persistence are missing.

While generic programming defines families of functions and types, generative programming describes parameterizable software modules, a space of possible combinations, and design rules for exceptional and forbidden instantiations as pointed out in [Eis96c]. In the context of transformation systems Batory defines a "generative generator as specifications written in common languages augmented by domain-specific extensions. Such specifications are components which transform abstract programs into (more) concrete programs" ([Bat96b]). Therefore generic and generative programming as philosphies of software programming vs. construction are different, but generative programming can be viewed as a superset and an extension of generic programming.

From this point of view several related approaches can be grouped as GP. A broad range of topics is covered by many contributions of [Sit96].

- For instance, GenVoca, is "a domain-independent model for defining scalable families of hierarchical systems from components" ([Bat92], [Bat96a], [Bat96b]). The two basic concepts of GenVoca are "components" and "realms". Components are formed from related and cooperating classes which act as a unit. A component has an interface and an implementation. A set of components with the same interface are grouped by a realm, which defines a basic abstraction, and an interface for a specific domain. Realms as well as components can be extended by inheritance. A component is parameterized by parameters of its realm, whereby these parameters are componentes of other realms. GenVoca is a holistic approach which covers as well the main concepts of transformative systems and object-oriented programming.
- Even transformative systems, like "intentional programming" (IP) ([Sim95], [Sim96]) refer to GP. The main idea of IP is to focus primarily on coding the pure "intentions" which are represented as nodes in a "source tree". Then programs in specific languages are generated from these nodes and optimized for various criteria by so called "enzymes". By selecting the appropriate enzymes specialized systems can be generated for any purpose. Other transformative technologies are applied for computer aided refactoring and rewriting of code as described in [Czar96b].
- Aspect-oriented programming ([Kic96], [Czar96a]) is another emerging approach to improve adaptability and reusability of software, which fits in the domain of generative programming. The main idea is to provide software modules with a meta-interface thus enabling modifications in the implementation of the module to perform necessary adaptations and improvements to new contexts.

All these approaches are labelled with a new name yet they share a great deal. Their commonality is that highly specific software systems are generated by combinig abstract specifications. Therefore in accordance with the terminology used in [Bat96b] the term "generative programming" seems to be appropriate for clustering these new approaches together.

1.2   Why GP?

There are four major issues to investigate GP:

- Increasing efficiency regarding execution speed and consumption of resources,
- increasing reusability,
- improving control of complexitiy,
- and managing a manifold of variants.

The goals and advantages of GP can be explained by contrasting them to object-oriented programming (OOP) which is currently a very popular and successful software development paradigm.

In OOP, real world objects as well as notions are modelled from a specific aspect. The more general these models are, the greater is the overhead of code in the final system which will be never executed or which slows execution by sending redundant messages between objects. System development, maintenance, and users have to pay a price for object properties and behavior which are never used but are incorporated in a system. Examples are persistence, instance counting, run-time checks for errors, specific interfaces, and so on.

In contrast, GP describes abstract models from which instantiations for specific requirements are generated. Only for those objects of the desired systems which should be persistent, is the necessary mechanism included, and the same applies for parts of the system which should be bounds-checked. So a maxim of GP is *that one should not pay for something which is not used.* This is also known as "zero-overhead rule" ([Str94], p. 120).

Focusing on the pristine semantics, the "programmer's intent", while preserving the possibility of any extensions is also a major principle of IP ([Sim95]). Even more important is that not only one mechanism or one treatment for realizing properties like persistence or bounds-checking can be applied, but that a module can be instantiated with any mechanism for implementing the desired properties in a consistent way. Furthermore, any arbitrary combination of particular properties must be possible for instantiating modules, yet exceptions can be formulated. Incompatibility and redundancy of class libraries and frameworks can thus be avoided. The developer no longer has to struggle with different implementations of object identifiers, persistency, 1:m associations, and so on.

OOP provides an improved means for modelling to control complexity. GP enhances the modelling power of OOP by generating systems, i.e. instantiating modules, that contain only required parts and interactions. This is similar to the difference between a very powerful model containing a description of all variants of car vs. a relatively simple construction plan which describes how cars can be configured by combining parts and which restrictions apply. This allows the production of a large variety of cars where each variant contains only specific configurations of components.

1.3   Statically vs. Dynamically Configured Systems

GP is an approach to generate specifically configured systems. The following types of system configurations can be roughly distinguished:

- Static systems which are configured completely at compile-time and which do not change during run-time, e. g. choosing a hash-table for holding matrix coefficients during compile-time,
- dynamic systems which are configured completely at compile-time and which can be combined with existing systems via polymorphism or which can be reconfigured during run-time in a predefined way, e. g. switching from vector to hash-table representation of matrix coefficients during run-time (design pattern *bridge*, [Gam95]), and
- dynamic systems which have a basic configuration at compile-time and the ability to generate new configurations during run-time and to replace existing configurations by them. Responsibility for controlling and generating configurations is at least partially transferred to those systems, e. g. generate persistent representations of matrix coefficients during run-time and subsequently employing them.

This paper deals only with the first two types of systems. The third type of system requires reflexive systems as a basis, i. e. systems that incorporate a mutable model of themselves like Smalltalk as well as a compiler or an interpreter, and many advanced techniques of artificial intelligence which are beyond the scope of this paper.

1.4   Why OOP as the Basis?

Theoretically, all programming language elements can be generated: functions, procedures, types, and so on. Why focus on classes and objects?

Because a class ties together an object's state and meaningful operations. If systems are generated in an object-oriented language with a type system, many implicit and explicit assertions and restrictions expressed within types can be checked and verified by the compiler. On the other hand, the object-oriented paradigm offers a great potential for modelling which allows easier design and understanding of generators. Additionally, it is more convenient if the same paradigm applies to generators and their products consistently.

2   Generative Techniques and Concepts in C++

2.1   Types and Polymorphism in C++

In Smalltalk a message can be sent to any object. If a corresponding method is implemented in the object's class or one of its antescendants, it will be executed. Therefore, the same message can be understood by objects of totally different classes, even if the method is not defined in a common superclass. In [Gol95] this sort of polymorphism is called "unbounded polymorphism". It could be also referred to as "signature-bound polymorphism" since it relies only on the evaluation of the method signature.

The situation is very different in C++. This language has two forms of polymorphism ([Eis95c]).

- This first is widely known. A virtual function of a base class can be overridden in derived classes. Pointers or references to a base class may contain instances of the base class as well as of derived classes. If a function is called for a pointer or a reference, the type of the actual object determines which function is executed. This form of polymorphism is called "bounded polymorphism" by [Gol95]. It seems appropriate to call it also "inheritance-bound polymorphism", to express that it relies on inheritance and virtual functions.
- Interestingly, the second form of polymorphism in C++ is very close to that of Smalltalk. Templates serve as the basis for this variant of "signature-bound polymorphism". If a variable a is of type T and a.hello() is compiled, it is only important that hello() is defined for T.

The main difference between the two forms of polymorphism in C++ is that inheritance-bound polymorphism will work at compile-time as well as run-time with the restrictions imposed by inheritance and virtual functions while signature-bound polymorphism will work at compile-time only but with no restrictions on inheritance and virtual functions.

The system developer has to choose between templates and virtual functions. If the foreseeable and preprogrammed reconfiguration of a system during run-time is essential, inheritance-bound polymorphism has to be used. If the configuration of a system is fixed at compile-time, templates offer interesting possibilities for modelling and optimization. Different requirements apply if a system should be able to generate new configurations by itself.

In the following, this potential of templates will be explored for GP.

2.2 Inhibiting and Specializing Instantiations

The simple template function:

```
template <class T>
void swap(T& a, T& b)
{   const T c = a;
    a = b;
    b = c;
}
```

defines a family of functions. It works well for all types defining the assignment operator in a semantically correct way. But what if char* is provided as template parameter? Perhaps it is not a good idea to swap these two pointers. So the designer of swap could decide to forbid the instantiation of this function for char*. A simple solution for doing this is:

```
void swap (char*, char*);
// This function may not be instantiated!
```

Because of the declaration only the linker complains about the missing definition if something like this is compiled:

```
char* a = "Jill"; char* b = "Jack";
swap(a,b);
```

Another example is a vector class which already implements an efficient swap operation. Instantiating the template function as shown above would not call the swap function of the vector. Moreover, by the temporary variable c the construction of a possibly very large vector would be forced. To avoid this, a specialization can be provided like:

```
void swap(Vector& a, Vector& b)
{   a.swap(b);
}
```

This style marks an important transition. It shows how first a family is defined which is followed by rules for using special implementations or prohibiting specific instantiations. What has been demonstrated for function templates works principially similar for class templates.

2.3   Compositional Use of Templates

The coefficients of a matrix can have different types and may be stored differently. Coefficients can be of type bool, int, double, complex, etc. and they can be stored in a two dimensional fixed-sized array, a dynamic array, or in a linked list or a hash table for sparse matrices. Additional optimiziations for representing the coefficients apply for triangular, symmetric, and diagonal matrices.

Trying to foresee all these possibilities using inheritance-bound polymorphism normally results in a large and complex class hierarchy ([Eis96a]), where special attention has to be paid to implementing the "orthodox canonical form" ([Cop92]) and controlling the generation of instances by design patterns like "factory" or "factory method" ([Gam95]). For example: What representation should coefficients of a matrix have that results from multiplying matrices using dynamic array and hash table representations?

To change the type of coefficients at run-time is very uncommon. Code for the static configuration of a matrix with respect to the type of coefficients and their representation could look like this (the example has been taken with small modifications from [Eis96a] and shows only an excerpt of the implementation):

```
template <class Type>
class FixedArray10x10
{   public:
        typedef Type type;
        FixedArray10x10(const unsigned& ro,const unsigned& co);
        const unsigned& rows() const
        {   return r;
        }
        const unsigned& columns() const
        {   return c;
        }
        const type& coefficient(const unsigned& i,const unsigned& j) const;
        type& coefficient(const unsigned& i,const unsigned& j);
    private:
        unsigned r,c;
```

```
        type coeff[10][10];
};

template <class Rep>
class Matrix
{   public:
        Matrix(const unsigned& ro,const unsigned& co):coeff(ro,co)
        {};
        const Rep::type& coefficient(const unsigned& i,const unsigned& j) const
        {   return coeff.coefficient(i,j);
        }
        Rep::type& coefficient(const unsigned& i,const unsigned& j)
        {   return coeff.coefficient(i,j);
        }
        const unsigned& rows() const
        {   return coeff.rows();
        }
        const unsigned& columns() const
        {   return coeff.columns();
        }
        Matrix<Rep> operator*(const Matrix<Rep>& m) const;
    private:
        Rep coeff;
};
```

Now matrices can be instantiated like this:

```
Matrix<FixedArray10x10<double> > m(3,2),n(2,2);
// assigning coefficients ...
Matrix<FixedArray10x10<double> > o(3,2) = m * n;
```

Note that the type, here double, for which the representation, here FixedArray10x10, is instantiated is passed to Matrix by the construct typedef Type type; in Fixed-Array10x10. This and the other public functions of FixedArray10x10 define the interface on which an instantiation of Matrix relies. Any representation for coefficients conforming to this interface can be used to instantiate Matrix. On the other hand FixedArray10x10 determines which interface Types must provide, so that the instantiation of FixedArray10x10 will work.

The fine thing about the compositional use of templates is that every combination of representations with types can be used for matrices, as long as the interface requirements are fulfilled, while the complexity of inheritance and virtual functions is completely avoided. The orthogonal design of components is also a major principle of the C++ Standard Template Library (STL) ([Ans95], [Bre96], [Ste94]).

Another example for the compositional use of templates is the "body-behavior idiom" which is fully described in the context of error detection and handling in [Eis95a] and [Eis95b]. By choosing different parameters for Vector one controls which errors are checked for and how the system reacts if an error is detected. In the following example Vector is the body class and the behavior classes are Checking and No-Checking.

```
class Checking
{   public:
        static void checkIndex(const unsigned& size,const unsigned& index)
        {   if (index >= size)
            throw("illegal index");
        }
        // other checks ...
};

class NoChecking
{   public:
        static void checkIndex(const unsigned& size,const unsigned& index)
        {   // do nothing
        }
        // other empty checks ...
};

template <class Behavior>
class Vector
{   public:
        // ...
        unsigned& coefficient(const unsigned& index)
        {   Behavior::checkIndex(size,index);
            // ...
        }
        // ...
};

// the following line causes an exception
Vector<Checking>(5).coefficient(6)=99;
// the error in the next line is not detected
Vector<NoChecking>(5).coefficient(6)=99;
```

2.4   The Static Equivalent to Pure Virtual Functions

A virtual function, especially a pure virtual function, provides the essential basis for constructing frameworks. The following fragment is a primitive "classical program" framework:

```
class Program
{   public:
        virtual void initialize() = 0;
        virtual void main() = 0;
        virtual void terminate() = 0;
        void run()
        {   initialize();
            main();
            terminate();
        }
};
```

A derived class must provide implementations for the pure virtual functions if they are to be instantiated and executed. The question is, what is analogous to a pure virtual function in a statically configured system? How can a template class be parameterized so that the parameter injects the necessary implementations?

The solution is to make use of a reverted inheritance order: The template class inherits from its template parameter which provides the necessary implementations. The implementations can be changed by substituting different template parameters. Here is an example:

```
template <class Base>
class Program: public Base
{   public:
        void run()
        {   initialize();
            main();
            terminate();
        }
};

class Demo
{   public:
        void initialize()
        {   cout << "initialize" << endl;
        }
        void main()
        {   cout << "main" << endl;
        }
        void terminate()
        {   cout << "terminate" << endl;
        }
}

Program<Demo>().run();
```

In a statically configured "framework" a function becomes "pure virtual" by just using it. Data and types can also be injected as a direct part of the class as well as functions.

Of course it is nonsense to say that "a Program *inherits* from Demo" or "a Program *is a* Demo" in this example, i. e. there is no *semantic* of inheritance. But it is correct to say that the *syntax* of inheritance is used to delay static injection of code.

2.5   Controlling Virtualization of Functions

Sometimes it may be important not to decide if a template class should behave polymorphic or not. This can be done easily also by the technique of inheriting from the template parameter.

If the class Vector in the following example uses its default parameter, all binding is done statically, i. e. during compile-time. If it is parameterized with Dynamic, all functions become virtual and a virtual destructor is added:

```
class Static
{};

class Dynamic
{   public:
        virtual ~Dynamic()
        {};
        virtual double& coefficient(const unsigned& i) = 0;
        // ...
};

template <class Binding = Static>
class Vector: public Binding
{   public:
        Vector(const unsigned& size);
        double& coefficient(const unsigned& i);
        // ...
};

Vector<> v1(5);              // non-polymorphic vector
Vector<Dynamic> v2(5);       // polymorphic vector
```

This technique can be applied if statically configured systems or predefined dynamically configured systems are to be generated from the same source.

2.6   Interface and Properties Extensions

The same technique can be used for adding properties like instance counting and extending the interface of a class, e. g. to dump the objects state to a file or to display its class name. It is a challenge if one tries to provide these properties and interfaces polymorphic and to make them arbitrarily combinable.

If a property is added which does not change the class interface it is sufficient if the template-class inherits directly from the appropriate parameter. Such property classes can by combined via multiple inheritance with no restrictions. Then this multi-property class is used as template parameter.

If the interface of a class is extended, a special class is needed which implements the necessary adaptation for a specific class. For instance an abstract class Displayable defining virtual void display() = 0 must be specialized for parameterizing a template class Vector to display its coefficients. The specializing adapter class must use a type cast to change itself to the type of the derived class.

```
class Displayable
{   public:
        virtual void display() const = 0;
};

template <class Property>
class Vector: public Property
{   public:
        Vector(const unsigned& s);
```

```
        double& coefficient(const unsigned& i);
        const unsigned& size() const;
        // ...
};


class DisplayableVector: public Displayable
{   public:
        void display() const
        {   const Vector<DisplayableVector>& self =
            static_cast<const Vector<DisplayableVector>&>(*this);
            cout << "( ";
            for (unsigned i=0;i<self.size();i++)
            cout << coefficient(i) << " ";
            cout << ")" << endl;
        }
};

Vector<DisplayableVector>(5).display();
```

It becomes very complicated if classes extending the interface of the derived class are to be combined in any way with themselves or with property classes. The reason is that the isolated adapter class no longer knows for which combination of classes the derived class is instantiated.

As a solution "type-donator" classes are introduced. They define a standard name for the specialization needed for typecasting. It would be more safe and less efficient to replace static_cast in the next example by dynamic_cast. But it is assumed that only a correct type specialization is given by the type-donator class. Of course it would be possible to make the kind of cast generative too. To preserve the understanding of the code it is refrained from doing so.

```
template <class Property>
class Vector: public Property
// as in the previous example ...


class Displayable
// as in the previous example ...


class Debuggable
{   public:
        virtual void debug() = 0;
        // ...
};


template <class TypeDonator>
class DisplayableVector: public Displayable
{   public:
```

```
      void display() const
      {   const Vector<TypeDonator::Type>& self =
          static_cast<const Vector<TypeDonator::Type>&>(*this);
          // ...
      }
};

template <class TypeDonator>
class DebuggableVector: public Debuggable
{   public:
      void debug()
      {   Vector<TypeDonator::Type>& self =
          static_cast<Vector<TypeDonator::Type>&>(*this);
          // ...
      }
};

template <class TypeDonator>
AllPropertiesVector:    public DisplayableVector<TypeDonator>,
                        public DebuggableVector<TypeDonator>

{};

class AllPropertiesVectorType
{   public:
      typedef Vector<AllPropertiesVector<AllPropertiesVectorType> > Type;
};

void display(const Displayable& d)
{   d.display();
}

void debug(Debuggable& d)
{   d.debug();
}

Vector<AllPropertiesVector<AllPropertiesVectorType> > v(5);
display(v);   // it works
debug(v);     // it works too
```

The technique of type-donators is discussed in more detail in [Eis96d].

2.7   Constraining Related Classes

When generating classes and frameworks (a set of related and cooperating classes) it may be important to ensure, that two classes are parameterized with the same argument. This can be easily done by nesting these classes in an enclosing template-class.

In the following example the instantiation of Vector and Matrix are forced to be of the same type.

```
template <class T>
class Domain
{   public:
        typedef T ScalarType
        class Vector
        {   public:
            T scalarProduct(const Vector& v);
            Matrix matrixProduct(const Vector& v);
            // ...
        };
        class Matrix
        // ...
};

typedef Double Domain<double>;
Double::Vector v(5);
// initializing coefficients of v ...
Double::ScalarType r = v.scalarProduct(v);
Double::Matrix m = v.matrixProduct(v);
```

Note that it is always possible to extend the template-class Domain as well as the classes defined inside Domain by inheritance as demonstrated in [Eis96d]. This provides much of the modelling power of realms and domains described in [Bat96a] and [Bat96b].

3   Summary and Outlook

After a short outline of the principles and goals of generative programming (GP), the basic elements for GP with C++ were introduced. Much more could be said about the importance of inlining, the usage of const-references, and different forms of attribute access for GP, which is partially discussed in [Eis96b]. But it is much more important to investigate how the basic primitives can be combined to powerful generative expressions and what patterns of GP will result. Perhaps some design patterns can be reused, possibly new patterns will emerge. Another important issue is to form a common understanding of GP and a language convention as well as neccesary extensions and adaptations to analysis and design methods. These efforts would be far beyond the intention of this paper. I sincerily hope that the presented techniques will be an incentive to investigate the potentiality of GP - even with "old" languages like C++.

4   Acknowledgements

I am indebted to Frances Paulisch (Siemens ZFE and OBJEKTspektrum) and Jim Coplien (Bell Laboratories) for proof-reading and commenting on the paper.

5   References

[Ans95]   ANSI X3J16, Working Paper for Draft Proposed International Standard for Information Systems - Programming Language C++, X3J16/95-0185, WG 21/N0785, 26. September 1995, *ftp://research.att.com/dist/c++std/WP*

[Bat92]   D. Batory and S. O'Malley, The Design and Implementation of Hierarchical Software Systems With Reusable Components, in: ACM Transactions on Software Engineering and Methodology, Vol 1(4), October 1992

[Bat96a]   D. Batory, Subjectivity and GenVoca Generatos, in: [Sit96], pp. 166-175

[Bat96b]   D. Batory, Software System Generators, Architectures, and Reuse. Tutorial Notes for the International Conference on Software Reuse '96 (Orlando), 1996

[Bre96]   U. Breymann, Die C++ Standard Template Library, Addison-Wesley, 1996

[Cop92]   J. Coplien, Advanced C++ Programming Styles and Idioms, Addison-Wesley, 1992

[Czar96a] K. Czarnecki, "Separation of Concerns" - objektorientierte Frameworks und das generative Paradigma, in: OBJEKTspektrum, 6/96, pp. 35-40

[Czar96b] K. Czarnecki, Transformationen in Smalltalk, in: OBJEKTspektrum, 6/96, pp. 86-95

[Eis95a]   U. Eisenecker, Exceptions in Libraries. In: Pre-Austin Mailing, Document Number X3J16/95-0006 (WG21/N0606)

[Eis95b]   U. Eisenecker, Recht auf Fehler, Strategien zur Fehlerbehandlung in C++-Klassenbibliotheken, in: iX, 6/1995, pp. 184-189

[Eis95c]   U. Eisenecker, Typisierung und Polymorphie in C++, in: OBJEKTspektrum, 5/1995, pp. 81-83

[Eis96a]   U. Eisenecker, Templates *statt* Vererbung, in: OBJEKTspektrum, 4/1996, pp. 92-95

[Eis96b]   U. Eisenecker, Attribute im Zugriff, in: OBJEKTspektrum, 5/1996, pp. 98-101

[Eis96c]   U. Eisenecker, "Das generative Paradigma" oder "Was kommt nach der Objektorientierung?", in: OBJEKTspektrum, 6/96, pp. 30-34

[Eis96d]   U. Eisenecker, Generatives Programmieren mit C++, in: OBJEKTspektrum, 6/1996, pp. 79-84

[Gam95]   E. Gamma, R. Helm, R. Johnson, and J. Vlissides, Design Patterns, Elements of Reusable Object-Oriented Software, Addison-Wesley, 1995

[Gol95]   A. Goldberg and K. Rubin, Succeeding with Objects, Addison-Wesley, 1995

[Kic96]   G. Kiczales, J. Irwin, J. Lamping, J.-M. Lointier, C. V. Lopes, Ch. Maeda, and A. Mendhekar, Aspect-Oriented Programming, A Position Paper From the Xerox PARC Aspect-Oriented Programming Project, position paper for the ECOOP'96 Workshop on Adaptability in Object-Oriented Software Development, 1996, http://www.parc.xerox.com/spl/projects/aop/

[Mus94]   D. R. Musser and A. A. Stepanov, Algorithm-Oriented Generic Libraries, in: Software Practice and Experience, Vol 24(7), 1994

[Mus96] D. R. Musser and A. Saini, STL Tutorial and Reference Guide. C++ Programming with the Standard Template Library, Addison-Wesley, 1996

[Sim95] Ch. Simonyi, The Death of Computer Languages, The Birth of Intentional Programming, Technical Report MSR-TR-95-52, Microsoft Research, 1995

[Sim96] Ch. Simonyi, Intentional Programming - Innovation in the Legacy Age, Presented at IFIP WG 2.1 meeting, June 4, 1996 (for more information about IP see *http://www.research.microsoft.com/research/ip/*)

[Sit96] M. Sitaraman (Ed.), Fourth International Conference on Software Reuse, April 23-26, 1996, Orlando Florida, IEEE Computer Society Press, 1996

[Ste94] A. Stepanov and M. Lee, The Standard Template Library, Hewlett-Packard Laboratories, California, 1994, *ftp://butler.hpl.hp.com/stl/*

[Str94] B. Stroustrup, The Design and Evolution of C++, Addison-Wesley, 1994

Seamless Integration of Online Services in the Oberon Document System

Emil Zeller

Institut für Computersysteme, ETH Zürich,
CH-8092 Zürich, Switzerland

Abstract. This paper presents our ideas of client/server integration by means of a highly integrating *document-oriented interface* (DOI) of unlimited functionality. By document-oriented interface we think of a unified stateless presentation of input data, output data and user-interface in the form of *self-contained documents*. The terms *unlimited functionality* and *integrating* address the possibility of integrating arbitrary local and remote services into the document-oriented interface of Oberon System 3.

1   Introduction

An important trend in modern operating systems research is towards global environments like distributed systems and client/server architectures. Because of the increasing importance of remote systems (cable and wireless), client/server environments will progressivley replace traditional operating systems operating on a single isolated workstation.

A very important issue in a client/server system is *integration*. It is unreasonable to require users of a client system to learn a different interface and access mechanism for every single service that they want to use. Thus services should be presented uniformly and called implicitly. Service-specific technical details should be handled by the system behind the scenes. Another very important issue is *portability* of executable code as well as of other resources.

Integration

We are interested in a general concept of documents because it provides a solid basis for a completely unified and integrating programming environment and user interface, especially in connection with inter-document links. For example, the same opening command and the same look-and-feel apply to local documents as well as to remote ones such as World Wide Web documents, electronic dictionaries or Teletext. Moreover, we want to smoothly switch between different kinds of documents (and thus between different applications) simply by clicking at links.

Portability

An interesting set of problems is raised by the desire to distribute documents in a consistent form. A consistent distribution is made by attaching all the required resources (auxiliary data files, libraries, executable code, ...) to a document so that the document is truly *self-contained*. If we want self-contained documents to be usable on all Oberon platforms, we have to keep in mind the following problems:

- In addition to data resources, we have to include the platform independent implementations of components. By components we mean objects with build in functionality.
- Portable documents must be as compact as possible.
- Installing resources should be done only once, and not each time the document is used.
- We have to find a way to identify all resources required by a document.
- If we include executable code, we must find ways to protect the system against viruses and other unwanted software.
- We must find ways to avoid name and version conflicts.

2 Documents in Oberon System 3

In the Gadgets system (the GUI of Oberon System 3) [6, 7], application user interfaces and application documents are unified with the concept of *documents*. As a consequence of this idea the distinction between applications and documents that are used with applications vanishes.

```
TYPE
  Document = POINTER TO DocumentDesc;
  DocumentDesc = RECORD (Gadgets.FrameDesc)
    name: ARRAY 128 OF CHAR;
    Load, Store: PROCEDURE (D: Document)
  END;
```

A document consists of a run-time part with its visual representation, and a data part with contents. The run-time part of a document is called a document gadget, a visual gadget that displays the document contents. The data part of a document is an entity identified by a document name (e.g. a file). Loading a document requires the entity identified by the document name to be read and linked to the document gadget. Storing a document writes the contents back to the entity identified by the document name. The exact interpretation of load and store is a matter of the document class, and often involves more than just reading or writing data from and to a file. We can think of the document names as a set of names intersecting with the set of filenames, but also intersecting with other name sets (e.g. names on a network).

Before we can load a document, we need an uninitialized document object of the correct class. Hence on opening a document, we need a mapping of the document name to the document class. Ideally we want a loose connection between the document name and the document class, so that users are able to name their documents almost in any way they want. For all file-based documents Oberon uses a standard document file format (in EBNF):

```
Document = Header [ MetaData ] { Contents } .
Header = Tag Generator X Y W H .
Generator = ModuleName "." ProcedureName .
```

Loading a document from a file is implemented by reading the document generator from the header and creating a new instance of this document class by calling the generator using the module loader. The filename is then copied to the name field of the document instance, and the Load method is invoked to load the document contents. The fields X, Y, W and H in the header are used as hints for placing the document gadget on the desktop.

For files that are not Oberon documents a table of filename extensions and associated document classes is maintained by the document system. When detecting an invalid document header in a document file, this table is consulted with the filename extension to generate a document gadget of the associated class. If needed, storing the document again will provide the document with a valid document header.

Figure 1 shows a typical Oberon desktop containing different local documents: a system log, a hypertext system tool, a cd player panel, a hypertext tutorial, the gadgets toolkit, the columbus object inspector and a new panel under construction.

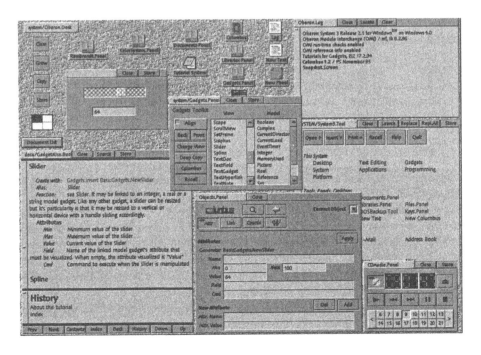

Fig. 1. In this snapshot, a desktop is presented showing some examples of local Oberon documents.

3   Internet Documents

Documents need not necessarily be restricted to (local) files. With today's high level of workstation connectivity we can imagine accessing documents that are located on remote machines or are published on the Internet.

3.1   Uniform Resource Locators

Fortunately, the problem of associating document classes with document names is already addressed by the *URL* (Uniform Resource Locator) [12] syntax, the way in which services and documents on the Internet are identified. In general, URLs are written as follows (in EBNF):

```
URL = SchemeName ":" SchemeSpecific .
SchemeName = "ftp" | "gopher" | "http" | \ldots .
```

A URL contains the name of the scheme being used (SchemeName) followed by a colon and a string (SchemeSpecific) whose interpretation depends on the scheme. Internet documents thus can be transparently included in our document framework by maintaining an additional table associating URL scheme names with document classes. Mappings in this second table have precedence over those in the filename extension table.

Using this model, end-users have a unified model of local and remote documents. The same commands are used to open, store, print and manipulate any of these documents (see table 1). One problem which arises with this approach is that only the

OpenDoc	Open a document. Desktops.OpenDoc http://www.ethz.ch/ will open the ETH homepage.
CloseDoc	Close the current document.
StoreDoc	Store the current document under its given name in a local file.
PrintDoc	Print the marked document.
ReplaceDoc	Same as OpenDoc, but the current document is exchanged in place with the new document. This is the basis for hypertext like browsing in the "document space".
CopyDoc	Open a copy of the current document.

Table 1. document commands

scheme being used to access the document is known in advance, but not the document class of the actual contents (html text, gif image, oberon document, ...) transferd. If we want to access a HTML (Hypertext Markup Language) page using the HTTP (Hypertext Transfer Protocol) protocol, the document manager will generate an instance of the class associated to the HTTP scheme. After this document has fetched the MIME-header (Multipurpose Internet Mail Extensions) for the requested URL across the network, its type has to be transformed into the associated HTML-browser document type. This transformation is problematic, since this feature is not supported by statically checked programming languages like Oberon. Nevertheless the exchange of a document class is possible since Oberon uses procedue variables to implement message dispatcher, rather than using class bound methods. This exchange is associated with a drawback: we must not make type extensions of Documents.Document. The example below shows how an implementation of a document class for a stateless protocol like HTTP might look like.

```
PROCEDURE LoadDoc*(D: Documents.Document);
  VAR
    host: ARRAY MaxHostStrLen OF CHAR;
    request: ARRAY MaxRequestStrLen OF CHAR;
    C: Net.Connection; D2: Documents.Document;
    key: LONGINT;
    port, res: INTEGER;
BEGIN
  Split(D.name, host, port, request, key);
  IF key # HyperDocs.UndefKey THEN
    Net.OpenConnection(C, Net.anyport, host, port, res);
    IF res = Net.done THEN
      SendRequest(C, request);
      D2 := ReceiveResponse(C);
      Net.CloseConnection(C);
      D^ := D2^; RETURN
    ELSE Texts.WriteString(W, "connecting failed")
    END
  ELSE Texts.WriteString(W, "invalid URL")
  END;
  Texts.WriteLn(W); Texts.Append(Oberon.Log, W.buf)
END LoadDoc;

PROCEDURE NewDoc*;
  VAR D: Documents.Document;
BEGIN
  NEW(D); D.dsc := NIL; D.handle := Documents.Handler;
  D.Store := NIL; D.Load := LoadDoc;
  Objects.NewObj := D
END NewDoc;
```

Procedure Split splits the URL contained in D.name into its parts host name, port number and request-string (e.g. path and document name). Once a connection to the server specified by the (host, port) tuple could be established, the request is sent by calling SendRequest. ReceiveResponse finally will generate a new document depending on the content-type returned by the server. If the server responds with some error code, ReceiveResponse will generate a text document displaying an error message.

3.2 Internet Client Software

Table 2 gives an overview on the URL schemes currently supported by Oberon. New

file	Accessing local files
finger	User Information Protocol
ftp	File Transfer Protocol
gopher	A distributed document search and retrieval protocol
http	Hypertext Transfer Protocol
mailserver	Access to E-Mail based Services
mailto	Sending E-Mail
news, nntp	Network News Transfer Protocol
telnet	Remote Terminal

Table 2. URL schemes

link schemes can be added dynamically to the system. E.g. a panel document (self-contained document) can contain the software to access a new kind of online-service. This software is automaticaly installed, and the first time a link to this new service is accessed the new software will be invoked. The same mechanism can be used to distribute the software to view a new content type (e.g. a PNG image). Self-contained documents are discussed in detail in Section 4. The current version of Oberon System 3 supportes the following content types:

- All Oberon Documents (Text, Rembrandt, Panel, Arc, ...)
- HTML 1, HTML 2 and HTML 3 (a subset only)
- GIF, JPEG [17], XBM and BMP images
- WAV, SND and AU sounds [2]
- VRML 3D scenes
- ZIP archives [1]

4 Self-contained Documents

Oberon documents require resources like modules and data files to work correctly. Most of the resources are included with the Oberon distribution. However, as Oberon is an extensible software system, programmers can add new resources to the system. Documents that use these resources will not work correctly should the resources not be available in the Oberon system where the document is opened. An example is a document that contains a gadget whose code is not available. Opening this document causes the gadget to be discarded. To solve the resource distribution problem we introduce self-contained documents which are documents that have their resources integrated into themselves. Should the resources required for opening a document not be available on that platform, the resources of the self-contained document are installed automatically by the document loader before they are used. Nothing happens should the resources already be available.

The resources of a self-contained document are stored in a compressed format inside the document. Installing the resources means unpacking and uncompressing them from the document into the Oberon file system. The resources remain in the document, ensuring that it remains consistent when transporting it to other Oberon systems.

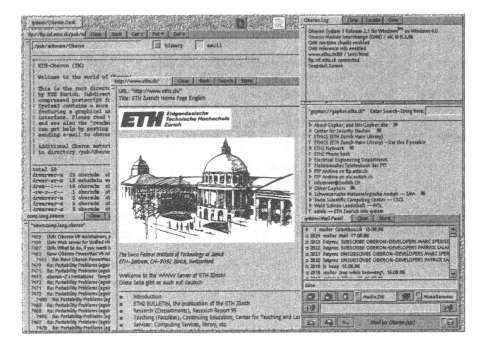

Fig. 2. This snapshot shows some examples of Internet documents.

4.1 Resources

Compressed versions of resources are attached to a document with a document linker [7]. Each attached resource is given a name corresponding to the module or filename and a programmer-definable version number to distinguish between successive versions of the same resource. A fingerprint or message digest could be generated automatically, but then we would be limited to a equality test. With programmer-definable version numbers we can check for compatibility by building the version number out of a major and minor part. E.g. version 3.1 is compatibel to 3.0 but version 4.0 may not be compatibel to versions 3.x. All resources and version numbers attached to a document are packed into a single object of type Resources.Obj, which is linked to the document under the name "Resource".

```
TYPE
  Resource = POINTER TO ResourceDesc;
  ResourceDesc = RECORD
    next: Resource;
    name: ARRAY 128 OF CHAR;
    version, pos, len: LONGINT;
    F: Files.File
  END;
```

```
Obj = POINTER TO ObjDesc;
ObjDesc = RECORD (Gadgets.ObjDesc)
  res: Resource;
  signature: Crypt.RegisterPtr;
  key: Crypt.Key
END;
```

On loading the document, the resource object is loaded and reconstructs its resource list. The fields F, pos and len identify the resource data inside the meta-data part of the document file. The fields signature and key are used by the authentication mechanism discussed below. Installation of a resource is dependent on its presence on the destination machine and its version number. A table of all already installed resources and their version numbers is maintained in a file. Installation occurs according to the following code, each time a document with attached resources is loaded.

```
PROCEDURE Install(obj: Obj);
  VAR
    r: Resource;
    base, ext: ARRAY 64 OF CHAR;
BEGIN
  r := obj.res;
  WHILE r # NIL DO
    GetExt(r.name, base, ext);
    IF ~Avail(r.name, base, ext) OR
       NewVersion(r.name, r.version) THEN
      IF (ext = "Mod") OR (ext = "POM") THEN
        Compile(obj, r) (* compile source code *)
      ELSE
        Unpack(obj, r)  (* unpack data file *)
      END
    END;
    r := r.next
  END
END Install;
```

Note that the resources remain in the document file until they are explicitly removed by the user. Thus document files remain consistent when transfering them to another computer. To avoid over-writing of existing files, resources are installed in a user-specified directory which can be purged at any time.

One major, yet unsolved, problem with self-contained documents are independently developed resources sharing the same name. For data files a simple solution would be to prefix the file names with the developers name. A far more sophisticated solution would be to introduce name scopes in the Oberon filesystem. Since in Oberon modules with the same name can only be loaded once, an enlargement of the module name space would be needed, too. A document could then load conflicting modules and files into its private name space.

Another yet unsolved problem is the detection of the resources needed by a document. With the currently implemented document linker the developer of a self-contained document has to explicitly list the resources he wants to link to the document. It would be desirable to have a mechanism to automaticaly detect the resources needed by a document. This could be achieved by means of a new message sent to all objects belonging to the document to be linked. In addition also the resources needed by modules should be taken into account. The IMPORT keyword can be used to recursively find all modules required, other resources such as fonts or auxiliary data files are only known by the programmer of a module. This problem could be solved, by either adding a new keyword to the Oberon programming language or just by defining the syntax for a special comment. Example, VBZ time-table panel:

```
MODULE VBZ;
   IMPORT Objects, Texts, Oberon, Gadgets;
   RESOURCES VBZTimes.Data, VBZStations.Data;
```

or

```
MODULE VBZ;
   IMPORT Objects, Texts, Oberon, Gadgets;
   (*$RESOURCES VBZTimes.Data, VBZStations.Data *)
```

Using this approach a document would require many parts of the standard Oberon distribution. So we need additional information as version numbers not only for the resources installed by self-contained documents, but also for all resources included in the Oberon distribution. Using this information we can then detect if a given resource has to be linked to a document or if it is part of the standard Oberon distribution.

4.2 Mobile Code

In principle, module resources of portable documents can be transported as source code installed by invoking the compiler. However, with this approach the source code has to be given away to all clients interested in the compiled module. Further disadvantages are the required compilation time and network bandwith. As an advantage, optimal runtime efficency is obtained in comparison with approaches based on interpreted bytecodes.

The number of ways modules can be transported, without taking into account source code and machine dependent object code, depends on how many ways we can cut up the Oberon compiler and still optain a platform-independent and serialisable module representation. The natural choices include a token steam or an intermediate representation (e.g. a parse tree). A parse tree representation of modules, based on the Oberon Module Interchange (OMI [4]), requires an adapted Oberon system. A token stream representation of modules is simpler to implement, as it only involves inserting an interface between the scanner and parser for reading tokens. In table 3 a size comparison of different module representations is given.

SourceCoder The token stream representation of a module is created by scanning the tokens of a module, and numbering identifiers as they are encountered. Unexported identifiers which have no influence on the module's interface are detected by a state machine and are omitted from the identifier table. This makes it harder to understand the source code after a reverse engineering step. The resulting token stream, consisting of the token numbers, identifier numbers and the identifier table, is further compressed using the common LZSS [19] compression algorithm. Decompression of the token stream representation is done by replacing the default text-based scanner by a scanner able to read the compressed token stream. For token stream representations a file format was defined, so the compiler does not need to know which scanner to install.

```
TokenFile = Header [ ExtraHeader ] Data .
Header = Tag ScannerInstaller .
ScannerInstaller = ModuleName "." ProcedureName .
```

When there is no token file tag in a file to be compiled, the compiler installs the default text-based scanner otherwise the scanner installer is called to install the scanner for that token file.

Oberon Module Interchange Oberon Module Interchange (OMI) [4], also called slim binaries, uses the parse tree representation of the Oberon two-pass compiler. This tree representation is externalized using an adaptive method similar to LZW, which has been tailored towards encoding abstract syntax trees rather than character streams. Loading a module rebuilds the parse tree and invokes the second compiler pass, which then will generate the code directly in memory.

OMI-based modules can be unpacked and loaded immediately, whereas the token stream representation will compile to an object file, which is then loaded by the module loader. Once the token stream is compiled, the cost of loading a natively compiled module is lower than loading an OMI module; the latter does the decompressing and compilation of the parse tree each time the module is loaded.

Storage Technique	Absolute Size	Relative Size
Source Code	76121	100 %
Intel Object File	58165	76 %
LZSS Compressed Source Code	24151	32 %
Oberon Module Interchange	19907	26 %
SourceCoder	17480	23 %

Table 3. A size comparison of module representations (HTMLDocs.Mod).

4.3 System Protection and Authentication

Self-contained documents introduce a certain level of risk in the Oberon system. It is easy to imagine that by simply opening a document, viruses or other unwanted software are transfered to the client computer. Oberon uses several mechanisms [3, 7] to protect itself against such cases:

- All resources are installed in a user-specified directory reserved for resources. This keeps the resources separate from the system files and allows deletion without affecting the system.
- Code resources are passed through the compiler to check correctness. Low-level features like using module SYSTEM are checked and disallowed. As module SYSTEM cannot be used, low level interfaces to the underlying hardware or operating system cannot be used to bypass security mechanisms.
- To prevent a resource from corrupting system files, files and directories can be marked read-only. Trying to change read-only files or files in a read-only directory immediately results in a TRAP.
- Self-contained documents are protected by a digital signature. The signature is signed by the author of the document, making him responsible for the contents of the document. So any changes to a document are detected. Certified signatures can be traced back to their owner, discouraging the distribution of malicious software. This process is called document authentication.
- Oberon users have to explicitly allow documents from developers they trust. Resources from untrusted authorities are not accepted.
- For sensitive Oberon installations, self-contained documents can be completely deactivated.

Digital Signatures Digital signatures, authentiction and public key cryptography are dependent on mathematical one-way functions. The digital signature mechanism used for portable documents is called RSA [16]. The signing of a doucment with RSA requires a large number of computations, which makes it unfeasible for signing the whole document with the one-way function. Instead a one-way hash of the document is signed. The one-way hash function used for portable documents is called MD5 [15]. The signature protocol is highly reliant on the public keys being authentic. To verify public keys so called key certificates are used. Thus a central authority signs the public keys of document developers, which can be verified using the authorities public key. Portable documents signed by a key without a certificate from the authority might have been compromised and must be rejected. In our implementation of digital signatures for portable documents, the public and private keys are visual key gadgets (see figure 4). For managing and generating keys a panel is provided (see figure 4). Keys are collected in three key rings: one containing the public keys, another containing the user's secret keys (private key ring) and a key ring identifying developers whose documents are trusted (access ring).

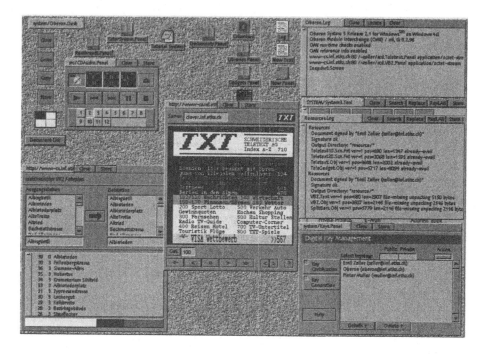

Fig. 3. In this snapshot, some examples of self-contained documents are shown.

5 Conclusions

If we recapitulate the requirements stated in the introduction, we come to the conclusion that we have reached the following:

- We are able to access and use remote and local services in a consistent document oriented manner, using only six commands.
- All implemented Internet services can be used to transparently transport Oberon self-contained documents.
- Using SourceCoder, the same module resources can be used with Native Oberon for PC, Oberon for Windows, Oberon for Windows 95, MacOberon and PowerMacOberon.
- Using Oberon Module Interchange we are even able to use the same object files with Oberon for Windows, Oberon for Windows 95, MacOberon and PowerMacOberon.
- Since digital signatures are used, any changes to documents can be detected and certified signatures traced back to their owner.
- System files can be protected against corruption.

The following points still require some work:

- Automatic detection of resources needed by a document

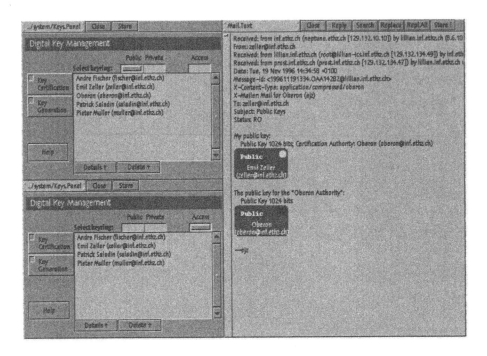

Fig. 4. key gadgets and keyring panel

- Local name scopes for files and modules
- Oberon Module Interchange for Native Oberon for PC
- A more sophisticated solution for associating meta-information to files
- An advanced Oberon Module Interchange plug-in [5] in for the NetScape browser, capable of loading self-contained documents
- HTML 3.x support in the HTML browser

References

1. T. Bralla: UNZIP für Oberon. Semesterarbeit, Institut für Computersysteme, ETH Zürich, July 1996.
2. T. Burri: Sound System für Oberon System 3. Semesterarbeit, Institut für Computersysteme, ETH Zürich, July 1996.
3. M. Dätwyler: Executable Content in Compound Documents. Master's thesis, Institut für Computersysteme, ETH Zürich, March 1996.
4. M. Franz: Code-Generation On-the-Fly: A Key to Portable Software. PhD thesis, ETH Zürich, 1994.
5. M. Franz, T. Kistler: Juice. http://www.ics.uci.edu/~juice/, University of California, Irvine, 17th June 1996.
6. Jürg Gutknecht: Oberon System 3: Vision of a Future Software Technology. Software - Concepts and Tools, 15:26-33, 1994.

7. J. Marais: Design and Implementation of a Component Architecture for Oberon. Dissertation, ETH Zürich, 1996.

8. J. Postel: Simple Mail Transfer Protocol. Request for Comments 821, 08/01/1982.

9. J. Postel, J. Reynolds: File Transfer Protocol. Request for Comments 959, 10/01/1985.

10. M. Horton, R. Adams: Standard for interchange of USENET messages. Request for Comments 1036, 12/01/1987.

11. F. Anklesaria, M. McCahill, P. Lindner, D. Johnson, D. John, D. Torrey, B. Alberti: The Internet Gopher Protocol (a distributed document search and retrieval protocol). Request for Comments 1436, 03/18/1993.

12. T. Berners-Lee, L. Masinter, M. McCahill: Uniform Resource Locators (URL). Request for Comments 1738, 12/20/1994.

13. J. Myers, M. Rose: Post Office Protocol - Version 3. Request for Comments 1939, 05/14/1996.

14. T. Berners-Lee, R. Fielding, H. Nielsen: Hypertext Transfer Protocol - HTTP/1.0. Request for Comments 1945, 05/17/1996.

15. R. Rivest: The MD5 Message Digest Algorithm. Request for Comments 1321, April 1992.

16. R. Rivest, A. Shamir, L. Adleman: A Method for Obtaining Digital Signatures and Public-Key Cryptosystems. Communications of the ACM, 21(2):120-126, February 1978.

17. D. Ulrich: JPEG - Dekodierer für Oberon. Semesterarbeit, Institut für Computersysteme, ETH Zürich, June 1995.

18. E. Zeller, W. Bock: A General Platform for Prototyping Electronic Newspapers and Related Services. ACTS Mobile Communications Summit, Granada November 1996.

19. E. Zeller: Data Compression Techniques. Semesterarbeit, Institut für Computersysteme, ETH Zürich, January 1993.

Lecture Notes in Computer Science

For information about Vols. 1–1122

please contact your bookseller or Springer-Verlag